THE LEARNING CEN
HAMMERSMITH ANI
LONDON COLLEGE
GLIDDON ROAD
LONDON W14 9BL

D0531330

INTRODUCING SOCIAL HOUSING

By Stephen Harriott and Lesley Matthews
(with Paul Grainger)

WITHDRAWN

Chartered Institute of Housing
Policy and Practice Series
in collaboration with the
Housing Studies Association

Hammersmith and West London College

322540

The Chartered Institute of Housing

The Chartered Institute of Housing is the professional organisation for people who work in housing. Its purpose is to maximise the contribution housing professionals make to the well-being of communities. The Institute has 18,000 members across the UK and the Asian Pacific working in a range of organisations, including housing associations, local authorities, the private sector and educational institutions.

Chartered Institute of Housing
Octavia House, Westwood Way
Coventry CV4 8JP
Telephone: 024 7685 1700
Fax: 024 7669 5110

The Housing Studies Association

The Housing Studies Association promotes the study of housing by bringing together housing researchers with others interested in housing research in the housing policy and practitioner communities. It acts as a voice for housing research by organising conferences and seminars, lobbying government and other agencies and providing services to members.

The CIH Housing Policy and Practice Series is published in collaboration with the Housing Studies Association and aims to provide important and valuable material and insights for housing managers, staff, students, trainers and policy makers. Books in the series are designed to promote debate, but the contents do not necessarily reflect the views of the CIH or the HSA. The Editorial Team for the series is currently: General Editors: Dr. Peter Williams, John Perry and Peter Malpass, and Production Editor: Alan Dearling.

ISBN: 1 903208 54 8

Introducing social housing
By Stephen Harriott and Lesley Matthews (with Paul Grainger)

Published by the Chartered Institute of Housing © 2004

Cover photographs supplied by Anglia Housing Group

Printed by Unwin Brothers Ltd, Old Woking, Surrey

Whilst all reasonable care and attention has been taken in compiling this publication, the authors, the publishers, the Editorial Team and its advisers regret that they cannot assume responsibility for any error or omission that it contains.

All rights reserved. No part of this publication may be reproduced, stored in a retrieval system or transmitted in any form or by any means, electronic, mechanical, photocopying, recording, or otherwise without the prior permission of the Chartered Institute of Housing.

Contents

HAMMERSMITH AND WEST
LONDON COLLEGE
LEARNING CENTRE

1 3 JAN 2005

322540   £22-50
363·511

Housing

322540

Foreword

Whatever your perspective, housing is a major item on the government's policy agenda and both housing associations and local authorities face many challenges with the ever-increasing demand for affordable housing.

I have worked in housing for over twenty years over which time I have seen many changes in the sector, most significantly the proliferation of housing associations and the establishment of group structures. When Anglia Housing Group was formed in 1995 it was the first of its kind and was described as an innovative structure that would shape the way forward for the next 20 or 30 years. The structure was subsequently adopted by many of the largest and most successful housing associations throughout the country, and we have expanded to become one of the leading providers of affordable housing in the East of England.

Today housing associations play a significant part in the development of communities and as a Group our priority is to provide high quality affordable homes that are safe, secure, energy efficient, and able to meet the requirements of a lifetime. We work with our partners and other agencies to ensure that we are meeting local needs and creating neighbourhoods where people want to live long term.

The new edition of *Introducing Social Housing* is long awaited and is a particularly important publication not just for those people studying housing, but for those working in the sector who need to increase their understanding of the fundamental role that housing plays in people's lives. It reflects the changes that have taken place in the sector and led to the creation of organisations such as ourselves and we are delighted to be associated with its publication.

This book provides key information on the significant challenges facing anyone working in the social housing sector. It clearly indicates that the social housing service of the future must move away from being a service of last resort. The housing agenda is a full one and meeting the needs of new housing supply and the targets set in the government's Communities Plan are near the top.

Especially welcome in the pages of the book are details of how housing organisations are getting involved in partnership arrangements to deal with common issues such as anti-social behaviour and the Supporting People initiatives. There is also much useful material on the development of new housing bodies through arm's length management organisations, stock transfer and Private Finance Initiatives. Finally, as it should, the book reminds us all of the importance of putting customers first.

Mark Rogers
Chief Executive, Anglia Housing Group

About the authors

Stephen Harriott is Group Chief Executive at Amicus Group, having previously been Chief Executive at St Pancras & Humanist Housing Association in London. He has worked at senior level for a number of housing associations and local authorities. He is a former Chair of the Northern Region Branch of the Chartered Institute of Housing and is an External Examiner for the BSc in Housing at the University of Greenwich.

Lesley Matthews is Director of Housing at Northumbria University, which is designated as the Northern Regional Centre for Housing Education by the Chartered Institute of Housing. She has lectured to housing and other students for many years and contributed to the development of a full range of CIH approved professional housing courses at the university. She is currently responsible for all housing programmes at the university and teaches a wide range of both full-time and part-time students.

Paul Grainger wrote large parts of chapter two of the book and assisted with the editing and updating of the book. He is an experienced housing manager who has held a number of senior positions in local authority housing departments. He is currently a senior lecturer in housing at the Northumbria University.

Acknowledgments

Many people have contributed, both intentionally and unintentionally, to the development of this book, not least the students on the various professional housing courses at Northumbria University as well as our colleagues in housing throughout England and elsewhere. Our respective families are also owed a debt of gratitude for readily accepting our many absences from family life during the writing of this book.

A special thanks to John Perry at the CIH who gave invaluable assistance and comments from his base in Nicaragua (getting comments on the Barker Review from John in Nicaragua when we had not had a chance to read it off the internet was a treat!).

Our thanks are also offered to those who have so generously and freely given permission to publish their work, especially to Edwin Trotter for permission to use his design drawings of Turnbull Street and other material; George Kennedy of G R Kennedy, Chartered Architects of Dunoon, Scotland, for so kindly supplying a range of materials relating to the redevelopment of Commercial Buildings; Newcastle City Council, which gave permission to reproduce their Tenants' Repairs Receipt; and Tees Valley Housing Association kindly allowed use of their repairs satisfaction survey card. Policy Press gave permission to publish Figure 5.11 taken from Smith and Merrett (1988) *The Challenge of Empty Housing*.

Any opinions expressed in the text are, of course, entirely our own, and we remain responsible for these as well as any unintended errors.

GLOSSARY OF TERMS and ABBREVIATIONS

ACG   Annual capital guideline. The government's limit for each local authority's capital spending programme. Replaced by Supported Capital Expenditure (SCE) in England from 2004.

ADP   Approved development programme. This is the Housing Corporation's total capital programme in any one year. It is normally broken down into rented housing, shared ownership and other home ownership initiatives.

AI   Architect's instruction. This is an instruction to a contractor in relation to a building contract.

ALMO   Arm's length management organisation. A separate organisation set up by a local authority to manage its council housing.

AMRA   Asset Management Revenue Account; under resource accounting in England, the account which funds local authority council housing debt repayments.

ASB   Anti-social behaviour.

BCA   Basic Credit Approval. The amount which a local authority is authorised to borrow annually for capital expenditure on council housing in England and Wales; replaced by SCE in England from 2004.

BES   Business expansion scheme. A scheme (no longer available) which allowed investors to invest money in the private rented sector and obtain significant tax benefits.

CCT   Compulsory Competitive Tendering. A government initiative which required local authorities to submit the delivery of parts of their services to competitive tendering. Introduced into housing management services from 1995 but replaced by the Best Value regime in 1999/00.

CDM   Construction, Design and Management Regulations. Introduced by the Health and Safety Executive placing obligations on clients in relation to health and safety. In particular they require most construction projects to have a planning supervisor appointed.

CFCR — Capital from current revenue; revenue income used for capital expenditure in Scotland, the equivalent of RCCOs.

CIH — Chartered Institute of Housing; the professional body for housing managers.

CIS — Cash incentive scheme. This offers a cash grant like TIS but is operated by local authorities with government support. The cash grant assists tenants to buy a property in the open market. The amounts vary between local authorities.

CSO — Conventional Shared Ownership. A scheme whereby a housing association builds or acquires properties for part sale to prospective or current tenants

CTB — Council tax benefit. A subsidy paid to low income households to reduce their council tax liability.

DIYSO — Do-it-yourself shared ownership. This is a housing association scheme where applicants can ask a housing association to buy a private property and the applicant part buys and part rents the property from the association. They can increase their share of the property by staircasing up; eventually to outright ownership. The scheme was only open to council or housing association tenants and the resulting vacancy must be let to an applicant in priority need. Substantially replaced by Homebuy.

Defra — Department of the Environment, Food and Rural Affairs.

DETR — Department for the Environment, Transport and the Regions; responsibilities largely taken over by the ODPM.

DoE — Department of the Environment; forerunner of DETR.

DTI — Department of Trade and Industry.

ERCF — Estates renewal challenge fund. A government initiative introduced in 1996 to offer grants to local authorities to transfer their stock to new landlords who would be able to carry out refurbishment works. The grant was necessary to enable transfer to take place, as most had a negative market value.

EU — European Union.

EUV-SH — Existing-use value for social housing; method by which stock is valued for resource accounting purposes in England and Wales.

GNI	Generalised needs index. A government compiled index of need used as a factor to allocate resources to local authorities.
GNP	Gross national product. The annual value of output of the United Kingdom economy.
GRF	Grant redemption fund. Established in the 1980 Housing Act to recoup revenue surpluses generated in housing association accounts from fair rent increases. Abolished in the 1988 Housing Act and partly replaced by the Rent Surplus Fund (RSF).
HAG	Housing association grant. A capital grant from the Housing Corporation/Communities Scotland/National Assembly for Wales to registered housing associations for capital works. Renamed social housing grant in England and Wales as a result of the 1996 Housing Act.
HAMA	Housing associations as managing agents. An initiative promoted in the mid-1990s where housing associations would manage empty properties on behalf of private owners and landlords and rent out the properties.
HAT	Housing action trust. Set up under the 1988 Housing Act to undertake large scale refurbishment of council housing stock. At the end of the trust's life the tenants had the option of returning to the local authority or to new landlords.
HB	Housing benefit. The main means tested benefit towards meeting the rented housing costs of low income households.
HC	Housing Corporation.
HIP	Housing investment programme. Refers to the local authority's annual bid for capital resources from the government.
HMP	Housing market package. A one-off initiative in 1992/93 which allocated HAG to housing associations to purchase properties in the private sector in an effort to kick-start the housing market.
HNI	Housing needs index. A Housing Corporation index of housing need used in resource allocations decisions.
HRA	Housing Revenue Account. This is the revenue account which all housing authorities have to establish for their council housing activities. Since the 1989 Local Government and Housing Act this account has been ring fenced and must balance.

HSE	Health and Safety Executive, responsible for overseeing health and safety procedures in workplaces.
ISMI	Income support for mortgage interest. Interest subsidy available to unemployed owners with mortgages through income support.
JCT	Joint Contracts Tribunal. A professional body which issues draft building contracts reflecting the needs of client and contractors.
LA HAG	Local authority housing association grant. This is similar to HAG except the grant comes from the local authority itself rather than through the Housing Corporation. Abolished in 2003.
LDF	Local Development Framework. These replaced local and unitary plans drawn up by local authorities.
LHC	Local housing company. This is a new form of registered social landlord created under the 1996 Housing Act. These bodies are set up by local authorities and associations and controlled by a board with typically councillors, tenants and independent members in equal proportions.
LSE	Leasehold scheme for the elderly. A form of shared ownership where a housing association develops a scheme for the elderly which is sold at 75 per cent of the market value.
LSVT	Large scale voluntary transfer. This refers to the transfer of the whole or most of a council's owned stock to a housing association, normally one which has been set up specifically to receive the council housing stock. The resulting associations have become known as LSVT associations.
MIRAS	Mortgage interest tax relief at source. An Inland Revenue scheme which enabled tax relief to be deducted from the mortgage interest payments due rather than via the individual's own tax code. Abolished in 2000.
MITR	Mortgage interest tax relief. Mortgage interest attracted tax relief at 15 per cent on the interest of the first £30,000 of a mortgage. Abolished in 2000.
MMC	Modern Methods of Construction are factory-based production methods.
MRA	Major Repairs Allowance. Revenue subsidy paid to English local authorities to help to maintain council housing stock; paid into a Repairs Account.

NFHA	The National Federation of Housing Associations. Following the 1996 Housing Act which introduced the concept of registered social landlords the NFHA changed its name to the National Housing Federation to enable non-housing associations, such as local housing companies, to join.
NHBC	National House Builders Council. The trade body for house builders. Offers ten-year building guarantees and undertakes building inspectors' work.
NHF	National Housing Federation. This represents the interests and concerns of housing associations in England.
NIHE	Northern Ireland Housing Executive. The NIHE provides 'council' housing in Northern Ireland, rather then the local authorities.
ODPM	Office of the Deputy Prime Minister.
OSM	Off-site manufacturing; a term for the use of prefabricated construction components (see also MMCs).
PFI	Private finance initiative. A government scheme designed to encourage private finance to provide public sector capital projects.
PPBS	Planning, Programming Budgeting Systems. A method of budget setting which focuses on objectives and alternative ways of meeting them.
PRS	Private rented sector.
PSBR	Public sector borrowing requirement. This was the annual amount which the public sector needed to borrow to meet its expenditure plans. Now called Public Sector Net Borrowing.
PSL	Private sector leasing. Similar to HAMA where associations and local authorities lease privately owned properties usually to house homeless households.
PSNB	Public Sector Net Borrowing; see PSBR.
QS	Quantity surveyor.
RCCOs	Revenue contributions to capital outlays. These are amounts of money set aside in the housing revenue account to pay for capital improvements to council housing out of rental revenue income.

RPI	Retail Price Index; a measure of annual inflation.
RSF	Rent surplus fund. Set up after the 1988 Housing Act to set aside part of the surpluses of housing associations as a result of fair rent increases to provide for major repairs to their stock.
RSL	Registered social landlord. A new term introduced into the 1996 Housing Act which refers to organisations registered with the Housing Corporation, Communities Scotland and National Assembly for Wales. These could be housing associations or local housing companies.
RSG	Revenue support grant. The annual sum of money made available by the government to subsidise a local authority's revenue spending.
RTB	Right to Buy. Introduced in the 1980 Housing Act which enables qualifying tenants to buy their property at a discount.
RTIAs	Receipts taken into account. These are the projected capital receipts from sales which the government took into account when deciding on capital borrowing allocations to local authorities. Now abolished.
SCA	Supplementary credit approvals. These are additional borrowing approvals granted to local authorities by government (in addition to the BCA) for specific purposes. Credit approvals superseded by SCEs in England from 2004.
SCE	Supported Capital Expenditure; the amount of capital expenditure taken into account in the calculation of Housing Revenue Account Subsidy in England (where it replaced ACG).
SCG	Specified capital grant. Allowances in the ACG for specific private sector grants such as improvement grants.
SFC	Strategic Forum for Construction.
SH	Scottish Homes; replaced by Communities Scotland.
SHF	Scottish Housing Federation.
SHG	Social housing grant. The new name for HAG in England and Wales as a result of the 1996 Housing Act. The name had to be changed as SHG is now payable to registered social landlords other than housing associations, such as local housing companies.
SLHA	Standard Local Housing Allowance; a flat rate housing benefit allowance piloted in a few English councils from 2003.

SO	Shared ownership. This is where associations develop schemes and sell them on a part buy part rent basis, with owners taking a 25 per cent, 50 per cent or 75 per cent share. The remaining equity is owned by the association which charges a rent for this. In later years shared owners can increase their equity stake and eventually staircase to full ownership.
SOE	Shared ownership for the elderly. This is like LSE although under SOE properties can be sold at 50 per cent of the value, with applicants renting the remaining share to 75 per cent of the value.
SOOTS	Shared ownership off the shelf. A former Scottish Homes scheme similar to DIYSO.
SRB	Single regeneration budget. Operated in England and included the budgets of many government departments concerned with regeneration.
SSA	Standardised spending assessment. A government assessment of necessary revenue expenditure by each local authority on individual services. It is used in the determination of the revenue support grant.
TCI	Total cost indicators. These are costs which the Housing Corporation and the Welsh Assembly Government publish annually which show maximum allowable costs for new developments to be funded by SHG.
THFC	The Housing Finance Corporation. A body set up to obtain private loans for a number of smaller housing associations in England who might find it difficult or more expensive to arrange loans on their own behalf.
TIC	Total indicative cost. Allowable capital costs for housing association schemes published by Scottish Homes (later, Communities Scotland). Similar to TCI.
TIS	Tenants Incentive Scheme. This is a housing association scheme which gives existing tenants a cash grant to assist them in buying a property in the open market. The amounts vary between local authorities. The resulting vacancy must be let to an applicant in priority need. Now abolished.
TMV	Tenanted market value. The assumed market value of an estate which takes account of the predicted net income from the stock.

TPAS   Tenant Participation Advisory Service. A consultancy set up to promote tenant participation. Used extensively by local authorities and housing associations.

UBR   Uniform business rate. Business rates, once set by individual local authorities, are now set nationally by the government.

VAT   Value Added Tax; the main indirect tax (on expenditure).

CHAPTER 1:
What is social housing?

1. Introduction

Despite the massive changes which have taken place in housing over the last 20 years or so, social housing – that is, housing managed mainly by councils or by housing associations – has a major role. It provides homes for more than one-fifth of the UK population. It is a major item on the government's policy agenda. It is a crucial issue in regional policy – whether the booming south or the declining north – and of course in devolved government in Scotland, Wales and Northern Ireland. Regeneration of poor neighbourhoods cannot take place if social housing is neglected. The way it is managed is a significant factor in tackling crime and anti-social behaviour. For these and other reasons, the government has recently increased housing investment for the first time for many years. This makes an understanding of social housing policy and practice of prime importance not only for those studying or practicing in housing itself, but for those interested in wider social and public policy too.

This book is primarily directed to students of housing who wish to learn about the nature of *social* housing in the UK, the key features of its management, and its place in the UK housing system. It has been written particularly for those pursuing (or interested in) a career in social housing, and for individuals new to the profession, since it reflects the requirements of Part One of the Chartered Institute of Housing's Professional Qualification. It is, therefore, especially suited to courses of study such as the BTEC Higher National Certificate in Housing Studies, foundation degrees in Housing and the Graduate Foundation Course of the CIH, as well as undergraduate degrees in Housing Studies. However, this text will also be useful to anyone with an interest in social housing, such as those taking a wide range of courses in social policy, public administration, estate management, building management, architecture, housing development or surveying.

This first chapter introduces the concept of *social housing*, initially by considering what is meant by social housing in the context of the UK and then tracing its historical development and the reasons for (and nature of) the involvement of the public sector in housing provision. It then identifies the types of organisations which provide social housing in the UK today, and considers how they vary in size and location. Finally, there is a brief examination of what is involved in the *management* of social housing provision by these organisations, which is the primary focus for much of the rest of the text.

Chapter two considers the wider context within which social housing is provided
by housing organisations, examining the place of social housing in the UK
housing system. Most housing in the UK is provided within a market system,
which essentially means that it is allocated according to the ability to pay. Social
housing is different in this key respect. This chapter explores the significance of
these different tenures, each distinguished by differing legal rights and obligations
attached to occupation. Tenures exhibit many differences, in terms of influences
on their provision, their changing size and importance, the types of households
they attract, the types of property they contain and the condition of those
properties. These differences are explored in some detail, as well as the ways in
which different tenures interact with each other. The social context in which the
housing system operates is considered, with a discussion of issues around social
exclusion, poverty and disadvantage. Other factors affecting the quality of life,
such as crime and anti-social behaviour are examined, along with the
government's policy initiatives for dealing with many of these issues through the
regeneration of neighbourhoods and measures designed to create sustainable
communities.

Chapter three resumes the examination of the management of social housing, with
an exploration of the financial framework within which social housing providers
operate. Since this is the first, essential step to achieving new affordable housing
development, it considers the significant influence of the *economic context* for
public housing finance, as well as the specific financial frameworks which govern
the provision of finance to social housing organisations. This is examined not just
in the context of differences applicable to different social tenures, but also in the
context of the targeting of financial subsidy to those most in need, via means-
tested housing benefit payments. It also examines other ways in which public
finance for housing has been re-directed in recent years, and the reasons for these
changed priorities.

As the next step in the achievement of sustainable social housing, chapter four
turns to the *process* by which social housing is *provided* in the UK, with a detailed
examination of the steps which are essential to achieving a social housing
development or refurbishment. It identifies the roles of different professionals in
the traditional approach to the development process, and considers the
requirements of the various stages in development, from a management
perspective. It identifies key aspects which will influence the likely success and
sustainability of the constructed scheme, both for its occupiers and for those who
must manage it. It concludes by exploring the reasons for the more recent
emphasis on 'partnering' approaches to the process and examines what is meant
by 'partnering'.

Having achieved the development of a new social housing scheme, chapter five
examines the tasks which are conventionally viewed as 'housing management',
identifying the key roles of social housing managers in allocating and letting

social housing, setting and collecting the rents, and ensuring that homes are adequately maintained. The chapter also examines the role of the housing manager in dealing with anti-social behaviour. These are the 'front-line' tasks of housing managers, the activities which will most directly affect tenants and hence their satisfaction with the service provided. Approaches to these key tasks are explored in some detail, and issues of 'best practice' identified.

Chapter six moves on to consider the delivery of the social housing service in more detail, by examining different possible approaches to *running a social business*. It considers the different ways in which the delivery of the key tasks can be structured in social housing organisations, and the reasons for this. In recent years, there have been a number of important influences on service delivery which have resulted in many different approaches. These include the growth of different forms of *tenant participation* in the management process, the *decentralisation* (and re-centralisation) of some key management tasks, and the introduction of *Best Value* for the management of social housing.

Chapter seven concludes with a review of the challenges facing housing managers in the first decade of the 21st century and the recognition that these challenges will require housing managers to have a good understanding of the past in order to inform their future actions. The chapter will also make clear the interaction between development, finance and management which will be needed if these challenges are to be met effectively.

2. Defining social housing

The term *social housing* means housing provided and managed by local authorities – commonly called *council housing* – as well as by housing associations and other organisations regulated by government. The essential characteristic of social housing is that it is provided by organisations which do not exist to make a profit for their owners in the way that a company in the private sector would aim to do.

Social housing organisations generally provide homes for those households which find it difficult to obtain a home of an appropriate size or quality in private housing markets. This may result from low incomes, which mean that private rents and prices are not *affordable*, or there may be other reasons why access to suitable housing is difficult, for example, for some households or individuals with special needs. The involvement of the public sector in the provision of housing was intended to help to meet these housing needs, to ensure that every household (regardless of income) could attain a decent home.

Since social housing providers exist to ensure that homes are available to households in *housing need*, the process of obtaining access to social housing is very different to the private tenures. In the private rented sector, or in owner occupied markets, the ability to obtain a home depends very heavily on the *ability to pay* for it. In general (unless there is discrimination), if households have sufficient income they can obtain a property of the type they want. Their *demand* for housing – the desire for housing, backed by the ability to pay for it – will, ultimately, be met by a private housing provider.

In contrast, in the social tenures the ability to pay is *not* a criterion. In the absence of any *supply constraints* – a shortage of available properties to let – social housing organisations could permit anyone who wanted a home to occupy, and pay rent for, one of their properties. However, in most areas of the UK, there are insufficient homes in the social housing sector to meet the requirements of everyone who might want properties. For this reason, social housing organisations must identify (and publish) the criteria by which they will determine which households gain access and which do not. These are known as *allocations or lettings policies*, and a range of traditional approaches, together with the move to using more consumer focused or 'choice based' lettings systems are examined in detail in chapter five.

In addition to providing homes, local authorities are also an important vehicle through which the government provides various types of financial subsidy to the housing costs of individual households, including those in social housing. For example, most households with low incomes may obtain *housing benefit*, which pays some or all of the property's rental costs. Indeed, a very large proportion of social housing tenants is in receipt of housing benefit, and this is examined in detail in chapter three.

The nature of the housing provided by local authorities and other social landlords varies considerably, in part reflecting differences in the housing needs which different organisations attempt to meet. A number of housing associations exist primarily to provide housing for one particular type of housing need, such as the elderly, so their properties will reflect this specialism. Until recently, local authorities were more likely to provide homes for general, family needs, so they tend to have higher proportions of houses than housing associations. However, some local authorities, particularly large urban authorities, have considerable numbers of flats in tower blocks; in Glasgow, for example, the newly-created Glasgow Housing Association, now the owner of the city's former council housing, has over 20,000 flats in tower blocks. The largest estates have been built by local authorities, some of them extremely large and typically located on the outskirts of large cities. In contrast, housing association developments tend to be small, and may only consist of a single building, such as a hostel, or two or three properties in a small rural scheme. Hence, there is no typical profile for the housing stock of different providers. Social housing is provided in all varieties of building and in a huge range of locations.

3. How has social housing evolved in the UK?

Prior to the advent of social housing provision in the UK, households with low incomes were unable to afford the private, market rents which were demanded for decent housing. They were forced to make do with whatever they could afford, which meant either renting sub-standard, *slum* housing and/or living in very cramped, overcrowded conditions. By the mid-nineteenth century, these problems had become particularly acute in the rapidly expanding urban areas of the UK. It was concerns about the impact of these overcrowded conditions on public health and the environment which first led to government involvement in housing issues.

Regulation: nineteenth and early twentieth century public intervention

In 1846, the *Nuisances Removal Act* permitted local authorities to take action against acute public health problems, such as the *middens* which provided working class sanitary facilities. The *Public Health Act* of 1848 permitted the setting up of local Health Boards, intended to address problems of sanitation and tackle the epidemics of cholera and typhoid, which regularly swept through the overcrowded dwellings in urban areas. Later, the *Torrens Act* of 1868 permitted local authorities to demolish properties which were *unfit for human habitation*, and an attempt was made to address the problems of poor quality building standards with the 1875 *Public Health Act*, which encouraged local 'bye laws' for minimum standards of construction. Shortly after, the *Cross Act* (Artisans' and Labourers' Dwellings Improvement Act) of 1875 extended the powers of *clearance* – demolition – to entire slum areas.

These Acts marked the beginning of attempts to *regulate* the private provision of housing, but the view of most politicians at that time was that housing provision, and its finance, were private sector concerns. In general, the Acts gave *enabling powers* to local authorities rather than statutory *duties*, and since local authorities' incomes were raised from their local populations, local voters were reluctant to take on any unnecessary obligations which would raise their taxes. These voters were also likely to be the landlords of the overcrowded properties. The result was that, when the *Shaftesbury Acts* (the *Labouring Classes' Lodging Houses Act* and the *Common Lodging Houses Act*) were passed in 1851, local authorities largely ignored their new powers to build housing.

The *Housing of the Working Classes Act* of 1890, which largely consolidated and amended earlier Acts, again permitted local authorities to provide council housing; but since no government subsidy was available and the finance had to be found by the local authorities themselves, few councils engaged in housing provision or slum clearance.

Around this time, however, a number of private benefactors, appalled by the housing conditions in which many households lived, set up charitable trusts to provide private finance for decent rented housing – individuals such as Peabody, Guinness and Rothschild – but the scope of the problem was such that they made little impact; and, due to the quality of the dwellings provided, the rents were relatively high, affordable only by skilled workers.

Octavia Hill, viewed by some as the founder of modern housing management, took a somewhat different approach, focusing on the improved management of existing properties *and their tenants*. She effectively combined improved housing management with social work, and

> *...was able to show that, by an authoritarian, labour-intensive system of management, using trained middle class women managers and rent collectors, it was possible to make profits out of housing the poor in decent conditions* (Malpass and Murie, 1999, p. 36).

The extent to which social housing management should reflect a 'social work' dimension remains, to this day, a topic for debate amongst social housing managers, and is explored in chapter five. Malpass and Murie argue that the later municipalisation of working class housing resulted in the re-definition of housing management as a 'bureaucratic-administrative activity done by men' (p. 37), with few elements of the Octavia Hill approach.

Towards the end of the nineteenth century, Joseph Rowntree in York and Charles Booth in London produced important social surveys which showed that approximately 30 per cent of the population of these two cities were living in poverty. This challenged the prevailing view of Victorian England that poverty 'was due to idleness' (Darke, 1979, p. 16).

In the early twentieth century, the government first intervened more directly in housing markets with the introduction of *rent controls* in 1915, in response to rapidly rising rents at the start of the First World War. This fixed private rents at pre-war levels, effectively forcing private landlords to subsidise the housing costs of their tenants. Some form of rent control – latterly known as 'fair rents' – largely existed from then until their abolition (for new tenancies) in the 1988 Housing Act. By reducing the returns available to private landlords, rent controls undoubtedly contributed to the decline of the private rented sector in the UK since 1915.

Twentieth century: the emergence of council provision in the inter-war years

The first significant involvement of the public sector in the *provision* of housing followed the end of the First World War. There were chronic housing shortages, and council house building was viewed as the best and quickest way to respond effectively to the situation. With the *Housing and Planning Act* (the Addison Act) of 1919, the government encouraged councils to build new homes by, for the first time, offering significant subsidies. The *Tudor Walters Report* of 1918 changed perceptions about house design, so that the preferred home changed from the tightly packed, 'high density' form of 19th century terraced housing for the working classes to more spacious environments of homes with a garden and inside amenities (baths and WCs). Many council homes were built to a 'garden village' layout in the 1920s, when the quality of council housing was high, but rents too, were beyond the reach of the poorest. The later *Wheatley Act* (Housing (Financial Provisions) Act) of 1924 improved the subsidy arrangements, so that by 1939, over a million council homes had been produced, representing around ten per cent of the total housing stock (Malpass and Murie, 1999).

In 1930, the *Greenwood Act* changed the emphasis of housing policy from simply expanding housing supply to *slum clearance*, encouraging councils to demolish sub-standard dwellings and provide new council homes for their occupiers. This was intended to supplement the provisions of the Wheatley Act, but by the early thirties, the government was under pressure to reduce public spending. As a result, the Housing (Financial Provisions) Act of 1933 repealed the Wheatley Act, so that subsidy was now available *only* to build new housing for households from slum clearance areas. Local authorities did succeed in re-housing large numbers of households – over a quarter of a million homes were demolished between 1931 and 1939 – but the quality of new council homes declined during this period, and councils now had new problems, with large numbers of much poorer tenants from the demolished slums.

Until 1935, the financial accounts of new council estates were effectively separated, depending on the Act (the subsidy system) under which they had been provided. This meant that tenants in properties built with lower subsidies had to pay higher rents. Partly as a way of helping councils to introduce *rebates* on rents for poor tenants, a new unified *Housing Revenue Account* was introduced by the 1935 Housing Act, so that subsidies could be transferred between schemes. Much later, this would permit councils to cross-subsidise newer schemes from the rents of older schemes. The more recent evolution of local authority housing revenue accounts is examined in chapter three, while rent setting is examined in chapter five.

Expansion of council housing and owner occupation following World War Two

The Second World War created new and acute housing shortages. During the war, there was very little construction or repair, and, in contrast to the First World War, around 400,000 homes were destroyed by bombing. Public sector attention was, therefore, directed once again to expanding the supply of housing, and for a time, slum clearance virtually ceased. The Housing (Financial and Miscellaneous Provisions) Act of 1946 introduced new subsidies, and in response to shortages, a system of building licences ensured that construction activity was undertaken largely by councils. This was also the period in which new, *system-built* techniques of construction were first introduced, employing factory produced components in an attempt to reduce the need for skilled labour.

By the early 1950s, there was a new Conservative government, which wished to encourage greater private sector provision. Building licences were phased out, and as council house building declined (except for slum clearance), there was a boom in the construction of properties for owner occupation. As subsidies were progressively reduced during the fifties and early sixties, councils were encouraged to build high-density developments, including high-rise and medium-rise blocks of flats (which attracted higher levels of subsidy from 1956 to 1967). Many of the system-built developments proved to be particularly problematic in management terms, due both to poor design and poor standards of construction, and a number have since been demolished.

The 1957 Rent Act removed rent controls from better quality private rented properties, with decontrol of the remainder as they became vacant. This was intended to revive the private rented sector, but probably had the reverse effect, by permitting landlords to sell their newly decontrolled dwellings for owner occupation. A further boost to owner occupation was provided in 1963, when the government abolished Schedule A income taxation – a tax on the *imputed* rent income which owner occupiers chose to forego. In effect, owner occupiers were choosing to take this income 'in kind', by occupying the property themselves, instead of renting it out. (This is similar to being taxed on the value of services received from, say, a company car – it is a benefit in kind, which nevertheless has value to the recipient and so is effectively another source of income). The abolition of Schedule A taxation therefore represented a significant tax advantage to owner occupiers.

The Housing Act of 1961 provided the first significant public funding for housing associations in England, with £25 million available as loans from the *National Federation of Housing Societies* to provide homes at *cost-rents*. The 1964 Housing Act set up the *Housing Corporation* to regulate and finance housing associations, extending their interests into co-ownership schemes. However, at this time, two-thirds of any finance had to be raised from the private sector – usually building societies – which is similar to the present system of housing association finance (examined in chapter three).

The new Labour government of 1964 promised a huge expansion of council house building, with a target of half a million homes a year. Rent controls were re-introduced for the private sector with the 1965 Rent Act – known as *Fair Rents*, and assessed by a rent officer (employed by the Civil Service). The 1967 Housing Subsidies Act increased the subsidies available to local authorities, and new minimum (and very generous) space standards were introduced as a result of the *Parker Morris* report.

Policies for social housing in the 1970s

By the late sixties, general economic problems had caused a reduction in council house building and slum clearance, and instead, there was a new policy emphasis on the rehabilitation of the existing, private sector stock. For example, in England and Wales the 1969 Housing Act introduced *General Improvement Areas*, followed in the 1974 Housing Act by *Housing Action Areas*. Similar legislation was passed for Scotland and Northern Ireland. These Acts encouraged local authorities to identify areas for systematic improvement, and more generous improvement grants were made available to private owners.

The *Cullingworth Report* of 1969 reflected a growing view that local authorities took too narrow a view of their responsibilities for housing. This recommended that all restrictions on the letting of local authority housing should be lifted, and in particular, that local authorities should look after the most vulnerable households in their area. (Lettings policies are examined in detail in chapter five). A new requirement in the 1970s, that local authorities produce *housing strategies* for their areas (see chapter three), was intended to force authorities to adopt a wider, more strategic role in housing. However, it was not until 1977 that, for the first time, local authorities were given a statutory duty to provide housing for some categories of homeless households, in the *Housing (Homeless Persons) Act*.

By the early 1970s, housing *finance* had become a key policy issue. The 1972 Housing Finance Act introduced, for the first time, a *mandatory* (compulsory) rent rebate scheme for council tenants. This was necessary because rent controls – *fair rents* – were also introduced for council tenants, with the intention of increasing council rents to private sector levels and removing their connection with the cost of provision. As a result, the housing revenue account – the rent income account – could now generate a surplus; rents could be higher than the amount required to repay debt interest and the costs of management and maintenance. Fair rents were later abandoned (for council housing) by the 1975 Housing Rents and Subsidies Act, because this was widely perceived as unfair to council tenants.

The 1974 Housing Act also extended the role of the Housing Corporation, by introducing the *Housing Association Grant* for housing associations. Similar provisions applied to Scotland and Northern Ireland. This was a very generous grant system, no longer requiring that associations obtain private finance. This marked the beginning of the considerable, recent expansion of housing association provision of social housing, albeit on a very small scale in comparison with local authorities.

Housing policy under the Conservative government from 1979-1997

The election of the Conservative government in 1979, under Margaret Thatcher, marked a turning point in the provision of social housing in the UK. In pursuit of a 'property-owning democracy', the expansion of owner occupation now became the central goal of housing policy. The Housing Act and Housing (Tenants' Rights etc.) Scotland Act in 1980 introduced the right of most council tenants to purchase their council home at a discount – the *Right to Buy* policy – as well as new public sector tenancies with new rights. The later *Building Societies Act* of 1986 deregulated the provision of housing finance for owner occupation, bringing 'high street' banks into the market, so that a great deal more finance was available, and many more households became eligible for mortgages.

As part of a substantial policy shift in favour of individual subsidies, the rent rebate system was reformed in 1982, to provide a new *housing benefit*. The results of this new policy shift were to influence housing in the UK throughout the 1980s, with policies which would continue to affect social housing provision throughout the 1990s.

In addition, the 1980s saw the beginning of large scale voluntary transfers (LSVTs) where local authorities began to divest of their housing stock to new housing associations which they had set up themselves. In some cases, transfers were politically motivated in the sense that some Conservative councils did not want to be landlords, but in others the need to raise private finance to fund stock improvements was the key driver of the policy.

Housing policy under the Labour government since 1997

The election of the Labour government in 1997 resulted in a number of key developments in the governance of the UK. The most fundamental of these was a change in the way in which housing policy is developed and implemented, following the devolution of aspects of government in Scotland, Wales and Northern Ireland. With the creation of the Scottish Parliament and Scottish Executive, and Assemblies in Wales and Northern Ireland, the government delegated responsibilities for housing issues to those new bodies. The differences in powers devolved to the different parts of the UK, and implications of these changes for the processes of providing, managing and regulating social housing, are considered in subsequent chapters of the book.

A further development of housing policy saw the government focus on partnership working as a fundamental tool in governing and monitoring the increasingly diverse social housing sector, and in tackling the key issues of community safety, social exclusion, the regeneration of neighbourhoods, and the creation of sustainable communities. Government policies have also stressed increased *choice*. This was seen, for example, through discounted home ownership schemes and the continued encouragement of stock transfers. Choice in terms of the individual's access to a home and its location have been supported through changes in the law relating to housing allocations (through, for example, the Homelessness Act 2002 in England), and the emphasis on choice based lettings. Developing approaches to the governance of housing associations, and particularly the local housing company model adopted for many stock transfers, has seen much greater representation of tenants on governing bodies.

The publication of the Communities Plan in 2003 heralded a major increase in resources for housing with a commitment to build at least 200,000 new homes in designated growth areas, funding for market renewal in areas of low demand and a commitment to bring existing social housing up to a decent standard. This injection of resources in housing was also accompanied by an increasing use of inspection as a means of regulating social landlords. In addition the government signalled its desire to reduce the role of local authorities as social housing providers by requiring all local housing authorities with housing stock to consider alternatives such as stock transfer, arm's length management organisations or the use of the Private Finance Initiative to bring the stock up to a Decent Homes Standard.

4. Who provides social housing in the UK?

Although owner occupation is the predominant form of housing, the social housing sector is a key tenure. In Great Britain the two key providers of social housing are local housing authorities and housing associations. Northern Ireland has the *Northern Ireland Housing Executive*, with roles and responsibilities in relation to social housing which are similar to local authorities in the rest of the UK. The table below sets out the dwelling stock by tenure in the United Kingdom as at March 2002.

Table 1.1: Dwellings by tenure 2002 in 000s (with %)

	England	Scotland	Wales	NI	Total
Owner occupation	14,901 (70.1%)	1,506 (64.2%)	930 (72.5%)	489 (74.7%)	17,826 (69.8%)
Private rented	2,190 (10.3%)	156 (6.7%)	112 (8.7%)	34 (5.2%)	2,492 (9.8%)
Housing association	1,467 (6.9%)	148 (6.3%)	52 (4.1%)	21 (3.2%)	1,688 (6.6%)
Local authority	2,708 (12.7%)	535 (22.8%)	188 (14.7%)	110 (16.8%)	3,541 (13.9%)
Total	21,266	2,345	1,282	655	25,548

Source: Wilcox, 2003

Local authorities

Although in recent years the government has attempted to reduce the role of local authorities as social housing *landlords* they nonetheless still remain the main provider of social housing in Britain. However, not all local authorities have housing responsibilities, for example, shire county councils in England only play a minor role in the provision of housing services.

For housing authorities in England and Wales, most of their legal duties are set out in the 1985 Housing Act which was a consolidating piece of legislation, bringing together a plethora of housing laws contained in earlier acts of Parliament. In Scotland the responsibilities of housing authorities are laid down in the Housing (Scotland) Act 1987. The new Scottish Parliament passed the Housing (Scotland) Act 2001. The 1996 Housing Act changed the responsibilities of local authorities in England and Wales significantly in relation to issues of letting of homes and dealing with homelessness and repeals the earlier provisions in the 1985 Housing Act. The implications of these Acts and additional changes brought about by the Homelessness Act 2002 are considered in subsequent chapters.

The key responsibilities of local housing authorities include;

- developing and keeping up to date a strategy for dealing with all the major housing issues – public and private – in their area;
- the assessment of housing needs in the area and the development of plans to meet those needs;
- the provision of rented accommodation and the management of that housing stock, including the letting of dwellings, rent collection, arrears recovery and the enforcement of tenancy conditions;
- assisting housing associations and private developers to provide housing within their area: the *enabling* role;
- the provision of accommodation and other services to the homeless;
- exercising powers to tackle disrepair in private sector housing and in relation to houses in multiple occupation;
- the provision of housing advice services;
- the administration of housing benefit for both private and public sector tenants.

The responsibilities of housing authorities for housing in their area are much more extensive than simply the management of their own housing stock; indeed there is no requirement in the legislation for housing authorities to manage their own housing. As we shall see below, increasingly local housing authorities have been transferring their housing stock to a variety of *stock transfer* organisations, or (in England) having it managed by arm's length management organisations (ALMOs).

In the development of their *local housing strategies* – annually updated plans for housing in their area, required as part of their bid for resources (and examined in chapter three) – housing authorities are required to take a wide ranging *strategic* view of the housing needs in their area, including the provision of both rented and owner occupied housing. This view of the local authority as having a wide ranging responsibility for housing in the area is reflected in a general desire of government to see housing authorities undertaking an enabling role – assisting other providers to achieve housing development – rather than providing new housing themselves.

The changing role of local authorities

The Labour government which came to power in 1997 developed a housing policy approach tied into their overarching aim of encouraging social inclusion. The Green paper *Quality and Choice: a decent home for all*, published in 2000 set out a series of aims and objectives which laid the foundation for subsequent policy initiatives. The Green paper emphasised the need for a much stronger strategic role for local housing authorities, the importance of partnership working, and the need to tackle areas of low demand. It outlined proposals to support those living in private sector tenures, improving the quality of social housing, encouraging choice in access to social housing, and the promotion of regeneration and balanced communities. The paper also emphasised the need to create a fairer system of affordable rents, improve housing benefit, and target support to those who are vulnerable, poor, or in fear of crime and anti-social behaviour.

As part of this raft of policy initiatives the introduction of the *Best Value* regime generated a need for local authorities to examine critically the range and detail of their service provision. The service provision, together with service standards, must be carefully specified, and accounted for as local authorities are subject to inspections by the Audit Commission's Housing Inspectorate.

In February 2003 the government published The Communities Plan, (*Sustainable Communities: Building for the future*), which emphasised a focus on the creation of affordable housing, dealing with regional demand issues, tackling homelessness, improving local environments and the 'liveability' of local areas, and ensuring that all social housing is brought up to a decent standard by 2010 (ODPM, 2003). The implications of this key policy development are considered throughout the remainder of the book.

Since the late 1980s financial constraints have also stimulated some local authorities to engage in the *large scale voluntary transfer* of their stock to a new or existing housing association, since associations face fewer constraints on their ability to obtain finance for spending to refurbish housing stock. By the end of 2003, housing associations managed over a third of all social sector dwellings, with almost half of these accounted for by transfer associations (Pawson, 2003).

However, in spite of these pressures, local housing authorities still remain significant landlords in their own right, as well as having the strategic and enabling role which the government has advocated.

Local housing authorities in the United Kingdom from April 1996

From the 1st April 1996 a new system of local government was introduced in Scotland and Wales (and also in some parts of England). The main result of this change has been to reduce the number of local authorities mainly through the abolition of the Welsh county councils, the Scottish regional councils and in England the abolition of some shire county councils and the amalgamation of other district councils. (Council housing in Northern Ireland is still provided by the Northern Ireland Housing Executive, with funding from the Department of Social Development).

Figure 1.1: Housing authorities in the United Kingdom

England:
- metropolitan district councils
- non-metropolitan district councils
- London borough councils (and the City of London)
- unitary district councils

Wales:
- unitary councils

Scotland:
- unitary councils

Northern Ireland:
- Northern Ireland Housing Executive

Housing authorities in England

English metropolitan district councils

Following the Local Government Act of 1972, 36 metropolitan district councils were established in England, within the main urban conurbations of Merseyside, Greater Manchester, South Yorkshire, West Yorkshire, the West Midlands and Tyne and Wear. For example, within Tyne and Wear the metropolitan districts of Newcastle-upon-Tyne, Gateshead, North Tyneside, South Tyneside and Sunderland were created. These metropolitan district councils are now the responsible housing authorities in their areas.

Following the abolition in the mid 1980s of the metropolitan county councils, the new metropolitan district councils became all purpose, unitary, authorities, responsible for all local government activities in their area. The metropolitan district councils vary significantly both in terms of population size and the housing stock managed; the largest is Birmingham City Council with 75,783 households living in homes rented from the council at the time of the 2001 Census.

English non-metropolitan district councils

Prior to April 1986 there were a total of 334 non-metropolitan district councils in England and Wales, but following a review of local government initiated in the mid 1990s a number of changes have taken place. In some cases, shire county councils have been abolished and their functions transferred to new all purpose district councils, whilst in other areas the shire county council lost part of its geographical area to a new unitary authority.

Where unitary district councils have been established (particularly in big, non-metropolitan districts like Nottingham and Leicester) these have responsibility for housing. In the shire areas where the two tier system remains the county councils have responsibility for key services such as education and social services whilst district councils take on responsibility for more 'local' services, such as housing, planning, leisure services and refuse collection.

London

Within London there are 32 borough councils which together with the City of London operate as unitary authorities and have responsibility for most local government matters, including housing, in their area. Each of these councils has a landlord function with the housing stock ranging from 2,250 homes in the City of London to 54,500 dwellings in the London Borough of Tower Hamlets. The Greater London Authority and its Mayor have broad responsibility for strategic planning in the metropolis and this has led to a number of significant interventions in London housing policy, particularly to encourage more affordable housing as part of new developments.

In 2003 the government passed the *Regional Assemblies (Preparations) Act*, which paves the way for referenda to be held on the creation of Assemblies within the English regions. The likely implications of this development for the administration of housing policy is considered in chapter three. Already the *Regional Housing Boards* are having an influence on policy and on the distribution of government grants and subsidies for housing.

Housing authorities in Wales

In Wales a review of local government was conducted in the mid 1990s by the Welsh Office and this review has led to the abolition of all of the previous eight county councils and the 37 Welsh district councils. In their place a new structure of local government was introduced consisting of 24 new unitary, all purpose, councils, all of which have a responsibility for their housing. Since 1 July 1999, the National Assembly for Wales has taken responsibility for, amongst other things, developing housing policy, social housing regulation and investment, and strategic issues.

Housing authorities in Scotland

Prior to April 1986 mainland Scotland had nine regional councils and 53 district councils. In addition there were three separate islands authorities for Western Isles, Shetland and Orkney. In Scotland the housing function had been carried out by the district councils and the islands authorities. Following a review conducted by the Scottish Office, local government in Scotland was reorganised in April 1986 with the creation of 32 new unitary authorities and the abolition of the regional councils, though the three authorities for the Scottish islands remain.

In the new structure all of the unitary authorities including the islands councils have responsibilities for all local government services including housing. The smallest authority is Orkney with a population of 20,000 and the largest is Glasgow City Council with a population of 624,000.

The Scottish Parliament was opened on 1 July 1999, directing the work of the newly created Scottish Executive, with more extensive powers and responsibilities than the Welsh Assembly. Among these is the power to pass legislation on housing issues in Scotland, although Social Security matters – and therefore housing benefit – are retained by the UK Parliament at Westminster.

Northern Ireland

The Northern Ireland Housing Executive is the provincial housing authority, responsible for a range of strategic enabling functions, together with the development and management of its own stock of 109,742 dwellings (NIHE, 2003).

Originally established by the Housing Executive Act (Northern Ireland) 1971 (since superseded by the Housing (Northern Ireland) Order 1981), the Housing Executive assumed the housing responsibilities of some 65 separate authorities and became Northern Ireland's single comprehensive housing authority.

As part of the government's policy of devolution, and a cornerstone of the Belfast Agreement (commonly known as the 'Good Friday Agreement'), the Northern Ireland Assembly was created through the Northern Ireland Act 1998. However, this was temporarily dissolved in April 2003 due to political difficulties between the different parties involved. At the time of writing the government is seeking to call new elections and to re-establish the Assembly.

Housing associations

Although local authorities remain the most important provider of social housing in Great Britain, the sector with the key role now in providing new social housing is the housing association sector. Under the 1985 Housing Associations Act, a housing association is defined as:

> *a Society, body of trustees or company;*
> *a) which is established for the purpose of, or amongst whose objects or powers*

> *are included those of, providing constructing improving or managing, or*
> *facilitating or encouraging the construction of, housing accommodation*
> *and which*
>
> b) *does not trade for profit...*

Housing associations are essentially non profit seeking organisations which exist
to provide housing for people in need. They are independent bodies usually
controlled by unpaid voluntary committee members (although English
associations are now able to make payments to board members within limits
established by the Housing Corporation). Most housing associations will have
received public subsidy in the form of grants from the Housing Corporation,
Communities Scotland, National Assembly for Wales or (in Northern Ireland) the
Department for Social Development and are therefore subject to public regulation.

Types of housing associations – England

There are a number of different categories of housing association which usually
reflect the type of housing they provide or the particular housing need that the
association wishes to meet. The majority of housing associations are general needs
associations. This means that the association has been established to meet a range
of needs and will provide housing for families, couples, single people and the
elderly.

However there are a number of specialist housing associations such as:

Abbeyfields
These are smaller housing associations, usually only owning a handful of
properties, which specialise in providing shared housing for the elderly. The usual
model is for three or four elderly people to share a house with a housekeeper being
employed to offer care and support to the residents.

Almshouses
These are perhaps the earliest form of sheltered housing (housing for older people
usually with a member of staff providing support services), with some having their
roots back to the 12th century. They provide sheltered housing for the elderly and
are found throughout the UK, often owning a handful of properties.

Hostels
Many housing associations provide hostel accommodation. Hostels will normally
provide shared accommodation with each household having their own bedroom
facilities but with cooking and bathrooms usually being shared, and with the
housing association normally providing support workers, usually with specialist
skills in meeting the needs of hostel residents. These needs will vary, and hostels
are provided to help amongst others women fleeing domestic violence, the
homeless, the mentally ill, people with physical disabilities and young people who
have left the care of the local authority.

Co-operatives and co-ownerships

Co-operatives are a form of housing association in which the accommodation is collectively owned and managed by the people who live in it, although the members' only stake in the equity (value) of the properties is their £1 membership share.

Co-ownerships are a very different form of co-operative housing, which gained popularity in the late 1960s and early 1970s. When a member leaves this rented accommodation they are entitled to a share of some of any increase in the value of the property, depending on how long they have lived there and paid rent.

Sale/leasehold associations

A number of specialist housing associations have been set up which have concentrated on providing housing for low cost home ownership, rather than for rent. This can take the form of shared ownership housing where residents will part buy their home on a mortgage and rent the remainder from the housing association, with the option of increasing their share (*staircasing*) to full ownership when their resources allow. Some specialist *leasehold schemes for the elderly* (now called shared ownership for the elderly) have been set up where elderly persons can buy a property at 75 per cent of its market value, the housing association retaining ownership of the remaining equity in the property. Many general needs associations now operate low cost home ownership schemes alongside their rented provision although in some cases they have set up specialist associations to deal with this particular type of provision.

Table 1.2 gives details of housing associations registered with the Housing Corporation in England at March 2003.

Table 1.2: English housing associations at 31 March 2003

General needs	632
(of which stock transfer 116)	
Abbeyfield societies	317
Other hostels	301
Almshouses	433
Co-operatives	254
Co-ownerships	32
Sale/leasehold	44
YMCA/YWCA	31
Total	**2,044**

Source: Adapted from Housing Corporation, 2003

The latest data available at the time of writing showed that at 31 March 2003 English housing associations registered with the Housing Corporation owned 1,643,000 homes (ODPM, 2003 data).

Types of housing associations – Scotland

A particular feature of the Scottish housing association movement is the development of co-operative and community based housing associations. Table 1.3 gives details on the number of Scottish housing associations. Between them they own over 128,000 homes.

Table 1.3: Numbers of Scottish Registered Social Landlords at 31 March 2003

General needs	176
Abbeyfield societies	57
Small specialist	16
Co-ownership	2
Total	**251**

Source: Communities Scotland on-line RSL directory

Types of housing associations – Wales

In Wales registered housing associations are regulated and funded by the National Assembly for Wales. At 31 March 2003 there were 77 associations registered with the Welsh Assembly Government, owning a total of 59,036 homes.

Table 1.4: Housing associations in Wales at 31 March 2003

General needs	35
Abbeyfield societies	34
Almshouses	6
Co-ownerships	2
Total	**77**

Source: National Assembly for Wales stock estimates

Types of housing associations – Northern Ireland

At 31 March 2003, 39 housing associations in Northern Ireland were registered with the Department for Social Development. Registration gives access to housing association grant aid, and places the association within the Department's regulatory regime. The 39 associations between them owned 20,297 dwellings (Department for Social Development, 2003).

Most of the associations manage housing. However the Northern Ireland Co-ownership Housing Association provides opportunities through equity sharing home ownership schemes and at 31 March 2003 NICHA had 17,482 owners with 13,024 of them now owning their home in full.

Table 1.5: Housing associations in Northern Ireland at 31 March 2003

General needs (including mixed general needs and supported)	33
Supported associations (including Abbeyfields)	5
Co-ownerships	1
Total	**39**

Source: Adapted from Department for Social Development data, 2003

The size of housing associations

The housing association movement is a diverse one with a large number of associations owning a handful of properties, and a small number of associations owning in excess of 10,000 properties. The list below shows the 10 largest associations in England at September 2003.

Table 1.6: Largest housing associations in England at September 2003

North British Housing Ltd	44,962
Sanctuary Housing Association	35,763
Anchor Trust	35,057
Home Group Ltd	31,239
Hyde Housing Association Ltd	28,731
London & Quadrant Housing Trust	26,173
Home Housing Association Ltd	25,197
Orbit Housing Association	24,093
Riverside Housing	23,162
Paddington Churches Housing Association Ltd	23,029

Source: Housing Corporation RSR Survey, 2003

Table 1.7 shows quite clearly the diversity in stock sizes.

Table 1.7: Housing associations in England, March 31st 2003

By size in units	No. of HAs		HA stock	
0-5	143	7.0%	300	0.0%
6-1,000	1,370	71.2%	140,000	8.0%
Over 1,000	412	21.4%	1,622,000	92.0%
Total	1,925	100.0%	1,762,000	100.0%
By stock owned				
General needs	1,593,000		90.4%	
of which keyworker units	10,000		0.1%	
Supported	135,000		7.7%	
Total social housing stock	1,728,000		98.1%	
Non-social housing stock	34,000		1.9%	
Total stock in ownershp	1,762,000		100%	
Shared ownership	148,000			

Source: Housing Associations in England, Key Facts 2003, Housing Corporation, 2004

As with England and Scotland, the majority of housing associations in Wales own only a handful of homes, with 38 of the associations owning 500 homes or less, and with only 22 associations owning more than 1,000 homes. Indeed these 22 Welsh associations own over 73 per cent of the total stock.

Table 1.8: Distribution of Welsh housing association stock by size of association

Units owned	No of HAs	% of HAs	Total stock owned
0-5	9	9.3	17
6-25	10	44.3	431
26-100	8	12.4	590
101-250	3	2.1	412
251-500	8	6.2	2,384
501-1,000	17	11.3	8,524
1,000+	22	14.4	34,057
Total	**77**	**100**	**59,036**

Source: The National Assembly for Wales stock estimates, 2003

Scottish housing associations own over 128,000 homes, but most of the properties are owned by the largest associations.

Table 1.9: Stock owned by Scottish housing associations 2003

Units owned	No of HAs	Total units
0-100	34	1,183
101-500	81	20,499
501-1,000	36	26,714
1,001-2,500	46	79,812
2,501+	6	19,038
Total	**197**	**128,208**

Source: Adapted from Communities Scotland RSL on-line register, 2003

The situation within the Northern Ireland housing association sector is again similar to the other countries. Of the 39 associations, 30 own 500 or less properties with only 4 owning more than 2,500 dwellings.

Table 1.10: Stock owned by Northern Irish housing associations 2003

Units owned	No of HAs	Total units
0-100	6	314
101-500	24	6,596
501-1,000	2	1,282
1,001-2,500	3	6,233
2,501+	4	14,872
Total	**39**	**29,297**

Source: Adapted from Department for Social Development data, 2003

5. The management of social housing organisations

The provision and management of social housing demands a wide range of knowledge and expertise. As shown in the previous section, most of the social housing stock is provided by relatively large organisations, though there are some which are exceedingly small. The task of managing them is a complex one, just as it is for any private sector organisation with a wide variety of functions. The main difference is that, since social housing organisations do not exist to make a profit, there is no simple measure of 'success', as there is for a private firm. As for all parts of the public sector, the social housing organisation cannot examine its profitability to see how well it has performed. For this reason, performance is gauged from a series of *performance indicators*, which relate to some of the key tasks undertaken by housing managers.

What are these tasks?

First, if properties are to be built or refurbished, the key requirement is that finance is obtained. In general, this will be from a combination of grants from the government, borrowing from the private sector, and from income generated from rents. Obtaining and managing this finance has become increasingly important for many social housing organisations. In addition, housing organisations must ensure that the income received from rents is managed wisely, to ensure that funds are available to provide an appropriate range and quality of services to the tenants on a week-to-week basis.

In those organisations where some or all of their services are decentralised, so that services are provided from a number of different locations, each manager may have control of a budget to pay some or all of the costs of management activities. These resources must be carefully managed to ensure that they are spent in an appropriate and timely manner. Indeed, in the light of increasing restraints on the resources available to social housing over recent years, good management of the organisation's financial resources has become a key issue.

A few, usually small associations, undertake no new housing development and very few local authorities now have sufficient resources to build new homes. However, all social housing providers will need, at some stage, to refurbish ageing properties, and most medium to large housing associations undertake new development. This demands the ability to undertake a range of development tasks, ranging from identifying suitable sites, to managing the design of the planned development or refurbishment and arranging for the building work. Hence, the management of social housing may also require knowledge of the process of development, the roles of the key professionals, and the ways in which a high quality of development can best be achieved.

Once the properties have been built, they must be let to new occupiers, the tenants, and suitable arrangements must be made to collect rent and minimise arrears, to manage the letting of vacant properties, and to arrange for their repair and maintenance. These latter tasks are perhaps conventionally thought of as the key tasks of social housing managers, and they are certainly the tasks which have the most immediate and direct impact on the tenants. Increasingly, however, as explored above, some knowledge of finance and development issues is also required for effective management.

Since the managers of social housing have an obligation to ensure that their properties are available to households in housing need, identifying and defining needs is also an important task. The aim is to identify all of those needs which are unlikely to be met by the private sector, usually because the households lack the ability to pay. As identified above, local authorities have an obligation to identify housing need in their area, and to plan an annual housing strategy which addresses these needs. Chapter two considers the nature of the housing needs which are generally met by social housing organisations, while chapter three examines the role of the Housing Plan in bidding for public finance.

Unlike private sector firms, the people responsible for strategic management issues in social housing organisations generally form an *unpaid, voluntary committee*, although in 2003 the Housing Corporation has begun to allow housing associations to pay members of their executive bodies, if they can show that it will improve performance. In local authorities, these are the *elected members*, the councillors, who sit on a committee such as the housing committee. Housing associations have management committees, and, as in local authorities, these committees take key decisions, with advice from the senior management team. Senior managers need, therefore, to be fully conversant with committee procedures and it is their job to 'operationalise' the decisions taken in committee – to turn the policies into reality in the organisation. However, these are high level management tasks, beyond the scope of an introductory text.

As might be anticipated from the wide variation in the numbers of properties controlled by different housing organisations, the numbers of staff employed to undertake the management of the stock varies considerably. In very small associations it is likely that almost all of the work involved in running the association will be carried out on a voluntary basis by committee members. Large associations on the other hand employ significant staff numbers – often rivalling the larger local authorities.

Local authorities with their own housing stock all employ some staff to undertake housing management – although some have set up arm's length management organisations which employ the staff. However, as you will discover in chapter six, there are huge variations in the scale and location of some of these tasks in the organisation, so some important management tasks may be undertaken by departments other than the housing department; for example, it is quite common for housing benefit payments to be administered by the Finance Department. In addition, local authorities have a much broader range of responsibilities for housing than associations, as identified earlier in this chapter. Hence, in a local authority, there will be strategic policy makers and other staff dealing with private housing, as well as housing managers.

This book mainly sets out to explore the nature of the management roles and responsibilities carried out by social housing organisations, and most of the remainder of the book is directed to that objective. However, before doing so, the next chapter examines the context within which social housing operates and its place in the housing system of the UK.

References and further reading

Anderson, I. and Sim, D. (2000) *Social Exclusion and Housing*, CIH, Coventry.

Burnett, J. (1978) *A Social History of Housing, 1815-1979*, David and Charles, Newton Abbot, Devon.

Cole, I., Gidley, G., Ritchie, C., Simpson, D. and Wishart, B. (1998) *Creating Communities or Welfare Housing?*, CIH for the JRF, Coventry and York.

Darke, J. and Darke, R. (1979) *Who needs housing?* Macmillan, Basingstoke and London.

Department for Social Development (2003) *Northern Ireland Housing Statistics 2002-03*.

Department of Environment, Transport and the Regions, (2000) *Quality and Choice: A Decent Home for All*, DETR, London.

Grant, C. (1992) *Built to Last? Reflections on British Housing Policy*, Shelter, London.

Housing Corporation (2004) *Registered Social landlords in England: Key Facts*, Housing Corporation.

Malpass, P. and Murie, A. (1999) *Housing Policy and Practice*, 5th edition, Macmillan, Basingstoke.

Merrett, S. (1979) *State Housing in Britain*, Routledge and Kegan Paul, London.

Mumford, K. and Power, A. (2003) *Boom or Abandonment: Resolving housing conflicts in cities*, CIH, Coventry.

Northern Ireland Housing Executive, (2003) *Housing Agenda 2003-4*, NIHE.

Office for National Statistics, (2003) *Housing Statistics*, ONS.

Office of the Deputy Prime Minister, (2003) *Sustainable Communities: Building for the future*, ODPM, London.

Paris, C. (ed.) (2002) *Housing in Northern Ireland*, CIH, Coventry.

Pawson, H. and Fancy, C. (2003) *Maturing Assets: The evolution of stock transfer housing associations*, Policy Press, Bristol.

Power, A. (1993) *Hovels to High Rise: State Housing in Europe since 1850*, Routledge, London.

Sim, D. (ed.) (2004) *Housing and Public Policy in Post-Devolution Scotland*, CIH, Coventry.

Smith, R., Williams, P. and Stirling, T. (2001) *Housing in Wales*, CIH, Coventry.

Wilcox, S, (2003) *UK Housing Review 2003/2004*, CIH and CML for the Joseph Rowntree Foundation, Coventry and London.

Web sites

www.communitiesscotland.gov.uk

www.esystems.communitiesscotland.gov.uk/pls/register/reg_home

www.odpm.gov.uk/housing

www.statistics.gov.uk/census2001

www.housing.wales.gov.uk

www.cih.org

www.housingcorp.gov.uk

CHAPTER 2:
The changing context

1. Introduction

The need for shelter is a fundamental human requirement and the quality and availability of housing affects all of us. However, 'housing' is not a single entity; it is a heterogeneous item, available in many different locations, in different sizes and styles, of variable quality, and in a number of distinct tenures. This chapter considers the various ways in which households in the UK might satisfy their need for housing, through a discussion of the UK housing system and the different ways in which housing is made available to households. It explores the context in which the social housing sector operates, to set the scene for the issues considered throughout the subsequent chapters of this book.

The chapter begins by examining key concepts relating to the requirement for housing, such as housing *desire*, *need*, and *demand*. It also identifies the main tenures, which have implications for the rights and responsibilities of the dwelling's occupants. It examines influences on the demand for housing, and the ways in which this can vary over time and between tenures. It considers the problems arising from the fact that private housing markets can only respond to the desire for housing when it is accompanied by an ability to pay. The inability of households to pay has resulted in the concept of housing 'need', as distinct from housing demand, and the provision of *social* housing to meet housing needs. It also explores the ways in which housing need has been defined by both governments and social housing providers and why this concept changes over time.

In the course of this discussion the chapter examines economic and social factors which impact on the social housing system and also introduces some government policy initiatives and key legislation implemented by successive governments to 'steer' the context in which social housing is delivered.

2. Housing desire, demand and need

Housing desire
This can be conceived as a household's *preferences* for housing. It will include not only preferences for the size of the accommodation, its physical attributes and qualitative standards, but also preferences for tenure type and location. This means that all households, or potential households, will have particular desires in relation to their homes.

Housing need

The assessment of housing need – the process of which is considered in more detail later – involves the identification of the minimum housing standards which are required by particular households, and the measurement of whether households achieve those standards. Some housing organisations have argued for the adoption of 'optimal' standards rather than 'minimum', especially when it involves potentially vulnerable people (CPA, 1984). Assessment involves a qualitative judgement about the requirements of different households, and as a result, perceptions of housing need can change over time. Different societies may also have quite different perceptions of housing need.

The concept of housing need is a crucial element in the allocation (or letting) of social housing. In general, only those households considered to be in *housing need* will be offered a social housing dwelling, which may, or may not, meet with their desires or aspirations. This is in contrast to private sector housing provision, which is allocated largely in response to demand. The recent introduction of choice based lettings by some social landlords is an attempt to recognise that households' preferences should also ideally be met. See chapter five for more discussion of these approaches.

Housing demand

The term *demand* (or, more accurately, 'effective demand') is used here as an economic term to describe the situation in which housing 'consumers' have a desire for particular accommodation and have the financial resources to pay it. In this precise economic definition, therefore, 'effective demand' only exists if individuals' desires or needs coincide with an ability to pay the market price (or rent) for that accommodation. The desire for housing, or the need for it, do not, in themselves, permit the household to demand it.

3. Tenure

Within the United Kingdom at any one time, housing may be located in any one of four main tenure types. The crucial determining factor of which tenure a particular dwelling is in will be the ownership of the accommodation. The four main tenures are owner occupation, local authority (council) housing, housing association, and private rented accommodation.

Owner occupied dwellings are owned by the occupants, either outright or purchased with the assistance of loans – usually mortgages, for which the home will act as security for the loan. Within the United Kingdom this is the far largest tenure type with over almost 70 per cent of the population living in such accommodation at March 2002 (Wilcox, 2003). The other three tenures consist of accommodation which is owned by someone other than the occupier, who pays rent to the owner.

Local authority housing is the stock of dwellings owned by local councils. As the owner occupied sector has continued to expand in recent years through the Right to Buy there has been a corresponding reduction in the stock of council housing. At the same time an increasing number of local authorities have transferred their housing stock to existing or newly created housing associations. The reasons for these changes are considered later in the section on housing supply. Together, local authorities and housing associations make up the *social rented sector*. This sector accounts for just over 20 per cent of the total housing stock in the United Kingdom (Wilcox, 2003).

The private rented sector consists of those dwellings owned by private individuals and companies, and let for rent usually with a view to making a profit. From a situation at the end of the First World War in which over 90 per cent of the UK housing stock was within this tenure, this sector has reduced to around 10 per cent of the total stock (Wilcox, 2003).

Owner occupied and private rented accommodation are secured in a private market context which means that the ability to obtain properties in these tenures is dependent on the ability to pay the market price or rent. The next three sections examine the operation of these private markets, first by examining how markets operate, and then looking at demand from households and exploring the influences on the supply of housing. Within the social tenures, potential occupiers are prioritised on the basis of housing need, which is examined in section seven.

4. Private housing markets

A market is any arrangement which permits the exchange of goods or services, whether for money or other consideration. In the case of housing, this refers to the arrangements by which dwellings are bought and sold, or let. Traditionally, economists have focused on the operation of markets, and the way in which markets are assumed to reach an 'equilibrium', when they achieve a balance between supply and demand. In the long term, the supply of housing should equal its demand, because price will provide the 'equilibrating mechanism' linking the two.

In very simple terms, the process by which a market reaches equilibrium is as follows:

> As demand for a product increases the price will rise, because the lack of sufficient supply will result in consumers 'bidding up' the price; they will be competing for a scarce product, which always results in a higher price.

> As the price increases, manufacturers (or, builders and sellers, in the case of houses) will be encouraged to produce (or sell) more of the item.

> As more become available, the price will stop increasing and a new equilibrium will be found where the number of articles (houses) demanded is

equal to the number being supplied. The price remains steady until levels of demand or supply alter again.

If supply expands so that it exceeds demand, or if demand falls, the price will soon start to fall. There will be insufficient buyers to take up the supply. Falling prices will eventually result in a contraction in the supply, as builders put off new developments and owners delay selling their homes. Eventually, equilibrium is restored, and prices become steady again.

Whereas the theory of supply and demand and price equilibrium may be particularly accurate in describing the market for many products, such as shoes or loaves of bread, the supply of housing is rather 'inelastic' (unresponsive to price changes), in that an increase in demand with an associated increase in price cannot quickly be followed by an increase in supply. Housing supply – the 'flow' of houses into the market, those offered for sale or rent at any one time – responds only slowly to changing prices. This is because of the long lead-in times involved in the production of new houses compared to shoes or loaves of bread.

The Barker Review into Housing Supply (December 2003) reported that:

...formal estimates of supply responsiveness suggest that housing output in the UK responds relatively weakly to changes in house prices. Against a background of rising demand, this will contribute to higher house prices than otherwise might be the case. International comparisons show that the supply of housing in the UK is less price responsive than in most other major economies. Our housing supply is only half as responsive as the French housing market, a third as responsive as the US market, and only a quarter as responsive as the German market. Studies also show that supply has become less responsive over time. Before the war it was up to four times as responsive as it was through most of the post-war period and the responsiveness of housing supply has declined further in the 1990s, falling almost to zero, implying no change in housing output in response to the increases in price. Increasing demand has therefore fed directly into higher house prices (Barker, 2003).

This means that the operation of housing markets is particularly complex. The complexity of factors affecting both the demand for and supply of housing, and the ways in which these differ between each tenure, are now considered in greater detail.

5. Demand

Demand arises from households either seeking to set up home for the first time or to move to a different property. The factors which influence the *overall* level of demand for accommodation will also have an influence on the levels and types of demand for accommodation within the different tenures in different ways.

The overall demand for housing is affected by a wide range of factors. These include:

Demographic factors

The demand for housing will be affected by a range of demographic (population) factors.

Size of the population

Self evidently, the size of the population will have an impact on the numbers of people requiring accommodation, and therefore on the level of demand. The United Kingdom population has undergone a fairly steady increase over the past four decades, rising from 50.25 million in 1951, to 59.8 million at the time of the 2001 census. However, the rate of growth has been reducing over this period, and future projections suggest that by the year 2031 the total population level will have begun to decrease (Census, 2001; ONS, 2002).

Composition of the population

Such changes in the total population will clearly have an influence on the number of people requiring accommodation, but this in itself will only be one factor affecting the numbers of homes required. A further influencing factor is the composition of the population, which means the numbers of people in different age groups, as well as the way in which it is structured – the relative size of each age-grouping.

Census data show that there has been a significant increase over the past 40 years in the proportion of the population which is over 65 years of age; and this is most marked in the group aged 75 years and over. In addition, future projections suggest that this trend is likely to continue through the next 40 years (Census 2001; ONS, 2002).

This pattern can be expected to have implications not only for the level of demand for accommodation, but also for the demand for housing of designs which are appropriate to the needs of older people. As such the changing age profile can be expected to have an impact on both the level of demand, and the types of accommodation being required.

Migration

Another demographic factor which will impact on levels of demand for accommodation is the extent of migration among the population. At a national level, the relative rates of outward migration (emigration) and inward migration (immigration) will affect the size of the population. However, levels of internal migration may also be significant. For example, during the 1980s and early 1990s rising levels of unemployment elsewhere in the country resulted in net migration of people into the south east of England with an associated impact on the levels of demand for accommodation in that region. During the late 1990s there was a net loss of population from London as people moved elsewhere in the south east and south west. Indeed, there has been a continuing urban to suburban and rural drift, resulting in population decline in many major cities throughout the UK (such as in Glasgow and Newcastle-upon-Tyne).

The Draft London Plan (Mayor of London, 2002) is particularly striking in its predictions for growth and migration, 'equivalent to a city the size of Leeds during the next decade'. Furthermore, the Mayor anticipates, '80 per cent (of growth) will be from black and minority ethnic communities. That will see London grow from 7.4 million to 8.1 million people by 2016 with the creation of 600,000 new jobs. The Mayor expects that this will require a target of 23,000 new build homes each year of which, 'affordable homes would make up half of all new provision in the majority of London boroughs'.

Levels of migration will also have a tenure specific impact. Traditionally in the UK young single people have always been the most mobile group within the population. In addition to the influence this will have on total demand for accommodation, there will be a disproportionate demand for particular tenures. The relatively long time taken to enter and exit from owner occupation through selling and moving elsewhere, as well as the high costs of this process (so called 'transactions' costs') will tend to discourage highly mobile groups from choosing this type of accommodation. Access to local authority and housing association dwellings have traditionally been lengthy processes due to high levels of demand and the bureaucratic rationing mechanisms adopted by many through their allocations and lettings policies as a way of dealing with that excess demand. As a result the private rented sector has tended to allow the quickest and easiest entry and exit for the highly mobile within the population, and young single people are the largest group represented among tenants of private rented dwellings.

Employment
Clearly demand can be influenced by issues related to the labour market. The requirement to move for employment purposes is, however, only one of a range of ways in which mobility impacts on housing demand. It will also be affected by the age of individuals, with young single people traditionally being the most mobile group within the UK population. As such, the numbers of this group in the overall population will impact on the overall level of demand.

Family life cycles
Family life cycles also have an influence on the levels of demand and the type of accommodation required. As the number of children in a family increases, larger accommodation is usually required. Similarly, as the household ages smaller accommodation or even a home suited to limited mobility may be required. Key times for households to move include leaving home for the first time, marriage, childbirth, changing employment, and retirement.

Household formation

As the children of the family grow, and begin to form new independent households there is a demand for more accommodation to house this increased number of household units. The rate at which new households form will therefore affect demand levels. The Office for National Statistics, in the 2003 edition of Social Trends, observes that:

> *The types of households and families that people live in today are increasingly diverse, reflecting changes in relationship formation and dissolution. People live in a variety of household types over their lifetimes. They may leave their parental home, form partnerships, marry, and have children. Some people experience separation, divorce, lone parenthood and the formation of new partnerships, leading to new households and second families. More people now spend time living on their own, whether before or instead of marriage or cohabitation, or because of divorce or the breakdown of a relationship.*
> (ONS, 2003a, p.42).

Census data show an expectation that the number of separate households in the United Kingdom will continue to increase throughout the near future. In 2001 there were 24.4 million households, an increase of almost a third since 1971 (ONS, 2003a).

As discussed above the total numbers in the population are expected to continue to increase throughout the same period. This increase, together with the increasing numbers of the population who are living in single person households, is likely to result in a significant increase in demand for accommodation, and an increased emphasis on single persons' dwellings.

Size of households

A further demographic factor which impacts on the level of demand is the size of individual households. This can also be expected to affect not only the number of dwellings required but also the size of those dwellings. Household size can also affect levels of demand resulting from households sub-dividing if existing accommodation is not sufficient to meet existing needs. For example, an older child of a family which is overcrowded in their present accommodation might be influenced to leave the family home and form a single person household earlier than would have otherwise occurred in order to ease the overcrowding situation.

Throughout the past four decades, as the number of households has steadily increased, the mean average of people within each household has steadily reduced as smaller family sizes, single person households, and divorce have become more commonplace. Government data indicates that the proportion of the population living in single person households increased from 14 per cent in 1961 to 29 per cent in 2002. At the same time the proportion of the population living in households of four or more people reduced from 34 per cent in 1961, to 21 per cent in 2002 (ONS, 2003a). Clearly such demographic and social changes impact on the level of demand for accommodation with more households requiring dwellings, and with a need for smaller individual units of accommodation. However, Barker (2003) cautions that one should not assume, particularly in an era of rising incomes, that all smaller households will 'necessarily want smaller housing'.

From 1991 to 2016, 28 per cent of the growth in English households is predicted to come from higher household formation rates. In other words where people are less likely to be forming a household as a couple (Barker, 2003).

Income and wealth

Levels of income, and the distribution of income throughout the population have an impact on demand. The level of a household's income will affect its ability to express its housing desires through the market. For example, a young person living with relatives, who aspires to independence will need to achieve sufficient income to fund the independent accommodation they seek.

Similarly, if a household aspires to move into larger accommodation, or to a dwelling in a more desirable area it is likely that their ability to achieve this wish will be linked to their level of income. As the level of this household's income increases, they are more likely to be able to afford their desired accommodation.

The *distribution* of income throughout the population is also important. Increasing levels of income among greater numbers within the population, i.e. a more equal income distribution, will multiply the above effect with more households being in a position to afford their desired accommodation.

A further relevant factor is, however, the perceived permanence of the income. A temporary increase in income is unlikely to result in a household expressing a different housing preference, for instance by moving from rented into owner occupied accommodation, as any such change would be unlikely to be sustainable in the long term. A subsequent fall in income could have serious implications for the household.

Incomes also have significance for the ability of households to choose particular tenures. There is a marked difference between the incomes of households in owner occupation and those in council renting, for example. The General Household Survey, conducted in 2001 (ONS, 2003b), found that the mean average weekly income of households in owner occupied dwellings was £600, whereas the average for council tenants was £208. Housing association tenants were seen to have similarly low incomes, with an average of £216; with private rented tenants falling in between the two extremes with an average of £382 for those in unfurnished tenancies, and £433 for those in furnished tenancies.

It can be concluded from these figures that as income increases households are more likely to move from social rented accommodation to home ownership. It can also be concluded that the first choice tenure for many of the UK population is owner occupation. When this accommodation is not available the option of renting will be considered. In most cases it could be anticipated that renting with the 'social' landlords – local authorities and housing associations – will be preferred, due to the emphasis on affordable rents. However, for some people the connotation of social housing being a tenure of the last resort and a form of welfare housing may lead them to seek private sector rented housing. For higher income groups, where owner occupation might not be an option due, for example, to the need for job related mobility, higher quality private rented accommodation might also be a preferred option.

In general, however, rising incomes will generally lead to an increase in demand for owner occupied housing. In the UK, although not necessarily elsewhere in Europe, the demand for rented accommodation tends to fall as incomes rise. Among households with lower income levels, however, the effect of rising income may be a qualitative one, stimulating demand for better quality rented accommodation if the costs of home ownership are still prohibitive.

Closely related to income is the concept of social class or 'socio-economic group' which will also influence tenure choice. The percentage of people in each socio-economic group are shown in Table 2.1.

Table 2.1: Proportion of UK population living in each tenure by socio-economic group

Socio-economic group by tenure, 2000/01 United Kingdom				Percentages
	Owned outright	Owned with mortgage	Rented from social sector	Rented privately	All tenures
Economically active					
Professional	12	68	3	17	100
Employers and managers	15	74	3	9	100
Intermediate non-manual	14	66	8	12	100
Junior non-manual	14	52	20	15	100
Skilled manual	18	58	14	9	100
Semi-skilled manual	12	47	29	13	100
Unskilled manual	14	38	35	13	100
All economically active	15	61	13	11	100
Economically inactive					
Retired	62	7	27	4	100
Other	18	13	54	15	100
All economically inactive	48	9	36	7	100
All socio-economic groups	27	41	21	10	100

Source: Social Trends 2003 from General Household Survey, Office for National Statistics; Continuous Household Survey, Northern Ireland Statistics and Research Agency

The main trends which emerge from the statistics are the decreasing use of rented accommodation when moving from 'lower' to 'higher' socio-economic groups. At the same time there is a converse trend toward an increase in the proportion of owner occupiers when moving from 'unskilled manual workers' to 'professionals'. Such statistics can support the contention that most of the population will aspire toward owner occupation, as those in the 'higher' socio-economic groups are more likely to be in a financial position, with secure employment or continuing expectations of a sustained level of income, to take on the financial responsibilities associated with home ownership.

This also means that at the local – or regional – level, the occupational distribution can have important implications for the demand for particular tenures. The extent to which the local economy of any particular area is dependent on industries with a preponderance of workers from a particular socio-economic grouping, will influence local demand for those tenures which are traditionally available to these groups. For example, in a local area in which there is a preponderance of industries in which there is a high concentration of unskilled manual workers we would expect to see a high demand for rented accommodation, and in particular social housing. In another area in which there was a high proportion of professional groups, for instance in a commuter belt, there is likely to be a higher demand for owner occupation and a lower level of demand for rented dwellings.

Wealth and the way in which it is distributed is also a key factor affecting the demand for accommodation. In the UK today most households' assets are held in the form of housing. The ownership of residential property is seen as socially desirable, a situation which has been encouraged by an intensification of the policies of successive United Kingdom governments to encourage owner occupation as the 'natural' tenure choice.

Another conclusion which might be drawn is that some of the increase in demand for this tenure is due to those households who can afford it deciding on owner occupation in order not to be 'left behind' by rising house prices which might exclude them from a future option to purchase their own accommodation. Households who, given other circumstances, might prefer to take advantage of the more flexible rented sectors as they experience life changes may decide to buy earlier than would have otherwise been the case fearing that house price inflation will take the option of home ownership beyond their financial reach.

The availability of finance

Since housing tends to be a very expensive item, most buyers rely on borrowing to fund their purchase. This means that it is not only the household's income which is significant, but also how readily they are able to borrow the necessary finance. During the 1980s and 1990s the expansion in the availability of housing finance through capital market deregulation undoubtedly contributed to the explosion in demand, which generated huge price rises in many areas. By 2003 the average advance loaned by UK building societies for first time buyers was equivalent to 76.9 per cent of the full cost of the property being purchased. At the same time societies were loaning on average an amount equivalent to 2.26 times the annual income of borrowing households (ODPM, 2003a). Such relaxation of the restrictions on lending both contributed to, and was a response to the increase in house prices which occurred during this period.

In addition, the returns available from substitute investments may affect demand, both from owner occupiers and from landlords. Potential purchasers of dwellings may choose to invest any additional income or wealth elsewhere, if this gives better returns than they would anticipate from the ownership of residential property. Existing private landlords might also decide under certain economic conditions that investment in other markets is more attractive and decide to move out of private landlordism. Any such decisions will reduce levels of demand for accommodation among this group.

Price

The price of accommodation, whether the cost of buying or the level of rents, has an impact on demand. As the effective demand for accommodation will be a function of the ability of potential occupants to pay for accommodation, it follows that when the price for particular accommodation is lower, the level of demand will be influenced by this situation and will increase. Conversely, price increases can have an influence on reducing demand.

As the price of accommodation fluctuates there will be an impact on rates at which new households form, with lower prices allowing more new households – or those 'concealed' households previously living with relatives – to be in a position where they are able to afford to pay for independent accommodation. Similarly, as prices rise fewer of these households will be able to realise their independent ambitions and will continue to live in multi-household situations. At the same time some households who were living in independent accommodation can find themselves unable to continue meeting their housing costs at times of rising prices and may be forced to enter into multi-household arrangements, moving to live with relatives or friends until such a time as they can once again afford independent accommodation.

The factors which will be considered to be the 'price' of accommodation within different tenures will vary but many of the impacts of changes in price will be the same. There are a number of elements making up the price of owner occupied accommodation. The purchase price of the dwelling is the main element. If purchase takes place with the aid of a mortgage the interest payments due in respect of the loan, together with any capital or endowment policy payments will be part of the 'price' of the accommodation. A further element of the price will be the costs of purchase transactions (including solicitors' fees, surveys, mortgage arrangement costs and valuation) as well as insurance and maintenance costs for which the owner occupier is responsible.

The main element of the 'price' of rented accommodation will be the rent due to the landlord. The attraction for many who choose to rent is the payment of a one-off rent to cover all of the different elements to be met by those who own their accommodation. The price of accommodation within any tenure will have an impact on demand. Expectations of future price levels are also crucial, particularly in relation to owner occupied property. As was suggested earlier there is a tradition, particularly in the United Kingdom, for owner occupation to be seen as an investment in addition to a method of satisfying an individual's housing need. As a result of this convention the impact of house price increases is for a corresponding increase in properties available for sale as prices reach a level at which owners will decide to cash in on their investment. One result of this phenomenon, as seen during the house price boom of the 1980s, is the increase in demand for more expensive properties as long standing owners within different property value bands 'trade up' to take account of the increase in equity caused by price rises. Equally, owners who hold residential property as an investment will choose to sell once they feel that house prices have reached a plateau, or if they feel that a fall in prices is imminent, in order to maximise the profit from their investment.

The impact of expectations of future price increases is lessened in the rented sectors because of the existence of housing benefit. A tenant of a private landlord who is entitled to housing benefit will see most of the increases in rent met by increased benefit payments, so long as the increase is considered to be within reasonable limits in terms of the rent officer's assessment of the *Local Reference Rents* for the area. (This is examined further in chapter three). A prospective tenant will not be dissuaded from taking up a tenancy which may have a relatively high rent if they will be entitled to housing benefit, and the benefit levels are such that the rent will be paid. As such the impact of an increasing 'price' – in this case rent – for the accommodation will have less impact on demand than the fluctuating price of owner occupied dwellings.

Similarly those tenants of social landlords who receive housing benefit will find the impact of any rent increases tempered by the benefits system. As such the impact of rising rents on the demand for rented accommodation has been, to date, fairly limited. However, as discussed earlier, rented accommodation, mainly in the private sector, has traditionally been used as a starting point, or stepping stone by new households setting up home for the first time and looking in the longer term to move into other types of accommodation. One likely impact of rising rents is therefore to discourage new household formation if this 'first step' is out of the reach of some who would otherwise seek to use it.

In addition to discouraging new household formation an increase in rent levels could also be expected to encourage multiple occupation with more than one household sharing accommodation, and 'concealed' households living with others due to their lack of financial ability to obtain their desired independent accommodation.

Increases in rent can also have an impact in reducing the differential cost between renting and owner occupation (during periods when the cost of owner occupied housing is static or reducing), and as such can be expected to encourage the decision to enter owner occupation among some tenants who might not otherwise have chosen this step. Similarly, those who see owner occupation as a long term aim may make the move earlier than planned if rent levels increase and the difference between the costs of the two tenures appears less prohibitive.

The price of accommodation, whilst influencing overall demand for accommodation in all tenures, as discussed earlier, can specifically affect the demand for owner occupied housing in different ways. In relation to first-time buyers, rising prices may have two opposing effects. As prices rise, the quality of dwellings which can be afforded will reduce. In addition, fewer first-time buyers will be in a position to enter the housing market. If, however, prices are expected to continue to rise, this may stimulate additional demand in the short run, as new buyers choose to enter the market earlier in an effort to 'beat' the increases. At the same time existing owners might be stimulated, by price rises, to 'trade up', selling their existing properties to release equity which can be used to buy more desirable and expensive properties.

Interest charges add to the 'price' of owner occupied housing. Any owner with a mortgage has to meet the cost of interest payments in relation to the loan. The level of interest rates at any given time will be a cost to the owner and will influence their economic decisions about continuing in their present accommodation, or whether it is possible or necessary to 'trade' up or down. Increases in interest rates may depress demand, as was seen in the house price crash in the late 1980s. During that period the government, faced with inflation in the housing market used an interest rate policy as the main tool for controlling inflationary pressures. The rise in interest rates reduced the amounts that individuals could afford to borrow – and therefore the amount they could afford to pay when moving house – with the net result that house prices fell dramatically. During the late 1990s and into the early 2000s the country saw the lowest interest rates since the 1960s, and this contributed to a boom in house prices. In 1998 the average dwelling price in the United Kingdom was £82,000 (ONS, 2000). By 2001, this had risen to £112,800. In the year between 2000 and 2001 alone the average house price rose by 11 per cent (ONS, 2003a). By the end of 2003 house prices had continued to rise, with a rise of 11 per cent to an average of £142,033 during 2003 alone.

Perceived availability

The level of availability of accommodation, or the perception among households of its availability, will have an impact on levels of demand. If there is a perception that dwellings are not available those new households who might be looking to form and seek independent housing will be discouraged from doing so. Similarly, if a particular tenure is perceived as unavailable, then those demanding accommodation will be forced to transfer to alternative tenures. For example in areas where the local authority has a lettings policy which precludes single people under a certain age from joining the waiting list, or has very little single persons' accommodation among its housing stock, young single people will have to look to other tenures, typically the private rented sector, to meet their housing need. Traditionally in the United Kingdom the private rented sector has often provided an essential first stage for young people leaving home, including students and those saving a deposit to buy their own home. It also complements the social rented sector in meeting demand for accommodation from those people on low incomes, and those who prefer to rent rather than to buy.

Research suggests that many new households appear to choose their parents' tenure type, possibly because it is the tenure with which they are most familiar. An OPCS *Survey Into Recently Moving Households* in 1984 looked at the 'housing pathways' followed by different households – that is, the history of the different tenures and types of accommodation occupied by a sample of those who had recently moved house. The survey identified that newly forming households were likely to move directly from parental homes into owner occupation (33 per cent of those surveyed) and furnished renting (35 per cent). A further 15 per cent moved directly into local authority rented accommodation. Whilst this balance is not equivalent to the proportions of the stock in each of the different tenures, there are limitations on access to social rented housing and owner occupation, and therefore these tenures might be under-represented among those taking the first step to independence. The survey showed, however, that a significant proportion of the population follow their parents' tenure choice, or would choose to if finance and availability allowed.

The impact of government policies

Government policies clearly have an enormous influence on demand for particular tenures. For example, rent controls and increased security of tenure following the 1977 Rent Act encouraged the demand for private rented accommodation, though this was increasingly unavailable due to the impact of these restrictions on the attractiveness of rented accommodation as an investment opportunity for private landlords, and much of the demand switched to public rented housing.

Successive governments of different political hues have promoted home ownership through a range of policies. For example, the Right to Buy provisions originally introduced in the 1980 Housing Act have contributed greatly to the increase in owner occupation over the past 25 years. After the implementation of the Right to Buy for tenants of local authorities and many housing associations, the levels of discount available on the sale price were periodically increased, thus reducing the cost of purchasing for many tenants. However, in 2003 the government responded to the concerns about the loss of rented stock through the Right to Buy by reducing the discounts available to a maximum of £16,000 (less than half the previous level) in 41 high demand areas such as London and the south east region. At the same time, changes in the financial regimes for both local authorities and housing associations have put pressure for rent increases, in turn lessening the differential between the cost of renting and purchasing as part of a government policy of encouraging owner occupation as widely as possible.

6. Housing stock and the supply of housing

The supply of housing is the overall quantity of accommodation made *available* to households either through the market system or through the social rented tenures. Hence it is the amount of property actually available to buy or rent at any given time. This is different to the stock of housing which is the total quantity of dwellings existing in a particular locality.

Since the 1980s there has been a continuing increase in the stock of housing in the owner occupied sector. At the end of 2002, around 70 per cent of the total housing stock of the UK was within this tenure, with 14 per cent per cent in local authority ownership, 10 per cent rented privately and 7 per cent within the housing association sector. A fuller picture can be gained by looking at the age and type of dwellings available within each tenure.

Composition of the stock in each tenure

Within tenures the stock tends to have different characteristics. This can be illustrated by considering the example of the English housing stock.

Table 2.2: Age and type of accommodation in each tenure (England)

	Percentages			
	Owner Occupied	Private Rented	Local Authority	Housing Association
Houses				
Pre-1919	22	30	2	11
1919-1944	18	10	17	6
1945-1964	14	5	21	5
Post 1964	25	7	12	10
Flats				
Pre 1919	5	29	2	19
1919-1944	1	4	3	4
Post 1945	5	10	35	41
Bungalows	10	5	8	4
Totals	**100**	**100**	**100**	**100**

Sources: Adapted from English House Condition Survey, 2001; ODPM Publications, 2003

It is clear from Table 2.2 that there are marked differences between tenures in the age of accommodation currently in use. Within the private rented sector over 70 per cent of properties were built prior to 1945. Of the dwellings owned by housing associations and owner occupiers 40 per cent and 46 per cent respectively are of this older stock. Local authority dwellings are of more recent construction with only 24 per cent being more than 50 years old.

It can also be seen that there are some differences in the types of accommodation between tenures. Within the owner occupied sector 79 per cent of the housing stock consists of houses, with only 11 per cent of dwellings being flats and 8 per cent bungalows. In contrast within the housing association sector 64 per cent of dwellings are flats, and only 32 per cent are houses with the remaining 4 per cent being bungalows. Whilst the total numbers of dwellings in each tenure indicate that the housing association sector is by far the smallest tenure, the preponderance of flats within this sector is significant in terms of the types of developments traditionally undertaken and the ethos behind much of the voluntary housing movement in catering for other than 'traditional' general needs family housing. The table also shows that 40 per cent of local authority dwellings consist of houses built prior to 1964, with only 12 per cent of the stock being houses built since 1964, reflecting the large scale local authority house building which took place following the first world war and the boom during the 1950s. It is also notable that only 5 per cent of local authority dwellings are flats built prior to 1945, reflecting the emphasis on building houses in the first half of the century. The immediate post-second world war policy of building as many new homes as possible, together with a commitment from governments of both political hues to clear slums and replace with large scale family housing is reflected in the table which shows that 35 per cent of the total local authority stock consists of flats built since 1945.

It is worth noting that England is unusual in the low proportion of flats in its housing stock, compared with the rest of Europe. Many other European countries have one third or more of their housing stock in the form of flats rather than houses, even in countries like Spain where home ownership is high. Within the UK, Scotland is more like the rest of Europe in having a much higher proportion of flats across tenures, than England, Wales and Northern Ireland (Perry, 2003).

General influences on the supply of housing

It will be useful to now look at some of the factors which will have an impact on the supply of housing within all of the tenures.

The supply of housing within tenures is affected by a range of factors, which include:
   a. Patterns of household life cycles have an impact on the availability of housing. As the numbers of households increase, causing an expansion in demand, so there will be an associated impact in reducing the supply as available accommodation is taken up in increasing numbers.

b. The mobility rates of existing occupiers will affect how often dwellings become available to rent or buy. Increasing supply can be expected, particularly in the private rented sector which is used by those groups such as young single households who, as seen earlier, are among the most mobile in the population. Clearly, high levels of mobility will result in high levels of turnover and thus increased availability of accommodation. Conversely, family housing within the public sector, for which there are usually longer waiting times to gain access, and greater security of tenure than in the private sector, will tend to have comparatively lower levels of turnover. The net outcome will be less supply of available accommodation within existing stock in this sector when compared to private rented accommodation.

c. Government policies in relation to taxation and planning regulations will also have an impact on the supply of housing. Tax concessions may be used to stimulate additional supply to particular tenures, whereas tax increases are likely to adversely impact on housing supply. Planning regulations may be used to influence the types, tenures and locations of new housing.

The Barker Review examined the constraints on housing supply which were seen as preventing the output of new housing responding to price signals. The Review identified a number of factors linked to market failures and the policy environment.

These included:

*   industry constraints such as the lack of competitiveness of house builders;
*   capacity constraints in relation to skills and innovation as well as the lack of availabile finance to house builders;
*   the impact of policy on such matters as tax, planning regulations and housing subsidies;
*   the lack of availability of land caused by risk averse attitudes of the house building industry, the complex nature of sites, difficulties in land assembly, the planning system's influence on land availability, the need to improve infrastructure, the unpopularity of building development to the general public.

We will now examine ways in which the stock of each tenure can increase.

The supply of privately rented housing

The rate at which new privately rented accommodation becomes available is affected by economic investment decisions reached by existing and would-be private landlords. The return on investments in private rented accommodation – chiefly the income from renting – is a major factor determining whether new housing stock will enter the tenure. The level of returns realised by landlords will be influenced by other factors, such as government regulation through rent controls, the restriction of housing benefit levels, and the existence of tax concessions. As house prices increase the attraction of housing as a longer term capital investment increases, and properties purchased for their long term investment value are likely to find their way into the private rented sector until the price reaches a level at which the landlord chooses to realise the capital tied up in the property. Asset values will be affected by a range of market factors, among them the security of tenure enjoyed by tenants. The deregulation of tenancies through the Housing Act 1988 was an attempt by central government to make private renting more attractive to potential landlords with decreased security of tenure enabling landlords to obtain vacant possession more easily and therefore liquefy (sell to turn into cash) their assets more quickly.

The upturn in the numbers of privately rented dwellings from the 1989 low point followed a number of government policy initiatives which had the stated aim of stimulating growth in the tenure. Assured tenancies, which had been a small scale and rarely used initiative within the 1980 Housing Act, were re-defined and extended by the 1988 Housing Act to cover all new lettings within the 'independent rented sector', a newly defined tenure grouping including both private renting and housing associations. The new 'assured tenancy' offered less security of tenure than the previous 'secure tenancy' by extending the mandatory grounds for a landlord to obtain possession.

The supply of housing for private renting is also affected by the availability of finance. Lending to private landlords is in turn affected by the perceptions of financial institutions about likely available rental income and long term asset value, and thus whether private renting is seen as a good investment. The availability of private finance is also of key importance to both the refurbishment of dwellings and the development of new stock by housing associations, as the reduction of grant levels from central government pushes them to rely increasingly on the money markets to raise funds.

The attractiveness to both lenders and landlords of investment alternatives impacts on the availability of finance to fund new private rented stock. If revenue and capital returns from residential property are expected to yield less than other investment opportunities, there will be less finance available to fund the purchase of housing stock for private renting purposes.

A further crucial factor is the mobility of existing tenants. Traditionally in the UK, the private rented sector has been seen as having the advantage of flexibility for tenants due to it being relatively easy to gain access quickly, subject to having the ability to pay, when compared to social rented housing or owner occupation. As such the more mobile sections of the community have traditionally made use of this tenure which allows swift entry and exit. High levels of tenant turnover within this sector can be attractive to potential landlords who will see only a few long term tenants inhibiting their ability to liquefy their assets through sale of the property once the market price is appropriate.

The supply of owner occupied housing

Since the supply of existing owner occupied accommodation relates to the movement decisions of households, those factors which contribute to demand for this tenure will also influence supply.

Unlike most of the rest of Europe and North America, most new building in the UK is speculative. As such the provision of new housing within this tenure is largely based on expectations of future price changes. These expectations in turn depend on the flow of funds to housing finance markets, the current level of vacant dwellings for sale, and the time taken to sell current houses – the rate of turnover. Unlike many other markets where an increase in demand will result in a fairly swift increase in supply, housing supply is relatively inelastic (unresponsive to price changes in the short term) due to the lead-in periods necessary to construct new housing stock. Housing developers will find the conditions for construction more favourable in a situation where the building societies and banks are able or willing to lend sufficient funds to potential buyers.

Equally, in a situation where there are less properties on the market and they are selling fairly quickly, prices are likely to rise, which will in turn encourage the development of new properties for sale.

Allied to these factors, the costs of land, construction costs, the cost of borrowing (interest rates) will all impinge on the decisions of developers, as will the availability of finance to builders, which in turn will be affected by costs and prices outlined above. It is clear then that each of the different factors influencing the cost of developing and the anticipated profits to be made from investing in new development are all closely linked and in many ways interdependent.

Developers will also take account of the profitability of other work – for instance, non-residential building work and renovations – in deciding whether to develop further housing. The inelasticity of supply in the housing market is also a product of the time lags and delays caused by factors such as planning controls, seasonal factors, and occasional shortages of labour and materials. Each of these factors will also have an influence on the rate at which new housing enters this sector.

As with other housing tenures government policy has an impact on the supply of owner occupied dwellings. One of the major policy initiatives in this area has been the Right to Buy provisions that were considered earlier in relation to the demand for accommodation. Right to Buy sales contributed markedly to the increase in the number of dwellings in the owner occupied sector since the 1980s. Some of those properties purchased by tenants will have also found their way into the private rented sector.

The supply of social rented housing

Unlike the other tenure types, social rented housing, whilst it has always operated within the context of the market, is far more dependent on the context of political and administrative decisions, from central government, local government and agencies such as the Housing Corporation. The new building of social rented housing in the UK has been heavily dependent on government policies in relation to borrowing and capital finance. Since 1979 policies to restrict levels of borrowing by local authorities have reduced their ability to provide new housing for rent, in line with a general trend in government policy toward the privatisation and deregulation of housing provision. At the same time there has been encouragement to housing associations to take over the role as the main developers of new social rented housing by making use of increased levels of private finance as grant levels have reduced. In addition, in any particular local area the political views of the local authority will also have an impact on the types of development and the way in which that development is carried out.

The supply of social rented housing is also affected by the use made of existing stock. The first key factor is the size of the housing stock. Clearly the more social rented housing stock there is, the more likelihood of housing within that sector becoming available to meet demand. This is not to suggest, however, that size is the only determining factor. Clearly the level of turnover within the stock is crucial. For example, a social landlord with a large stock in which there was no turnover is never going to be in a position to meet the housing needs of any but its existing tenants.

An example will illustrate the impact of turnover and its relationship to stock size. Assume that there are two social housing landlords, one with a stock of 20,000 properties and the other with 5,000 dwellings. If the smaller landlord has a turnover of ten per cent of dwellings during a year, this would equal 500 properties becoming available for re-letting. If during the same period the larger landlord has a turnover of two per cent of its dwellings, this would equal 400 homes available for new letting. Leaving aside considerations of the popularity of areas with these respective turnovers, it is clear that in terms of total dwellings being supplied from within the existing housing stock for letting, turnover can have a bigger impact than total stock alone.

Related to the issue of turnover is the mobility of existing tenants. Traditionally, social rented housing has been more difficult to gain swift access to than private rented accommodation, due to the often bureaucratic processes used to administer the rationing process. This has tended to reduce the use of social rented housing among the most mobile groups in society; however a certain level of mobility will obviously occur, and will impact on the level of turnover in the housing stock. As the level of mobility among tenants increases, whether due to factors such as movement to seek employment elsewhere, or tenants choosing to leave the tenure to move into other accommodation, then there will be an increase in supply of dwellings from within the existing housing stock.

Just as the supply of new dwellings affects the level of supply, so the rate at which accommodation leaves the social rented sector will have an impact. Earlier there was consideration of the impact on the supply of owner occupied dwellings of the provisions of the 1980 legislation which gave certain social rented housing tenants the Right to Buy their homes. There has at the same time been a substantial reduction in the numbers of social rented dwellings.

As noted above, whilst the numbers of properties owned by both local authorities and housing associations being bought by tenants under the Right to Buy has fluctuated year by year there has been a steady continuing sale under this policy. At the same time the numbers of new properties being produced within the social housing sector has been consistently substantially lower than the numbers of properties leaving the sector. The net result of this disparity has been a reduction of the number of properties in the social rented sector.

Levels of supply will in addition be influenced by the void management policies of social landlords. Clearly, efficient policies will reduce void times and thus speed turnover to ensure swifter availability for renting of properties vacated. The policies of the landlord will also have a differential impact on the availability of dwellings for different groups within the population. If a landlord has a policy of allocating dwellings only to tenants above a certain age, or with certain family characteristics, then clearly those who fall outside those limits will have less access to the stock of social rented housing. Similarly an increased willingness on the part of the landlord to transfer tenants between properties will increase the supply of accommodation appropriate to the needs of tenants and potential tenants.

Changes in housing supply between tenures

So far there has been consideration of a range of factors which might affect the rate at which housing becomes available within each of the tenures. There is however scope for substantial movement of properties from one tenure to another. The total number of dwellings in Great Britain has steadily increased throughout the past century. For example, in 1901 the total national housing stock stood at 6.3 million; by the end of 2002 the figure had increased to 21.3 million. During the past two decades the stock of owner occupied dwellings, and the stock within the housing association sector have increased. The stock within the owner occupied sector has risen from 12.17 million to 17.04 million, whilst the stock held by housing associations has increased from 472,000 to 1.5 million during the same period. The stock of dwellings in the private rented sector remained fairly steady, changing from 2.37 million to 2.69 million. The only sector to have experienced substantial reductions during this period is the local authority housing stock, falling from 6.57 million to 3.96 million between 1981 and 2001 (Wilcox, 2003).

Factors affecting the movement of dwellings between tenures are considered further in chapter three.

7. Assessment of housing need

As discussed during the introduction to this chapter, inherent in the market system is a requirement for households to have the ability to pay for their preferred accommodation if such housing desires are to be transformed into demand. Analysis of market conditions such as price levels, and effective demand (i.e. demand which is backed up by the ability to pay) can only give part of the picture of the overall levels of housing needed, and what types of accommodation are required. It cannot give the full picture because any such consideration will not take account of those households in need who do not have the finance required to satisfy their needs. Instead it is necessary to draw together information from a number of sources in order to arrive at a complete assessment of housing need.

Traditionally many local authorities in the United Kingdom relied on their waiting lists as a measure of housing need. They would often base decisions for new building on the perceived shortfalls reflected through the types of accommodation, and in the locations, for which they had the greatest numbers registered on waiting lists. During the immediate post-war period, when large scale local authority housing development was taking place – particularly in Scotland and the north of England – the numbers of applicants for whom the authority could not provide accommodation was often the major factor influencing the type of new development taking place. At the same time many local authorities had waiting lists through which lettings were solely based on date order. Many authorities had restrictions on who could join their lists with, for example, applicants having to have reached a certain age or have lived in the local area for a given period of time before becoming eligible to register on the list. Such restrictions clearly distort any assessment of 'need' using the lists as a basis.

As the role of local authorities as developers of new social rented housing has diminished they have been subject to increasing encouragement from central government to expand and develop their role as 'strategic enablers'. Whilst the strategic planning role had already existed for local authorities for some time the emphasis on this aspect of their activity was brought into sharper focus by government proposals in the 1987 White Paper, *Housing: The Government's Proposals*, which specifically stated that:

> *...the future role of local authorities will essentially be a strategic one: identifying housing needs and demand, encouraging innovative methods of provision by other bodies to meet such needs, maximising the use of private finance, and encouraging new interest in the revival of the independent rented sector.*

The crux of this role, then, is for authorities to take overall responsibility for assessing the level of housing need within their area, and for the encouragement of partnership arrangements with both the private sector and housing associations to facilitate the development of accommodation to meet that need.

It was noted earlier that the census measure of the total numbers of the population will not give a fully accurate picture of the level of demand for housing. It is, however, a useful starting point for the analysis of housing needs. The census data that were considered earlier in relation to the total population, numbers of households, and household size give a useful basis for assessment, looking at the way in which the population is structured in terms of the age profile and the way in which households are structured. Factors such as the birth rate and mortality rates can also contribute to building up a picture of likely future housing need in terms of overall stock, and also the types and sizes of dwellings which will be required.

Guidance issued by the Office of the Deputy Prime Minister in 2000 recognises that local authorities will have their own specific local circumstances and recommends that approaches to measuring housing need are largely adopted to reflect those local situations. It suggests that authorities begin by looking to establish the backlog of existing need and the rate of newly arising need. The guidance also suggests that authorities should go beyond this to consider indicators of levels of supply of affordable dwellings and should incorporate stock condition surveys to allow consideration of the availability and standards of available dwellings.

The guidance suggests that local authorities might commission housing needs surveys, and consider them together with other available administrative data, such as social landlords' transfer lists, data showing the numbers housed and awaiting re-housing by housing associations, records on Right to Buy and low cost home ownership demand, and data kept by housing aid and advice agencies.

Authorities are also recommended to consider demographic, economic and market data, by considering forecasts of the total population and number of households from census data, household projections and migration estimates. In addition, information on house prices and private rent levels adds to the overall view of need and likely access for those seeking housing in the local area (ODPM, 2000).

Communities Scotland introduced a *Local Housing Need and Affordability Model for Scotland* in 2003, which aims to provide a snapshot picture of the annual net need for affordable housing in each Scottish local authority area. The model recognises the need for local authorities to use its data when considering stock size imbalances and stock which is unsuitable or in poor physical condition.

8. Housing quality

As has already been stated, there is a range of factors influencing the supply of dwellings to each housing tenure. A further crucial issue for consideration is the impact of such socio-economic and demographic factors on the quality and standard of the accommodation. A useful starting point in any consideration of the quality of accommodation is to look at a definition of what might be considered to be standards of 'reasonableness' or 'fitness' in relation to dwellings.

Condition surveys

Regular, five yearly, house condition surveys are carried out for England by the government and within the three devolved governments. Each of the surveys considers whether dwellings have a range of basic amenities and the physical condition of the properties.

The 2001 English House Condition Survey found that the number of dwellings which did not meet the Decent Homes Standard (unfit, in disrepair, in need of modernisation or failing to provide sufficient thermal comfort) had fallen to 7 million (33 per cent of the total stock) from 9.4 million (46 per cent) at the time of the last survey in 1996.

The reason for most properties failing to meet the Decent Homes Standard was a lack of thermal comfort – 5.6 million homes (80 per cent of all non-decent dwellings). Two million were in disrepair, the number of unfit homes (the statutory measure and one element of decent homes) was 900,000 (4.2 per cent), and 500,000 required modernisation.

The Northern Ireland survey in 2001 found that 31,600 dwellings, 4.9 per cent of the total housing stock, lacked basic amenities. The condition of the dwelling stock was not uniform, with 8.5 per cent of rural dwellings failing to meet basic standards compared with 3.1 per cent of urban dwellings. The main causes for properties being defined as unfit were unsatisfactory facilities for the preparation of food (19,600), disrepair (19,600) and dampness (16,300). 5,500 dwellings were found to be lacking a kitchen sink, 5,500 had no piped water, 8,400 no internal WC, 8,700 no bath or shower, and 8,100 no wash hand basin. The majority of these dwellings were vacant at the time of the survey. The survey concluded a clear relationship between age and the Decent Homes Standard. One half of those dwellings built before 1919 were non-decent, and this proportion reduced steadily until it was minimal for those properties built since 1980.

Elderly heads of household were more likely to live in non-decent homes – 46 per cent compared to the overall average of 30 per cent for all households.

The Welsh House Condition Survey of 1998 identified 98,200 dwellings failing to meet the fitness standard, representing 8.5 per cent of the total housing stock at that time. Of those dwellings built before 1919, 14.9 per cent were unfit, a level which reduces steadily with newer properties with only 2.4 per cent of those properties built since 1965 failing to meet the standard.

The Scottish House Condition Survey of 2002 identified that less than 1 per cent of the housing stock fell *below the tolerable standard*, due to reasons such as dwellings being structurally unstable; damp or poorly ventilated; lacking a wholesome water supply, WC or bath/shower facilities; effective drainage and facilities for cooking food. The Housing Bill introduced in December 2003 aims to replace the current unfitness standard with a new Health and Safety Rating system.

Who lives in poor housing?

As might have been anticipated, the proportion of the housing stock which is unfit reduces in properties of more recent construction. There are, however, a number of factors in addition to age which impact on the standard of dwellings. The English House Condition Survey gives information on the household make up of those households in the worst 10 per cent of dwellings. Consideration of this data provides some useful insights.

Some 6.7 million households live in non-decent homes, of which 5.2 million are in the private sector and 1.5 million in social housing tenancies. Older households are more likely to live in non-decent homes in the private sector, with 39 per cent of those households including someone over 75 years of age, 40 per cent of single persons over the age of 65, and 47 per cent of households who have been resident for 30 years or more living in non-decent private sector housing.

In the private sector some types of households are more likely than average to live in non-decent homes: 43 per cent of the poorest fifth of private sector households are living in non-decent homes, as are 42 per cent of those below retirement age who are either economically inactive or unemployed and some 41 per cent of ethnic minorities. In contrast there is relatively little difference between the quality of housing occupied by different groups within the social rented sector.

Ethnic minority households (27 per cent) are nearly three times more likely to live in poor neighbourhoods than white households (10 per cent). Poor neighbourhoods have relatively high concentrations of pre-retirement households on low income, those who are unemployed or economically inactive, lone parents, and other people living alone or sharing.

Residents of poor neighbourhoods are much more likely than those living elsewhere to view their neighbourhood as having a wide range of problems linked to the environment and its upkeep and to criminal and anti-social behaviour. The most common problems indicated by residents of predominantly local authority-built poor neighbourhoods are the amount of litter and rubbish around (60 per cent of all households in these neighbourhoods), fear of being burgled (50 per cent), vandalism and hooliganism, troublesome teenagers/children, and the general level of crime (all 44 per cent). For households in private sector poor neighbourhoods (who are most likely to live in city and other urban centres) the most common problems are the amount of litter and rubbish (55 per cent), street parking (55 per cent), fear of burglary (44 per cent) and heavy road traffic (42 per cent).

Survey data also suggests that age and income levels are key factors as to whether owner occupiers are likely to carry out repair and maintenance work on their homes. As income increases the likelihood of people spending more money on repairs to their property increases. Data from the survey indicates that households in the lowest income bands were most likely to live in the worst dwellings. This would suggest that those with the lowest income are able to only afford the worst property and are less able to afford repairs.

As owner occupiers age the likelihood of spending money on repairs would appear to decrease. A greater proportion of both the elderly and the younger age groups were found to live in the worst dwellings. As with income, this suggests that the dwellings these groups inhabit were in poorer condition to begin with and that repairs are less likely to have been carried out (ODPMb, 2003).

There is also a link between age and income. The younger the occupier is, the more opportunity there is to earn money which might be spent on improvements in the house. In the same way that the above data shows the link between the income and the dwelling condition of owner occupiers, there will also be a link between the availability of finance to landlords and stock condition. If finance is available to landlords, both in the private and public sector, there are more options available to them in maintaining their dwellings. In relation to local authority landlords there is a crucial impact of government financial controls in determining the amount of resources available to repair and maintain the stock. An associated factor will also be the spending decisions made by local politicians in how to ration and allocate the central government determined total sum.

A further influence on private landlords' decisions to spend on maintenance will be the rate of return on rented accommodation. At the present time there is a relatively poor rate of return for private landlords, and therefore a lack of incentive to invest in improving the condition of housing stock among this group.

As the owner occupied sector has increased, an increasing proportion of home owners will be relatively poorer. Some commentators have noted that the government's push to increase the owner occupied sector has taken numbers beyond limits which are sustainable by the market. In the worst cases the result might be repossession for those encouraged to take on financial responsibilities they cannot afford to meet. For others the impact will be a lack of ability to meet the costs of repairs and maintenance.

Improving housing quality

The English House Condition Survey (which is carried out every five years) last reported in 2003 (based on a survey in 2001). The survey showed that 4.2 per cent of the English housing stock was classified as unfit for human habitation (in that homes failed to meet the basic standards for housing as laid down in the 1985 Housing Act). This represented a total of 885,000 homes. The new survey showed a significant improvement from previous years in that the 1986 survey showed that 8.8 per cent of the housing stock had been deemed unfit. The English House Condition survey also looks at the costs required to remedy unfitness and disrepair in the housing stock and this shows that the total costs for remedying unfitness and completing the backlog of repairs is £80 billion, with requirements to spend

£59.5 billion in the owner occupied sector and £12.5 billion in the private sector. 33.1 per cent of the English housing stock (6.993 million dwellings) failed to meet the Decent Homes Standard – 37.7 per cent of all social housing and 31.9 per cent of all private sector homes (Wilcox, 2003).

Table 2.3: English housing conditions: repair costs and unfitness 2001

Tenure	Stock (000s)	Average comprehensive repair cost per dwelling £	Total comprehensive repair cost for tenure £m	Number of unfit dwellings (000s)	Total cost of remedying unfitness £m
Owner occupied	14,771	4,027	59,483	468	5,247
Private rented	2,191	5,729	12,552	238	2,877
Local authority	2,790	2,384	6,651	132	638
Housing association	1,388	1,418	1,968	47	211
Total stock	21,140	3,816	80,670	885	8,973

Source: Adapted from Wilcox, 2003.

Table 2.4: English housing conditions: unfitness

	2001	
	(000s)	%
Owner-occupied	423	2.9
Private rented	207	10.3
Local authority	110	4.1
Housing association	40	3.0
Vacant	106	15.5
Total stock	885	4.2

Source: Adapted from Wilcox, 2003.

The government has prioritised the need for housing conditions to be improved and made available additional resources for housing as part of the Spending Review and as part of the government's stated intention to link increased spending to better outcomes, the government introduced a new Decent Homes Standard for social housing landlords in July 2000 which required that:

All social housing meets standards of decency by 2010, by reducing the number of households living in social housing that does not meet standards by a third between 2001 and 2004 with most of the improvements taking place in the most deprived local authority areas (ODPM website, *A Decent Home: the revised guidance*, February 2002).

The **Decent Homes Standard** states that all housing must:

- be above the statutory minimum standard (i.e. the fitness standards);
- be in a reasonable state of repair;
- provide reasonably modern facilities and services;
- provide a reasonable degree of thermal comfort.

A similar standard applies in Wales, set by the Welsh Assembly.

In Scotland the Scottish Executive announced in February 2004 the details of its housing quality standard. Under the proposal homes have to be free from serious disrepair, energy efficient and safe and secure. Landlords have been given until 2015 to achieve this target and have to produce a delivery plan by April 2005 setting out how they intend to achieve the target.

The **Scottish Housing Quality Standard** states that dwellings must be:

- compliant with the tolerable standard;
- free from serious disrepair (this applies to all elements of the building);
- energy efficient (effective insulation, insulated hot water systems, energy efficient full central heating);
- provided with modern facilities and services (bathrooms with a WC, bath/shower and hand basins in 'good and usable' condition, kitchen fittings in good condition with adequate storage);
- healthy, safe and secure (lead free internal pipes, mechanical ventilation where appropriate, external noise insulation, smoke detectors, safe electrical and gas installations, internal common areas in a good and safe condition, secure front and rear doors and entry systems operative).

English Decent Homes Standard

a. Meeting the statutory minimum standard

In England, this is the Fitness Standard as set out in the Housing Act 1985 as amended. Dwellings unfit under this standard will also fail the Decent Homes test. Fit dwellings are homes which should:

- be free from serious disrepair;
- be structurally stable;
- be free from dampness prejudicial to the health of the occupants;
- have adequate provision for lighting, heating and ventilation;
- have an adequate supply of wholesome water;
- have an effective system for the drainage of foul, waste and surface water;
- have a suitably located WC for exclusive use of the occupants;
- have a bath or shower and hand basis with hot and cold water;
- have satisfactory facilities for the preparation and cooking of food, including a sink with hot and cold water.

→

In blocks of flats there are additional requirements applying to the whole building in that:

- the building or part is structurally stable;
- it is free from serious disrepair;
- it is free from dampness;
- it has adequate ventilation;
- it has an effective system for the drainage of foul, surface and waste water.

b. Meeting the reasonable repair test
A property is in reasonable state of repair unless:

- one or more key building components are old and because of this need replacing. Key components are:
  - external walls (80 years+);
  - roof (50 years+);
  - windows and doors (40 years+);
  - chimneys (50 years+);
  - central heating boilers (15 years+);
  - gas fires (30 years+);
  - storage heaters (30 years+);
  - electric supply system (30 years+).
- Or, two or more other building components are old and because of their condition need replacing or major repair:
  - kitchens (30 years+);
  - bathrooms (40 years+);
  - radiators (40 years+).

c. Meeting the reasonably modern facilities and services test
If three or more of the following are lacking then the home is not decent:

- kitchen 20 years old or less;
- kitchen providing adequate space and layout for food storage and food preparation;
- bathroom 30 years old or less;
- appropriately located bathroom and WC;
- adequate noise insulation;
- adequate size and layout of common entrances for blocks of flats.

d. Meeting the thermal comfort test
A dwelling must have both:

- efficient heating (programmable central heating systems);
- effective insulation (cavity insulation where possible, plus 50 mm loft insulation for gas/oil heating and 200 mm for electric systems).

The requirement to meet the Decent Homes Standard is a factor which impinges on the financial planning of all social landlords. The implications of the issues arising are considered in the next chapter.

Housing Health and Safety Rating System

In December 2003 the government introduced a new Housing Bill which proposes to replace the Fitness Standard in England with a new Housing Health and Safety Rating System (HHSRS). This will become an evidence based system which numerically rates the level of risk of harm (or potential harm) to any vulnerable actual or potential user of a dwelling. This measure will replace the statutory minimum standard test to be included in the Decent Homes Standard.

Conclusion

From this chapter we have seen that there is a range of contextual factors which impact on the housing system and the types and quality of housing available within different tenures. We have also noted that many economic and social factors have an impact on access to housing and the type of housing available. It can also be seen that government policy initiatives are used to steer and encourage changes in the housing system, through a range of measures from setting standards for decent homes to encouraging the privatisation of public sector housing. Often the government will use legislation to change the legal rights of tenants (such as the introduction of the Right to Buy) or to alter the role of local government, or the housing associations.

References and further reading

Barker, K. (2003) *Review of Housing Supply: Securing our Future Housing Needs: Interim Report – Analysis*, ODPM, London.

Centre for Policy on Ageing (1984) *Home Life*, CPA, London.

Communities Scotland (2003) *Scottish House Condition Survey 2002*, Scottish Executive/Communities Scotland.

Kemp, P. (2004) *Private Renting in Transition*, CIH, Coventry.

Mayor of London (2002) *Draft London Plan*, Greater London Authority, London.

Northern Ireland Housing Executive (2003) *Northern Ireland House Condition Survey 2001*, NIHE.

Office of the Deputy Prime Minister (2003a) *Housing Market Report: September 2003*, ODPM, London.

Office of the Deputy Prime Minister (2003b) *English House Condition Survey 2001*, ODPM, London.

Office for National Statistics (2000) *Social Trends 30*, HMSO, London.

Office for National Statistics (2002) *Social Trends 32*, HMSO, London.

Office for National Statistics (2003a) *Social Trends 33*, HMSO, London.

Office for National Statistics (2003b) *General Household Survey*, HMSO, London.

Perry, J. (2001) 'International Comparisons', in Wilcox, S., *Housing Finance Review 2001/2*, CIH/CML/JRF, Coventry and London.

Wilcox, S. (2003) *UK Housing Review 2003/4*, CIH and CML for the Joseph Rowntree Foundation, Coventry and London.

CHAPTER 3:
Finance for social housing

1. Introduction

This chapter provides an overview of the main features of finance for social housing in the UK, and highlights the key reasons for, and implications of, a number of recent policy changes.

It begins by considering the nature of housing and the reasons why housing finance is an important policy issue, and examines the key influence of the economic context. It next considers the nature of public finance for social housing, by both local authorities and housing associations. It explores the specific arrangements for the funding of development and rehabilitation of social housing – called capital spending – as well as finance for spending on management and repairs and maintenance, called revenue spending. It next examines the importance of budgets and budgetary control in managing financial resources and achieving financial objectives. It then considers the arrangements for the provision of personal, financial subsidy to tenants, the housing benefit system, as well as the help available to owners. Finally, the chapter examines various approaches to financing tenure transfer and concludes with a brief evaluation of the overall effects of recent changes to social housing finance for housing in the UK.

Readers requiring a more detailed guide to aspects of housing finance should consult *Housing Finance* (Garnett and Perry, forthcoming 2004).

The nature of housing and the need for finance

The term housing finance includes all sources of funding for housing, whether public or private. Housing is a commodity much like any other, in that it can be produced, bought and sold, whether by private developers, social housing providers, landlords or individual owners. So, why is finance such an important issue in housing markets?

Housing is a very expensive item to produce and, for most households, it is by far the most expensive item in their household budget. The high cost of housing means that those who wish to buy property invariably have to find external sources of finance to help them, usually borrowing funds from financial institutions, such as building societies and commercial (high street) banks.

However, housing is not simply a consumer good, wanted only for the service it provides in giving households shelter and security. It is a very durable commodity; with proper maintenance, it lasts for a very long time. This means that people view housing as an *asset*; they can put money into housing, and feel reasonably secure that, at some future date, they can sell the property and get their money back. Unlike assets such as stocks and shares, however, the service which housing provides can be used by someone other than the owner, without it (necessarily) affecting its ultimate asset value. This means that property owners can either live in the dwelling themselves – as owner occupiers – or they can let someone else live there, as tenants, for a regular payment – a rent. Renting permits those who either can not afford to buy, or do not wish to buy, to obtain the services of a home. However, since landlords buy housing as an asset, they will wish to ensure that the income they earn from it, the return on their investment, is at least comparable with the return from other investments. If it is not, they will cease to keep their housing assets, and sell them to invest their money elsewhere.

House prices (or rents) in private markets

The term private markets, as explored in chapter two, refers to a situation in which prices for goods or services are determined by the interaction of supply (the goods or services offered by the sellers) and demand (the willingness and ability of customers to purchase or pay rent). In private housing markets, you can observe the way that changes in demand and supply affect prices most easily in owner occupied markets. When very many people are keen to buy, prices are pushed up – as we saw during the housing 'booms' of the mid to late 1980s and then again in the late 1990s/early 2000s. Conversely, when the demand for owner occupied homes collapses (perhaps due to increased interest rates causing an increase in the monthly loan repayments, or rising unemployment causing falling household incomes), prices will be driven down. This happened mainly in parts of England from around 1990 to 1995 (depending on the region), as Table 3.1 shows. Prices had risen fastest in London and the south of England in the late 1980s, so the market collapse occurred earlier there and with a greater effect on prices.

Table 3.1: Average regional house prices (selected years and English regions), 1985-1995

Region	1985	1990	£ 1992	1993	1995
North	22,786	43,655	48,347	49,337	**47,062**
North West	25,126	50,005	56,377	**54,890**	56,537
Greater London	44,301	83,821	**78,254**	78,399	89,527
Rest of the South East	40,487	80,525	**74,347**	74,605	80,949

Source: Wilcox, 2003

Notes: the 'trough' (lowest average price level) for each region in the slump of the early 1990s is emboldened

When landlords let properties in private rented housing markets, assuming there are no rent controls (price ceilings set by the government), a similar process operates. As already identified, rents must offer a reasonable return on the investment made by the landlord. If private market rents fall to levels which do not provide a sufficient return to landlords, they will withdraw from renting, causing the supply to fall. This will, ultimately cause rents to rise again, until the supply from landlords prepared to stay in the market just equals the demand at the market rent.

Access problems for low income groups

At market rent levels, there are likely to be many households who wish to rent, but who cannot afford the price. They may have a need for housing, but cannot turn this need into a demand for housing. This is the case in many parts of the UK where there is a shortage of decent homes available at rents that many people can afford. So, rents, like house purchase prices, are relatively expensive and unless landlords receive a reasonable return, they will not let property.

Before the public sector became involved in the provision of finance for housing, families with low incomes were forced to live in very overcrowded, poor quality properties, often sharing with a number of other families. The government first became committed to the provision of finance for house building after the end of the First World War. It provided capital subsidies toward the cost of building council homes, which is examined in chapter one. Much later, councils were urged to introduce rent subsidy schemes, in the form of rent rebates. Public finance was then used to provide lower-cost homes via *capital* subsidies, but also directly to reduce weekly housing costs for households via *revenue* subsidies. The current provision of public finance for housing still has these two distinct elements, as you will see.

In more recent years, the main role in developing new social housing has switched substantially to voluntary, not-for-profit organisations – the housing association movement, also called registered social landlords (RSLs). Local authorities have, increasingly, been forced to take an enabling role, facilitating the production of housing by other providers. However, the resources available from the public sector for housing are constrained by broader economic factors – such as whether the UK economy is expanding or contracting, and whether there is ample employment, which generates more tax revenues from income tax, VAT, etc. The next section, therefore, considers the importance of the economic context to housing.

2. Housing in the economic context

Section one began by pointing out that housing is a commodity that must be produced like any other. It is expensive and the production process takes a relatively long time because of its complexity. (This process is examined in detail in chapter four). Housing construction is a very important industry, with a significant impact on the national economy. As with any industry, it is also affected by economic factors, and the economy tends to grow unevenly and is subject to cyclical patterns, with periods of strong growth followed by periods of falling output, or recession.

The significance of economic growth

As the economy grows, output is rising, so more income is created. Higher incomes mean higher tax receipts for central government. The demand for many goods, including housing, grows strongly too, which stimulates high levels of output from the construction industry. However, since housing takes a long time to produce, the main initial effect of rising demand is to push up house prices, as more buyers chase the same number of properties. As shown in Table 3.1, this could be seen clearly during the late 1980s to early 1990s, when despite rising housing starts, house prices rose dramatically.

When the economy ceases to grow, and then goes into recession (also called negative economic growth), there is falling output and national income. This means higher unemployment and lower household incomes. Uncertainty leads households to put off buying property or moving to a larger, more expensive home, and renovations are delayed. This results in reduced demand for housing output, which adds to the growing numbers of unemployed, further reducing national output and incomes.

At the same time, house prices face downward pressure as demand falls. In a severe recession, as in the early 1990s, house prices may even fall in real terms; this means that after allowing for inflation (the general increase in prices felt across the whole economy), housing becomes cheaper relative to other goods and services. Unemployed owner occupying households, unable to afford their mortgages, may fall into arrears and suffer 'repossession' – which means that the institution from which they borrowed the finance for the home takes possession of it, in order to sell it and re-coup the loan. The 'owners' are evicted. Similarly, unemployed renting households may fall into rent arrears, and may be evicted as a result. This increase in homeless households will generate higher demand for social housing provision, as local authorities have a statutory duty to provide accommodation for certain priority groups (see chapter five), and housing associations also are expected to provide housing for these households.

It is evident that during these booms and slumps, public sector expenditure will tend to move in the opposite direction to national income. Higher levels of unemployment mean falling tax receipts, but this also means higher expenditure on welfare payments, such as jobseeker's allowance, income support and housing benefit. Government expenditure is rising whilst it is collecting less revenue. It can choose to fill the gap by more borrowing – increasing public sector net borrowing (PSNB) – or it must reduce public expenditure. This choice depends on the policies of the government for the whole economy, known as macroeconomic policies.

The impact of the government's macroeconomic policies

Macroeconomics is concerned with the operation of the economy as a whole. In the UK during the 1950s and 1960s, the main macroeconomic concern of the government was unemployment. In recession, falling output means increasing unemployment. This also means falling government revenues from taxes. In an effort to maintain output and employment levels, the government would attempt to make up for the fall in private expenditure by raising public sector spending. This, of course, necessitates an increase in public borrowing, because public sector receipts fall at the same time. This *demand management* approach was first advocated by an influential Cambridge economist called John Maynard Keynes, following the Great Depression of the 1920s/30s. He argued that the government must manage demand, and be prepared to borrow during recession, if such economic catastrophes are to be avoided.

However, by the mid 1970s, the government was faced with a new and persistent concern: that of chronic inflation. Inflation is a sustained increase in the general price level, such that goods in general become relatively more expensive over time. By the end of the 1970s (due partly to government policies as well as huge increases in the price of an essential raw material, Middle-east oil), inflation in the UK reached record levels, approaching 25 per cent per annum. This meant that each year goods in general were costing almost a quarter more. The key macroeconomic goal now became low inflation. *Monetarists*, such as Milton Friedman in the USA, argued that inflation was due to increases in the supply of money in the economy, fuelled significantly by increased public sector spending and increased borrowing. Therefore, the key role for the government was to spend less and curb borrowing. Keynesian demand management approaches were viewed as unacceptably inflationary.

Monetarists argued that the more that the government borrows, the more that it has to pay to induce people to lend – i.e. interest rates have to rise. This has implications not only for government costs, but also for all industries' and households' costs. Some firms may be put out of business as a result, and households with mortgages will certainly face higher repayments. Hence, more recent government policies have focused on controlling public spending in order to reduce the amounts borrowed by the public sector. This has implications for all aspects of public expenditure, of course, and not just housing.

Fiscal rules
The present government places particular emphasis on three main 'fiscal rules' for managing public finances, which to some extent reflect European Union requirements such as those set out in the Maastricht Treaty:

1. The 'golden rule', which says that in the long term, the government will borrow only to invest, not for current (revenue) spending.

2. Public debt must be at a sustainable levels, currently regarded as below 40 per cent of national income.

3. Only bodies owned and controlled by the private sector are exempt from these rules. This means, of course, that, while HAs are exempt, LAs are not, and, as a result, their borrowing counts as public borrowing and is part of the total that is monitored carefully by the Treasury according to these fiscal rules.

The role of interest rates

In addition to a commitment to controlling government expenditure, interest rates have also been used by UK governments as a key weapon in the fight against inflation. If inflation is rising, an increase in interest rates deters borrowing, which reduces the amount of money available to spend. Less money to spend means less demand, and so less upward pressure on prices. In the UK, a substantial part of consumer spending is undertaken with borrowed money, most importantly in housing markets for home purchase and for home refurbishment, but also for goods such as cars and major household items. Hence, increasing interest rates and so raising the cost of borrowing should reduce demand and limit the upward pressure on prices. Reduced consumer spending should also force firms to remain more competitive if they are to continue to sell their goods.

At one time, interest rates were entirely under the control of the Chancellor of the Exchequer, but, in the 1990s, there were growing concerns that political pressures had resulted in interest rate changes that were not necessarily in the best interests of the economy. Hence, control over these was passed to an independent *Monetary Policy Committee* of the Bank of England, whose members meet monthly to take decisions on interest rate changes, based solely on economic data (such as output and inflation).

Unfortunately, as we have seen over recent years, the emphasis on interest rates as an economic weapon has also had major implications for private housing markets. High interest rates, as a result of rising inflation, were partly blamed for the collapse of housing markets early in the 1990s (see Table 3.1), as households were deterred from entering owner occupation or moving home. Rising interest rates had resulted in rising mortgage costs, causing repayment problems for large numbers of households. This resulted in rising numbers of house repossessions by lenders, increased homelessness, and increasing mortgage arrears. Private sector housing output also fell as a result.

In more recent years (late 1990s to date), low interest rates have contributed to rapidly rising prices (see Table 3.2), as they did from the mid to late1980s, because mortgage repayments become much more affordable. Especially in the southern parts of England, this was compounded by rising demand due to a booming economic situation.

Table 3.2: Average house prices (selected parts of the UK), 1998-2002

	1998	1999	£ 2000	2001	2002
England:					
North	57,765	63,501	64,995	71,100	79,457
North West	65,730	71,997	78,166	82,495	92,417
Greater London	115,183	142,690	163,288	182,536	206,839
Rest of the South East	104,323	118,176	137,217	152,836	176,014
Wales	61,180	67,669	72,243	79,850	87,950
Scotland	64,083	69,366	69,877	73,704	76,893
N.Ireland	59,645	66,200	72,471	80,103	112,865

Source: Wilcox, 2003

3. Public finance for housing

Types of finance

As indicated above, the public sector may spend money on housing in two key ways:

a. Capital investment

This pays for, or provides subsidy towards, the building (and rehabilitation) of homes. Thus, it helps to create or protect housing assets, increasing the stock of housing – the total quantity available – as well as its quality. Local authority capital investment, mainly in improving council housing, is undertaken largely by borrowing. Except for certain limited purposes, councils do not receive capital subsidy from government. Housing associations, though, do receive capital subsidy in the form of Housing Association Grant (in Scotland) and Social Housing Grant (in England, Wales and Northern Ireland). In addition, like local authorities, they also borrow money for capital investment. An important distinction, however, is that this borrowing – unlike that by LAs – does not count as public borrowing under the Chancellor's fiscal rules, because HAs are not public sector bodies (see section 2 of this chapter).

Capital subsidies can also assist some households to purchase properties (see section 8, later), but, in general, this does not result in any additional stock being created.

b. Revenue finance

Revenue spending by housing organisations broadly consists of three elements of costs for:

- managing properties;
- repairs and maintenance;
- financing borrowing (paying interest and repaying the original loan).

Government revenue subsidy may assist towards these annual, operational costs of housing organisations, so that rents are lower (for example, Housing Revenue Account Subsidy for LAs in England, which currently takes account of all three elements of revenue costs). Revenue subsidy may also take the form of a personal subsidy for individual households towards the costs of purchasing housing *services* – either mortgage repayment costs or rents (such as housing benefit) – see section 7. Hence, revenue subsidy does not create any new or improved housing assets, but instead focuses on subsidising the housing costs of (mainly) low income households.

An important distinction between council housing and housing association housing is, therefore, the form of subsidy each receives: capital subsidy for HAs and revenue subsidy for LAs. Tenants in all sectors, however, may receive housing benefit subsidy. Some of the main forms of public subsidy to providers and consumers are summarised in Table 3.3, and these are examined in more detail in this and subsequent chapters.

Table 3.3: Examples of public sector housing subsidies

Paid to: Subsidy type	Local authorities	Housing associations	Consumers
Capital	(Limited) specified capital grants (e.g. to pay for disabled facilities' adaptations) Assistance available to offset any remaining ('overhanging') debts after LSVT	Housing Association Grant (Scotland); Social Housing Grant (England, Wales and N. Ireland)	**For ownership** Right to Buy discount; Right to Acquire; Homebuy; Cash Incentive Scheme; Do It Yourself Shared Ownership (DIYSO); Conventional Shared Ownership
Revenue	Housing Revenue Account (HRA) Subsidy (England and Wales); Housing Support Grant (Scotland)	N/A	**For renters** Housing benefit **For mortgagors** Mortgage benefit (in income support)

Declining public subsidy

The desire to 'level the playing field' between tenures, arguably to improve incentives and choice for individual households, has resulted in public sector subsidy to housing declining substantially, by a staggering 67.4 per cent in real terms between 1980/1 and 2001/2 (Wilcox, 2002). In addition, the early 1990s saw a change in focus, such that:

What has occurred has been a major transfer of resources from those programmes conventionally defined as public expenditure on housing (mainly subsidies to public sector housing and new capital investment) towards other expenditure (Housing Benefit and support to owner occupiers). (Malpass and Murie, 1994, p. 109).

This is demonstrated clearly by Figure 3.1.

Figure 3.1: The changing balance of subsidy

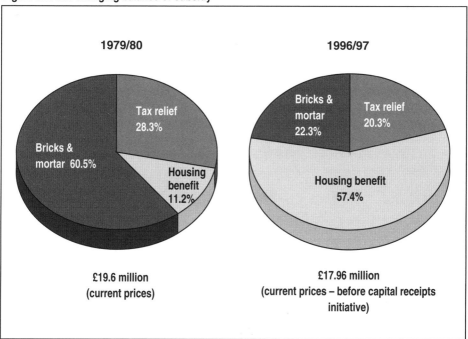

Source: Garnett, 2004

Hence, over the past two decades, there has been both a decline in the quantities of public investment and a shift in focus, from capital programmes to revenue spending. This decline in capital investment has affected English local authority housing particularly badly, as demonstrated in Table 3.4

Table 3.4: Housing capital investment by local authorities in England
£ million at 2000/01 prices (i.e. in real terms)

1980/1	1985/6	1990/1	1995/6	2000/1
6,637	5,242	3,975	2,869	2,777

Source: Wilcox, 2003

Planning public expenditure on housing

The central government's plans for expenditure on housing are set out in their bi-annual Spending Reviews, which cover spending by all government departments. Most of the funding for housing in England comes via the Office of the Deputy Prime Minister (ODPM). In Scotland, Wales and Northern Ireland (when devolution is operating), the devolved governments (via the Scottish Executive, the Welsh Assembly Government and the Northern Ireland Department for Social Development) plan spending on housing (except housing benefit, which remains centrally controlled). These spending plans permit the devolved governments and the UK government to plan their borrowing needs with greater certainty.

As shown in Table 3.5, the trend of falling subsidy, identified above, has only just started to reverse. By 2002/03, housing received only 1.2 per cent of total public expenditure, the lowest of all the main spending functions, followed closely by Agriculture, fisheries, food and forestry (at 1.4 per cent) and Culture, media and sport at 1.6 per cent (Wilcox, 2003).

Table 3.5: Total Managed Public Expenditure on housing
£ billion at 2000/01 prices (i.e. in real terms)

1980/1	1985/6	1990/1	1995/6	2000/1	2001/2
14.0	7.7	6.7	5.9	3.2	4.6

Source: Wilcox, 2003

Financial accounts

Capital and revenue spending must be recorded by all social housing providers in separate financial accounts. Accounts are simply records of financial transactions over a period of a year.

Both LAs and HAs have *capital accounts* to record capital income and spending, but whereas HAs are free to borrow capital funding (from financial institutions) as they see fit, local authorities are heavily constrained by central government policies. As identified above, HAs may also receive significant public capital subsidies, called Social Housing Grant (SHG) in England, Northern Ireland and Wales, and Housing Association Grant (HAG) in Scotland, which is examined in section 5.

The revenue account for a local authority's housing is called the *Housing Revenue Account* (HRA) whereas for a HA it is usually called the *Income and Expenditure Account* (like private landlords). These contain records predominantly of rent income and expenditure on management, maintenance, and loan charges, though local authorities may also receive some government subsidy to the HRA.

In addition, LAs have a *General Fund Account* (which also receives government revenue subsidy) for all other local authority (including non-council housing) activities (such as homelessness services and renovation grants). The New Financial Framework has also recently created another two accounts for English local authorities, which are examined in detail in section 4.

In Scotland only, the capital account is divided into Blocks A and B. Block A is for expenditure on council housing and is also known (confusingly) as the 'HRA' element of capital expenditure. This is because any borrowing for council stock (in the capital account) will appear as annual debt repayments in the housing revenue account (HRA). Block B is for expenditure on other stock, such as private sector renovation grants or mortgages for Right to Buy purchasers. This is also known as the 'non-HRA' element. A small amount of virement (transfer) may be permitted between the two blocks of capital expenditure.

4. Finance for local authorities

This section examines the funding of local authorities, both for council and non-council housing activities. It begins by examining a key piece of legislation which set the rules for LA finance in England and Wales throughout the 1990s, the 1989 Local Government and Housing Act, while identifying some key differences in Scotland. It examines the key implications of the act, firstly for capital spending and then for revenue expenditure. It then identifies a number of key changes introduced during the early 21st century, and examines some key reforms to be introduced from 2004/5.

It should be noted that this section applies mainly to England, Scotland and Wales, as local authority housing does not exist in Northern Ireland. Former council housing there is controlled by the Housing Executive (NIHE), an agency responsible to the Department for Social Development.

In the early 1980s, the government introduced a requirement that local authorities offer their tenants the 'Right to Buy'. This was intended both to satisfy the desire by lower income households in council tenure to become owner occupiers, as well as to promote local authorities becoming, increasingly, 'enablers' rather than 'providers' of housing. This policy has had an enormous impact, reducing council housing stock both quantitatively and qualitatively. This is examined further in section 8.

In an effort to reduce public spending and borrowing throughout the 1980s, the government tried various measures to control housing expenditure by local authorities. Borrowing was permitted only for 'prescribed' capital spending, but local authorities were very creative in finding ways around these controls – for example, by using leasing schemes for capital items, which evaded the borrowing controls. This led to the government in 1989 to enact new legislation, which attempted more effectively to control all elements of LA finance for housing.

The Local Government and Housing Act 1989

This Act set out substantial mechanisms of control, as follows:

a. Borrowing
The annual amount which local authorities can borrow for housing capital expenditure is controlled via an annual allocation of 'credit approvals', 'borrowing consents' in Scotland, following a bidding process – see later in this section. (However, this is changing, under new 'prudential borrowing' arrangements, also examined later in this section)

b. Capital grants
A few specific capital grants are available from central government sources, for purposes viewed as desirable by central government, but these are allocated competitively, as part of the bidding process. Councils that actively pursued central government goals, such as partnerships with the private sector, were most likely to be 'winners' in the bidding process.

c. Capital receipts
Capital receipts arise when any assets, such as houses and land, are sold, but the main source of capital receipts has been the sale of council housing to tenants, through the *Right to Buy* policy (see above and section 8). Controls on the use of capital receipts were strengthened by the 1989 Act, except in Scotland; English local authorities could now use only 25 per cent from housing sales (but 50 per cent from land sales) to fund capital spending, with the remainder used to pay off past debts or simply to earn interest for the local authority. In Wales, 50 per cent from house sales could be spent, and 30 per cent from others. This meant that some capital receipts were defined as 'useable' (for local authority expenditure) while the rest were not.

The system in Scotland, whereby councils could use all of their receipts, remained until 1996, which helped to sustain investment levels in Scotland. However, there was an effect in terms of mounting Scottish council housing debt, which later would affect the ability of Scottish councils to transfer their stock (see section 8); unlike in England and Wales, until recently, Scottish councils have not been using capital receipts to repay debts, so average debt levels remain much higher.

Capital receipts have been boosted over recent years, particularly in England, by large scale voluntary transfers (LSVTs), which are examined in section 8. The government is introducing a system to 'pool' capital receipts in England – see later in this section.

d. Revenue income
Revenue income is largely income from council rents together with central government subsidy. The 1989 Act 'ring fenced' the HRA in England and Wales, which means that income from sources other than council housing, such as the council tax, can not be used to subsidise the HRA. So, any contribution to capital

spending from the HRA has to come from rents, called *revenue contributions to capital outlays* (RCCOs), or *capital from current revenue* (CFCR) in Scotland. The government wanted to see rent increases, so that council rents would better reflect the value of the housing, so this provided an important means by which council rents were levered upwards.

However, towards the end of the 1990s, the government became concerned that local authority rents were rising too rapidly, resulting in a spiralling cost for housing benefit payments. Hence, more recent policies have focused on restraining rent increases. We return to this point later.

Capital finance since the 1989 Act

a. The allocations process for capital spending

The process for allocating the government's planned capital expenditure on council housing to specific local authorities differs somewhat in each country, with slightly different rules, different names and different time scales. The description, which follows, is based largely on the capital allocations arrangements in England. However, the general approach elsewhere is similar. Over recent years, the process has become increasingly competitive (in England, Scotland and Wales), with larger proportions set aside each year for specific, competitive funds (known as 'top sliced' allocations).

The key stages in the process are:

i. Compiling the housing strategy and business plan
The first stage requires that each local authority (and the NIHE in Northern Ireland)) produces an annual housing strategy – called the *Housing Strategy and Housing Investment Programme* (HIP) in England, the *Housing Strategy and Operational Programme* in Wales, the *Housing Plan* in Scotland, and the *Annual Housing Strategy* in Northern Ireland. This sets out the local authority's assessment of housing need in its area, together with proposals for a capital programme to implement its *housing strategy*. Since 2001/2, in support of the Decent Homes Standard, LAs in England must also produce a *business plan*, to permit longer-term planning to meet the targets (see later in this section).

A good strategy will have several features – it:

- takes account of the views of relevant local authority departments, such as social services and planning, as well as housing;
- identifies housing needs across all tenures in the local authority area, requiring local authorities to undertake research into their housing markets and housing need in their areas;
- takes into account the relevant housing association *Approved Development Programme* (ADP) – the planned capital spending – for housing associations in the area (see section 5);

- explores opportunities to promote specific government housing policies, particularly stock transfer and/or other initiatives to involve the private sector and/or private finance.

A fuller description can be found on the ODPM and Scottish Executive websites.

ii. Evaluation of the strategies and business plans
The strategies and plans are assessed by the ODPM, DSD in Northern Ireland, Scottish Executive or Welsh Assembly Government (as appropriate), so that the allocation of total expenditure between local authorities and to the NIHE can be determined.

Each part of the UK has a different system for allocating capital resources. As an example, the ODPM allocation is based on:

- The *Generalised Needs Index* (GNI), which is an index of the need for capital expenditure by each local authority, accounting for 80 per cent of any potential allocation. It includes elements for a range of indicators of need, including overcrowding, homelessness and temporary accommodation, benefit dependency, vacant stock, and stock condition in both social and private sectors.
- A discretionary element, determined by the 'quality' of the housing strategy and the local authority's management performance (informed by Best Value inspections), which can add another potential 20 per cent to each council's allocation.

Until 2002/3, the weighting for these two elements was 50/50, so the change to 80/20 has resulted in reduced allocations for many better performing councils (Martin, 2003) – though, of course, more to those with the greatest need. This is intended to ensure that the properties in worst condition are tackled effectively to meet the Decent Homes Standard (see later in this section).

Annual Capital Guideline/Supported Capital Expenditure
After the strategies have been assessed, each authority receives a capital allocation for housing. Until April 2004, this was called the Annual Capital Guideline (ACG) and is now known as Supported Capital Expenditure (SCE) for housing. In England, this is part of the Single Capital Pot – see later in this section – and thus forms part of the whole capital allocation for the authority.

The ACG carried permission to borrow the capital sums required, and was allocated as Basic Credit Approvals (BCAs) and Supplementary Credit Approvals (SCAs) for particular projects approved by the government – called 'borrowing consents' in Scotland. However, under the 'prudential borrowing regime' which now applies, the SCE is simply the amount of borrowing recognised by the government for HRA subsidy purposes (see later in this section).

Currently, in England, with the Single Capital Pot, it is up to the authority to determine how these funds will be spent; they need not be allocated solely to housing. In recognition of the fact that some authorities used leasing agreements to get around previous attempts to control capital spending, the ACG/SCE also has to cover any commitments that the authority might have for leasing charges. Large leasing costs mean that less is available for other spending.

b. Sources of borrowing

The local authority Treasurer (or equivalent) is responsible for all borrowing by a local authority. It is the task of the Treasurer's Department to ensure that the authority obtains its funding at a fair price (rate of interest) and at timely intervals – that is, it should not unnecessarily be taking out loans which are not immediately needed. The Treasurer must also ensure that all rules affecting the operation of accounts are complied with.

The borrowed money is placed in the local authority's *Loans Fund*. Local authorities have a major advantage over housing associations, in that they represent a much more secure 'home' for investments, as local authorities cannot go bankrupt. Local authorities also generally have a much larger *asset base* (the total amount of capital assets owned), so are viewed as very low risk by lenders and generally are able to obtain much more favourable rates of interest.

Local authorities have two main sources for borrowing:

i. The Public Works Loan Board
Finance for this fund is borrowed by the central government, so it should be a cheaper source than the local authorities' own external borrowing, as central government is even more of a 'safe bet'. Each authority receives a quota allocation from the Board, based on its capital programme and existing debts. The Board will also provide short-term emergency funding – i.e. it acts as *lender of last resort* for local authorities – should an authority find itself temporarily short of funds.

ii. Capital markets
Local authorities can issue their own financial instruments, such as bonds, which are sold on the capital market (through the Stock Exchange). Hence, LA bonds compete for buyers with central government and large private sector firms' borrowing. The original purchaser can sell the bond to someone else (who then receives the annual LA interest payments), so the bonds are *tradable* on the capital market. This also enhances their attractiveness to lenders.

c. The impact of capital constraints on local authorities

Since the 1980s, local authorities have virtually ceased to build new homes. For example, housing starts by councils in England, Scotland, Wales and Northern Ireland (by the Northern Ireland Housing Executive) since 1980 are shown in Table 3.6, which illustrates clearly the scale of the decline to 2002.

Table 3.6: Local authority housing starts

	1980	1985	1990	1995	2000	2002
England	27,869	18,076	6,533	579	151	208
Scotland	4,281	2,017	913	288	81	15
Wales	2,343	770	338	45	62	20
N.Ireland (NIHE)	2,901	2,352	1,059	994	22	(N/A)

Source: Wilcox, 2003

The decline in capital funding over more than two decades also put severe pressure on housing renovation programmes, forcing most local authorities to increase rents to fund expensive rehabilitation from revenue sources. As large proportions of LA tenants are in receipt of housing benefit, there was an awareness that most tenants would not themselves have to pay for the rent increases. Unfortunately, for those not in receipt of housing benefit, this provided a greater incentive to move out of council tenure, mostly via Right to Buy, providing a further twist to the 'residualisation' spiral – the process by which council tenure is increasingly the home of the most disadvantaged and poorest households in the UK.

The increased use of competition to allocate capital funds, particularly in England, had the effect of forcing most local authorities to pursue policies that were favoured by the government, including reducing their role as landlords and encouraging partnerships with HAs and the private sector. As identified earlier in this chapter, since 1988, many authorities have chosen to pursue large scale voluntary transfers, transferring all of their stock to (in general) a newly created housing association, to escape restrictions on spending. Since 2001 in England, councils have also been able to bid to set up ALMOs (arm's length management organisations), and though these authorities remain constrained in their ability to borrow for housing expenditure by the government, they have received additional credit approvals. ALMOs seem to have proved popular partly because tenants view them more favourably than transfers (as the council retains ownership of the stock), but primarily because the government has made available significant additional borrowing (subject to a minimum two star Best Value rating). This is examined further in section 8. However, it has been suggested that they may eventually have more financial freedoms under 'prudential borrowing' rules – see later in this section.

Revenue finance

a. The General Fund Account
The General Fund Account is the main revenue account for the whole council, paying for expenditure on schools, libraries, cleansing, leisure centres, etc, as well as funding general housing services which are provided for private sector residents

of a local authority (such as advice centres and help for the homeless). Revenue *income* is obtained from local taxes (the council tax), business rates (collected from businesses and redistributed by the central government), government grants and interest on any unused capital receipts. Expenditure is on a wide range of non-housing and private housing services, and includes housing benefit.

The General Fund Revenue Support Grant
Revenue Support Grant is based on *Standard Spending Assessments* (SSA). This is the amount that the government believes will permit each council to deliver equal service provision, having regard to the needs in the area. The SSA is then reduced by:

- the 'local contribution'; the amount which the government determines can be raised from the council tax (which is levied on households and is based on a 'band' for their properties' value);
- payments from the business rate pool, which is the 'local' tax charged to businesses; this is also determined and distributed by the central government.

Taken together this determines the amount of RSG.

Local authorities have lost the ability to control most of their General Fund income, because, not only is RSG determined by the central government, so also effectively is the council tax (because if this is increased beyond the levels assumed, the grant will simply be reduced) and business rates. Only the level of charges, such as rents for temporary accommodation, remains under their direct control. Furthermore, many would argue that the assessments for Revenue Support Grant have not recognised sufficiently the ever-widening scope of local authority responsibilities – for example, *Community Care* responsibilities, or *Children Act* requirements. Within the General Fund, housing services have to compete with all other types of council provision. Increased expenditure on one element generally demands reduced expenditure elsewhere. This is the main reason why some councils have made significant cut-backs to their provision of housing services to the private sector, closing advice centres or hostels for the homeless, for example.

b. The Housing Revenue Account (HRA)
This is the main account for council housing revenue income and expenditure. The main elements are:

Expenditure:
- Debt interest payments.
- Maintenance costs, which cover day-to-day repairs and planned maintenance programmes (such as re-painting), but *substantial* improvements would be capital expenditure.

- Management costs, such as the costs of paying employees, office expenses, staff training, and so on.
- Revenue contributions to capital outlays (RCCOs) – CFCRs in Scotland – which is revenue income used to help fund capital projects.

Income:
- Rents and charges to council tenants.
- Housing Revenue Account Subsidy (Housing Support Grant in Scotland). an annual subsidy from the government to many local authorities.
- Interest received – paid to the council for Right to Buy mortgages and other loans (Interest received from invested capital receipts from HRA assets must be paid to the General Fund).

Housing Revenue Account Subsidy
The revenue subsidy from central government was originally intended to help to provide councils with a 'level playing field' in the provision of services to council tenants. It was recognised that, for various reasons, some councils would necessarily incur higher costs (e.g. due to higher costs for building and land, resulting in higher loan costs), or may receive less income, than others. So, it was fair that central government took a role in redistributing some income to councils.

Like the system for capital finance, the revenue arrangements underwent substantial revision in England and Wales in 1989. To explain why, we need first to examine briefly the operation of revenue funding under the 1980 Act – a system that largely continues today in Scotland.

i. The 1980 Housing Act paid revenue subsidy in two main parts:

- a housing subsidy to fund any anticipated deficit and hence to restrain rent levels

and
- a rent rebate subsidy, to reimburse the council for actual rent income lost through rent rebates (housing benefit) to their tenants.

The government calculated subsidy on the basis of the estimated income and expenditure for council housing, assuming also a contribution from the General Rate Fund – as the General Fund was then called. As an aim of this subsidy system was to increase council rents, the government assumed both rising rent levels and increasing subsidy from the general rate fund, in making the subsidy calculations – i.e. it used 'notional' figures to calculate the anticipated deficit, rather than real ones. This meant that subsidy could be progressively withdrawn. Any council that chose not to increase rents in line with the assumptions could increase General Fund contributions and/or reduce costs.

In the event, council rents rose rapidly, and eventually, many councils became ineligible for subsidy – the government had lost its ability to exert a lever on council rent levels, in all but 95 English and Welsh councils, by 1987/8. In some cases, rate fund contributions had grown well beyond the assumptions made for subsidy purposes; in others, they were well below the notional figure. Some councils, still in receipt of subsidy, were transferring funds out of the HRA into the General Rate Fund. It became clear that the subsidy was not necessarily being used for the purposes intended.

The government also took the view that the substantial transfers to or from the General Fund were making it impossible to assess how efficient and effective the council housing service was; it permitted the real performance of housing managers to be obscured.

As with capital spending, the central aim of the 1989 Local Government and Housing Act was greater control over council revenue in England and Wales by the government. The government wanted rents to increase, to reflect more closely the real value of council housing. It was intended that councils would be forced to become more efficient in their delivery of the service, by restricting management and maintenance allowances. The HRA was now 'ring fenced' in England and Wales, so that funds could not be paid from the General Fund. The aim was that it would become clearer just what councils were spending their rent (and other revenue income) on. Most importantly, from the government's perspective, all councils would be brought back into entitlement to subsidy; this would restore the government's ability to apply an upward lever on council rents

ii. The HRA subsidy system under the 1989 Act
The main features of the current HRA subsidy system are:

- a rent rebate element, to repay housing benefit costs for council tenants (since local authorities pay this on behalf of central government);
- a general housing element to cover any income deficit, *which can be negative if a surplus is anticipated*;
- the HRA is 'ring fenced' to prevent contributions from the General Fund;
- local authorities receive specific annual allowances for management and maintenance costs, rather than general ones, applicable to all, as before;
- each authority has an annual *guideline* rent, which changes each year.

The calculation of subsidy depends on the ODPM-determined balance in a *notional* housing revenue account for each local authority, not the actual HRA balance. The level of subsidy is set to cover the difference between notional income and expenditure. *Notional income* is calculated from guideline rents. If a local authority charges less than the notional guideline rent to its tenants, the subsidy will be less than is needed to balance the account; costs will have to be reduced to balance the account, or rents increased. There is no allowance for arrears; the government assumes that all the rent is gathered, which is intended to place some pressure on councils to ensure that rents are collected efficiently. Voids are assumed at two per cent. Average rents will, of course, have to be higher to cover any sums lost through arrears or voids greater than two per cent.

Calculations of *Notional Expenditure* include:

    a. Management costs.
        An allowance is made for management costs, taking into account the characteristics of the authority's stock, and is specifically intended to squeeze costs to encourage greater efficiency. If a local authority decides to spend more than its notional allowance on management, then rents will have to be higher than the notional average rent to balance the Housing Revenue Account.

    b. Maintenance allowance (per property).
        This is the notional amount that the local authority needs, based on indices of need and regional cost variations. In England, there is now also the Major Repairs Allowance (see later in this section).

    c. An assessment of loan charges; in England, this is now the 'cost of capital', a 'depreciation allowance', currently six per cent of the stock's value – see later in this section.

    d. Some additional allowances may be made, for example, to cover the cost of the introduction of resource accounting in England (more later in this section).

The government does not allow for any extra spending on capital projects outside the credit approval system. So, if the local authority decides to make Revenue Contributions to Capital Spending (RCCOs)/Capital From Current Revenue (CFCRs), then rents have to cover that extra money.

iii. Housing Support Grant in Scotland
The 1989 Local Government and Housing Act did not apply in Scotland, so the system there is essentially the 1980 system, but with some adjustments. The HRA subsidy is called the *Housing Support Grant*. The Secretary of State for Scotland had the power to limit rate fund contributions to the HRA from 1985/6, which had the effect of causing Scottish rents to rise, but they still remain below English and Welsh rents, and generally *below* the guideline figures. For example, in 2001, average weekly rents in England were £47.71 (guideline, £41.18), £43.28 (guideline, £40.93) in Wales, but only £39.35 (guideline £43.67) in Scotland (Wilcox, 2003).

Unlike in England, where HRA subsidy (under the 1989 Act) still exerts a powerful influence, by 2002, hardly any councils in Scotland (only the Western Isles and Shetlands) qualified for Housing Support Grant. However, revenue-funded capital investment (CFCR) has become relatively more important there, since constraints on the use of capital receipts were introduced from 1996.

c. Impact of the post 1989 HRA subsidy system in England and Wales
The subsidy for housing benefit payments – the rent rebate element – is generally positive, since most councils (except those which have transferred all of their stock through a large scale voluntary transfer) have some tenants (now, a

majority) in receipt of benefit. But the assumptions about rising notional rents (rising incomes), and strict limits on management and maintenance allowances (expenditure), resulted in the general housing subsidy element becoming negative in a large number of cases – i.e., the HRA is assumed to have a surplus rather than a deficit. Since HRA surpluses are not permitted, the notional negative housing subsidy element is deducted from the rent rebate subsidy element – so the total HRA subsidy may not cover the full costs of housing benefit payments. For example, in 2000/1, councils' assumed surpluses resulted in a negative general subsidy totalling -£1,008 million in Great Britain (Wilcox, 2003). According to the DETR (1998), in 1999/2000, in 60 English authorities, the Housing Element surplus exceeded the rent rebate element, so that, even after deducting rent rebates, the authorities still had a surplus (known as being in 'negative subsidy'). This assumed surplus has to be transferred to the General Fund to subsidise council tax payers, and cannot be used to reduce rents.

The government has now (from April 2004) removed rent rebates from the HRA (and hence from the HRA subsidy calculation) and transferred them to the General Fund (from which RSL and private landlord tenants' housing benefit is paid). However, 'once rent rebates are removed from the HRA, authorities in assumed surplus on the housing element will pay it into a pool' (ODPM, 2002a). So, the government clearly still intends that any surpluses are redistributed nationally.

Recent changes (to 2003)

There have been a number of new policy initiatives for local authority housing since 1998, reflecting the new focus of the Labour government, which have had – or promise to have – a major impact on local authority finance in England.

a. Single Capital Pot
The first significant financial change was the establishment of a Single Capital Pot for English local authority capital spending, announced by the DETR in 1998 and introduced from 1999. This means that the capital allocations for each local authority from the central government – the Annual Capital Guideline, or now the Supported Capital Expenditure – are no longer earmarked for specific activities (such as housing or transport). Instead, local authorities can (in theory) spend their capital funds to reflect their own local priorities.

According to the DETR (1998), the single pot would:

- increase local autonomy to make capital spending decisions;
- increase local accountability;
- permit a more holistic approach to tackling cross-service issues and problems;
- provide greater stability through reduced annual variability in resources for particular projects and less dependence on central government.

However, there remain some concerns about the realism of these objectives in relation to the degree of autonomy actually possible, particularly since local authorities are still monitored extensively by central government. In addition, although LA housing capital allocations, historically, have tended to be amongst the highest, housing's potentially lower, current political priority could result in it losing out to other programme areas. These issues will need to be monitored over time as the policy outcomes become more apparent. From 2004, new Regional Housing Boards in England have a strategic responsibility for capital spending in their areas, so there is now a 'regional' pot (see later in this section).

In Scotland, a more limited 'capital pot' has recently been introduced, specifically excluding spending on council housing. All non-HRA capital spending has been rolled into a General Fund pot, but HRA (council housing) capital spending remains separate.

b. Best Value
While the new Labour government abolished Compulsory Competitive Tendering (CCT) for local authority services – the requirement to invite competitive bids to run council services from the private sector – it instead introduced the Best Value regime from 2000, involving the need to demonstrate continuous service improvements, benchmarked against similar local authorities. Inspectors examine and rate the service provision by three star categories, with an indication of the likelihood of continuing improvement. So, the best achievement from an inspection is three stars and likely to improve; the worst, no stars and unlikely to improve. This is examined in detail in chapter six. However, it is mentioned here because, as you saw in the 'bidding process' (earlier in this section), it has implications for the capital funds which local authorities are permitted to borrow and spend by central government.

c. Decent Homes Standard/Housing Quality Standard
In July 2000, the government introduced a new Decent Homes Standard in England, to:

> ...ensure that all social housing meets set standards of decency by 2010, and reducing the number of households living in social housing that does not meet these standards by a third between 2001 and 2004, with most improvement taking place in the most deprived local authority areas.

The latter point indicates that this policy heralds a major re-allocation of capital resources between local authorities; indeed, this quickly occurred through changes in calculations for the allocation of credit approvals in England (see earlier in this section). In addition, the requirement that one third of properties must meet the standard by 2004 is likely to have caused a shift in priorities within local authorities. For example, if there are many serious problems which, due to time as well as resource constraints, cannot effectively be tackled by 2004, the authority may need instead to prioritise spending on properties in better condition which are much closer to meeting the standard. These can more cheaply and quickly be brought up to standard, thus (potentially) meeting the one third target, but leaving the major problems still to be tackled.

The government recognised that the condition of council stock in many local authorities fell well below this standard, with 40 per cent non-decent in England in 1996 which had fallen slightly to 37.7 per cent for all social housing in 2001 (Wilcox, 2003) and committed itself to increased capital resources for housing from 2001/2.

Wales also introduced a new Housing Quality Standard, to be met by 2012, and Scotland's standard was introduced in 2004, to be met by 2015 (see chapter two).

The Welsh standard is rather higher than the English and Scottish ones, with housing required to be in 'good' repair, not merely meeting the current statutory minimum.

The Decent Homes Standard applies equally to housing association stock but the position on compliance with the standard is mixed. A survey in 2002 indicated that 32 per cent of association homes in England currently failed to meet the standard (Housing Corporation, 2002,). Associations with stock built more recently should have fewer problems reaching the Decent Homes Standard. Large scale voluntary transfer associations will also have factored into their business plans on transfer a substantial modernisation programme and achieving the standard may be easier (although in some cases associations who are facing falls in income through reduced sales or negative rent restructuring may struggle to raise resources to meet the investment required).

Associations with older stock face particular difficulties; for example Peabody Trust has indicated (May 2004) that it requires £156 million to bring 40 per cent of its stock up to the standard. As a result the Association has reduced its development activity and made some of its development staff redundant. This failure also contributed to a critical inspection report from the Audit Commission in May 2004 which said that the service provided had scope for considerable improvement.

It should also be recognised that the Decent Homes Standard is very much a minimum standard and there is likely to be pressure in the coming years for the standard to be strengthened to ensure that the stock meets the increasing expectations of tenants.

d. Rent restructuring

During the 1990s, a widening gap developed between housing association and council rents, with higher rents in the HA sector primarily as a result of the need for associations to borrow privately to fund development, following the 1988 Housing Act (see section 5). As a result, rent restructuring was introduced from April 2002 for councils and housing associations in England. This is intended to ensure that LA and HA rent levels converge over the next decade (by 2012), and so become 'fairer', but while still remaining at below market rent levels.

The implication is that many council rents will have to rise relative to HA rents, so HA rents are (in general) being held back while council rents rise. The long lead-in time is intended to permit gradual changes, with no annual increases exceeding RPI + 1½ per cent + £2 per week for council properties, and maximum increases of RPI + ½ per cent for HA tenants. (The RPI – retail price index – is a measure of the annual rate of inflation).

The **formula rent** for each property reflects:

- its condition and location, and 'other qualities that tenants value' (Ch 2, p. 1);
- local earnings;
- property size.
  (ODPM, 2003)

It is assumed that property values reflect the relative attractiveness to tenants of different properties in different localities, so this is taken as a proxy for the first element. Property valuations are based on Existing Use Value (EUV) – in effect, just like private house valuations – at January 1999. This value will normally remain the same during the whole period of restructuring, unless there have been substantial major works which radically affect the value (ODPM, 2003).

The formula rent is weighted:

- 70 per cent for earnings (which also takes into account the property size)
  Calculated from:
  average LA rent (*national (English) average council rent at April 2000*) x relative county earnings (*average manual earnings in the county divided by national average manual earnings*) x bedroom weight
- 30 per cent for property values
  Calculated from:
  average LA rent x relative property value (*individual value divided by national average value of council properties, at January 1999 prices*).

It is intended that the rent for each council property will move towards the formula rent in roughly 10 equal steps over the decade, though there is a **rent cap** (maximum amount) to protect tenants from excessive increases in high property value areas.

To permit an element of discretion, LAs (in consultation with tenants) may take some account of local factors, to vary rents for particular properties by up to 5 per cent + or – the formula rent.

e. The New Financial Framework

The *New Financial Framework* was introduced by the Department of the Environment,Transport and the Regions (DETR) – now, the Office of the Deputy Prime Minister (ODPM) – in a consultation paper in 1998 and was gradually introduced into all local authorities in England from 2001/2.

The key elements of this new framework are:

i. The Major Repairs Allowance (MRA)

This was introduced in 2001/2 and it 'represents the estimated long term average amount of capital spending required to maintain a local authority's stock in its current condition' (ODPM, 2002a). In practice, it is paid as an additional item of revenue subsidy for LAs (see earlier in this section), though Basic Credit Approvals (also earlier in this section) have been reduced to take account of it.

According to the ODPM (2002a), 'the MRA has made a very substantial difference to the national picture (of Housing Element Subsidy)...in 2001/2...there is an overall net housing element deficit, and central government make a contribution of some £400 million to the housing element'. So, the good news for English local authorities is that the negative subsidy (of -£1,008 million) in 2000/1 had become a positive subsidy (of + £402 million) by 2001/2 (Wilcox, 2003).

ii. Resource accounting

Until recently, the value of councils' housing stock was recorded in the capital account as its **historic value** – i.e. what it cost to produce at the time it was built. However, beginning in 2001/2, English councils were required to introduce resource accounting – i.e. they must record the **current value** of the stock (as HAs and private landlords do). The stock is valued according to its *Existing Use Value for Social Housing* (EUV-SH) – that is, its value allowing for the fact that it has secure tenants, which is lower than a vacant, free-market valuation. Note that this is a different valuation to that required by rent restructuring (see earlier), because the 'for social housing' (-SV) element reduces the EUV valuation (ODPM, 2003).

This is intended to:

- encourage more efficient use of housing assets (by ensuring an adequate return on investment, much like the private sector);
- increase the transparency of the HRA, to present 'more fairly' the financial position of the local authority;
- assist authorities to plan their housing strategy;
- bring accounting procedures into line with the private sector and HAs
- achieve consistency with central government and other local authority accounting practices.
  (ODPM, 2002b)

The stock must achieve a rate of return on investment of 6 per cent p.a. – in effect, a 6 per cent profit or surplus – which must be shown in the revenue account, the HRA. As mentioned earlier, under resource accounting, rent rebates are being removed from the HRA and transferred to the General Fund, so that there is greater clarity about the amounts paid in housing benefit.

New revenue accounts for resource accounting

The Housing Repairs Account
In England only, created specifically for the Major Repairs Allowance (MRA) paid by the government. The HRA, which previously funded all maintenance and repair, now makes a contribution to the Repairs Account.

The calculation of the MRA is based on the proportions of different house types, and their ages, in an authority's stock – for example, ranging from £403 per unit for pre-1945 1-2 bedroomed houses to £793 per unit for high flats in 2002/3. These figures are adjusted regionally, by a *regional adjustment factor*, to ensure that higher cost regions (such as the south-east of England) get relatively more than low cost areas (such as the north-east) (ODPM, 2002). This sum is paid to the HRA as part of the central government's HRA Subsidy (see earlier in this section), but causes the amount of Basic Credit Approvals – the amount that can be borrowed for capital spending (see earlier in this section) – to be reduced by an equal amount.

The Asset Management Revenue Account
Created for debt repayments by English councils only. Currently six per cent of their stock's value is charged for the 'cost of capital', and payment is made from the HRA. This account is then used to pay actual debt interest charges and repayment of capital borrowed. Since this is likely to be much less than the six per cent cost of capital (since the historic cost of the housing is much less than its current value), the government requires any excess to be paid to the ODPM.

(iii) HRA business plans

Supported by resource accounting, from 2001/2, English local authorities have to produce HRA business plans, to show how they intend to manage and enhance their housing assets over the longer term (up to thirty years). These are intended to enhance the existing Housing Investment Programme (HIP) bidding process for capital funds (examined earlier in this section) by providing the opportunity to undertake longer term planning. This is similar to the business planning process which HAs have had to undertake since the need to borrow private finance was introduced by the 1988 Housing Act and Housing (Scotland) Act (see section 5).

However, some view these changes mainly as an extension of the previous privatisation/enabling policies, because, as part of their business plans, local authorities must undertake 'stock appraisals', to consider the options of a stock transfer, arm's length management organisation (ALMO) or the private finance initiative (PFI). ALMOs were first encouraged from 2001 in England as an alternative to LSVT, in recognition that LSVTs were proving (demonstrated by rejections at ballot) not to be wholly acceptable to many tenants, despite the borrowing freedoms (and hence, rehabilitation possibilities) which these created. ALMOs permit local authorities to retain ownership of their stock, whilst also creating a new management organisation to undertake all management functions. There are additional, earmarked, borrowing permissions for ALMOs, but attached to success (currently, a minimum two stars) in the Best Value inspection (see earlier and section 8).

f. Changes in Scotland and Wales

Except for some aspects of the Best Value regime and the 'single pot', the recent policy changes just examined apply only to England. In particular, in neither Scotland or Wales is rent restructuring taking place, although, in Wales, earlier rent policies meant that the problems of divergence between LA and HA rents were avoided. Also, Scotland and Wales decided not to introduce the new financial framework or resource accounting, and there is no Major Repairs Allowance. This means that the financial pressures toward stock transfer (see section 8) are greater, because resources for council housing are now more limited than in England. This may change over the next few years in Scotland, where (as in Wales) the prudential borrowing regime (see later in this section) will apply, but, because of their subsidy system, will enable Scottish councils with low debt levels to raise rents to finance new borrowing and investment.

Reforms from 2004/5

a. The Local Government Act 2003

This act was preceded by a government consultation paper, *The Way Forward for Housing Capital Finance*, in 2002, which was intended to generate wide discussion of possible reforms – the 'blue skies debate' – to the capital subsidy system. This paper signalled an end to local authority SHG in 2003 – capital subsidy provided by LAs to HAs (via the Housing Corporation). This ties in with the new Regional Housing Boards' strategic responsibilities (see part b. below), to determine investment priorities in their areas. However, abolition was subsequently delayed slightly for some councils with advanced plans for LA SHG allocations.

The 2003 Act *applies only to local authorities in England and Wales*, and key features include:

i. A system to pool RTB receipts nationally for redistribution

In effect, the 75 per cent 'set aside' capital receipts, formerly used largely to repay debt, must now be paid to central government, so that receipts 'rich' LAs can be used to subsidise other councils and housing associations (via SHG). This also permits the government to capture the non-usable receipts from debt-free local authorities. Non-RTB receipts – i.e. those under the LA's direct control, such as receipts from the sale of land – will not be affected if recycled into regeneration or housing projects.

ii. Supported Capital Expenditure

The system of credit approvals established under the 1989 Act (see earlier in this section) is being abolished, and replaced by 'Supported Capital Expenditure' or SCE. It is determined as part of the annual capital allocations process (e.g. the HIP allocation in England – see earlier in this section) and is based on an estimate of what the government thinks each LA needs for capital spending, which borrowing will support. The SCE is allowed for as part of the HRA subsidy calculation.

The SCE is actually split into two elements:

- SCE (Revenue) – which determines the support offered through the HRA subsidy system, and
- SCE (Capital grant) – which determines what were previously known as specified capital grants.

The total pooled capital receipts (see i. above) will be used to offset a large part of the SCEs and the Housing Corporation's ADP (see section 5). Similar reforms are taking place in Scotland and Wales.

iii. Prudential borrowing
A new system of 'prudential borrowing' starts in April 2004, which effectively shifts responsibility for borrowing decisions back to the councils. However, overall local authority borrowing will still be controlled by the Treasury, through the SCE system.

LA borrowing is to be undertaken in accordance with a professional code, drawn up by the Chartered Institute of Public Finance and Accountancy (CIPFA). This code provides a set of 'prudential indicators', which include items such as past borrowing levels, usable receipts, borrowing support available from the government (SCEs) and revenue sources of finance. The level of support available from the government – the SCEs – will be a key borrowing constraint, because any attempt to pay for extra borrowing beyond this via higher rents will simply result in reduced HRA subsidy (see later in this section). In addition, LAs cannot borrow against the value of their assets or their projected future rental streams (unlike HAs). Hence, tight borrowing constraints, in reality, remain.

b. Regional Housing Boards
The Government has indicated that all capital allocations in England will, from 2004, be determined by new Regional Housing Boards. They will not only be responsible for allocating councils' SCEs (see ii. above), but also for allocating the ADP for HAs (see section 5), via the Housing Corporation. This suggests that the allocations' process – for both LAs and HAs (see earlier in this section and section 5) – will face further revision in the near future. However, for the first two years, the government has indicated (ODPM, 2002c) that 70 per cent of the HIP will be distributed according to the existing formulas (see earlier in this section).

The Boards comprise representatives of the:

- *Government Office for the Region*
  This regional body represents departments of the UK central government, so comprises civil servants.

- *Housing Corporation*
  The body which allocates ADP funds to HAs in England, appointed by and responsible to the central government.
- *Regional Development Agencies*
  These were founded in 1999, to promote economic development and contribute to sustainable development; appointed by and responsible to the central government.
- *Regional Assembly*
  These too were set up in 1999, to scrutinise the work of the Regional Development Agencies, and contain government appointees. All regions are to be given the opportunity, through a referendum, to opt for directly elected assemblies in future.
- *Regional Housing Forums*
  Regional representatives from all organisations with an interest in housing – e.g. tenants' groups, Council of Mortgage Lenders (CML), House Builders Federation.
- *English Partnerships*
  The national (English) regeneration agency, to promote regeneration and brownfield development; appointed by and responsible to central government.

These new boards must produce a Regional Housing Strategy by July each year, which must take account of the Regional Economic Strategy (produced by Regional Development Agencies) and the Regional Planning Guidance (drawn up by the Regional Assembly). The Strategy has to be approved by the ODPM, but the intention is that it can better reflect regional needs and priorities than a centralised system.

However, there are concerns about exactly how decisions will be made, and whether they will adequately take account of local community, health and social services concerns (Delargy, 2003). Readers will need to monitor this developing system through examining regional housing strategies, the ODPM website, and the housing press.

5. Finance for housing associations

The Housing Corporation is the main funding body for housing associations in England. In Scotland, Communities Scotland, directly administered by the Executive, was formed from the old Scottish Homes, which was an agency similar to the Housing Corporation with its own board. In Wales, the equivalent body, Tai Cymru, was absorbed into central government before devolution took place, so that HA funding and regulation are now the direct responsibility of the Welsh Assembly Government. Funding and regulation of HAs in Northern Ireland is shared between the Department for Social Development and the NIHE. The description which follows is based largely on the English system but arrangements elsewhere are very similar.

Capital finance

a. The pre-1988 regime

Like local authorities, the arrangements by which housing associations obtain capital finance for housing saw significant changes at the end of the 1980s. In order to understand the reasons for these changes, as well as to appreciate their implications for housing associations, it is necessary first briefly to explore the earlier arrangements.

The Housing Act of 1974 first introduced *housing association grant* (HAG), which provided a large capital subsidy from the public sector to housing associations registered with (and hence, regulated by) the Housing Corporation. HA rents, like most private sector rents, were controlled *fair rents*, determined by rent officers.

The public funding regime for HAs was very generous. The Housing Corporation (HC) provided all necessary funding as the scheme was built, then, once the fair rent had been determined, the HA's annual revenue stream from the development could be calculated. The value of a loan which these rents could support in loan repayments was then loaned to the HA by the HC; the remainder of the cost was simply HAG. This was, of course, very expensive for the government and there was little incentive for associations to control development costs; basically, if costs rose, so too did HAG. Hence, the risks lay entirely with the government. Although rents were re-assessed upwards periodically by rent officers, the sums repaid to the HC remained at the same level as originally determined. Hence, according to Malpass (1999, p. 883), 'In the period 1974-88, housing associations had enjoyed a sheltered and effectively risk free financial framework'.

The government wished to expand the role of housing associations, but without substantial increases in HAG costs, as well as to provide incentives to housing associations to achieve better value for money. As a result, the 1988 Housing Act and 1988 Housing (Scotland) Act introduced a 'new regime' for housing association finance, designed to address the main problems of the previous system.

b. Features of the 1988 Housing Act regime for capital finance

i. The grant rate

The proportion of the costs of a scheme paid by HAG (now, Social Housing Grant – SHG – in England, Northern Ireland and Wales) are determined at the start, set by the applicable *grant rate*. Grant rates are revised annually. Initially, a target of 75 per cent (of scheme costs) was set for England and Wales, and 85 per cent for Scotland (where associations are generally much smaller), but these rates fell rapidly in subsequent years, particularly in England and Wales. However, they have recovered somewhat under the current Labour government; for example, the average outturn grant rate fell as low as 44.23 per cent in England in 1997/8, but was predicted to rise to 68 per cent in 2002/3 (Housing Corporation, 2001).

ii. Private finance
Associations may have to supplement HAG/SHG by borrowing funds from private sector lenders – so-called, mixed funding – though this did not apply until much later in Northern Ireland.

iii. Major repairs fund
Associations must fund major repairs costs for schemes themselves, whereas under the pre-1988 regime, grants were available from the Housing Corporation. All schemes are expected to contribute to a *major repairs fund*, so that associations build up sufficient funds to pay for all future work.

iv. Higher rents
New lets (and re-lets of old regime properties) are assured tenancies, instead of the old housing association secure tenancies (see chapter five) on fair rents. These can be let at higher rents, which better reflect the scheme costs. Furthermore, whereas fair rents can be re-assessed only every two years, assured rents can be revised annually.

Much like local authorities, rents have to cover:

- the repayments of the private loan;
- management and maintenance costs;
- voids and arrears;
- future major repairs.

However, unlike local authorities, housing associations receive no revenue grant. By far the largest element in the rent calculation is the loan repayment. The lower the grant rate, the larger the private loan. This increases the repayments, so rent levels are higher. The government, nevertheless, requires that they be 'affordable', but has so far declined to define this.

In contrast to local authorities, in 1989 few associations operated rent pooling systems, which shares the costs of more recent, higher-cost developments between all tenants. With rapidly rising new rent levels over recent years, many more associations are now operating rent pooling.

However, the *rent restructuring* policy introduced in 2002 (see section 4) has now effectively constrained the ability of English associations to increase rents, with increases (where these fit with the new, *formula rents*) limited to RPI (the retail price index, a measure of inflation) + ½ per cent. Many have argued that, for HAs, rent restructuring simply represents a new form of rent controls.

v. Cost controls
The funding bodies introduced cost indicators for different types of development, to control scheme costs more effectively. These vary between different local authority areas, depending on local cost conditions (including land costs), and on

property types and sizes. Ordinarily, the costs of any proposed development must be within the relevant cost limits.

Once the level of HAG/SHG is determined, in general, cost-overruns have to be funded by the HA. This shifts the risks heavily towards the associations themselves, and provides them with a strong incentive to keep a tight control over scheme costs.

c. The capital funding bidding process

Under the current system, HAG/SHG is determined at the outset, so that it is up to the HA to ensure that costs are constrained within these limits. Rents are determined at the end, at the level needed to cover all annual (revenue) costs.

The precise details of the allocations process differ between each of the funding bodies, and are also subject to regular revisions. Hence, all that we can provide here is a *general* indication of the stages in the process. The process examined below is based on the Housing Corporation's requirements, but the other funders have adopted similar approaches. For simplicity, the term SHG is used to apply to all funders.

1. The government determines the total expenditure available for housing associations.
2. The relevant statutory funders then issue an Approved Development Programme (ADP) (or similar), setting out the amounts available for each HC region. The amounts for each local authority's area in England are currently based partly on the Housing Needs Index (HNI), which (like the LA's GNI – see above) is indicative of relative housing need. It comprises 75 per cent weighting for new provision (based on demand factors such as overcrowding, temporary accommodation, proportions on housing benefit) and 25 per cent related to private sector stock condition.
3. Each RSL bids for a share of the ADP, indicating the types of schemes it intends to develop for those sums; this bid is judged both on past performance and on how well it conforms to the relevant local authorities' housing strategies (examined in section 4), as well as costs (related to the appropriate Cost Indicator/Value for Money).
4. If this receives approval, the funder undertakes to provide an amount of SHG, based on current grant rates for the type of development.
5. The HA arranges private finance for the remainder of the scheme's costs.
6. SHG is released in pre-determined proportions, at various stages in the scheme's progress. Costs beyond this have to be temporarily covered by the association, by borrowing and/or from reserves.
7. On completion, the private finance is released to the HA, and monthly repayments of the loan and interest commence.

Note that, from 2004 in England, recommendations about allocations from the regional ADP (as well as council SCEs) come from the new Regional Housing Boards – see earlier section 4.

Rent limits

These were introduced by some funders in the 1990s due largely to the increasing proportions of housing association tenants on housing benefit (see section 7). It became apparent that there were reducing incentives for associations to curb rents, if very few of their tenants would actually have to find the costs of the higher rents. It also meant that the actual cost to the government was very much higher than simply the SHG costs, as there was a rising revenue cost in the form of a rising housing benefit bill.

The first funding body to attempt to tackle this was Tai Cymru. In 1994, it introduced limitations on the size of housing association developments to which it would give HAG. It wished to fund only those associations with annual development programmes in excess of £3 million. These were *Approved Development Bodies* (ADBs). Associations with smaller programmes would have to join with an ADB to gain funding. However, for 1995/6, they also introduced a new requirement in relation to rents. Funding would be offered only if rent levels were reasonable – called rent-bidding. However, as it proved very difficult for ADBs to be sure that they could achieve programmes requiring £3 million in funding, approved developer status was later abandoned.

Similarly, the Housing Corporation introduced a form of rent limits from 1996/7, in the form of *benchmark rents*. These were related to the cost of development for the type of scheme, the relevant Total Cost Indicators (TCIs). Associations had to take these figures into account when setting rents for new schemes, and their bids were examined in the light of proposed rent levels. If rent levels for a project exceeded benchmark rents, the additional rent was assumed to attract housing benefit, and the annual value of this was calculated and added to the SHG bid as a capital sum. So, for example, if the SHG bid was for £2 million, but rents were above the benchmark, the capitalised value of anticipated additional housing benefit costs was added to the £2 million SHG, to give the total, real capital cost to the government. Another association, bidding for more SHG but with lower rents, might therefore seem to be offering better value.

From 1997/8, additional controls on association rent levels were introduced for all new HA schemes in England. The association had to charge the rent indicated in the bid to the HC, and thereafter, rent increases must not exceed the rate of inflation + one per cent. So, if inflation were two per cent, the maximum rent increase that year would be three per cent.

Of course, English HAs (since 2002) are subject to the *formula rents* from the **rent restructuring** policy (see above and section 4), so that rents are expected to be harmonised with LA rents for comparable properties over a period of ten years, and increases limited to RPI + 0.5 per cent. Restructuring will have major implications for some HAs' rents (HACAS Consulting, 2000) and the formula has proved controversial for some associations (Hebden, 2003, p. 2).

In addition, these new 'rent controls' are of particular concern for some HAs, due to the implications of meeting the government's Decent Homes Standard (see section 4). Housing Corporation research in 2002 suggested that almost a third of HA properties did not meet the standard, though 'there were large variations in fail rates' (Housing Corporation, 2002, p. 2). Yet, government subsidy to help achieve the Standard has been substantially focused on LAs.

As indicated earlier, in England, Regional Housing Boards will play a key role in the allocation of development subsidy from 2004, for both LAs and HAs (see section 4.5). According to Martin (2003), the final Housing Corporation ADP in 2003 is planned to increase the share of funding for home ownership schemes to more than 20 per cent (from 11 per cent in 2002/3). These are examined in detail in section 8.

d. The calculation of HAG/SHG

i. Cost indicators

Cost indicators are devised by each of the funding bodies to reflect estimated development costs in particular areas. They may be revised periodically, down as well as up if appropriate. Each funder has their own particular system, though in general, the cost indicators will vary by:

- the nature of the development (new build or rehab);
- the location (council district);
- the type of household (e.g. family, elderly or special needs);
- the size of dwellings.

The association must generally demonstrate that the scheme's costs are within the indicative costs.

ii. Grant rate

The grant rate is the proportion of scheme costs that will be provided by HAG/SHG. So, the maximum payable is cost indicator x grant rate. If estimated scheme costs are lower than the indicative costs, then HAG/SHG is estimated costs x grant rate.

As a simple example, suppose that scheme costs are assessed as £400,000, and this is within the cost indicator for the type of scheme and number of dwellings. If the current grant rate is 50 per cent, then the amount of HAG/SHG payable is £400,000 x 50 per cent = £200,000.

Grant rates vary considerably between funders. They fell fastest in England and Wales during the early 1990s while Scottish Homes' grant rates generally remained higher. However, this changed somewhat from the mid-90s, when Scottish Homes started to reduce average grant rates (though they still remained above English and Welsh levels). Every cut in grant rates potentially puts up rents for new association properties (through higher borrowing), or may cause a reduction in quality in an attempt to reduce costs.

e. Private finance

As we have seen, with the decline in HAG/SHG rates during the 1990s, virtually all HAs had to secure private finance for new development. Indeed, a number of housing associations have developed some schemes without any HAG/SHG at all, raising all of the finance privately (sometimes in conjunction with a private development company), and charging near-market rents.

The need to access private funds has forced a more 'business-like' approach on HAs. Private lenders view associations as they would any company seeking finance from them, and seek always to minimise any risk that they could lose money. This means that they want detailed financial information about the company, including rent levels, voids, arrears and details of its other housing assets. Associations with a large asset base (generally, a large stock, with high proportions dating from pre-1988) are, therefore, more likely to be viewed favourably by private financial institutions, because this will help to reduce any risk of default (failure to repay).

The requirements of private lenders include a business plan prepared by the association. Business plans set out the present state of the organisation, indicate plans for the future, and, most importantly, show (with careful financial analysis) how those plans can be achieved. Planned schemes must, of course, be consistent with the agreed business plan.

f. Effects of the 1988 Act for housing associations

i. Increase in use of private finance

The expansion in the use of private finance by HAs has been significant. According to Wilcox (2002), more than £15 billion was borrowed between 1989 and 2002.

> *Private finance now accounts for 40% of the capital base of the sector, so it has to be concluded that associations have been highly successful in raising (and repaying) loans. As the market has developed, associations have been able to improve the terms attached to private loans, and they have achieved all this in the context of falling grant rates, and, more recently, tighter rents policies* (Malpass, 1999, p. 886).

ii. Rising rents

As we have seen, the main result of increased dependence on private finance was rising rents for housing association tenants, particularly in England and Wales where the grant rate reduced most rapidly. Table 3.7 shows that, as a percentage of average male earnings, assured rents rose rapidly in the early 1990s – though by much less in Scotland and Northern Ireland, due (as a result of a more generous grant regime) to lower dependence on private finance. Research in 1995 by Chaplin *et al.* suggested that some HA applicants were having to reject tenancy offers because the rents were not affordable. However, the effect of restrictions on rent increases in the late '90s are evident in England and Wales.

Table 3.7: Housing association assured rents as a % of earnings

Region	1990	1995	2000	2001
England	12.1	16.6	15.8	15.3
Scotland	11.1	12.6	13.8	14.0
N. Ireland	–	12.4	13.7	13.9
Wales	13.7	14.8	13.4 (1999)	N/A

Source: Wilcox, 2003

However, even these figures may disguise the full impact, because:

- these are *average* rents: new rents are generally higher than the previous average;
- this is based on *average* earnings; many RSL tenants earn well below average earnings, and many are female, whose earnings remain well below average male figures.

Concerns about whether HA rents are *affordable*, especially in relation to council rents, are a key reason for the government's current rent restructuring policy (see section 4).

iii. Increased risks

The issue of risk has become very significant for HAs. Risks have greatly increased in two main ways. First, as identified earlier, associations must bear the risk of costs rising during the development phase. The desire to reduce these risks has contributed to the increased use of approaches to development which reduce the overall time period, and offer greater certainty about costs. Arrangements such as *package deals* or *design and build* contracts combine much of the design and construction elements, so the association can agree a fixed price for everything in advance. These are examined further in chapter four.

As noted above, there were some fears in relation to design and construction standards, as there could be a temptation to 'cut corners' in an attempt to curtail costs, so the funding bodies have devised various approaches to maintain quality; for example, the Housing Corporation introduced 'Scheme Development Standards'. In England, where grant rates fell fastest, there has also been a large reduction in rehabilitation work, simply because this is inherently more at risk of cost increases, as new and unforeseen problems emerge. New build is less risky.

Secondly, there is also a growing body of evidence from housing associations that rapidly rising rents have increased the difficulties of letting to low income households in some areas. Increasingly, it is only households entitled to full housing benefit (where benefit payments cover all of the rent) which can afford new housing association properties. In areas with depressed property markets and pockets of low demand (such as the north of England), RSL rent levels on new properties may be well above what is considered 'usual' in the area. This has forced some HAs to diversify their lettings policies, so that they now accept households which would not have previously been considered.

iv. Significance of size

As examined above, private financial institutions, in general, adopt a very cautious approach to lending funds. They prefer to have a large amount of *security*, to guarantee that they will get their money back whatever happens. Small associations, with few assets, can offer little extra security; furthermore, they might be considered more at risk of failure – going bankrupt – which resulted in a certain amount of merger activity between housing associations during the 1990s, keen to expand their asset bases.

In England, with a large number of small-to-medium sized associations, a new financial institution was set up under the 1988 Act, specifically to help these Housing associations to access private funding. *The Housing Finance Corporation* (THFC) assembles the funding requirements of a number of associations into one 'package', and then finds a private lender willing to lend on this larger portfolio of schemes. Other associations also join together to make collective applications for private funding. Scotland's smaller sized associations were, instead, largely protected initially via higher grant rates, so that their borrowing requirements were lessened.

g. Reforms from 2004/5 in England

With encouragement from the ODPM, the Housing Corporation wholeheartedly embraced the Egan Report (*Rethinking Construction*, 1998) agenda for reforming the construction industry. This report proposed 'partnering', involving the whole supply chain, together with greater use of 'modern construction methods' (such as more factory produced components), to improve efficiency. This partnering approach is examined in some detail in chapter four, section 8.

As well as requiring associations to adopt partnering approaches for their development schemes, the Corporation has piloted the introduction of partnering values to its own process for allocating the ADP. It was concerned that, by permitting small organisations to take SHG funding for very small schemes, it was not encouraging greater efficiency in social housing development. It pointed out that, by funding 350-400 associations annually, it was achieving an average output of only 50 homes per association. Hence, for 2003/4, it established a pilot Challenge Fund of £300 million, which funded a total of 50 HAs. These had to enter into 'partnering agreements' with the Corporation, and the scheme was widened significantly during 2004/5. There are strict criteria which must be met before an association can apply to enter a partnering agreement, and these are explored in detail in chapter four, section 8. The partnering agreements will last, initially, for two years, and bids are made to the HC on the basis of funding for the entire capital programme for those two years.

Allocating SHG to partner associations

For associations with a partnering agreement, the HC introduced a number of changes to the process of bidding for a share of the ADP. For 2004/5, these include:

- *Discarding the TCI framework*
  The Corporation considers that the focus on cost limits will deter partner associations from making greater efforts to achieve continuous efficiency improvements. Hence, the HC has ceased to take costs into account, because,

  > It will be for associations to determine the cost of development. We believe that this is the right place for this responsibility, as associations need to live with the long term consequences of development costs. (Housing Corporation, 2003, p. 8).

- *Discarding the grant rate framework*
  This means that it is up to associations to decide how much SHG they need to bid for, for the whole capital programme that they have determined for 2004/6. These bids will be assessed in the light of other bids in order to ensure that Value for Money can be demonstrated.

- *Quality standards*
  As well as the schemes meeting the HC's Scheme Development Standards (see chapter four), the bid must include Housing Quality Indicators (HQIs), and associations will have to match – or better – minimum 'scores' for unit size and unit layout. This is intended to ensure that costs (in terms of SHG) are not driven down at the expense of housing quality standards.

The evaluation of the 2003/4 pilot Challenge Fund has not yet taken place, but it is anticipated that this may result in subsequent changes to the partnering and/or bidding arrangements, so readers are advised to consult the HC website and/or the housing press for the most recent changes.

Revenue finance

HA revenue (income and expenditure) accounts are not subject to the strict controls placed on local authority housing revenue accounts. On the contrary, they are encouraged to make surpluses, to ensure that they generate sufficient funds to pay for future major repairs.

a. The income and expenditure account

The main elements of the Income and Expenditure Account as shown in the following box.

Income and expenditure account

Main elements of expenditure

- Loan repayments, which generally include elements of both capital and revenue; Housing associations cannot borrow over such long periods as local authorities and will generally have to pay higher rates of interest to reflect higher risks.
- Management costs, which are actual rather than (as for councils) allowances; furthermore, costs are generally higher than for most local authorities, reflecting the much smaller size of most association stock, with fewer possibilities of 'economies of scale' in management.
- Maintenance costs are not a significant problem for most HAs, because, being relatively recent social housing providers, they generally have much newer stock than most local authorities.
- Major repairs' provision. The statutory funding bodies make recommendations about the amounts to be set aside from *post-1988* schemes; schemes completed before this (with no private funding) make contributions to the *Rent Surplus Fund* (examined in section c. below)
- Depreciation, to allow for reduced value of the stock through deterioration. This is generally a set percentage of the stock's value, related to an annual revaluation of assets.

Main elements of income

- Rents and charges. Some rents from pre-1988 schemes may still be *fair rents*, determined by the rent officer, but rents on all assured (post 1988) tenancies are determined by the association. However, this is now constrained by rent restructuring (section 4). Rent setting issues are examined briefly below, as well as in chapter five. Voids and arrears will, of course, reduce rent income.

---

b. Rent setting

One of the main effects of the revised, 1988 regime was to make rent setting policy a key activity, because previously, rents were determined by the rent officer. Rents on new schemes funded by private finance must generally cover all scheme expenditures, but, as we have already seen, these increased substantially, as grant rates declined. However, housing associations could choose to reduce the rents payable on new schemes by cutting scheme costs, or making contributions from their reserves – in effect, contributions from the rents of other tenants. Some form of rent-pooling is allowed, in recognition of the fact that existing tenants in older properties may be paying significantly less than new tenants. A major issue became how to set rents fairly under a pooled system and what factors to vary rents for and by how much.

Rent restructuring (see section 4) is likely to have a significant impact on some HAs, particularly those with a higher proportion of recent – and hence, higher cost and higher loans – schemes. In addition, there may be implications for particular groups of tenants. Recent research for the Housing Corporation (Kiddle and Banks, 2002) suggests that smaller properties are likely to suffer the largest increases under rent restructuring, since two thirds are currently below their average target (formula) rents. This indicates that it may be single people and couples who will be hardest hit by rent restructuring.

---

c. Rent Surplus Fund

As rents increased on pre-1988 schemes (with low borrowing), housing associations started to make a surplus of income over expenditure. They were required to pay this into a *Grant Redemption Fund*, to permit the government to make use of these surplus funds. The 1988 Housing Act replaced this with the Rent Surplus Fund (RSF). The RSF applies only to pre-1988 schemes, in which some tenants are likely to remain on fair rents (in secure HA tenancies), whilst others (in re-lets) will have assured tenancies on rents determined by the housing association. Initially, the RSF was to be shared between HA reserves and a Major Repairs Fund, but, from December 1997, English HAs were required to create a RSF Reinvestment Fund, from which they could draw RSF funds (subject to certain conditions) for reinvestment in their existing stock (Housing Corporation, 1998).

6. Planning and controlling expenditure

Housing organisations, just like any private firm or individual, have to plan how they will spend their financial resources. Someone (or group, such as the management committee) must take decisions about *priorities* for expenditure, and must plan to ensure that income will be sufficient to cover this.

Sections 4 and 5 identified the ways that social housing providers bid for and are allocated capital finance; however, having received these funds (or the prospect of them), they will have to plan *how* they will be spent, on *what*, and *when*. Similarly, for revenue finance, they must determine income levels (principally by setting rents) based on the amount they wish to spend. This means that they have to prepare budgets, for both capital and revenue spending, which set out planned income and expenditure.

Budgets

The treasurer or finance manager/director will have to compile capital and revenue budgets for the whole organisation, which identify broad categories of expenditure and income, approved by the relevant committee.

The time period covered by the budget may depend on its purpose. Generally, revenue budgets are *annual*, covering the organisation's *financial year* (April 2003 – March 2004, for example). Capital budgets may cover a longer period, say two to five years, to reflect the time scale of capital projects.

These main budgets may be specified in a number of ways:

- *By department*
  For a local authority, the council's budget will be allocated to particular *departments*, such as housing, social services, environmental services, etc.

- *By location*
  A large organisation may need budgets for each *location*, such as a budget for each area office. Many local authorities have *decentralised* budgets, so that smaller units (the neighbourhood office, or the estate) are responsible for the allocation of their own budgets, within the overall limits defined by the centre.
- *By category*
  This focuses on the *nature* of the income or expenditure, known as l*ine-items*. For example, in a revenue budget, line items might include employees (salaries, wages, pensions, etc.), office expenses (stationery, telephones, etc.), staff travel/transport costs, repairs and maintenance.

The process of budget preparation
There are a number of possible approaches to preparing a budget.

i. Incremental budgeting
For revenue budgets, this is a fairly common approach, which concentrates attention on the **reasons for change**, but its essential assumption is that service provision will continue as before.

It takes the *current* budget as the starting point, and concentrates on the *elements that need to change* in the budget. For example:

- costs may be rising due to inflation, or falling because prices (e.g. for maintenance) have become more competitive;
- employees may be entitled to increments, increasing the salary costs ;
- there may be a need for new/additional services (e.g. for *Community Care* and *Supporting People* provision, or tenant involvement initiatives);
- income may be falling, for example due to reduced revenue grants.

Each line-item in the budget is adjusted for these changes. Of course, if income is static or falling, and costs are rising, then further adjustments will have to be made. Some elements may need to be reduced – for example, it may be decided to close a hostel, or to make some staff *redundant* (in which case, redundancy costs will have to be taken into account).

ii. Planning Programming Budgeting Systems (PPBS)
This approach is particularly relevant for capital budgeting, because it focuses on the objectives of the organisation, and identifies alternative ways of meeting these objectives. For example, the objective of providing 200 new dwellings may be met through a number of different possible programmes. The costs of each of the programme elements are identified, and compared to their possible benefits – the expected output. This enables the organisation to allocate capital resources between different programmes effectively. However, in practice, it is a difficult approach to implement, firstly because the objectives of organisations are usually complex and difficult to define precisely, and secondly, because the outputs from services (such as housing) may be difficult to measure.

iii. Zero-based budgeting

This approach starts with the assumption that *nothing is essential*. Each element of cost is identified and compared to the benefits that it provides. This is useful where alternative levels of provision are possible for each function, since it makes explicit the benefits and costs of each alternative. Alternatives are identified as decision packages, and are assessed against stated criteria – for example, the need for the activity (is it a statutory requirement?), its political acceptability, its contribution to the organisation's objectives. The decision packages are then ranked in priority order, and resources allocated to agreed budget levels (i.e. the anticipated capital or revenue funds).

The advantage of this approach is that it focuses attention on *value for money*, and develops a questioning attitude in the organisation – is this activity *really* necessary? However, it is also very time consuming, and may require a large amount of *subjective* assessments, permitting decision makers to favour 'pet' interests.

Budgetary control

Having *set* the budgets – i.e. set out anticipated income and expenditure, and ensured that they balance (are equal) – the budget manager(s) must ensure that each budget is monitored regularly. Responsibility will vary, depending on the 'level' at which the budget is set. For example, the treasurer/finance director who is responsible for the whole of a local authority's budget, and must maintain regular checks to ensure that overall spending is constrained within budget limits. A number of local authorities operate decentralised budgets, which permit particular managers (on an estate or in an area office) to control their own budgets. These will have to be monitored regularly, not just by the managers responsible, but also by their managers.

If it seems that a budget is danger of becoming overspent, then urgent action must be taken to adjust planned expenditure so that it remains on target; if this is not possible (for example, if storm damage has resulted in much higher than expected expenditure on repairs), then the 'higher' level of management control needs to be alerted, so that other budgets can be adjusted.

Perverse incentives?

While budgets must be monitored with the intention of ensuring there is no overspend, the goal is not necessarily to spend less than the amount allocated; particularly in the case of capital projects (with credit allocations from the government), anything unspent is 'lost'. Similarly, an area manager who spends less than the revenue budget allocation may find the office budget cut in the next year, particularly if the incremental approach to budgeting is adopted.

Far from ensuring that money is spent sensibly, this will provide a *perverse incentive* to spend any excess money urgently, and possibly wastefully, before the end of the budget period. Any system of budgeting that penalises saving in this way will virtually guarantee waste.

Cash flow

It may not be sufficient simply to monitor overall spending to ensure that it remains within budget. Particularly in the case of a housing association, budgets may need to be monitored to ensure that *at any one time* it does not spend more than the resources available – meaning that the *cash flow* into the organisation must be monitored.

If there are expected to be insufficient receipts to cover payments in a particular time period, the organisation will need to decide whether it can:

- delay some payments, until the cash flow situation improves;
- obtain temporary finance to cover the shortfall; this is much easier for a local authority;
- permanently reduce some planned spending.

For capital projects, it is particularly important that an RSL monitors its cash flow, because the amounts involved are potentially very large. Usually, they will undertake a cash flow analysis, which sets out anticipated payments and receipts in each time period (e.g. each month). The building contractor may need to receive regular payments for work completed (called interim payments, and examined in chapter four), but income may not be received until much later, since SHG is paid at much less regular stages, called tranches.

Having completed the cash flow analysis, the association may find it has to delay some activity – such as the start date for a particular project – in order to ensure that sufficient funds remain in the capital account each month; or, it may need to arrange additional, temporary borrowing. Any association which fails to do this risks bankruptcy, if it tries to spend more than the resources it currently has available.

This contrasts with the situation for a local authority housing department, which does not have to concern itself in the same way with 'day to day' sources of funding for expenditure. The treasurer/finance director is responsible for monitoring the cash flow for the whole authority, and has access to short term borrowing to accommodate any short term deficiencies. The main concern is that, over the financial year, the budget for the whole authority is balanced.

7. Individual subsidy for housing services

Subsidy for tenants

a. Housing benefit

Housing benefit (HB) is the main personal housing subsidy payable to tenants, whether in the social or private sectors. It is a *means-tested* subsidy, so applicants must have relatively low incomes to qualify. The present HB scheme was introduced in 1988, following a rationalisation of the means-test requirements for different types of benefit. It forms part of the Social Security budget and is administered by local housing authorities on behalf of the Department for Work and Pensions.

Generally, anyone entitled to housing benefit will also receive council tax benefit (CTB) – a reduction in the amount of tax payable to the local authority for local services – but this is also available to low income owner occupiers.

As the government pursued a policy of pushing up rents in the social sector during the 1990s, housing benefit was intended to 'take the strain' for low income households – which resulted in a rapidly rising subsidy bill. In the private sector also, the abolition of rent controls, in the form of 'fair rents' for private sector tenancies from 1989, resulted in rising numbers of tenants on housing benefit as well as large increases in the amount of benefit payable.

i. The allocation of housing benefit

Housing benefit 'payments' – rent rebates – to council tenants simply reduce (or eliminate) their weekly rent. Until April 2004, any such spending on housing benefit simply appeared as an item of expenditure in the Housing Revenue Account along with other HRA related costs such as spending on management and maintenance. Only the shortfall between the *total* notional expenditure in the account and the total notional income from rents (net of rebates) was reimbursed by the government (except in Scotland). Private and HA tenants receive actual payments – which may be paid direct to the landlord – from the LA, and this is recorded in the General Fund. The cost of administering HB also falls on the General Fund, though local authorities receive payment for the vast majority of this expenditure (95 per cent) from the government. However, from April 2004 onwards subsidy for rent rebates will be paid in a similar way to that for other housing benefit payments – to the General Fund. The actual payments are then reimbursed to the Housing Revenue Account.

HB is very expensive to administer, partly because there are so many elements to the calculation (as shown below) which need the claimant to provide proof. Then, any further change of circumstance such as an increase in income no matter how small will require a new assessment to be made. In addition, a complex *verification framework* (from 1999) introduced minimum standards of evidence that the LA was required to check on each aspect of the claim (income, rent payable, household size etc.) before benefit could be paid. This has in many cases resulted in lengthy delays in benefit payments. Late payments have left many claimants without sufficient resources to pay their rent, private tenants at risk of eviction, and deteriorating arrears figures for many HAs. For this reason, during 2001/2, a number of HAs were involved in a pilot scheme to permit them to undertake HB verification themselves, which was intended to improve the speed of assessments and hence arrears, and follow up research suggests that this was successful in a number of cases, if not as much as had been hoped. Nevertheless, there were plans to 'roll out' the project during 2003.

ii. The assessment of housing benefit

There are four key elements in housing benefit assessments, shown in the following boxes:

---

1. The household's expenditure needs

The government determines what each household reasonably needs to spend each week on essentials (excluding housing costs), and these figures are revised annually. There are two elements to this:

i. **Personal allowances,** which relate to the household's size and age; for example, those under 25 (unless married) are given smaller allowances, couples get more than single households, and there are additional amounts for each dependent child, depending on age.

ii. To the personal allowances are added **premiums**, to reflect the additional expenses of some household types and members; associated with age, disability or caring responsibilities, for example families with children.

---

2. Eligible housing costs

i. Currently these are based on the **rent payable** including any service charges which are related to maintaining the dwelling or any communal areas, but excluding any personal care or support services (which are eligible for Supporting People benefit, see later in this section and chapter seven). If there are adults living in the claimant's home (such as grown-up children, or grand-parents), they are assumed to make some contribution to the rent (even if they don't). These adults are known as **non-dependents**. The assumed contribution varies with their income but the net result is a reduction in the eligible costs and therefore the amount of benefit payable.

ii. An additional set of **restrictions** apply to private sector tenants, or occasionally housing association tenants where their rents are considered to be unreasonable. The purpose of these restrictions is to avoid abuse of the scheme and ensure benefit only covers the costs of accommodation that the claimant reasonably needs. These rules are extremely complex but can be summarised as four main types. HB will not cover:
    *   any rent in excess of what would normally be expected for that property in the open market (this prevents the landlord and tenant agreeing an artificially high rent);
    *   any rent in excess of the rent for a property which is large enough to accommodate the claimant and their family;
    *   any additional rent which is attributable to the property being at the very top end of the market (i.e. luxury sector); and
    *   any rent in excess reasonably priced accommodation appropriate to their needs. This means that within the normal range of rents that would be expected for an appropriately sized property. HB will only cover the rent up to the mid point of that range and not any excess. This is known as the **local reference rent**.

In the case of the last restriction what is considered to be appropriately sized accommodation for single claimants under the age of 25 is limited to a room in a shared property (which is known as the single room rent). Where more than one of these restrictions apply the eligible costs are calculated on the lowest figure. Each of these valuations is carried out by a rent officer and not the local authority. The lowest of the rent officer's valuations sets a 'maximum rent' which is binding on the authority. Rent officers are independent valuers who are employed by an executive agency of central government.

---

3. Income

Since HB is means-tested, this means that the income of the household must be assessed to determine whether it is sufficient to cover both their non-housing related needs as well as their housing costs. Income includes:

i.   earnings, pensions, benefits and any other regular or irregular earnings. In an attempt to offer some incentive to claimants to take employment, there is an **income disregard**, i.e. a small amount of any earnings is not taken into account.

ii. an assumed amount of interest received on capital or savings above £3,000 (£6,000 for those aged at least 60) even if no interest is actually received. If capital exceeds £16,000, the household is ineligible for housing benefit. Note that tax credits, introduced boost the incomes of those in low paid employment and intended to make it more worthwhile to work, increase income and hence potentially reduce HB entitlement.

4. The taper

If households have income in excess of the expenditure deemed necessary, they are expected to contribute 65 per cent of this toward their housing costs. In other words, for each £1 of income above the maximum permitted amount, the household is assumed to pay 65 pence of towards their rent. This is known as the taper – the rate at which benefit is withdrawn for each £1 increase in income. The severity of the taper contributes significantly to the poverty and unemployment traps – see below.

Steps in the calculation

1. **Assess income**
    *   calculate income, from wages, benefits, tax credits, pensions, etc. and add assumed income from capital;
    *   deduct any *income disregard* – the actual amount depends on the household type (single, couple, etc.).

2. **Assess income needs**
    *   calculate the value of relevant *personal allowances*;
    *   add any relevant *premiums*.
    This gives the *applicable amount* of income thought to be needed by the household.

3. **Calculate excess income**
    *   if the *applicable amount* is greater than the income, then it is deducted from it to give the excess – in any other case the excess will be zero.

4. **Assess eligible costs**
    *   identify rent payments and some service charges;
    *   if the accommodation is thought to be unreasonably large or expensive, the rent officer can determine what the rent should be as described in the section on eligible housing costs earlier;
    *   deduct any *non-dependent deductions* from the eligible costs.

5. Deduct 65 per cent of excess income from eligible costs
This is the entitlement to housing benefit.

Any household with an assessed income (less non-dependent deductions) which is equal to or lower than the applicable amount will be entitled to full HB – i.e. 100 per cent of the rent (after any restrictions) will be paid. Other households, with excess income, may be entitled to *partial* HB – that is they will be expected to make some contribution towards their rent.

Who is ineligible?
There is a wide range of exclusions. Some of the more important are:

- those with capital in excess of £16,000 (as identified above);
- full-time students, except the disabled or those with children;
- people in residential care;
- those who do not have a 'commercial arrangement', e.g. living with a close relative;
- persons from abroad; this rule excludes most people who need a visa to enter the UK such as non-EU nationals, as well as asylum seekers. However, it does not exclude foreign nationals who have a permanent right of settlement in the UK such as those whose asylum claim has been accepted.

iii. The claims process
There are two routes into HB:

1. *For tenants in receipt of income support*
   These tenants automatically receive a HB claim form from the Department for Work and Pensions (DWP), via the Jobcentre Plus or Pensions Agency, which assess income support claims. This results in a two-stage process, because, having been investigated by the DWP, they are then re-investigated (about some aspects) by the council. Furthermore, there may be delays in the DWP forwarding HB claims to the local authority, which further delays HB payments. LA performance indicators (see chapter five) include 'percentage of HB claims processed within 14 days' – but this *excludes* any delay by the DWP.
2. *For tenants not in receipt of income support*
   They must apply directly to the local authority. The authority is responsible for producing its own HB claim forms, and while some are very good, others may be complex and very difficult for tenants to complete.

iv. Problems of the present HB system
The housing benefit system creates a wide number of disincentives, for the administrators of the system, for claimants, and for the government. These include:

- *Complexity*
  As is apparent from this section, the housing benefit system is very complicated, difficult to understand and complex to administer. The

complexity occurs because rules were devised to limit take up, and over the years these have been further tightened so there is now a proliferation of limitations and penalties within the system. These have reduced the cost of HB overall, but have led to rising costs and delays in administration, and also to a situation where few people understand the system and know why they are receiving particular levels of support.

- *Disincentive to work*
  This arises because of the operation of the *poverty and unemployment* traps. When income rises, whether by taking a job (and leaving unemployment), or taking a better paid job, the combined effects of withdrawal of benefit, tax credits and extra taxes can leave the household little better off. Although the HB *taper* is 65 per cent, the overall withdrawal rate can be much greater when combined with the withdrawal of council tax benefit and working/and or child tax credits. In the worst cases this used to result in an effective marginal tax rate of 93p – i.e.. the household could lose up to 93pence from each extra £1 earned. The overall effect was to leave them much worse off, after taking account of the additional costs of employment, such as clothing, travel, lunches etc.

  However, in recent years the numbers of claimants caught facing the very highest rates of withdrawal (in excess of 90 per cent) has been considerably reduced by the introduction of tax credits. In many cases these have been sufficient to boost the incomes of working families to such an extent that they no longer qualify for HB and as such are not subject to its very high withdrawal rate. However there is still a residual problem for those households who qualify for both HB and tax credits and those who do not qualify for tax credits at all and so remain dependent on HB.

- *The effects of rising rents on work incentives*
  The disincentive to work provided by HB has been considerably worsened by rising levels of rent in all tenures. Table 3.8 shows that the main effect of rising rents is to considerably extend the *breadth* of the poverty trap. This arises because, for those on full HB, all of any increase in rent is paid by HB. Rising rents simply expand the amount of household costs paid by the benefit system, so that the wage that has to be earned before the household escapes the 'traps' rises with every rent increase.

Table 3.8 – Gross *weekly* earnings at which housing benefit entitlement ceases (selected households and rent levels)

Household type	Rent levels			
	£30	£50	£70	£90
Single person	£109.16	£151.49	£196.74	£241.99
Lone parent, 2 children	£68.65	£107.25	£192.32	£292.87
Couple, 2 children	£84.35	£146.02	£243.63	£344.18

Source: Wilcox, 2003

Research by Ford *et al.* in 1996 for the Joseph Rowntree Foundation found that around half of all households on benefit calculated whether they would be better off before accepting employment, with owner-occupiers more likely to accept work regardless of financial implications than tenants. This suggests that the work disincentives generated by the benefit system are indeed significant for many households, and it was particularly marked in the case of single households. As mentioned above, the recent introduction of a system of tax credits for working households is intended partially to address this disincentive effect, though this may be limited by reductions in HB entitlement.

- *Disincentive to economise*
  Since housing benefit pays the full cost of rent increases, it has been suggested that this provides a disincentive to *economise* on housing – i.e. it encourages households to take accommodation which is too expensive and/or too large for their needs. The removal of rent controls may have permitted some private sector landlords to charge exploitative rents and the availability of HB has enabled tenants readily to accept these inflated rents. It is also possible for claimants to move to better properties, offering standards of accommodation well above their needs. This is the primary reason for the introduction of the various rent restrictions, examined above.

- *The high costs of housing benefit*
  The cost of rent rebates to council tenants is estimated to be £5,379 million in 2002/3, with rent allowances to RSL and private landlords' tenants reaching £6,763 million. It is anticipated that the cost of rent rebates will continue at similar levels up to 2003/4, but the cost of rent allowances is predicted to increase to £7,396 million by 2003/4 (Wilcox, 2003). Part of the rationale for the pilot standard allowance reforms (see section v. below) is to address the problem whereby rent increases are seen to be driving the housing benefit budget.

v. Reform of housing benefit

During 2003, the government introduced a pilot HB scheme for private sector tenants, in which the eligible housing costs are based on a flat rate standard allowance (called the Standard Local Housing Allowance, SLHA) rather than the actual rent charged. The SLHA is modelled on a slightly modified form of the local reference rent. The idea is that a fixed allowance will encourage tenants to 'shop around' to find a cheaper rent, enabling them to keep any savings made as a result. However, there are some doubts about the likely impact of these 'incentives', particularly for elderly households (who may be reluctant to move) and those in high demand areas (where landlords may simply be able to charge higher rents, up to the allowance). Since HB will no longer be based on the actual rent, it is also intended that it will no longer be paid direct to the landlord. Overall the plan to end direct payment of HB has caused particular concern amongst HAs and their private lenders, as well as private landlords, who fear rising arrears as a result

(Ambrosi, 2003b). It is feared that this could lead to private landlords withdrawing altogether from the sector.

In the longer term the government intends to extend this idea to the social sector when wider reforms such as choice based lettings (see chapter five) and rent restructuring (see this chapter, section 4) have 'created the right conditions'. The government has made it clear that it will be looking for areas where these conditions have been reached early on, so that it can run a pilot when rent restructuring (in England) is complete.

vi. Supporting People

In order to clarify how much of any rents and charges were for non-housing elements, the government introduced this new subsidy in 2002. Basically, it took over the funding of all non-housing aspects of rent charges, which were previously covered by housing benefit. As a result, housing benefit payments should now cover only the cost of the housing service (providing and maintaining the properties).

Subsidy for owner occupiers

While this text is primarily about social housing, it is important that this is viewed in the context of financial resources made available to other tenures. We have already shown that the main subsidy to social tenants, housing benefit, is also available to the private sector tenants. However, owner occupation has been viewed, for many years, as the 'preferred' tenure by government, which explains why, historically, owner occupiers have tended to receive a wider range of subsidies than social housing tenants. Furthermore, a number of these are *general* subsidies, available to any household, and, as a result, may provide relatively higher levels of subsidy to the wealthiest households in the UK. However, they are mainly given in the form of 'tax reliefs', which reduce the household's tax bill rather than paying a direct income supplement, so the real cost is not counted by the government and largely remains hidden.

a. The main subsidies
These include:

- *Capital gains tax exemption*
  When most assets are sold, any gain in value (after allowing for inflation) – the capital gain – is subject to tax. In the case of the only or main dwelling of an owner occupier, this tax is waived. This represents a significant subsidy, and is doubtless part of the reason why housing as an asset is more attractive in the UK than many other assets, such as stocks and shares. However, since this is a tax *exemption* rather than a payment, estimates of the cost of this subsidy are difficult to make or obtain, and its value will fluctuate considerably depending on the state of private housing markets and hence the numbers and values of homes sold.

Again, it should be noted that the greater the value of the property sold, the larger is the value of this tax exemption. This suggests that it is the richest who gain most, with the poorest owner occupiers gaining relatively little in comparison.

- *Exemption from schedule A income taxation*
  Since owner occupiers choose to take the benefits of the value of their properties' services 'in kind' – instead of renting the homes out, to earn rent income – they used to be charged income tax on the 'imputed' (estimated) value of those services. However, this estimate was based on the rateable value of the property, which was the basis for local taxation (the 'rates'), but which had not been revised for many years, resulting in ridiculously low rental estimates. From 1963, therefore, this tax was abolished for owner occupiers. Again, it is very difficult to assess the value of this tax exemption, because it would involve estimating the 'rental value' of all owner occupied homes in the UK, and then making some assessment of the likely tax liability of each individual occupier (since some may have insufficient income to be eligible to pay tax in any case, and others would be liable at the highest tax rate of 40 per cent). However, we can be certain that this represents a substantial saving for many owner occupiers, especially for those in expensive properties – suggesting that the wealthiest potentially gain most.

- *Income support for mortgage interest (ISMI) payments*
  This is a means-tested benefit, available only to those on income support who are unable to work – whether through unemployment, sickness, disability or old age. However, because it is a mortgage subsidy, it necessarily excludes large numbers of low income owners without a mortgage – predominantly the elderly. Claimants must have assets (excluding the house) valued at less that £8,000. From 1987, the scheme paid half of all mortgage interest payments for 16 weeks, and the full amount thereafter. As the numbers of unemployed owner occupiers rose during the recession at the end of the 1980s, the government sought ways to reduce the cost of this benefit, which had reached about £1.1 billion by 1994. Hence, a mortgage ceiling of £150,000 was introduced in 1992, reduced to £100,000 in 1994, and from October 1995, new borrowers were ineligible for any interest payments for nine months. For pre-existing borrowers, there was no entitlement for four months, and only 50 per cent for the next four. For all claimants, interest is calculated as the average variable rate charged by mortgage lenders (regardless of what is actually paid). Nevertheless, mortgage benefit in income support still cost £484 million in 2001 (Wilcox, 2003).
  For first-time buyers, whose mortgages (particularly in the southern parts of England and some property 'hot spots' such as Edinburgh) are likely to far exceed £100,000, this level of support is clearly inadequate. It is the government's belief that private insurance should be taken out to

cover mortgage interest for periods out of work, but many commentators have suggested that this fails to recognise that the most vulnerable mortgagors – those with insecure employment, on temporary and part time contracts, which are increasingly common in today's 'flexible labour markets' – find insurance difficult or too expensive to obtain. In order to support some households in this situation, Communities Scotland has introduced a *Mortgage to Rent Scheme*, through which an RSL buys the property – subject to valuation limits – to rent it back to the occupiers.

- *Improvement grants*
  These means-tested grants are available for essential repairs to properties, to help to bring them up to acceptable standards. They include assistance with the provision of essential sanitary facilities, adequate heating, and hygienic kitchen facilities, and are available to low income landlords as well as owner occupiers. However, in practice, many authorities operate a lengthy waiting list. It is, therefore, unlikely that this present system adequately addresses the problem of poor house condition in the private sector, especially in the light of expanded numbers of low income owners (partly as a result of government policies such as the Right to Buy).

b. Poverty among home owners

Recent research has suggested that there is a growing problem of poverty amongst home owners (Burrows, 2003), with 50 per cent of all poor households living in owner occupation. 18 per cent of these households are outright owners and 32 per cent are paying a mortgage. While the poverty *rate* – the proportions which are poor in the tenure – is lowest in owner occupation (at 15 – 17 per cent), the large size of this sector means that these low income owners form this significant portion (half) of all poverty. Despite being 50 per cent of the poor, home owners receive only 8 per cent of targeted (means-tested) state support for housing costs. A key, earlier subsidy, Mortgage Interest Tax Relief (MITR), which reduced the cost of interest payments for home owners with a mortgage, was finally abolished in April 2000. As indicated above, there is now only very limited, means-tested help with mortgage costs, and there has never been an equivalent to HB for low income owners.

8. Finance for tenure transfer

As examined in the earlier sections, government policies over the past couple of decades have emphasised the *enabling* role of local authorities rather than their role as *providers* of social housing. This has resulted in new approaches to subsidising council housing, largely conditional on a requirement to transfer tenure. In general, these initiatives are intended both to encourage the transfer of social housing tenants to owner occupation, and to encourage council tenants in particular to transfer to another rented tenure.

In the brief examination of some of these initiatives which follows, they are classified by:

- the transfer tenure (the tenure to be transferred to);
- who and what transfers (only the *tenant*, or the *tenant and the property*);
- the target tenure (which tenure the property and/or tenant moves from).

This is summarised in Table 3.9.

Table 3.9 Summary of tenure transfer initiatives

Transfer tenure	By whom/what?	Examples
1. Owner occupation	LA and HA tenants and property	Right to Buy Rent to Mortgage Right to Acquire Right to Purchase Voluntary Purchase Grant
2. Owner occupation	Current and prospective social tenants	Homebuy TIS, DIYSO, CIS, Conventional shared ownership
3. HA (or PRS)	Current LA tenants and properties	(Tenants' Choice) LSVT Partial transfer
4. HA	PRS tenants and properties	HAMA
5. Council owned (arms-length) company	Council properties and tenants	ALMO
6. Private ownership (but remain council tenants)	Current LA properties	PFI

Each of these types is next examined in turn.

Tenure transfer type 1

To: owner occupation
By: tenants and property
From: council and housing association tenures

The Right to Buy policy was the first and most significant attempt by the government to encourage council tenants to become owner occupiers. It was introduced in the 1980 Housing Act and Housing (Scotland) Act, offering substantial discounts on the market value of the property for existing council tenants. Over time, the discounts were increased (to a maximum of 70 per cent for flats) to encourage further purchases. The impact on council housing has been enormous, with over £35 billion secured as capital receipts since 1980, as Table 3.10 shows.

Table 3.10: Right to Buy cumulative receipts from 1980 to 2002 (£ million)

England	29,274.1
Scotland	4,441.6
Wales	1,388.5

Source: Wilcox, 2003

However, this policy has affected not just the quantities of council properties available for new tenants, but also the qualities, since, in general, it is the best properties (predominantly houses), in the best localities, which have sold. In addition, recent research by Jones (2002) in London suggests that up to 40 per cent of Right to Buy purchases are now being let out (in the private rented sector), with up to a third (in Lambeth B.C., a London borough) owned by property companies. Concern was expressed also that there are abuses in regeneration areas, with tenants hoping to gain from subsequent compulsory purchase by the local authority. In 13 per cent of cases, relatives were financially involved, and a fifth were expecting a financial return.

As a result of these perceived abuses, the Scottish Executive introduced new controls, and the British government curbed the Right to Buy in some English LA areas with acute housing shortages (mainly London and the South east) during 2003. New legislation has reduced the maximum discount (from £38,000) to £16,000, extended the initial qualification period from two to five years, makes tenants repay the discount if they move within five (instead of currently three) years, and allows local authorities to refuse Right to Buy sales where demolition is expected. There will also be a five year ban on letting, and applications steered by private companies will be illegal (Ambrosi, 2003a).

A *Rent to Mortgage* scheme was introduced when it was perceived that Right to Buy sales were declining, in the 1993 Leasehold Reform, Housing and Urban Development Act, but this stimulated very little interest from council tenants and was later abolished.

Tenants of non-charitable housing associations were also given the Right to Buy by the 1980 Acts (with some exceptions, such as schemes for the elderly).

However, with the introduction of *assured* tenancies for housing association tenants in the 1988 Housing Act, outside rent controls, new association tenants lost this right (though old tenants, on housing association secure tenancies – subject to rent controls – retained it). This was because (as examined in section 5) new association developments were to be funded partly by private borrowing and private lenders would not wish to see their security, in the form of the dwellings, sold off cheaply.

However, under the Housing Act (1996), some HA tenants (in post-April 1997 schemes) were given the *Right to Acquire* in England, once again giving them a discount (of between £9,000 and £16,000, depending on LA area) to buy. Scotland also has a *Right to Purchase* scheme. However, housing associations that develop in rural areas were concerned about the effects that this policy could have on the availability of land for future developments. In some cases, they obtain land cheaply from local landowners on the understanding that the properties will be made available only to local people in housing need. As a result, rural properties in some small villages are exempt.

For English tenants in properties built before April 1997, who do not have the Right to Acquire, there is a *Voluntary Purchase Grant* scheme, but it is up to the HA as to whether this is offered, and on which properties.

Tenure transfer type 2

To: owner occupation
By: current (and prospective) tenants only
From: council and housing association tenures

Finance to permit tenants to move into a different property in owner occupied tenure became more important as RTB sales declined. These schemes are intended to 'free up' existing homes for new, homeless tenants. Since they provide properties for new or existing tenants *that would not otherwise be available*, at a much lower price than the cost of building a new property, they are considered by the government to offer good value. However, they do not result in any additional homes being produced, and the stock of housing in the area remains the same.

Homebuy is a scheme offered in England and Wales which enables LA and HA tenants, as well as those in priority need on LA waiting lists, an interest free equity loan to fund 25 per cent of the cost of buying a property on the open market. Hence, it is technically offering shared ownership (see below), since the RSL owns a 25 per cent share, but does it not involve any rental payments. This replaced the earlier *Tenants Incentive Scheme* (TIS) and *Do It Yourself Shared Ownership* scheme (DIYSO) (see below) for HA tenants, which had offered cash grants to tenants, to permit them either to buy a private sector home outright (TIS) or a share in one (DIYSO) – both usually with the aid of a mortgage. Under

Homebuy, the tenant takes a conventional mortgage for the remaining 75 per cent of the property's value, and only repays the 25 per cent public sector loan when the property is sold. However, repayment is of 25 per cent of the property's value at the time of sale.

Council tenants may – at the discretion of the LA – also be offered a *Cash Incentive Scheme* (CIS), which provides a (means-tested) cash grant toward owner occupation.

Conventional Shared Ownership (CSO) schemes apply only to housing association tenure. The HA builds or purchases a property which is then part-bought (on a mortgage) and part-rented by current or potential tenants. The initial 'bought' share is usually between 25 per cent and 75 per cent. All shared ownership schemes must permit *staircasing* – i.e. the part owner can progressively buy a larger share of the property, until they own 100 per cent.

Do it yourself shared ownership (DIYSO), which permits a council tenant (or prospective tenant) to select a home on the private market for shared ownership with the LA, can still be offered by English LAs, but at their discretion.

Tenure transfer type 3

To: other rented tenures
By: properties and tenants
From: council tenure

The possibility of council tenants transferring their properties to another landlord was introduced in the 1988 Housing Act. Under *Tenants' Choice*, tenants had to be balloted and agree the transfer, though there was a great deal of debate about the role of the statutory funders for housing associations in this (which oversaw the procedures), because usually the proposed new landlord would be an association. In the event, the policy was largely unsuccessful, and it was abolished by the 1996 Housing Act.

At the same time, *Housing Action Trusts* were announced for a few run-down council estates in specific areas, such as in Lambeth, Sunderland and Leeds. The private sector trust would take over the council housing, and would receive very large amounts of public funding to rehabilitate the estates. They were to be time limited, when the dwellings would pass to other private landlords. In the event, however, many tenants proved unwilling to take up the offer; generally, they did not wish to leave the security of council tenure. The scheme was rescued only after a major policy reversal, when Hull managed to persuade the Department of the Environment (DoE) that tenants should be able to opt *back* into council tenure at the end of the trust period. A number of other LAs later followed Hull's lead and persuaded tenants to agree to a HAT, including Waltham Forest, Birmingham and Liverpool.

A second initiative to boost LSVT was the DoE's Estates Renewal Challenge Fund (ERCF). Under this scheme, launched in November 1995, local authorities bid (competitively) for funding to transfer highly run-down estates to new social landlords. The ERCF funded essential repairs, and subsidised the new landlord if the estate had a negative *Tenanted Market Value*. The TMV, the assumed 'market' value of the estate, takes account of the predicted net income (rents less essential management and maintenance costs), assuming that it stays in social ownership. The ERCF also funded any set-up costs of the new landlord, but private finance must also be used.

However, before this there had been a large number of landlord-initiated transfers, known as large scale voluntary transfers (LSVT). As Malpass (1999, p. 889) argues, 'LSVT is essentially about demunicipalising social housing and about remortgaging to fund essential capital investment in an ageing stock'. By March 2003, some 120 English councils had (with the consent of their tenants) transferred *all* their housing stock to housing associations (Wilcox, 2003). Usually, these have been newly created associations, funded through private borrowing. This has involved the transfer of some 737,106 dwellings, at a transfer price of £5,503.3 million (Wilcox, 2003). The average price per dwelling paid by the transfer organisation has averaged a tiny £6,067, but these transfers have nevertheless produced 'usable' receipts (see section 3) of £1,229.6 million for the councils concerned. However, the transferred stock is valued as the *present value* of a 30-year income stream from rents, so future income streams must be *discounted* to give this present value. It has been argued by some councils that the government's choice of interest rate (used to discount the future income streams) was much too high, which resulted in much lower values. A lower interest rate would result in higher valuations, and hence greater receipts, and the rate has recently been revised downwards by the ODPM.

LSVT has transformed the composition of the HA sector: '57 new associations with more than 2,500 dwellings were formed by April 1999... (and) these associations constituted half of all associations with more than 2,500 dwellings' (Malpass, 1999, p. 889). Hence, the HA sector in England is becoming one increasingly of large organisations.

In contrast to the relative success of LSVT in England, in Scotland by 2002, there had been only one LSVT (Berwickshire). However, the Scottish Borders and Dumfries and Galloway transferred in 2003, with Glasgow City (the largest LSVT to date) also adding around 90,000 dwellings to the transfer total during 2003. This latter transfer is receiving enormous public funding: £900 million is committed from the Treasury at Whitehall to cover outstanding debt repayments, together with £700 million in HAG from the Scottish Executive, as well as a £100 million 'contingency fund'. In addition, private finance (from the Bank of Scotland, the Royal Bank of Scotland, Abbey National and Nationwide) is providing £850 million in loans. (Evans, 2002a). There are widespread concerns that the huge public finance commitment to Glasgow will be to the detriment of other Scottish housing for many years (Evans, 2002b), as well as concerns about the likely impact on the Glasgow construction market (Inside Housing, 2000).

However, many smaller scale transfers have taken place in Scotland, often to community based housing associations (unique to Scotland, these are managed by a locally-based committee), from former Scottish Special Housing Association (SSHA) stock. Scottish Homes (now, Communities Scotland) has provided substantial HAG funding for transfers. In contrast, in Wales, there has so far only been one successful ballot for transfer, in Bridgend in November 2002. This may open the gates for further LSVTs there.

LSVT is not, however, all gain for the public sector, because the LSVT councils are no longer able to subsidise housing benefit costs from their housing revenue accounts (examined in section 4). As housing benefit costs to the Treasury rose, so the government introduced a 20 per cent 'levy' on LSVT receipts that remained after all housing debt had been cleared. This levy had raised £256.4 million for the Treasury by March 2003 in England (Wilcox, 2003).

Tenure transfer type 4

To: housing association tenure
By: properties
From: private tenures

Compared to efforts to persuade council tenants into other tenures, these have been very small scale. The *Housing Associations as Managing Agents* (HAMA) scheme was intended to bring more properties into housing association management from the private sector, by persuading private landlords that it was worth remaining in the sector if management were taken from them. Essentially, a housing association lets and manages the property on behalf of the private landlord, for a defined period of time, to households that qualify for an association letting. However, take-up of this scheme has not been high.

Tenure transfer type 5

To: a new management company
By: council owned stock
From: council management

This most recent development in England, called arm's length management organisations (ALMOs), is now being actively encouraged by the government, with significant additional permitted borrowing to tackle stock rehabilitation. However, this is conditional on achieving a two star Best Value inspection rating, and this has deterred many councils who might otherwise have been considering the creation of an ALMO.

An ALMO involves the setting up of a new, separate ('arm's length') organisation to manage the council's stock. The board of the new company will usually include councillors, tenants and independent members. The properties remain council owned and the tenants remain local authority tenants.

There were eight proposed ALMOs in the first bidding round, created by councils in Ashfield, Derby, Hounslow, Kirkless, Stockton, Westminster, Wigan and Rochdale. The Audit Commission has since suggested that ALMOs can provide rapid improvements to service delivery, borne out by the fact that all 8 initial ALMOs successfully achieved a two or three star rating. The first round councils were followed by an additional 25 successful bids to form ALMOs in rounds 2 and 3, and 14 more councils put in bids for round 4. Altogether the 33 ALMOs already manage 530,000 council homes. In general, tenants have seemed to find ALMOs more acceptable than LSVT, since they remain council tenants and the houses remain council-owned – only their management is transferred to the new organisation. However, the first rejection by ballot of an ALMO, by council tenants in Camden, occurred early in 2004.

Tenure transfer type 6

To: private company ownership
By: council owned stock
From: council ownership (but retaining council management of tenancies)

The most recent 'privatisation' policy development has been to extend the Private Finance Initiative (PFI), used for many years now to provide roads, schools and hospitals, to council housing. PFI essentially involves a private company developing or improving, and managing/repairing, the *asset* (the road or building), while the public sector manages the *service* (provided by the hospital, school or house). In return, the private company is paid an annual fee by the public sector – rather like a leasing agreement. From the public sector's point of view, it is exchanging a capital cost (to provide the asset and undertake any major repairs) for a revenue cost (the annual 'rental' sum). It is also argued that this transfers any risk, that there may be major problems with the building or road (needing extra expenditure), to the private sector.

Pathfinder PFIs for council housing have so far involved some demolition and new build as well as refurbishment in Manchester and London, beginning in 2003. It is anticipated that others will follow.

9. Conclusion

This chapter has indicated that throughout most of the 1980s and 1990s, local authorities were encouraged to become enablers rather than providers of housing. This was achieved via Right to Buy as well as a variety of financial mechanisms including:

- tight control over the ability to borrow for capital projects as well as to spend capital receipts;
- reducing levels of housing revenue support grant, particularly in England and Wales, causing rents to be levered up (until the late 1990s);
- various policies with financial incentives to remove housing from council ownership to alternative landlords, particularly HAs.

At the same time, there was increased emphasis on HAs as social housing providers, though with reducing levels of public grant support (HAG/SHG) and increased reliance on private borrowing. These increased loans encouraged HAs, particularly in England and Wales, to increase rents, until (as with local authorities), there was a growing government awareness of the rising costs of high rents through the housing benefit bill. As a result, curbs on rent increases were introduced by the late 1990s for both types of provider in England and Wales, and additionally in England, there is now a requirement to restructure their rents to bring them more in line with each other.

The 1990s saw rising numbers of LSVTs in England, where a number of government financial inducements made transfer attractive. However, not all tenants were persuaded by the 'carrot' of refurbishment and there have been a number of high-profile failures at the tenant-ballot stage in the process, including England's largest proposed transfer in Birmingham. The largest LSVT yet, in Glasgow, occurred in 2003.

More recently, there has been some encouragement, via promised additional borrowing, of ALMOs, which permit the (English) local authority to retain ownership but remove the management functions to an 'arm's length organisation'. This model has received praise from the Audit Commission – the equivalent of the Accounts Commission in Scotland – for delivering rapid service improvements. In addition, local authorities in England have seen some recent expansion in capital funds, which, together with the new 'prudential borrowing' rules and the introduction of the Major Repairs Allowance, are designed to ensure that council housing is able to achieve the Decent Homes Standard by 2010. The move to resource accounting and the creation of an asset management fund is designed to encourage English councils to take a more strategic, long term approach to managing their housing assets.

English RSL stock is generally more recent, so there will be fewer problems for some of them in achieving the Decent Homes target – though those with older properties have expressed some concerns. Of more significance, perhaps, for HAs, is rent restructuring, which requires their rent levels to harmonise with council rents, so that over ten years, the two become directly competitive, to improve both competition and choice. It is, as yet, unclear how the extension of Best Value, via a Single Housing Inspectorate (under the Audit Commission) to English HAs, may influence capital allocations, particularly once these are transferred to the control of the proposed new Regional Housing Boards from 2004.

Subsidy to customers remains a highly problematic aspect of housing finance, with housing benefit supporting a majority of social housing tenants but also creating disincentives both to work and to economise. The recent pilot fixed-allowance scheme in England from 2003, to promote 'shopping incentives', will be watched with interest. The assistance available to the housing costs of owner occupiers has declined considerably since the abolition of mortgage tax relief, and, together with the expansion of home ownership to lower income groups (primarily through the Right to Buy), this has resulted in many more poor households in owner occupation.

References and further reading

Ambrosi, M. (2003a) 'Discounts Cut to Size', *Inside Housing*, 24 Jan, p. 1.

Ambrosi, M. (2003b) 'Shopping Incentives Spark Landlord Cash Flow Fears', *Inside Housing*, 18 April, p. 13.

Burrows, R. (2003) *Poverty and Home Ownership in Contemporary Britain*, JRF, York.

Chaplin, R., Jones, M., Martin, S., Pryke, M,, Royce, C., Whitehead, C. and Yang, J. (1995) *Rents and Risks: Investing in Housing Associations*, JRF, York.

Delargy, M. (2003) 'Calling the Shots', *Roof*, May/June 2003, pp. 18-21.

Department of the Environment, Transport and the Regions (1998) *Handling of Rent Rebates under Resource Accounting*, Consultation Paper, November, DETR, London.

Evans, R. (2002a) '£100 Million Fund Will Prop up Glasgow Transfer', *Inside Housing*, 20 December, p. 3.

Evans, R. (2002b) 'Funding Fears Dog Transfer Plans', *Inside Housing*, 4 April.

Ford, J., Kempson, E. and England, J. (1996) *Into Work? The impact of housing costs and the benefit system on people's decision to work*, Policy Press, York.

Garnett, D. and Perry, J. (2004 forthcoming) *Housing Finance*, CIH, Coventry.

HACAS Consulting (2000) *Impact and Implications of Restructuring Rents in the Registered Social Landlord Sector*, DETR, London.

Hebden, P. (2003) 'Rent Formula Set to Survive Review', *Inside Housing*, 11 April, p. 2.

Housing Corporation (1998) *Revised Uses of the Rent Surplus Fund*, January, Housing Corporation, London.

Housing Corporation (2001) *Total Cost Indicator, Grant Rate and Rent Analyses for 2002/3*, October, Housing Corporation, London.

Housing Corporation (2002) *Decent Homes; Sector Study 19*, Housing Corporation, London.

Housing Corporation (2002) *Decent Homes, Assessing Housing Association Properties Against the Decent Homes Standard*, Housing Corporation, London.

Housing Corporation (2003) *Re-inventing Investment*, Housing Corporation, London.

Inside Housing (2000) 'Transfer Jobs May Overload Construction Industry', *Inside Housing*, 28 Sept.

Jones, C. (2002) quoted in Ambrosi, M. (2002) 'Right to Buy Owners are now the Landlords', *Inside Housing*, 13 December, p. 3.

Kemp, P. (2001) *Shopping Incentives*, JRF, York.

Kiddle, C. and Banks, D. (2002) *Sector Study 20, Housing Associations and Changes in Rent 2001 to 2002*, Housing Corporation, London.

Malpass, P. (1999) 'Housing Associations and Housing Policy in Britain since 1989', *Housing Studies*, Vol 14, No 6, pp. 881-893.

Malpass, P. and Murie, A. (1994) *Housing Policy and Practice*, p, 109, Macmillan, Basingstoke.

Martin, D. (2003) 'How Green Does Your Garden Grow?', *Inside Housing*, 10 Jan, p. 11.

Office of the Deputy Prime Minister (2000) *Decent Homes Standard*, ODPM, London.

Office of the Deputy Prime Minister (2002a) *Housing Revenue Account Manual*, p. 5, ODPM, London.

Office of the Deputy Prime Minister (2002b) *Guidance on Stock Valuation for Resource Accounting*, ODPM, London.

Office of the Deputy Prime Minister (2002c) *Local Authority Housing Finance – A Guide to the New Arrangements*, ODPM, London.

Office of the Deputy Prime Minister (2003) *A Guide to Social Rent Reforms in the Local Authority Sector*, ODPM, London.

Wilcox, S. (2002) *Housing Review 2002/3*, CIH and CML for the Joseph Rowntree Foundation, Coventry and London.

Wilcox, S. (2003) *Housing Review 2003/4*, CIH and CML for the Joseph Rowntree Foundation, Coventry and London.

CHAPTER 4:
Developing social housing

1. Introduction: the context of social housing development

Housing development may involve the provision of new dwellings, or the refurbishment/rehabilitation of existing buildings. The ability of social housing organisations to engage in development work is partly dependent on the policies of the central government, since subsidy is usually required to produce 'affordable' rents.

The emphasis of recent government policy has been on local authorities as *enablers* of social housing development, rather than as providers. They have been encouraged to sell land cheaply to housing associations, and, (as examined in chapter three), to transfer part or all of their stock to associations for refurbishment and/or management. As a result, local authorities have virtually ceased to build new housing, as Table 4.1 clearly shows.

Table 4.1: Housing completions by local authorities

	1970	1980	1990	2000	2002
England	118,943	67,337	13,873	190	254
Wales	6,513	3,493	610	17	26
Scotland	31,570	6,167	1,203	95	51
N. Ireland*	7,692	2,507	1,299	77	19

(*Housing Executive in Northern Ireland)
Source: Wilcox, 2003

Housing associations were encouraged to take over the main role of developing and refurbishing social housing, initially via a large expansion in Housing Association Grant (HAG) from the government. More recently, as explored in chapter three, subsidy has been declining and associations encouraged to depend more on private finance. Nevertheless, they remain the main providers of new social housing in Britain, though in much smaller quantities than their local authority predecessors, as Tables 4.1 and 4.2 (overleaf) show.

Whether by a housing association or a local authority, this chapter aims first to describe the main features of the *traditional* process of developing or rehabilitating social housing schemes. This involves the housing organisation leading the process of development as the client organisation, and assembling (or using 'in-house') specialist consultants to advise and produce the design. In this

Table 4.2: Housing completions by housing associations

	1970	1980	1990	2000	2002
England	8,176	19,299	13,821	17,058	13,699
Wales	73	917	1,685	958	735
Scotland	244	881	1,963	4,894	5,120
N. Ireland	18	325	442	915	891

Source: Wilcox, 2003

traditional process, the contracting company, the builders, will only be employed after this stage. The chapter aims to provide an overview of the process, to promote an awareness of its essential features, so that the potential advantages of, as well as possible problems generated by, this traditional approach can be better understood. Finally, the chapter examines changes to the process which have been encouraged by the Egan Report, *Rethinking Construction* (1998), involving *partnering*. This idea of partnering has also recently extended into the Housing Corporation's approach to allocating the Approved Development Programme (ADP) in England (see Chapter three, section 5), which is also examined. The repair and maintenance of social housing, which directly involves many more housing managers, is examined in chapter five.

However, it should also be recognised that it is possible for housing organisations to acquire additional properties in other ways, such as buying existing properties from a private developer or local authority (for example, via large scale voluntary transfer or smaller scale transfer – see chapter three), or leasing (a form of long term renting) from private sector landlords.

The housing development process includes all activities, which are necessary to achieve the construction of a new housing scheme or the refurbishment of existing dwellings. The stage with which everyone is familiar, when construction work actually begins on site, is in reality often just the final stage of a long and complex process. Many separate issues first have to be resolved by the housing organisation, and most of these decisions will require the advice and assistance of a number of other parties, with different skills and areas of expertise. The next section identifies and briefly describes the main people with important roles in the traditional approach to the process. Their specific responsibilities at each stage will become clear in later sections, as the process itself is examined.

2. The main parties in the traditional development process

The *client* requires the development, initiates the process and pays for the design and construction.

This may be a person or organisation. The client must ensure that everyone involved in the scheme's design and construction is very clear about the requirements for the scheme, by setting them out in a number of clearly defined ways – which are examined as the process unfolds. One or two people, sometimes employed in a separate development section, known as the client's representatives usually represent housing organisations in this role. Housing managers may be involved in some or all of the activities required of this role.

The client employs a number of professionals to direct and manage the development process. Some large social housing organisations may have a number of their own 'in-house' consultants, able to provide all or most of the specialised roles. Many others will undertake insufficient development work for it to be worthwhile to employ specialist skills internally, so they will need to employ external specialists.

> The *consultant* generally designs the development and oversees its construction.

This person (or persons) is most often an *architect*, who has detailed knowledge of both house and estate design, so can advise on the best solutions to development problems and issues. When the development is a rehabilitation project, a *building surveyor* will usually be involved with the architect, or may replace the architect in the consulting role. This is because building surveyors have detailed knowledge of *existing* buildings – both of their design, and of the sorts of problems which arise from this. Building surveyors are also employed by social housing organisations to inspect property which needs repair, so will often work with housing managers engaged in maintenance work. This is examined further in chapter five.

> The *quantity surveyor* (QS) is the client's cost consultant, responsible for costing the design.

The QS costs the designs prepared by the main consultant, ensures that *value for money* is being obtained, and later, values construction work as it progresses to permit payments to be made to the contractor. Although the QS will have to work closely with the architect, they must be appointed separately by the client, because the QS checks that the architect's design is within the organisation's cost limits and/or offers good value for money. For rehabilitation projects, the building surveyor will usually also undertake the QS role.

> Other *consultants* may be necessary for some projects.

For example, where there are difficult site conditions, such as old mine workings, a *civil or structural engineer* may be engaged to undertake detailed examination of the site and advise on the design of the buildings' foundations. This professional can also advise on buildings which have special structural requirements, such as high rise flats. *Electrical, mechanical or building services engineers* may be needed when there are lifts; *landscape architects* specialise in the external areas of an estate; and *highways engineers* can resolve complex road layout or access difficulties. Generally, the main consultant will advise when any of these are necessary.

The *contractor* is the organisation which undertakes the construction work.

Sometimes, in the case of a local authority, the contractor appointed will be the in-house 'direct works' section, but in most circumstances, an outside contractor – a building company – will be engaged. It is important that the client and consultant maintain good communications with the contractor, in order to ensure that the work is of the right quality and is completed on time.

The contractor's main representative on site is the site agent, who supervises and co-ordinates the work of all of the different skills, such as bricklayers, joiners, plumbers, electricians etc.

Sub contractors may be engaged to undertake some aspects of the work

---

The client may nominate these, or the contractors themselves may engage them, because they have greater expertise in some field. They operate under the direction of the lead contractor.

The *clerk of works* closely supervises the construction work on behalf of the client.

Once the construction work is underway, it is overseen by the consultant, but not usually on a day to day basis. For this reason, most projects will have a clerk of works, who is employed on the site to work closely with the consultant to ensure that what is built is exactly what is required by the architect's design. This role is particularly important for a refurbishment project, because, very often, new and unforeseen problems emerge once the work begins. A poor standard of work may result, unless closely monitored.

The *planning supervisor* co-ordinates all requirements relating to health and safety matters for a scheme.

This role, required by the Construction (Design and Management) Regulations (CDM) from 1995, resulted both from the concerns of the Health and Safety Executive (HSE) – the body which oversees work-place safety in the UK – and the European Union (EU) about high accident and fatality rates on construction sites. These regulations now impose duties on clients, consultants and contractors to ensure that there are adequate health and safety controls at all stages of the development process, in order to reduce the likelihood of accidents. This function need not rest with one person, but may be undertaken by the design team or contractor where appropriate. What is important is that someone or somebody always takes the responsibilities of the planning supervisor, and this must to be stated in any contracts (which are examined at a later stage).

The responsibilities of the planning supervisor include:

* informing the HSE of planned projects which are likely to last more than 30 days or involve more than 500 person working days on site (so, minor maintenance projects are excluded);
* reviewing and co-ordinating arrangements to avoid risks to health and safety;
* preparing a *health and safety plan*, identifying potential hazards, safety issues and procedures;
* creating a health and safety file, containing all details about the site.

Solicitors are employed to advise on legal aspects and draw up contracts.

In general, a solicitor will be needed to complete the purchase of a site or buildings, and to draw up any contracts, which specify the conditions under which the client is employing the different parties. This helps to ensure that the client has *legal redress* – can go to court for compensation – in the event of a party failing to perform adequately.

In addition to the parties employed directly by the housing organisation, there are a number of other people whose roles are important to development. Most are public sector employees with specific statutory responsibilities – i.e. they have some obligations by law for aspects of the development process. The role of the Health and Safety Executive has already been identified, in overseeing matters affecting the safety of the public and employees whilst construction work is continuing.

Development control, exercised by the *planning authorities*, is intended to ensure that the quality of the physical environment is maintained and protected from inappropriate developments, and that new buildings, or significant changes to existing buildings, fit in with the local area.

The planning authorities, in general, are local authorities. The planning process is overseen by central government, via the ODPM. An important function of the planning system is also to ensure that there is an adequate supply of land for housing. As part of this role, the planning authorities are required to draw up *development plans*, which indicate how such requirements are to be met.

In most areas, where there is only one tier of local government, there is a single (Unitary) Development Plan, the UDP. Where two tiers remain, the plans are in two parts: the first drawn up by the county council and the second, by the district council. Overall, however, all development plans must cover similar issues:

- *a structure plan*, which defines requirements in broad terms, taking account of factors such as demographic trends, government policy, and housing demand in the area. It specifies the target number of new dwellings to be permitted, which are distributed amongst the districts;
- *a local plan*, which identifies specific locations in the area considered suitable for residential (and other) development, as well as local policies for development control.

However, the government is proposing to amend the current system (ODPM, 2002d), to introduce:

- *Regional Spatial Strategies* (Spatial Development Strategy in London), prepared by the regional assemblies, replacing the current county-level structure plan. It is intended that this will also consider sub-regional issues, and that counties will be consulted on their preparation.
- *Local Development Frameworks* (LDFs), replacing the structure/local plan or UDP and prepared at district (or unitary authority) level.

Each LDF will consist of three key elements:

1. A core strategy, identifying policies for delivering the spatial strategy, and including a Statement of Community Involvement, which sets out benchmarks for community participation in the preparation of the LDF.
2. A proposals section, with site specific policies and proposals.
3. Area action plans, for key areas of change or conservation.

It is planned that these separate elements can be updated as necessary.

Planning officers are responsible for drawing up the development plans and recommending whether applications relating to the types and location of buildings and the use of land should be approved.

The *planning committee* grants approval for development, but is advised by its professional officers. A development scheme is likely to attract planning consent if it conforms to the development plans. This is intended to ensure that:

- The interests of other occupiers in the locality are protected. So, planning consent is needed for the construction of new buildings, most changes of the use of a building (e.g. from a residential use to an estate office), and for some extensions. Neighbours have the opportunity to object to any plans, before the council considers them.
- The visual appearance and environmental quality of an area is protected.

This may result in special conditions being attached to the consent, such as a requirement to use particular types of building materials, in keeping with other properties in the locality. Some sites may have specific planning requirements; for example, old trees may be protected by *tree preservation orders*, and the plans will have to include measures to protect these trees during construction work. Some buildings are *listed*, as being of special architectural interest. There are strict limitations on the extent to which such buildings can be altered by construction activity. In rural areas, where it may be difficult for local people to access housing, local authorities may require, as a condition of planning consent, that only those who live or work in the area may rent or buy. In England and Wales, these are called Section 106 agreements.

In addition to controlling the location and types of construction work, local authorities have a duty to oversee the standards of construction. These are governed by the *building regulations*.

Building inspectors are responsible for checking that standards of construction conform to the building regulations

---

Building regulations' approval must be obtained before any work can commence. In addition, a local authority building inspector (or other authorised person, such as a representative of the National House Builders Council) checks the progress of construction at various stages, to ensure compliance with the regulations before the next stage can commence.

In addition, a number of other public officers may need to be involved in some projects. For example, properties which are intended for multiple occupation, such as flats, need to be approved by the fire service. This is to ensure that there are adequate, safe exits in the event of fire, and that suitable measures are taken to deter the spread of fire, such as fire-resistant doors to hallways. The police may advise on security measures, such as door and window locks, alarms, and the use of video surveillance equipment, under the *Secured by Design* scheme.

3. The main stages in the traditional process

There are a number of different stages in the traditional process of developing a housing scheme. These can be classified in a variety of ways, but for housing managers, it is useful to conceive of three main, (largely) sequential phases. The boxes provide a brief summary of what takes place at each stage, and subsequent sections examine each stage in some detail.

Stage I: Initiating the development

The first stage includes all of the activities which need to be undertaken before there is a firm decision to go ahead with the project. This involves a consideration of the *need* for housing in the locality, whether the development is likely to be sustainable, and identifying exactly *what is required* of the development. Next, (for new build only), identifying and assessing potential sites and then establishing the feasibility (in cost terms) of schemes. The consulting architect (or building surveyor) always becomes involved during this phase, but, in addition, key housing managers, social services, the police, employment services, health authority etc., may provide advice in any sustainability assessment.

Stage II: Detailed design

This includes all of the activities which contribute to the final detailed plans for the project, generally produced by the consultant and guided by a briefing from the client. This stage will determine whether the organisation achieves the sort of new development or refurbishment that it requires, because the outcome is the final design, which will be constructed.

Stage III: Constructing the development

This final stage is concerned with getting the project built. The client must first appoint a contractor to undertake the work, and there are several possible approaches to this. The consultant oversees the process of constructing the properties, with close supervision provided by the clerk of works.

There are some approaches which provide 'short-cuts' through the traditional development process, by assigning some or all of the design stage to the contractor, and these are explored at the beginning of stage III. More recently, the government has also encouraged 'partnering' approaches, and these are examined at the end of the chapter. However, the key tasks in achieving a housing development remain basically the same, it is a question more of who is responsible for, and involved in undertaking, these tasks at each stage.

4. Stage I: Initiating the development

This is a critical stage because key decisions will be taken which could have important implications for the organisation. This stage will determine whether any development is undertaken at all, and if so, the type and location. Key questions are, therefore:

1. What type of development is needed?
2. For new schemes, how can we identify a suitable site?
3. Is the development likely to be sustainable?
4. Will planning consent be given for the development?
5. Is the development feasible?

And finally, if it is decided to go ahead,
    6. How do we acquire the site?

Subsequent sections address each of these key questions in turn.

Type of development needed

The social housing organisation should have clear ideas about the sorts of housing needs which it wants to develop housing for. These local needs are identified in the local authority's housing strategy – such as the Housing Investment Programme in England, or the Housing Plan in Scotland – which include data from housing associations in the area (examined in chapter three). It involves a systematic and comprehensive needs assessment, as well as an assessment of the local housing market, so that the organisation is confident, before continuing with any development plans, that a need – and hence likely demand – exists.

In the past, local authorities built predominantly for general (family) needs, so they produced largely two and three bed houses. Due mainly to land constraints, most urban authorities also built flats, and during the late fifties and sixties, many were encouraged to build high rise homes for families (with very mixed success). Since local authorities concentrated largely on housing families, a number of housing associations were started with the aim of meeting more specialised needs, such as homes for the elderly, or for young single people. This resulted in a much higher proportion of flats being constructed in the housing association sector. Nowadays, severe financial constraints mean that few local authorities are able to engage in new build, and housing associations have largely taken over the role of producing new homes for general needs, as well as continuing to provide homes for other needs groups. Meanwhile, substantial numbers of (largely) houses have been lost to the LA sector through Right to Buy. In addition, the *large scale voluntary transfer* (LSVT) of some local authority properties to housing associations is adding significant numbers of houses to housing association stock. The proportions of houses in the housing association sector have increased as a result, while the relative proportions of houses in the LA sector have been falling, so that, as Table 4.3 shows, the property profiles in both sectors are now quite similar.

Table 4.3: Property types in social tenures, Great Britain, 2001
(Percentages of households)

	Local authority	Housing association
Houses:		
Detached	1	2
Semi-detached	26	18
Terraced	29	32
All houses	56	52
Flats:		
Purpose built	42	41
Converted	2	6
All flats	44	48

Source: Wilcox, 2003

Properties which are to be refurbished will often have existing tenants, who will wish to return to their refurbished homes. If, however, the properties are empty, then a decision will have to be taken about the need which it is intended they will meet, because this will affect the design requirements.

Identifying a suitable site

For a new build scheme, having identified the type of development needed and where, the process then moves to identifying an appropriate site; clearly, for rehabilitation projects, the site already exists.

a. Finding a site

There are many different possible sources of information about sites. The main ones include:

- Individual landowners; these may be a particularly important source in rural areas, where the local authority may be prepared to grant *exceptional* planning permission for a social housing scheme.
- Estate agents, who sell development sites on behalf of owners in most areas
- Development or construction companies, who may have land which is surplus to their requirements. This is most common when the market for speculative, owner occupied dwellings is slow, so the contractors may be unwilling to risk building on their own account. In return for making the land available, however, they will often require that the contract to construct the properties is placed with them.
- Local authorities; they will have identified possible development sites in their area as part of their local development plan – which is examined in section 2. It is increasingly common for local authorities to make land available to housing associations at low (or zero) prices in return for *nomination rights* over a certain percentage of lettings, often 50 per cent to a 100 per cent. This is the right to nominate new tenants for the scheme

from their own waiting list. Some local authorities may have assembled information about development sites as a *land bank*.

- Other housing organisations (who may have been offered a site unsuited to their own requirements, but who think it may be suitable for other housing uses).
- Other public sector organisations, such as health trusts and education authorities, which may have unused sites where facilities have been closed down.

b. Initial site appraisal

Someone in the organisation, such as a development manager, needs to make an initial assessment of the physical suitability of each potential site. Key factors should be considered systematically, so that nothing of importance is overlooked. This approach also permits alternative sites to be compared more easily.

The initial assessment looks at the site from both the perspective of its potential to provide affordable development and the needs of the customers who will be housed. The ODPM's *Housing Quality Indicators* (2003) indicate key physical factors likely to affect housing quality as experienced by residents, and so these should form part of the assessment of a potential site. These may include:

i. Location

Consideration of the availability of support services (e.g. GP, public house, café, community facilities, etc.); retail provision; schools; play and leisure facilities; public transport; 'liabilities', meaning negative impacts such as derelict sites nearby or polluted water; and noise (e.g. near major road). The significance of each of these elements may, of course, vary, depending on the need to be met (e.g. elderly or families).

Figure 4.1: A good site for development with services already available

ii. Visual impact, layout and landscaping, open space

The overall likely impact of the development, in relationship to the character of the area; likely relationship of buildings to each other, such as aspects and views; landscaping of public areas, such as trees and other planting; private spaces.

iii. Routes and movement

This includes connections with other roads within the neighbourhood; pedestrian access; the need for traffic calming; lighting requirements, etc.

A detailed *site survey* may also be necessary if there is any possibility of underlying physical problems, such as landfill, contamination or mine-workings, which may involve bore-hole drillings (to check samples below the surface) and soil testing.

Practical issues need also to be considered, such as:

iv. Availability of services

These include electricity supplies, telephones, gas, water, and sewers. It can be expensive to provide new sources of supply, but services are more likely to be readily available in urban locations. This partly explains why development costs on rural sites tend to be higher.

v. Special conditions affecting the site

The landowners may wish to specify the type of development which can be constructed, or there may be existing controls affecting land use, such as *covenants*, which restrict rights.

vi. Value for money of the site

The issue here is whether the asking price is 'fair'. This will depend partly on current market conditions – are sites in high demand? – as well as the particular features, locality, etc. of the site. This is likely to present particular problems in some high demand areas (such as parts of the south east of England, or Edinburgh), where the organisation may be competing with many private developers.

vii. Affordability of the rents

Even if the site is available at a fair price, it is critical to estimate the rent levels which are likely to be necessary to cover anticipated costs. This a key issue for housing associations, since they do not, in general, have a large historic stock over which to share the costs of new development by rent pooling (see chapter five). Rent levels may be particularly problematic for some English providers due to the need to achieve formula rents in the current rent-restructuring policy (see chapter three), but all statutory funders will be concerned about the affordability of any schemes which they support with SHG/HAG.

Assessing the sustainability of the development

A sustainable development is one which meets all of the needs of its potential residents, whether physical, social or economic. Will households want to live here and will they continue over time to view it as a 'good' place to live? Many HAs and LAs are currently experiencing problems of low demand and anti-social behaviour, with socially and economically excluded tenants who exhibit high levels of benefit dependency. As a result, there are whole areas and estates which have become so stigmatised that no-one wants to live there. The housing organisation must ensure that it will not be wasting money either building a new scheme, or to refurbish an estate which will still remain unpopular; and, in this latter event, demolition or other options (such as selling to the private sector) may have to be considered.

In a wider sense, sustainability is also about, 'development which meets the needs of the present without compromising the ability of future generations to meet their own needs' (ODPM, 2001, p. 1). Hence, it is also about minimising energy use, using renewable resources, etc., which must be 'built into' the design stage.

There has been considerable research over recent years into indicators of sustainability and how housing providers can prevent or reduce social exclusion and safeguard future sustainability. Suggested indicators of sustainability (EIUA, 2002, p. 13) include:

a. Current demand – including indicators such as voids, waiting lists and sales in the locality.
b. Anticipated long-term demand – influenced by factors such as household formation trends and demographic change.
c. Crime and anti-social behaviour.
d. Reputation – including current residents' satisfaction surveys and rejections of offers.
e. Social exclusion indicators – including current rent arrears in the locality, unemployment, educational achievement, mortality and morbidity ratios, and benefit dependency.
f. Accessibility, to services, employment, transport.
g. Quality of the environment – including derelict land, boarded up properties, pollution.
h. Housing quality, including stock condition, repair costs, quality indicators.
i. Social cohesion, such as attendance at community meetings, 'community spirit', electoral turnout.
j. Community mix (demographic, social and ethnic).

Such an assessment inevitably will involve many more people than those in the development section, as only a few of these indicators involve purely physical (development) issues. Housing managers, therefore, are likely to be at the heart of assessing the likely sustainability of any proposed new development or refurbishment, based on their knowledge of this estate (for refurbishment) or other estates in the locality.

Planning consent

All new developments require planning consent and some refurbishment schemes may also require consent if there will be external, physical changes. However, some minor works may not require planning consent – see box.

The likelihood of obtaining consent must be checked with the planning officers of the local planning authority (see earlier section 2).

What requires planning consent?

The need to obtain the approval of the local planning authority applies to the following changes:

i. Building, extending or altering a property
Some types of development, defined by Development Orders issued by the Secretary of State, do not need specific consents. For example, the Town and Country Planning General Development Order, 1988, lists 28 categories of development which are exempt. In general, these are minor alterations, so are likely to apply only to refurbishment schemes, such as:

- extensions which add *no more* than 50 cubic metres or 10 per cent of the existing building size, whichever is the greater;
- small buildings, which are 'incidental to the enjoyment of the house' – such as a greenhouse or garden shed (but not a garage);
- a porch, with a floor area no larger than two square metres.

Most other changes require planning consent. *Listed buildings,* which have some special importance or architectural interest, may be removed from general permitted development. National Parks, Conservation areas and Areas of Outstanding Natural Beauty are also subject to specific restrictions.

ii. Changing the use of the property
In addition to the general exemptions provided by development orders, the planning acts define 'use classes' – such as class C3 dwelling houses, or class C2 residential institutions. A change of use will require planning consent in most cases. So, if, for example, a housing association wishes to convert a former warehouse into several flats, or the housing department wishes to convert an estate dwelling into a 'neighbourhood office', it will have to obtain consent.

Planning applications are usually granted, in two stages: outline and detailed. At this stage, the organisation need only be concerned that outline consent is (or will be) available – though, in practice, many housing associations will opt to obtain both stages at the start, which minimises delays.

Outline applications require:
   a.   a brief description of the proposed development, and
   b.   a site plan, to identify the land.

This permits the planning authority to check that the proposed development conforms to the development plans. Outline planning consents are generally granted, subject to further approval of specific items. These are called *reserved matters*.

Reserved matters may deal with:

- siting
- design
- external appearance
- means of access
- landscaping.

The local authority will generally have some standard requirements relating to, for example, car parking requirements and the provision of play areas. If the client wishes, information about these reserved matters *can* be included at the outline stage.

Full (detailed) planning permission requires:

- detailed information about the design, layout, etc of the development.

This will usually be obtained when the detailed design has been prepared.

Local authorities have to undertake slightly different procedures for planning permission. If the development will be undertaken by the authority itself, it must obtain 'deemed consent', which requires:

- a *first resolution* passed by the Housing Committee, and
- a *second resolution* passed by the Planning Committee.

The second resolution can be made only after publicity of the application, and notice being served on the owners of the land (if not the local authority). If the local authority owns the land but the development will be undertaken by someone else (such as a housing association), the second resolution may include conditions on the development, which are viewed as *reserved matters* and remain to be approved.

What if consent is denied?

If consent is refused, the applicant has the right to appeal to the Secretary of State. The appeal may be granted or refused. In recent years, the government has taken a more relaxed approach to planning issues, and appeals have had a greater chance of success.

If all elements in this initial site appraisal are acceptable, the next stage is to appoint a consultant to undertake a full *feasibility study*.

Feasibility study

a. Selecting and appointing a consultant

The consultant must be reliable and responsive to the client's needs. For this reason, the client organisation should undertake some checks on any new consultant, to determine whether:

- they have previous experience of similar types of project;
- past projects were completed on time, within cost budgets and to the client's satisfaction;
- their past designs are liked by the client.

Some clients will have in-house consultants (e.g. the architect's department of a local authority), but they should nevertheless meet the standards required of external consultants.

A formal *letter of appointment* – in effect, a binding contract – is not normally offered until the consultant has shown that the project is feasible and is worthwhile. At this stage, therefore, the consultant generally receives only a *letter of intent* (to appoint once feasibility is demonstrated) from the client organisation.

Once the organisation decides to proceed with the scheme, the consultant will receive a letter of appointment (agreed with the organisation's solicitor) which:

- defines the roles of client, consultant and any other relevant professionals;
- identifies the conditions of the appointment;
- specifies the fees and expenses payable;
- requires indemnity insurance, to cover the client in the event of any design failures.

This is an important document, because it effectively defines the service which the client expects of the consultant.

b. Undertaking the feasibility study

The consultant will begin by sketching out possible estate layouts for different property types, suitable for the desired type of scheme, and identify possible construction methods. From these initial ideas, they will generally select one for further consideration. This will be the scheme which appears to meet the client's requirements best, within the client's budget.

In addition to the importance of site features and location (discussed above), the ODPM's housing quality indicators suggest standards in relation to:

- unit size/facilities (e.g. number of WCs needed);
- unit layout (adequate circulation and activity space);
- noise control, light quality (e.g. windows with open views) and services (sockets, TV points, etc.);

- accessibility especially for the elderly and disabled;
- energy and sustainability (e.g. SAP ratings – of energy efficiency – low emissions, water metering).

On the basis of this initial draft design, the feasibility of the scheme will then be assessed. In general, a project is considered feasible if:

- **The estimated costs** suggest that it is likely that it can be constructed within budget constraints.

The consultant will draw up more detailed drawings from the initial sketch, to show broad design details. These enable the quantity surveyor to estimate:

- construction costs;
- the cost of site acquisition (for new build);
- fees for professionals, such as consultants and solicitors (to undertake the legal work), known as *on-costs*;
- fees for statutory requirements, such as building regulations' approval and planning consents;
- interest charges on any money which will have to be borrowed during the construction phase, in order to make regular *stage payments* to the contractor as work progresses.

The social housing organisation should also consider likely future maintenance costs, and may wish to build an allowance for these into the costings; for housing associations, this is particularly important, since rents will have to cover these future costs. In general, they will also need to ensure that total costs are within the cost limits imposed by their statutory funding body if they require grant-aid, such as *Housing Association Grant* (HAG) in Scotland, or *Social Housing Grant* (SHG) in England, Northern Ireland and Wales.

- **The rent levels** which are necessary to cover scheme costs are viewed as affordable and acceptable (e.g. in the light of rent restructuring in England – see chapter three) to the funding body or regulator.

These will be much more certain than the estimates produced at the initial feasibility stage, since the costs are known with much greater certainty. If housing associations expect to receive HAG/SHG for the scheme, they will have to provide a feasibility report for the funding body, which shows the rent levels which will be generated by the scheme costs. These levels must conform to current rent policies (such as rent restructuring requirements – see chapter three) and the organisation must also feel confident that the properties can be let successfully at these rent levels.

- **Assessed levels of risk** are acceptable.
  All projects contain risks that may affect cost, quality and/or time. Risk management is the identification and statistical analysis of these risks,

*followed by the formulation of an action plan to control them throughout
the life of a project* (Communities Scotland, 2002, p. 50).

Projects to rehabilitate existing buildings may be especially risky, because
structural problems may only become apparent when work begins. It is this
element of higher risk that has resulted in reduced rehabilitation by housing
associations, most of whom must bear all of the risk of cost increases (see chapter
three).

There is also the possibility that the properties cannot be let (or sold, for low cost
or shared ownership projects) once completed, so these risks must be taken into
account. The demand for homes to buy is affected greatly by general economic
conditions, such as interest rates and levels of unemployment, none of which are
under the control of social housing organisations. As housing association tenants
must cover the organisation's costs via rents, increased voids or unsold properties
mean higher rents for the other tenants.

Different organisations will be able to tolerate different levels of risk. Local
authorities and very large housing associations will generally have more scope to
absorb higher costs than small housing associations, for which the level of
reserves to deal with possible cost increases will be crucial. The number of
schemes in progress will also affect acceptable risk levels, because if the worst
happened and *all* went wrong, this could create real problems.

A number of **approaches to risk assessment** are possible; two of the more
common methods are:

- *Sensitivity analysis*
  This approach attempts to identify, and quantify, particularly high risk
  elements in the costs – such as the risk that interest rates will increase
  during the construction period, resulting in higher loan repayments. The
  financial calculations relating to the scheme are re-worked – usually using
  a computer programme – making different assumptions about these risky
  factors. So, for example, loan repayments may be calculated assuming
  interest rates of 4 per cent, 6 per cent and 8 per cent; voids may be
  assumed to be 3 per cent, 5 per cent or 10 per cent; or, completion time
  may be varied.
    It is then possible to see the extent to which the viability of the project
  is affected by these changes. If it became clear that, with very few changes
  to the assumptions, the project would cease to be feasible, then this would
  suggest that it was a very high risk undertaking.

- *Classifying risks*
  This is a simpler approach, which involves grading (from 1 to 5) the:
  a. likelihood of risk, and
  b. the impact of the risk.

Communities Scotland's (2002) suggested grading is shown in Table 4.3.

Risks to be graded may include:

- cost increases;
- problems with the contractor;
- late completion dates;
- letting difficulties.

Table 4.3: Classifying risks

	Likelihood of risk		Impact of risk
5	Highly probable	5	Catastrophic
4	Very likely	4	Critical
3	As likely as not	3	Serious
2	Could happen	2	Marginal
1	Improbable	1	Insignificant

Source: Communities Scotland, 2002, p. 52

The overall rating of the risks can be seen from the total score, as shown in Table 4.4. If the project goes ahead, the risks identified need to be actively managed and controlled, as far as possible.

Table 4.4: Quantifying risks

	Insignificant	Marginal	Serious	Critical	Catastrophic
Improbable	2	3	4	5	6
Could happen	3	4	5	6	7
As likely as not	4	5	6	7	8
Very likely	5	6	7	8	9
Highly probable	6	7	8	9	10

Source: Communities Scotland, 2002, p. 52

c. The feasibility report

All of this information is set out in a feasibility report, for the consideration of the development manager, management committee, or whoever is responsible for taking decisions about development. The assumptions made for the calculations –

such as interest rates, construction period, completion date, etc. – must be clearly identified. A decision is then made about whether to go ahead with the project.

Once the decision to proceed has been taken, the next step (for new build) is to acquire the site – though not before outline planning consent has been obtained, as examined in the last section. (In reality, unless this was thought likely to be granted, the scheme would not have progressed to feasibility study stage).

Site acquisition

This, of course, is required only when the housing organisation does not already own the site.

a. Agreeing the price

The cost of the site may be a substantial part of total costs, so it important to obtain value for money. Before the sale price is agreed with the vendor, social housing providers **must** obtain a valuation from an 'independent' valuer, such as (in the case of local authorities) the district valuer, a civil servant employed by the Inland Revenue Service. Housing associations are not generally permitted by the statutory funders to pay a price higher than the valuer's price. In any event, it is a sensible precaution against potential corruption.

It is usual to obtain an initial, informal valuation, to use as a guide for negotiation purposes. If the vendor's price remains above the valuation price, it may be possible to discuss this with the valuer, before the formal valuation is undertaken.

b. Purchasing the site

Before any money is paid, the client's solicitors must ensure that the vendor does actually own the land – in legal terms, has the *title* to the land. If the title is not registered (at a registry set up by the government), this will involve checking back through all previous purchases in the *title deeds* to ensure that the title (ownership) was properly transferred. In England and Wales, this is transferred by a *conveyance*, in Scotland by a *feu charter* or *disposition*.

If the title has been registered – at the *Land Registry* in England and Wales, or the *Register of Sasines* or *Land Register of Scotland*, then checking ownership is quite simple.

For housing associations purchasing leasehold sites in England and Wales, the statutory funders will generally require minimum lease expiry terms as a condition of receiving SHG funds. This is because the leaseholder regains ownership of the land once the lease expires. Minimum expiry times are generally shorter for rehabilitation schemes than for new build, reflecting the different life-expectancies of the two types of development.

The solicitors will then draw up a contract, and this is *completed* when payment is made and ownership is transferred in the *deeds*, which confer a *title* to the land. After this, the housing organisation is free to begin construction work on the site.

5. Stage II: Detailed design

The next step is to determine the detailed design requirements, so that the briefing (from which the consultants will design the detailed scheme) can be prepared. This will be influenced by current ideas about what constitutes good design.

What is 'good' design?

Design issues apply both to dwelling design and to external (or 'urban') design issues – the physical context of the dwellings. According to the ODPM (2001),

> *...urban design should be taken to mean the relationship between different buildings; the relationship between buildings and streets, squares, parks, waterways and other spaces which make up the public domain; the nature and quality of the public domain itself; the relationship of one part of a village, town or city with other parts; and the patterns of movement and activity which are thereby established: in short, the complex relationships between all elements of built and unbuilt space (p. 3).*

These issues will be considered particularly important by the planning officers, who will advise on planning consent.

Dwelling design is a somewhat controversial topic, because few designers can agree, objectively, about what makes a good design. However, it can be argued that if the design 'works' for its inhabitants, so that they feel that it gives them the main things that they want from a home, then it is, subjectively, a good design. Good dwelling designs seem to fulfil two key, human requirements:

1. *Functional*
   Homes need to provide adequate shelter, comfort and security for their inhabitants. Both dwelling and estate design can affect these functional matters.
2. *Symbolic and aesthetic*
   Homes are also seen as a physical expression of their inhabitants, so they can 'confer' social values such as status, a sense of worth and success, 'respectability'. Most people prefer to live in a 'nice' home, which is aesthetically pleasing to them, and gain a sense of well-being from this. It is not only house *types* and *styles* which are important, but *locality*.

Social housing providers in the past may sometimes have overlooked the symbolic requirements of dwellings, focusing exclusively on the functional aspects of the design; for example, the tower blocks built in the late 1950s and 1960s may have been functionally good (though many weren't, with problems of damp penetration and poor security, for example), but symbolically, they offered little to residents. The importance of the 'image' projected by the home is perhaps most clearly demonstrated by the actions of tenants freed from landlord constraints when they purchase under the Right to Buy policy; almost inevitably, the external, 'public' appearance of the property is changed, with a new front door, for example, or a porch.

Recent influences on ideas about design

It is worth examining, briefly, some research findings, which have been influential on ideas about the significance of design, because these ideas affect social housing design today. An influential work, which suggested that estate design influenced social groups and the sense of community, contrasted life in a traditional inner-city area with that in a new suburban estate, following slum-clearance was *Family and Kinship in East London* (Willmott and Young, 1957). This suggested that the new estates resulted in social isolation, in contrast to the supportive social networks which existed in the old areas. This study was influential in moving housing policy away from slum clearance to the rehabilitation of old housing areas. Where slum clearance could not be avoided, attempts were made to keep social groups of neighbours together on the new estates.

A study in the USA in 1959, by Festinger, Schachter and Back, found that the *layout* of homes affected the number of contacts made between residents, which in turn influenced social group formation. A later study in Essex by Peter Willmott (1963) also found that layout mattered, with short culs-de-sac best promoting community links. However, later work by Carey and Mapes (1972) in the north midlands suggested that social factors were most significant, such as class and family life-cycle stage. Where these were similar, then better social links would be formed. However, the physical environment does provide the framework within which these social links take place. Most estate designs today attempt to cluster dwellings together rather than stringing them out along a road, for example.

Another key influence has been the concept of 'defensible space', which originated from Oscar Newman's work in the USA in the 1960s, and which concentrated largely on functional aspects of design. He suggested that public spaces that were not under the control of any particular residents made these areas more vulnerable to crime. So, the design should ensure that these spaces are visible, so that someone can assume responsibility for them: they become 'defensible'.

Newman's work was partially reinforced by a study by Alice Coleman in the UK (*Utopia on Trial,* 1987; revised in 1990), which identified problems of the surveillance of some public spaces. This resulted in greater anonymity and provided easy escape routes for criminals. However, Coleman went further, suggesting that large scale, high-density flats *created* conditions which resulted in criminal behaviour and low levels of respect for others.

These ideas have been highly influential on recent social housing design; few organisations would now build high-rise flats for families, and new build design as well as refurbishment generally attempts to maximise *defensible space*, with more private gardens, for example, and the eradication of interconnecting walkways, shared stairwells, etc. from blocks of flats, where possible.

Figure 4.2: Recent designs seek to cluster homes together, with good visibility over any public spaces

Figure 4.3: Indefensible space creates problems – in this case litter

Ensuring sustainability through partnerships

Whilst the ideas mentioned above have been influential, few believe nowadays that design changes are sufficient to resolve or prevent problems. Recent approaches emphasise the need for attention to management issues (e.g. lettings policies), economic development issues and community involvement and development, as well as design initiatives, for unpopular estates. The work of the *Priority Estates Project*, emphasising decentralised management and tenant involvement, was very influential, and more recent policy initiatives have emphasised the necessity for an approach which goes well beyond simple physical (design) changes for unpopular, run-down estates. Physical rehabilitation, whilst important, is unlikely to be enough. Research by Power and Tunstall (1995) confirmed that local management initiatives and tenant involvement were crucial to improving unpopular estates. As examined in section 4, there is an emphasis on ensuring the *sustainability* of all new or refurbished schemes, which includes attention to social and economic elements as well as purely physical and environmental issues. The Mayor's draft London Plan and the development of the Thames Gateway area as part of the Communities Plan both exemplify the need for sustainable planning to look at issues such as re-use of old buildings alongside the development of mixed tenure housing and an adequate transport system.

Ensuring sustainability requires *partnership* approaches to development, which means involving a wide range of organisations and agencies at the outset. According to the ODPM's (2002a) Summary of Good Practice (for 'Regeneration that lasts'), factors likely to encourage effective partnership working include:

- recognition of the need for an integrated, comprehensive approach;
- commonality of purpose between the partners;
- clear leadership;
- treating all partners (including residents) equally;
- continuity of policies and, (as far as possible), personnel.

To involve a range of income groups, many schemes will provide mixed development, meaning that there is a mix of tenures – often, some social housing to rent, low cost or shared ownership, and possibly some full cost housing for sale. Such developments will usually involve partnerships with private developers. Research for the JRF (Carley *et al.*, 2000) suggests a need also in regeneration to actively involve Health Trusts, the Employment Service, the Benefits Agency and the Police, and to build in a budget for community capacity building at the start. Hence, it is critical that, by this stage of the project, all key partners are involved in the plans.

Preparing the briefing

The briefing is the document which specifies exactly what the client wants, so the more detailed the briefing, the better. Only if the designers are very clear about the client's requirements will they be able to produce a design, which fully meets them.

The briefing will be developed by the person(s) in the organisation responsible for the development. In a social housing organisation, ideally those who will have future responsibility for the development should also be consulted; managers know which design features cause management problems, and maintenance staff can advise about aspects with high maintenance costs. Indeed, some organisations attempt to adopt a *lifetime* approach to scheme costs, so that repair implications are automatically incorporated into the scheme appraisal.

Tenants' views are also invaluable. For rehabilitation work, the people who will actually occupy the scheme can often be consulted; for new build, potential tenants may be identified for consultation, or the views of tenants on other new developments should be routinely surveyed (after a period of occupation), so that they can comment on good and bad design aspects and influence future developments.

In practice, the first version of the brief will usually develop over a short period of time, as new information comes to light. This will be added to the initial brief, until, eventually, the *full brief* emerges. By the time the design is complete, the *final brief* should have been amended to include all of the information given to the consultants. This is necessary so that, when the scheme is completed, the organisation can evaluate the consultants by checking whether the requirements of the final brief have been met. If they have, but the scheme is still felt to be unsatisfactory, then the fault lies with the client. The brief was not adequate. In this event, future briefs should be modified, to take account of the weaknesses identified in this brief.

Contents of the briefing

There are usually two key aspects:

1. The **general** requirements of the organisation, applicable to all schemes, and developed over time.
    The briefing must cover *all* aspects of design about which the organisation has clear requirements and preferences. Some organisations design to *Lifetime Homes* standards (Trotter, 1997) – also called 'barrier-free' homes in Scotland – which ensure that properties are readily adaptable to residents' changing needs; for example, will easily accommodate a wheelchair or stairlift. There will also be the requirements of the statutory funding bodies (such as the Housing Corporation's Scheme Development Standards) to incorporate. Over time, additional knowledge derived from experience will also be incorporated into the general requirements. If the consultants have designed many schemes for the organisation, they may be familiar with their *general* requirements, but will still need detailed briefing about the specific requirements of another particular scheme. This fact is often overlooked when *in-house* architects are employed to design a range of schemes.

2. The **specific** requirements of the particular site or property, to meet identified needs.
    There are a number of possible approaches to developing specific design briefs, and they may be set out in slightly different ways. In general, they will need to cover:

i. Details about the site
These include:

*   physical aspects (location, boundaries, size, slope, aspect, soil characteristics, existing vegetation, existing buildings and whether these are to be retained, existing services and positions, etc.;
*   environmental aspects such as adjacent buildings and uses, local amenities such as shops, parks, bus routes, etc.;
*   legal aspects such as public *rights of way* over the land and ownership of boundaries such as fences.

Rehabilitation schemes will, obviously, impose many more constraints on the possible design, so the brief should identify these constraints fully, as well as indicating the changes desired.

ii. Cost limits for the development
Most social housing organisations face severe cost constraints, including the statutory funders' cost indicators, which have helped them to become more conscious of *value for money* and less likely to engage in unnecessary expenditure. However, there are growing concerns about declining quality as a result, and organisations must try to ensure that the brief does not permit cost-limits to reduce design standards.

iii. Procedural aspects
This includes statutory bodies which need to be consulted, the consents required, procedures for approval by the client, etc. In general, this will include information about the planning authority, the highway authority and public utilities (which include gas, electricity and water). If outline planning consent has been obtained, any reserved matters affecting requirements should be identified.

iv. Time limits
The *programme* sets out *target dates* for achieving each stage in the construction process, though the consultant may negotiate about these.

v. Requirements of the accommodation design
This is likely to form the bulk of the briefing and is highly detailed. It must cover both the general requirements of the organisation – accommodation features which are always wanted – and the specific, dwelling design requirements of this development. A list of common contents for this aspect of the briefing is shown in the next box.

In addition, dwellings must be designed to permit normal activities to be undertaken in the home, so designs should be checked to ensure sufficient space is allowed for circulation of people, furniture removal, eating around a table, etc.

Social housing providers, as discussed above, are increasingly aware of the symbolic importance of design, so dwelling designs should also be attractive to an average person.

Sample contents of a briefing for accommodation design

a. General requirements
Mainly for new build:
- type of buildings (detached, terraced, flats etc.);
- dwelling numbers, mix and sizes – this will reflect the need(s) to be met as well as desired densities (number of units per hectare);
- maximum number of storeys; higher densities may be required when land costs are very high – such as some inner city areas – and generally require more storeys.

For all schemes:
- car parking, including whether garaging is required and how many, the numbers of car parking spaces, etc.;
- other facilities, such as play areas (for general needs housing), meeting rooms (for supported housing), laundry rooms (for hostels), etc.;
- land use distribution, indicating the proportionate share for dwellings, car parking, roads and other facilities.

b. Dwelling design requirements
For new build, the organisation may prefer to use a previous *standard* design for each type of dwelling, because this will reduce design costs. However, whether the designs are to be *standard* or one-off, the same details need to be reproduced in the brief. These include:

- general design requirements, such as minimum space requirements for net floor area (which excludes garages), storage areas, plot sizes, etc.;
- room relationships, such as access to rooms from hallways, from room to room (e.g. kitchen may not open off living room), and external access requirements (to external doors, road, etc);
- requirements for living areas, such as the type and siting of heaters and fires, radiators, TV sockets, thermostats, etc.;
- kitchen requirements, such as minimum provision and height of units, unit types, power sockets, sink position (e.g. in natural light), ventilation requirements, space for eating, laundry needs, work surfaces, etc.;
- bedrooms, such as fitted wardrobes, the position of radiators and windows, ventilation, and lighting;
- bathroom and WC, such as requirements for ventilation (e.g. extractor fan), sound insulation, a second, ground floor WC;
- storage areas, for the storage of refuse, fuel, meters, linen, prams, bicycles, garden equipment, etc.;
- doors and windows, such as UPVC windows to reduce maintenance; windows with external panes which can be cleaned from inside; security fittings, etc.;
- provision of services, including the type of heating system, requirements for water supply, electricity and gas connections (e.g. in kitchen), etc.;
- energy efficiency requirements, indicated by SAP ratings, including roof and wall insulation, double glazing, etc.

---

vi. Environmental design requirements

This concerns site layout, and how the dwellings will 'fit into' their surroundings. For a rehabilitation scheme, there may be little scope for altering environmental aspects such as:

- the distribution of dwellings (such as how they are to be grouped);
- vehicle and pedestrian circulation, such as footpaths, specific vehicle access needs, and adequate access for emergency vehicles (such as fire engines);
- aesthetic and social criteria, such as dwelling orientation (what they face) and any requirements for privacy and safety;
- landscape features, like existing trees, hedges, and any *preservation orders* which prevent the felling of trees.

Figure 4.4: Speed reduction measures are becoming much more common to reduce traffic speed

Figure 4.5: A sheltered scheme for the elderly, which makes creative use of a very large, old (protected) tree in a circular driveway

vii. Construction standards

This section details any special requirements for the construction *methods and materials* to be used, which requires expertise in construction technology and is beyond the scope of this text. As identified at Stage I, construction standards are controlled by the Building Regulations, which ensure that only safe methods and materials are used, and approval must be obtained from the local authority. However, knowledge acquired by the organisation from previous schemes should also be incorporated, so that methods or materials that have caused problems are avoided. Additionally, there may be a desire to standardise some elements (such as door and window types, or heating systems), which will permit the holding of spare parts to be minimised, and may allow for reduced maintenance contracts to be negotiated. Since the publication of the Egan Report (1998), the government has encouraged increased use of factory produced components (such as wood or steel frames) in social housing construction, which would need to be specified here.

The design drawings

Once the consultants have the briefing, they can proceed to producing some drawings to show their ideas for interpreting the brief. Drawings are a physical representation of the scheme, which enable the client to see what is proposed, as well as, ultimately, enabling the contractor to build according to the design. These are produced in two stages:

a. Outline drawings

The consultant must design in line with the brief, but is free to interpret these requirements as they choose. This means that, for any given briefing, a large number of possible approaches are possible. The consultant will have already produced some outline plans for the feasibility study, but ideas now need to be 'firmed-up'.

Outline plans will be sketched out, and these need to be considered by the client, to ensure that they conform to the brief. If any aspect is unsatisfactory, the consultant will need to revise as appropriate.

b. Detailed drawings

Once the client is happy with the outline scheme, the consultant proceeds to draw up detailed drawings. These are more numerous and detailed than the outline plans, and will have to be drawn carefully *to scale*. This means that a specified distance on the plan corresponds to a larger area on the ground. For example, a scale of 1:1000 means that 1 mm on the plan represents 1 metre on the site. The smaller the scale, the more closely the two distances match. All drawings will clearly indicate the scale.

A number of different drawings have to be made, in order to give a full picture of the scheme. These drawings are submitted for detailed planning consent, and are needed by the contractor so that it is clear what is to be constructed.

The main ones are:

Location plan

This places the site within its locality, showing adjoining roads, buildings, etc. It indicates the position of north with an arrow, and is usually drawn to a scale of 1:2500 or 1:1250.

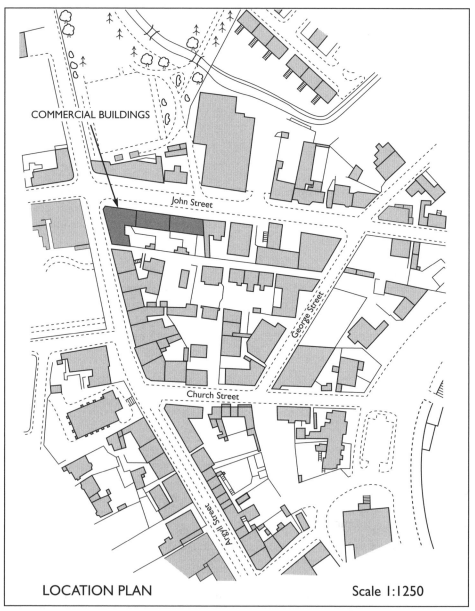

Figure 4.6: Location plan for Commercial Buildings; a rehabilitation project of tenement flats (Scale 1:1250)

Site layout plan

This shows the position of the dwellings in the site, with roads, trees, etc. indicated. The scale is usually 1:500, or 1:200.

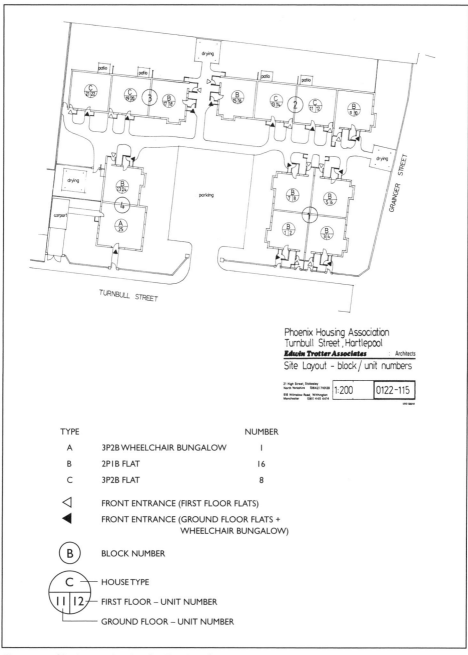

Figure 4.7: Site layout drawing for Turnbull Street, Hartlepool; a new build project of flats and bungalows (Scale 1: 200)

Floor plans

These are produced for *each* floor of each dwelling type, at a scale of 1:100 or 1:50. Possible furniture layouts should be included, so that it can be seen whether the layouts are feasible.

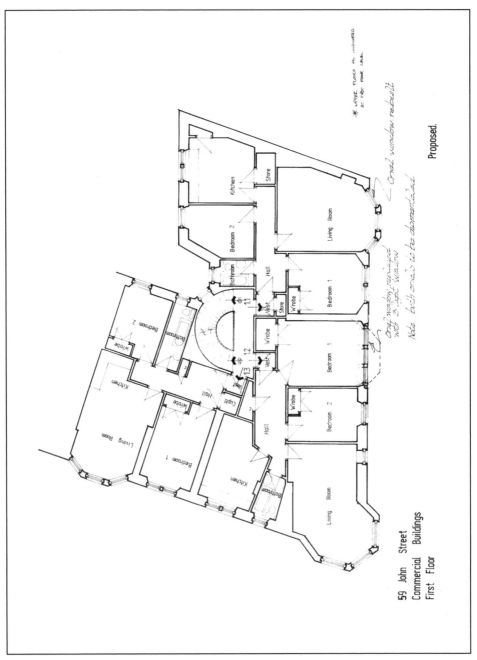

Figure 4.8: Commercial Buildings; first floor plan (scale 1:100)

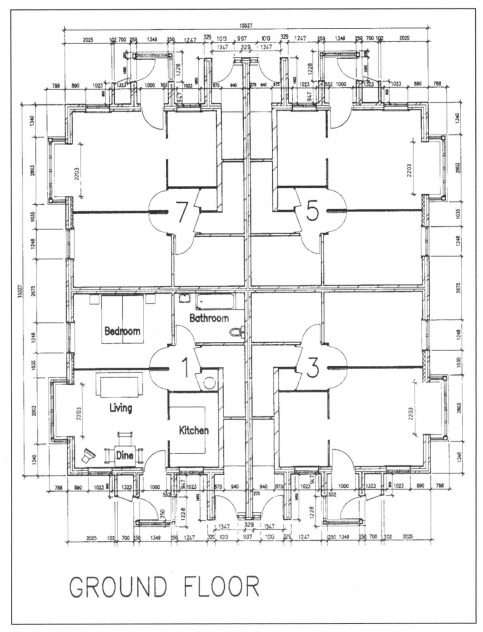

GROUND FLOOR

Figure 4.9: Turnbull Street; ground floor plan (scale 1:50)

Elevations

These view the properties from various positions, such as the front, side and rear. They give an impression of what the dwellings will look like from the outside, and will generally indicate wall and roof colours. See Figures 4.10, 4.11 and 4.12

Figure 4.10: Turnbull Street elevation; North and South

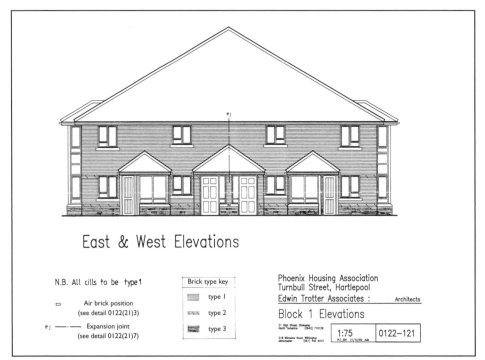

Figure 4.11: Turnbull Street elevation; East and West

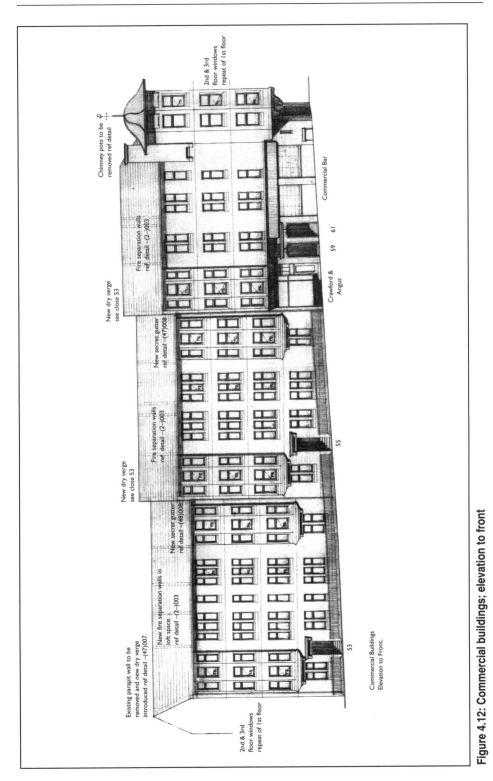

Figure 4.12: Commercial buildings; elevation to front

c. Construction drawings

These are much more detailed drawings, which show information about methods of construction for different parts of the dwellings and the provision of services. They have to be submitted for approval under the Building Regulations, and form part of the instructions to the contractor about how the scheme is to be built.

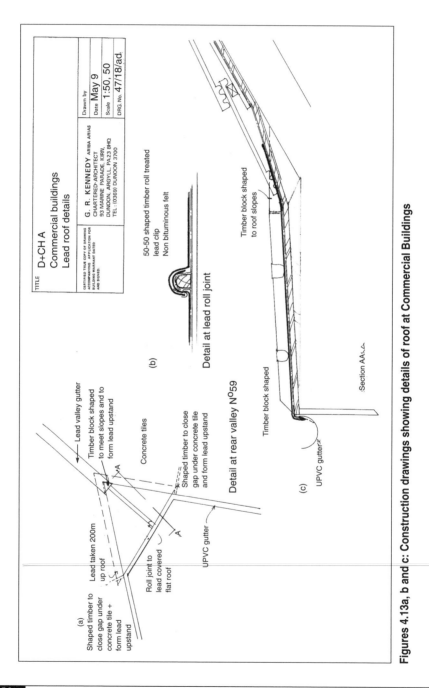

Figures 4.13a, b and c: Construction drawings showing details of roof at Commercial Buildings

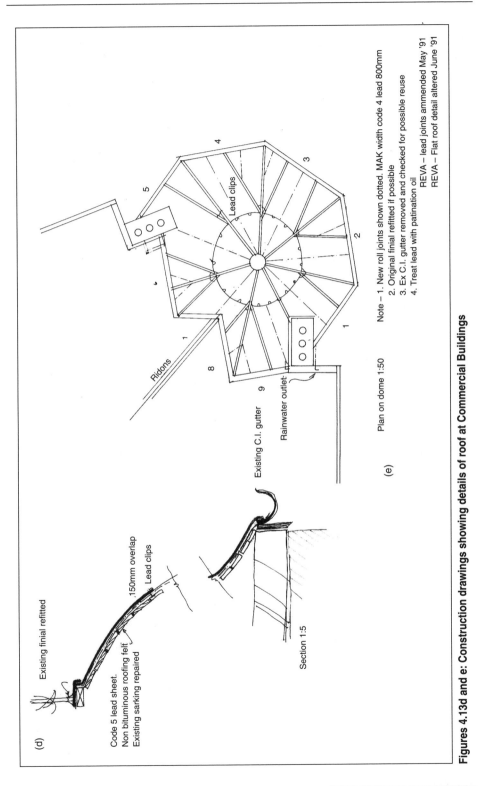

Note – 1. New roll joints shown dotted. MAK width code 4 lead 800mm
2. Original finial refitted if possible
3. Ex C.I. gutter removed and checked for possible reuse
4. Treat lead with patination oil
REVA – lead joints ammended May '91
REVA – Flat roof detail altered June '91

Plan on dome 1:50

Lead clips

Ridons

Existing C.I. gutter

Rainwater outlet

(e)

(d)

Existing finial refitted

Code 5 lead sheet.
Non bituminous roofing felt
Existing sarking repaired

150mm overlap
Lead clips

Section 1:5

Figures 4.13d and e: Construction drawings showing details of roof at Commercial Buildings

The construction specifications

The specifications identify, in detail, the construction methods and the quality of materials to be used. These are, necessarily, highly detailed and technical. They are produced so that the contractor knows exactly what standards are expected for all work. Generally, they will incorporate all relevant national and European standards of performance, as determined by bodies such as the *British Standards Institute*. This awards products which comply with relevant performance standards – such as electrical fittings – a BS number, which refers to their standard for the product.

6. Stage III: Constructing the development

Selecting the contractor

a. Traditional approaches
There are two main traditional approaches to selecting a contractor (Communities Scotland, 2002):

i. Single stage competitive tendering
This involves requesting quotations from a number of firms. However, in order to reduce the possible number of tenders (or *bids*) to manageable proportions, the consultant will generally advise on drawing up a *select list* of contractors. However, it is important that there is sufficient competition to encourage keen pricing by contractors, so generally, the list will consist of about six firms. Local authorities must advertise (in the European Union as well as the UK) for firms to apply for inclusion on their select list of tenderers, whereas housing associations will generally draw up a specific list for each project. However, both must undertake a series of checks, to ensure that potential tenderers are capable of undertaking the work.

Checking potential contractors
Many organisations will ask potential contractors to complete a standard 'Organisation and Capacity' questionnaire, which covers key aspects such as:

- financial records, with information about turnover (the value of work undertaken in a year) and financial stability (assets and debts); a banker's reference is also usually required;
- details of past experience of constructing similar projects;
- references from past clients, commenting on things such as the quality of their work, their ability to complete on time, and their willingness to co-operate.

The client's quantity surveyor (QS) will usually also check whether the contractor's previous tender prices have been competitive.

Inviting tenders
When the selected firms are invited to tender, they are sent the *tender documents*, which are generally prepared by the QS. They usually comprise:

- information about the site (location, characteristics);
- the detailed design drawings;
- detailed specifications;
- information about the sort of contract which the firm will have to enter into;
- a form on which the tender price is entered;
- a *bill of quantities*, which itemises all construction activities (the *quantities*), for individual pricing by the tenderer.

Having received the tender documents, the contractor will be in a position to calculate the likely costs of the work, and can decide whether to put in a tender. The *closing date* and *time* for receipt of tenders must be clearly specified, and the tender must be supplied in an unmarked envelope, so that the tendering firm cannot be identified until the tenders are opened.

Selecting a tender
The sealed envelopes are opened, at the appointed time, by the consultant, client, QS and other relevant parties such as committee members. This ensures 'fair play'. The client's QS will then check the accuracy of the prices, and having assessed whether the bids are reasonable, will make a formal recommendation about which (if any) tender to accept. This need not be the lowest price, if there are suspicions that the contractor might be unable to complete the project for unrealistically low sums. If all bids are too high, the QS will need to consider how lower bids might be obtained – for example, by making alterations to the design.

Once a tender has been accepted, but before the legal contract is signed, the consultants will undertake pre-contract planning with the contracting firm (see below).

ii. Two stage selective competitive tender
When it is desirable to involve the contractor at an earlier (design) stage, the contractor is appointed on the basis of a tender that is based only on preliminary design information. Similar checking procedures to those described above will, of course, have had to be undertaken. Cost certainty will not be achieved until the second stage tender, when a firm design is available. This may be particularly appropriate when a *partnering* approach is adopted (see section 8).

b. Non-traditional approaches
During the 1990s, out of a desire to achieve greater cost-certainty, it became more common for housing associations to take 'short-cuts' through the development process, with contracts that give the contractor a greater role in relation to design. Some of these alternative approaches are:

i. Package deals

These offer the quickest way to achieve a development, because a complete scheme is purchased 'off-the-shelf' from a building company, usually to the builder's own design. It is paid for in one lump sum, on completion. This largely eliminates the role of the consultant, and can offer good value for money.

ii. Design and build

Under this approach, the contractor provides the design as well as the construction work, so this also reduces the traditional consultant's role. The client can have an input into the design, by setting out precise details of the organisation's design requirements in a briefing called the *employer's requirements*. In this case, the client is represented on site by an *employer's agent* – usually a quantity surveyor – to oversee standards of work, rather than the consultant. Again, the price is usually fixed in advance.

iii. Develop and construct (or detail and build)

This approach is closer to the traditional approach. The consultant will produce *outline* designs, which will define very clearly what the client requires. The contractor then takes over and is responsible for turning these outline designs into *detailed* designs, which are then built. Again, an employer's agent represents the client, because the design cannot change once work commences. There is usually a fixed-price contract.

What are the advantages of these approaches?
They reduce:

- the length of the development process, which means that the client obtains a completed scheme much more quickly, and so begins to earn income sooner;
- costs; or as a minimum, offer more certainty about costs;
- the risk that the organisation will have to find additional resources to fund extra costs; this has become particularly important with mixed funding, under which the Social Housing Grant and Housing Association Grant (SHG in England/HAG in Scotland) is set very early in the process, so additional costs must be met by the organisation.

What are the disadvantages?
They offer:

- less client control over the design (to varying degrees), which may in turn:
  - reduce the possibility of standardising designs, fixtures and fittings, which can increase future maintenance costs;
  - result in a scheme which is less suitable for particular needs than developments which are specially designed;
  - eliminate the possibility of changing the design as work progresses;
- reduced possibilities to monitor and control standards of construction; this can be particularly important in rehabilitation work, where problems can easily be hidden.

Partnering approaches are now advocated to overcome some of these disadvantages, which are examined in section 8.

Pre-contract planning

Pre-contract planning ensures that no time is wasted; if various details are sorted out in advance, the contractor can get on with the actual construction work as soon as the contract is drawn up and signed. Pre-contract planning meetings will be arranged to sort out matters such as:

- The contract commencement date.
  This may depend on the completion of site acquisition, or arrangements to decant existing tenants.

- The contract completion date.
  Usually, the organisation will want the work to be completed as soon as possible, since faster completion means quicker letting and more rent income. If it involves the rehabilitation of existing tenanted stock, then the decanted tenants will be able to return more quickly.

- The programme of work.
  The programme of work enables the consultant to monitor progress, and initiate appropriate steps if work falls behind.

- The role of the planning supervisor.
  The location of this function must be clearly agreed, so that the requirements of the CDM regulations can be fulfilled.

- Arrangements for informing other parties.
  The building inspector must be informed about start dates, so that they can make regular inspections as work progresses. In the case of existing premises, the council tax authority should be informed, as no tax will be payable. Electricity and gas boards should also be contacted to take meter readings. This will ensure that the client is not liable for unauthorised use during construction work.
  Anyone likely to be affected by the construction work must be advised about works that directly affect them. This is important not simply because it is good *public relations*; the works could interfere with a neighbour's business, with perhaps serious legal implications as a result.

- Site security.
  Building sites are regularly subject to vandalism and theft. Responsibility for secure storage for materials must be agreed, particularly in high risk areas. Both the client and the contractor should have adequate insurance.

Agreeing the contract

A **written contract** ensures that all parties are clear as to what has been agreed. It reduces the possibilities of misunderstandings, and, importantly, offers the possibility of *legal action* if either party to the contract fails to deliver as agreed.

The contract is drawn up by the QS, and will generally be a standard contract type, approved by the construction industry. This was, until recently, normally the JCT (Joint Contracts Tribunal) contract, but, in the context of partnering (see section 4) this is now considered to be confrontational, and others, such as NEC Option C, are considered more amenable to team working (Communities Scotland, 2002). The PPC2000 contract has been developed by the Association of Consultant Architects for use in a partnering agreement, and is currently being tested in the context of Communities Scotland's 'Building a Better Deal' action plan (2002).

The contract sets out what has been agreed, and will cover:

- the **basis for payment** – the value of the contract, which will generally be for a *fixed price*;
- the **contract period** – how long the work will take;
- the **construction design details** – what, exactly, is to be built, and where.

The form of the contract may vary slightly, depending on whether it is for new build or rehabilitation, and whether there are to be *nominated sub contractors*. These are specialist firms, which the client may want for some specialised activities (e.g. for wood treatment in rehabilitation work). In addition, the organisation itself, or its funders, may have particular requirements for adjustments to the standard forms.

Once the contract is signed, the contractor can commence work on site.

The progress of construction

a. Traditional construction techniques

There are many possible approaches to constructing dwellings, which are beyond the scope of this text. However, many new, low-rise dwellings built today use traditional methods, with cavity-walls (a double wall of brick, with a space or *cavity* between to improve insulation and deter damp penetration) and tiles fixed to sloping roofs.

These schemes might be expected to progress roughly as indicated in the box. It is, of course, the duty of the consultant to oversee the quality and progress of this work, with day to day monitoring by the clerk of works.

Progress of work for traditional approaches to new build house construction

- Clear the site (of existing buildings, unwanted vegetation, and top-soil).
- Dig and lay the foundations (on which the walls are constructed).
- Build the walls.
- Construct the roof.
- Fix the external joinery (such as windows and doors).

This provides a relatively secure shell for the next stages.

- Fix some internal joinery such as floors and stairs, and internal wall-partitions.
- Fix internal utilities, such as electricity cables, gas pipes, water and heating supplies.
- Complete internal finishes – plastering walls, skirtings and door casings.
- Install fixtures, such as fitted kitchen units.
- Paint internal walls and complete final finishes.

The stages in a rehabilitation project are much more variable, since the exact nature of the refurbishment will vary greatly from one scheme to another.

---

b. Non-traditional approaches to construction

The main, current non-traditional approach involves the use of timber-framed construction. A factory-produced, timber-frame provides the main structure of the dwelling, and the walls (usually of brickwork) are constructed around the frame. Initially, this proved more popular with private (speculative) builders, because it permits faster completion; but, more recently, many more HAs have taken it up. For larger buildings, steel frames may be used. The Egan Report (*Rethinking Construction*, 1998) advocated much greater use of factory-built components – called off-site manufacturing (OSM) techniques – arguing that this provided not only faster construction but also at lower cost and to higher quality standards. This led the Housing Corporation to offer 'kick start' funds to RSLs partnering with selected, off-site manufacturers from 2001/2. This is discussed further in section 8.

Variations to the contract: architect's instructions

Unless the development is being constructed under some sort of 'package' arrangement, the consultant may make changes to the design details as work progresses. The commonest causes of changes by the consultant are last minute economies due to unforeseen financial constraints, or changes to design details, perhaps caused by supply problems.

Additionally, external factors may force changes. The likelihood of unforeseen problems arising on site is reduced, but not eliminated by, a site survey. However, such problems are more likely in rehabilitation schemes, when many problems may become apparent only after demolition work.

All variations to the contract details must be specified in *architect's instructions,* also known as *variation orders*. These are instructions issued by the consultant, which specify the alteration required (or agreed to), and, most importantly, identify the *cost* of the change. If the instruction is simply intended to clarify something, there may be no financial implication. But, where there is an added cost, the client should insist on strict limits to the amounts that can be agreed by the consultant, without *prior* approval. This is an important method by which the client can exercise tight control over costs.

Extending the contract period

If the effect of an instruction is to extend the construction period, then an *extension of time certificate* will need to be issued. The cost implications of this depend on the cause of the delay:

- Extensions due to consultant's changes or errors will have to be paid for by the client. Clearly, if the contractor has to spend longer on site, it will increase the firm's costs – for labour, plant hire, insurance, etc.
- Extensions may be allowed for factors outside the contractor's control, for which no extra payment is made. These include bad weather, delays caused by the contractor's own sub contractors, or strikes.
- Extensions that are the fault of the contractor result in the client being eligible for some payment in compensation. These are called *liquidated and ascertained damages*, and are deducted from any payments due to the contractor.

Monitoring information available to the client

The client will wish to monitor the progress of development, to ensure that it is satisfactory and that excessive numbers of expensive or delaying variation orders are not being issued. The main sources of information about progress include:

Site meetings

These provide a regular forum for the consultant, QS and contractor to discuss progress. The client may attend, but should certainly receive copies of the *minutes* of site meetings, which record what was discussed and agreed – including any need for architect's instructions and extensions of time.

Progress reports

The consultants will make their own regular reports to the client, identifying progress to date and any problems. They should cover the two key elements for control: costs and time – which will be the subject of architect's instructions and extensions of time certificates. These should be identified and explained. Quality issues should be resolved as the dwellings are being built.

Site inspections

The consultant will, of course, make regular site inspections, as part of the supervisory role, and normally, a clerk of works will report to the client.

Issued by:	Edwin Trotter Associates	
address:	21 High Street, Stokesley	

Architect's Instruction

Employer:		
address:	Phoenix Housing Associations Ltd	
	27 Yarm Road, Stockton on Tees	
Contractor:	Ideal Homes (Northern) Ltd	
address:	Ideal house, Allensway	Job reference: 0122-L
	Thornaby on Tees	Instruction no: 2
Works:		Issue date: 8th July 1993
situated at:	25 New Dwellings	Sheet: 1 of 2
	Turnbull street, Hartlepool	
Contract dated:	3rd June 1993	

– 9 JUL 1993

MANAGER   GO
ACTION
FILE

Under the terms of the above-mentioned Contract, I/we issue the following instructions:

	Office use: Approx costs	
	£ omit	£add
1. Arrange for the provisions of the Clause 21.2.1 insurance cover all as you letter and enclosure dated 22nd June 1993.		800
Omit the provisional sum of £800.00 in the Bill of Quantities (item C page 7/3) for insurance cover.	800	
2. Place an order and pay all all costs incurred with Northern Electric for the provision of the electricity supplies to the above dwellings (including landlord's supply) all as their letters and enclosures dated 3rd February 1993 and 4th February 1993. Please liaise with Northern Electric at all times and use the application forms enclosed as requested by them.		
Omit the provisional sum of £7,900.00 in the Bill of Quantities (item B page 7/1) for service connection charges.	7900	

To be signed by or for the issuer named above Signed *J Spencer*	8700	7300

Amount of Contract Sum	£	764925
± Approximate value of previous Instructions	£	+ 150
	£	765075
±Approximate value of the Instruction		−1400
Approximate adjusted total	£	763675

Distribution

☐ Original to: ☐ Copies to:

☐ Contractor   ☐ Employer   ☑ Quantity Surveyor   ☐ Clerk of works

☐ Nominated Sub-Contractors   ☐ Consultants   ☐ File

Figure 4.14: Architect's instruction at Turnbull Street

However, it is also useful for the client to make occasional inspections; *not* to give instructions, which might over-rule the architect, but to check generally on quality and progress. Any problems that are noted on inspection should be taken up with the consultant.

Paying the contractor during construction

It is usual to make payments to the contractor in *stages* as work progresses, because the firm has to pay for all materials and labour as they are used. Workers will not wait until the end of the contract to be paid! If the contractor should cease work, the client will be left with the portion of the scheme which has already been completed – it can not be taken away – so there is little risk in making *interim payments*.

Interim payment procedures

a. Interim certificates

The procedure for making interim payments to contractors involves the issue of *certificates* by the consultant. The quantity surveyor undertakes a valuation of the work completed, which is *certified* by the consultant. Valuations are usually undertaken at specific stages in the progress of construction; for example, when foundations are completed, when the building has reached first floor level, etc. Since the valuation relates to all of the work completed, the value of *previous payments* is then deducted, to calculate the payment due.

b. Retention monies

Some percentage will normally be retained, so that the contractor is never paid *fully* for the work completed. This is intended to provide an incentive to complete the work; if **full** payments were always made, the contractor could leave the site without losing anything.

The contractor will be keen to receive as high a payment as possible, so may contest the QS's valuation of the work. The consultant must then take the final decision about the valuation, and, in effect, arbitrate between the QS and the contractor.

If valuations include payments to *nominated sub contractors*, the contractor will normally have to pass this payment on to the sub contractor. For the contractor's own sub contractors, it is the contractor's responsibility to agree their share of any payments.

c. Receipt of HAG/SHG

Housing associations receive their public funding (if applicable) in pre-determined percentages (called *tranches*), at three *key* stages in the construction process. The tranche percentages depend on the type of scheme – new build or rehabilitation, and the key stages are:

    i.   Site acquisition.

   ii.   Start on site of main works.

  iii.   Practical completion – when the work is largely finished.

Since these stages do not correspond with normal stage payments to the contractor, which are made during the progress of construction, the client organisation must ensure that there are sufficient reserves, or access to borrowed funds (such as a bank overdraft), to make payments to the contractor prior to completion.

Ending the contract

This will occur only in extreme circumstances, when, for example, the contractor is declared bankrupt, or consistently fails to deliver the standards of work required. This is known as *determining* the contract. Another contractor will have to be found very quickly to finish the work – which is why the determination of contracts is comparatively rare. Since there are complex legal requirements to determining a contract, the organisation's solicitors have to be involved at an early stage.

Agreeing completion

The client will need to ensure that the properties are substantially completed and ready for occupation, before formally accepting the work as complete. This is known as *practical completion.*

The consultant is responsible for agreeing the date of practical completion, but it is important for the client to check personally, since the consultant's perspective is different to the client's.

a. Snagging inspection

The *'snagging'* inspection is intended to identify any outstanding work for completion, and occurs about two weeks before the date for practical completion. It is undertaken by the client with the consultant and contractor. Other interested parties may also attend. When the client is a social housing provider, the important issue is whether the properties are ready for occupation, well built, and with everything operating properly. A systematic approach to the inspection must be adopted, ensuring that possible problems are not missed. The approach suggested by the National Federation of Housing Associations appears in the box below, and provides a useful indication of the sorts of details that must be carefully examined at the snagging inspection.

b. Work to be completed

Following the snagging inspection, the client and consultant will need to agree a list of work that remains to be completed satisfactorily. This is then given to the contractor, who must ensure that this is undertaken prior to the date for practical completion.

The snagging inspection

It is important to have a system which can be used in a variety of circumstances rather than to wander around in an aimless fashion just saying that the colours look good: instead, the association needs a critical and systematic review of the building. Start at the top of the building, proceeding downwards; check the internal parts of the building first, then the external parts. Check each room carefully and systematically:

- Do the windows fit properly? Are they sticking?
- Do the doors fit properly?
- Have the floorboards been fitted properly and securely?
- Has all the painting and decoration been carried out to a reasonable standard?
- Check all the services to the building as applicable.
- Check bath, basin, toilet, to ensure they are not leaking.
- Make sure the heating system is working.
- Ensure all manholes are lifted to check that the drainage system seems to be working properly.
- Check there is a separate water stopcock for each house.
- Check that all stopcocks are properly labelled.
- Check that the interior and exterior of the building are clean.
- Check that the builders' rubbish, tools, etc. have been cleared away.

Source: NFHA, 1988 pp. 36-7

---

c. Practical completion inspection

The official 'handover' of the scheme occurs at practical completion – which does not have to mean perfection. A few minor items may still need to be completed by the contractor, but the social housing organisation must be certain that the property is fit to be *occupied*. Outstanding items would not have to affect tenants in any significant way. For this reason, it is usual for there to be a final inspection of the properties, to ensure the client is satisfied that the work is substantially finished.

d. Handover of the Development

The consultant issues a *Certificate of Practical Completion*, and the contractor hands over all items relating to the completed properties, such as keys, and operating instructions for electrical and heating equipment. See Figures 4.15, 4.16 and 4.17.

e. Management issues

Arrangements for letting or selling the completed properties must begin well in advance of completion. Rents or prices must be determined, and the properties assessed by the valuation officer for *council tax*. Social housing organisations will normally have a *waiting list*, or a *transfer list*, from which prospective tenants may be selected. If the waiting list is not relevant to the type of development under construction – perhaps because the need being met is not usual for the organisation, such as shared ownership – then the organisation will need to place

---

Figure 4.15: Commercial Buildings on completion

Figure 4.16: Turnbull Street on completion

Figure 4.17: Close-up of Turnbull Street on completion

advertisements in the local press, to invite applications from eligible persons. If a choice based lettings system is in operation then the properties will be advertised in the usual ways (see chapter five). Interviews may have to be arranged, and time allowed for offers to be accepted or rejected, and replacement tenants or buyers found. If the local authority has *nomination rights* to a housing association development, there must be close liaison to ensure that tenants have been selected and informed. It is important, for sustainability reasons, to ensure an appropriate tenant mix – see chapter five.

For rehabilitation schemes, where existing tenants will be returning, they should receive regular reports of the progress of the development, and be informed of the date when they will be able to return.

Depending on the nature of the scheme, there may be other requirements prior to completion. For example, the appointment of wardens, project workers, or caretakers; or the selection and ordering of communal furnishings and equipment.

It is important that all of these management issues are resolved in sufficient time for the new tenants to move into their dwellings at practical completion, otherwise the organisation will lose valuable rental income – or incur higher interest charges on outstanding debts, in the case of properties for sale.

7. After completion

Defects liability period

No further outstanding payments are made until the expiry of a *defects liability period*. Normally, the contractor remains responsible for any defects that are the result of poor materials or workmanship for a period of six months after practical completion. The consultant determines which defects are the builder's responsibility, so they should learn of all reported defects. While serious defects should be dealt with promptly by the contractor, most trivial ones can wait until the end of the defects period, so that they can all be completed together. It is expensive for a contractor to keep sending workers to rectify small problems.

The contractor has an incentive to rectify defects, because the final monies have not yet been paid. Once the defects have been rectified, the consultant issues a *Certificate of Completion of Making Good Defects*. Only then is the *final account* settled.

Final account

The contractor will usually have prepared the final account shortly after the date of practical completion. This sets out the total sums payable, less any monies already paid. It is generally prepared in conjunction with the quantity surveyor, and then checked by the consultant. This can take many months; even with a fixed price contract, *variation orders* may have resulted in changes to the total contract sum, so the preparation of the final account is not always a simple matter.

Final certificate

Once the client approves the final account, the consultant issues the *final certificate*, releasing all remaining retention monies to the contractor. This will, of course, have been adjusted for any *liquidated and ascertained* damages, which may be due to the client in the event of late completion caused by the contractor.

Latent defects

Some defects may not be apparent at the end of the defects liability period. The contractor, nevertheless, remains responsible for *latent* defects, usually for a period of six years from practical completion. However, the contractor may well prove reluctant to accept responsibility, and it is expensive to pursue this through the legal system; so the client should take advice about whether this is likely to prove worthwhile.

Evaluating the development process

This vital step is sometimes overlooked by the client, but it is essential if lessons are to be learned for future projects.

- The performance of all of the parties in the development process, including the client and any partners, should be evaluated. These assessments should enable the organisation to decide whether the same people should be engaged in future, whether internal procedures and external partnership collaboration were adequate, as well as whether to adapt their approaches – including the briefing – where necessary.
- The design should be evaluated, both by the tenants and by the housing managers responsible for the scheme. This should include both house and estate design issues and will have to be undertaken at a later stage than the evaluation of the roles of the main parties, because it may take some time for design problems to become apparent. Particular attention should also be paid to elements that may have significant maintenance and repair implications, with a view to ensuring that these are not replicated in future schemes.
- Of critical importance is the sustainability of the completed development. After a little time, it is necessary to consider whether it has 'worked', not just in design terms but also in social and economic terms. Is this community 'working'/functioning well, and likely to continue to do so? The indicators suggested by the EIUA (2002) – see section 4 – should prove useful in this assessment.

Clearly, all partners will be involved in this assessment, which must include an analysis of the reasons for any less successful elements. This is critical to enable all partners to learn from mistakes and improve future approaches.

8. Partnering

Rethinking Construction

a. Introduction
Rethinking Construction (1998) reported on the results of an enquiry into the industry by the Construction Industry Task force, commissioned by the DETR, and chaired by Sir John Egan. This was set up in the belief that the construction industry was 'underperforming', both from a client and contractor perspective. Whereas many other industries had seen huge improvements in efficiency during the 1980s and 90s, construction appeared to have made none of these gains.

The Egan report dismissed notions that this was because construction was significantly different to manufacturing; on the contrary, Egan argued that:

> *Not only are many buildings, such as houses, essentially repeat products which can be continually improved, but, more importantly, the process of construction is itself repeated in its essentials from project to project. Indeed, research suggests that up to 80% of inputs into buildings are repeated. Much repair and maintenance also uses a repeat process...The parallel is not with building cars on the production line; it is with designing and planning the production of a new car model* (Chapter 3, p. 1).

The report pointed out that the UK construction industry would have an output of roughly £58 billions in 1998, equivalent to around 10 per cent of GDP (national income), and employing about 1.4 million people. 'It is simply too important to allow it to stagnate' (Egan, 1998, chapter 1, p. 1).

b. Drivers for change

Egan identified 5 *drivers for change* within the industry, which would set the change agenda:

1. committed leadership;
2. customer focus;
3. integrated processes and teams;
4. a quality driven agenda;
5. a commitment to people.
   (Egan, 1998, para. 17)

This implies a significant change in the way the industry operates. The traditional approach, examined in earlier sections, tends toward an adversarial, 'us' and 'them' approach (client vs. contractor), with little emphasis on either the customer or quality standards. Projects were, too often, completed late, over budget, and with too many defects.

c. Targets for improvement

The report proposed a series of very ambitious, annual targets for improvements to efficiency. The traditional approach, accepting that a range of defects would be evident, both before and after completion (see section 4), was simply no longer deemed acceptable.

The annual targets were:

- a 10 per cent reduction in capital costs and construction time;
- a 20 per cent reduction in defects and accidents;
- a 10 per cent improvement in productivity, turnover and profits;
- a 20 per cent improvement in predictability.

d. Changes to the construction process

Egan argued that the targets could be met only by making radical changes to the project process, which must become fully integrated. This is, of course, in stark contrast to the traditional, highly fragmented approaches explored in earlier sections. The report claimed that integration must occur around four key elements:

1. Product development.
2. Project implementation.
3. Partnering the supply chain.
4. Production of components.

In addition, the poor safety record of the industry must be addressed through better working conditions and improved management and supervisory skills. This would be assisted by greater use of standard components and processes – more factory-produced elements – where quality control is easier to achieve.

In contrast to traditional approaches, then, the report argued that the process must involve building long term relationships in the supply chain, based on clear performance targets which anticipated sustained improvements in quality and efficiency. According to Communities Scotland (2002), partnering promotes 'a climate of trust and agreement on mutual objectives and are applicable to most contracts, whether for development, planned or reactive maintenance' (p. 34). Hence, competitive tendering, involving project-specific, one-off relationships, is inappropriate.

e. Features of partnering

Basic features include:

1. agreed mutual objectives, which include long term goals of sustained profitability (rather than quick profits) and 'open book' relationships;
2. a systematic approach to problem resolution, which seeks to avoid blame and disputes, and achieve 'win-win' solutions;
3. a commitment to continuous improvement, based on agreed and quantified targets, which is customer-focused.
(Communities Scotland, 2002)

The partnering arrangement is normally agreed by a Partnering Charter. Ideally, it is a strategic (long term) alliance, and will certainly involve the client, consultants and contractor, but, ideally, will also include others (such as manufacturers and sub contactors), as 'experience has shown that the benefits are significantly greater if partnering is applied throughout the supply chain' (Communities Scotland, 2002, p. 35).

f. Housing demonstration projects

Following the publication of the report, 56 'demonstration projects' were approved, with the intention of demonstrating clearly the improvements that could be achieved by partnering. Pressure from the Housing Corporation to be 'Egan compliant' ensured that 75 per cent of these were English social housing providers. 'Off-site fabrication of components dominates the strategies for improvement' (Housing Forum, 2000, p. 2), and all projects had to be benchmarked against previous projects, so that improvement could be rigorously demonstrated. In addition, a set of key performance indicators (KPIs) was developed, with the DTI collecting annual data for analysis and comparison.

Further projects were added later, and various bodies were set up to encourage the industry to respond positively to the report. These included:

- the Movement for Innovation (M4I) for general construction;
- the Housing Forum for house building;
- The Local Government Task Force, to assist local authorities.

In April 2002, these were streamlined into an 'umbrella' group to disseminate best practice, called Rethinking Construction Ltd.

Accelerating change

The Strategic Forum for Construction (SFC) was established in the wake of the Egan Report, and its subsequent report, *Accelerating Change* (2002), built on the results of the earlier work. Comparisons made by M4I, covering 2000-2001, found substantial gains under all KPIs, but particularly for safety improvements (100 per cent improvement); time predictability (design) 76 per cent; fewer defects (48 per cent); and cost predictability (construction) 42 per cent (SFC, 2002). The report argued that the traditional, lowest cost tendering approach was both wasteful and unpredictable.

By 2002, a survey for the SFC found that a third of the public sector was actively partnering in construction (Inside Housing, 20 Sept 2002). The Housing Corporation began to advocate 'partnering through the ADP' in 2002 and also initiated 'kick start' funding to promote the use of off-site manufacturing (OSM) techniques, targeted on a small number of suppliers of both timber and steel frame systems of construction (HC, undated).

The Corporation argues that these pre-fabricated approaches:

- Improve supply chain relationships.
- Reduce component delivery times.
- Reduce construction times.
- Increase predictability.
- Enhance build quality.

Research for Communities Scotland (Davis Langdon, 2002), however, suggests that, although there is a broad awareness of the Rethinking Construction principles in the Scottish house building industry, implementation is still relatively low. Contractors are particularly keen to move away from competitive tendering approaches and establish partnerships, but they felt that this would need to be client (i.e. social housing) led.

Regarding construction techniques, the Communities Scotland research found that timber frame technology is now used in most new build developments, but there is little off-site fabrication for other components. This may result from lack of production volume – a problem that has also been recognised in England. There appears to be a 'chicken and egg' situation; until there is ready availability, social housing providers are reluctant to specify OSM components – but, without substantial orders, manufacturers are unwilling to invest in the necessary factories. Concerns were also expressed about the possible impact of partnering in remote and rural areas of Scotland, where there are few potential clients for construction firms.

Partnering reforms in England by the Housing Corporation

The government recognised that there would be some resistance to the idea of partnering in the construction industry as a whole, so encouraged the Housing Corporation to take the lead, by encouraging social housing providers in England –

predominantly now housing associations – to adopt Egan's principles. The Housing Corporation indicated it was expecting all HAs to be moving towards Egan compliance by 2004, though it did not necessarily expect all transfer organisations (see section 3 earlier) to be so advanced (ODPM, 2002b). However, they are expected to draw up an action plan for compliance (HC, 2002/3). In addition, the ODPM anticipates that the procurement of repairs and maintenance (see chapter five) will now reflect Egan 'partnering' principles (2002c).

In pursuit of Egan compliance, in 2001, the Housing Corporation established the 'Client's Charter' for all associations undertaking regular development, and in 2002 established a 'Mini-Charter' for small and occasionally developing associations. From 2003/4, only associations able to demonstrate the achievement of Charter status qualify to apply for Housing Corporation SHG funding (see chapter three) for significant construction works (Housing Corporation, 2003).

In 2002, a discussion paper, *Partnering through the ADP*, set out the Corporation's ideas for more collaborative relationships with the 'best' developing associations, culminating in a new approach to its capital investment programme, 'Re-inventing Investment', in 2003. The Housing Corporation argued that:

> ...*the procurement of new housing in this country is too segmented, leading to competition which can be wasteful, distrustful and inefficient...We are confident that through selective partnering we will be able to achieve economies of scale, more efficient procurement, higher quality and increased end user satisfaction* (p. 4).

The Corporation pointed out that their previous approach had funded a very large number of associations (between 350 and 400), producing an average programme of only 50 homes per association, offering little opportunity to achieve economies of scale (cost reductions from increasing the scale of production). By 2003, they had begun to introduce a more selective approach to funding HA development, targeting 56 per cent of their ADP on just 42 associations in 2003/4, and setting up a new Challenge Fund of £300 million to pilot new construction techniques (Housing Corporation, 2003).

From 2004/5, they are pursuing the partnering approach much more vigorously, introducing a new framework for funding development (Housing Corporation, 2003) with six key elements:

a. Partner programme agreements
These are available to the best associations, and offer a two year agreement (though it is hoped that this will eventually be extended) for funding of at least £10 million in each year. The associations must be able to show that they can provide 'added value' from their programme, as well as that they comply with the regional housing strategy (see chapter three, section 4) and help to create or maintain sustainable communities (p. 6).

b. Working with developers and house-builders

The ODPM has required the Corporation to promote modern methods of construction (MMC) – i.e. greater use of factory produced components – amongst housing associations, and more standardisation of products and processes. To this end, the Corporation has been working with suppliers of MMC to produce standardised house layouts, which also meet Corporation Scheme Development Standards. Associations using these 'accredited' layouts 'will not need to have their internal arrangement proposals scrutinised again' (p. 7).

The Corporation has also indicated that it will, in future, be prepared to fund private developers and house-builders directly (with SHG), and has developed a closer relationship with English Partnerships to help to secure access to land for future development.

c. Changing the operational framework

This refers to changing the Total Cost Indicator (TCI) framework for determining permissible costs, explored in chapter three, section 5. Though the TCI system will remain for small associations, 'partner associations' (see section a. above) are expected to achieve significant cost reductions and the Corporation is keen to encourage this by removing the requirement that schemes are within 110 per cent of TCIs (since that encourages less concern to drive down costs). Instead, the key focus is the subsidy required to deliver the whole programme, and is subject to negotiation. This is explored in more detail in chapter three, section 5.

d. Developing the investment strategy

The Housing Corporation's national investment policy 'draws together key priorities from the regional housing strategies produced by the Regional Housing Boards' (see chapter three), and has three main objectives (2003, p. 9):

- *Providing affordable homes in areas of economic and demographic growth including rural areas and the 'growth areas'.*
  The 'growth areas' are mainly the parts of England identified by the government as having an acute shortage of affordable housing for 'keyworkers' (like policemen, teachers and nurses), such as London and the south east, and new development is expected to focus primarily on these areas. It is also a main aim of the Communities Plan in the four areas of the south east (ODPM, 2003).
- *Contributing to regeneration and neighbourhood renewal and housing market re-structuring.*
  This focuses primarily on issues of low demand and abandonment, centred on parts of the north of England and the midlands with Housing Market Renewal Pathfinder status from the ODPM.
- *Meeting the needs of a wide range of vulnerable people.*

There is an initial target that 25 per cent of new build schemes will use MMC.

e. Developing the regulatory framework

The Corporation has two key strands to regulating those associations seeking to become partners for the two year partnering pilots, beginning in 2004/5 (2003, pp. 10-13):

i. Entry criteria

This refers to determining which associations will be able to become partners with access to subsidy through the ADP. The criteria are likely to include:

- *Overall competence*
  As well as the three main headings in the current regulatory code – viability, governance and management – this will include investment performance. The association should ideally have a 'green light' (meaning entirely satisfactory) under all four headings.
- *Financial capacity*
  This is based on the HA's financial projections and uses a credit-rating methodology.
- *Management competence*
  This refers not only to competence in managing development projects but also to the association's housing management performance.
- *Development track record*
  This will centre on the HA's past development performance, particularly against its targets in the 2002/3 ADP.
- *Efficiency*
  This will require the HA to show plans for continuous improvement in their efficiency.

ii. Regulating partners

Having met the entry criteria and become a partner, the association's performance, both overall and specifically in relation to the SHG-funded programme, will be monitored. This will focus on compliance and self-assessment, though 'we shall generally expect external verification' (2003, p. 13).

Senior Housing Corporation officers have been designated as *Lead Investors*, whose role is to manage partner associations and negotiate subsidy.

f. Evaluating proposals

The development proposals submitted by the partner associations for 2004/5 were evaluated by:

- the extent to which they would meet the national (HC) and regional (Regional Housing Board) objectives;
- the timetable for delivery (the shorter, the better);
- to assist in the creation of sustainable communities, the proposed client groups and the mix of tenures;
- the procurement methods proposed, and the extent to which MMC are employed;

- arrangements for managing the completed development;
- the amount of SHG required;
- other benefits.

An investment programme worth £3.3 billion was announced for 2004/6 and 80 per cent of this was allocated to only 71 'partner' associations (Inside Housing, 2004b). It was intended that this would produce:

- 9,700 homes in the growth areas;
- 4,000 homes in small, rural settlements;
- 4,800 homes in the pathfinder areas;
- 16,000 homes for keyworkers.

g. Evaluation
The 2003/4 Challenge Fund pilot based on partner associations is be carefully evaluated, so that any lessons can feed into the 2004-6 programme of two year partnering agreements.

It is clear that small associations are already losing out in the allocation of SHG, with only 20 per cent going to traditional (non-partner) applicants for 2004/6.

Concerns have also been expressed by the Local Government Association (LGA) that this new, partnering approach to allocating the ADP may result in local authorities' views being sidelined from the process (Inside Housing, 2004a). They fear that the emphasis on lower development costs may be to the detriment of meeting housing needs, and point out that local authorities must have a key role to play. It is they who have detailed knowledge of local housing markets, grant planning consent and operate section 106 agreements (to limit housing in shortage localities to local people in housing need). It remains to be seen whether their fears prove well-founded. Readers should, in any event, monitor future partnering agreement developments via the Housing Corporation's web-site as well as the housing press. It will be interesting also to observe to what degree other funding bodies adopt the Housing Corporation's pioneering partnering approach to allocating subsidy in the next few years.

9. Conclusion

Most social housing development is now undertaken by HAs, and the development process involves the knowledge and skills of a range of key, professional parties to ensure its success. The traditional process is essentially three stage, consisting, firstly, of steps to initiate the development, followed by the design stage, then the construction phase. There are very specific requirements at each stage, to ensure that nothing is overlooked and that risk is minimised. It is also important that the sustainability of the development is fully considered, which will usually require the involvement of a range of partners in the process, including, for example, residents, planners, social services, benefits agency staff, the police, the education authority and the health authority.

Cost pressures over recent years have forced HAs increasingly to adopt 'short cut' development procurement methods, which generally involve engaging the contractor at the (earlier) design stage in the process, to give greater cost certainty. However, the publication of the Egan Report in 1998 heralded the introduction of key changes in the development process for social housing providers, involving 'partnering' with the whole supply chain and an encouragement to use Modern Construction Methods (MMC) which incorporate more factory-produced components. Partnering is a system based on mutual trust and shared objectives, and focused on continuous improvement, for the benefit of all partners and customers. This, it is argued, will produce better quality homes, at lower cost, with shorter development times, better safety and greater customer satisfaction. For this reason, both HAs and LAs are being encouraged to adopt partnering approaches by the government and the key funding bodies. However, the Housing Corporation has gone much further than the other funders, by introducing a partnering agreement for selected associations for two years from 2004/5. This targeting the ADP subsidy on fewer, generally larger, associations, with the intention of achieving large efficiency gains over time, but this will, of course, be to the detriment of some smaller associations. Local authorities also fear that their role may be diminished as part of this new approach.

References and further reading

Carey, L. and Mapes, R. (1972) *The Sociology of Planning*, Batsford, London.

Carley, M., Chapman, M., Hastings, A., Kirk, K. and Young, R. (2000) *Urban Regeneration through Partnership: a study in nine urban regions in England, Scotland and Wales*, The Policy Press, Oxford.

Coleman, A. (1990) *Utopia on Trial*, Hilary Shipman, London.

Communities Scotland (2002) *Building a Better Deal*, Communities Scotland, Edinburgh.

Davis Langdon Consultancy (2002) *Rethinking Construction in the Scottish House building Industry*, Communities Scotland, Edinburgh.

Egan, J. (1998) *Rethinking Construction*, Department of the Environment, Transport and the Regions, London.

European Institute for Urban Affairs (EIUA) (2002) *Sustainability Indicators*, Housing Corporation, London.

Festinger L. *et al.* (1959) *Stanford Studies in Psychology*, Stanford University Press, Stanford, CT.

Greater London Authority/Mayor of London (2002) *The Draft London Plan*, GLA, London.

Housing Corporation (undated) *Kick Start Programme*, Housing Corporation, London.

Housing Corporation (2003) *Re-inventing Investment*, Housing Corporation, London.

Housing Corporation (2002) *Partnering Through the ADP*, Housing Corporation, London.

Housing Corporation (2002/3) *Guide to the Allocation Process*, Housing Corporation, London.

Housing Forum (2000) *The Housing Demonstration Projects Report*, April 2000, The Housing Forum, London.

Inside Housing (2004a) 'Pilot Partnering May Overlook Local Needs', 23 January, p. 5.

Inside Housing (2004b) 'Pressure on for Developers', 26 March, p. 1.

Mumford, K. and Power, A. (2003) *Boom or Abandonment: Resolving housing conflicts in cities*, Chartered Institute of Housing, Coventry.

National Federation of Housing Associations (1988) *Development, a Guide for Housing Associations*, NFHA, London.

Newman, O. (1981) *Community of Interest*, Anchor Books, Garden City, New York.

Office of the Deputy Prime Minister (2001) *Planning Policy Guidance Note 1: General Policy and Principles*, ODPM, London.

Office of the Deputy Prime Minister (2002a) *Regeneration that Lasts*, ODPM, London.

Office of the Deputy Prime Minister (2002b) *Housing Transfer Guidance 202 Programme*, ODPM, London.

Office of the Deputy Prime Minister (2002c) *Effective Housing Strategies and Plans: repairs, maintenance and improvements*, ODPM, London.

Office of the Deputy Prime Minister (2002d) *Sustainable Communities – Delivering Through Planning*, ODPM, London.

Office of the Deputy Prime Minister (2003) *Housing Quality Indicators*, ODPM, London.

Office of the Deputy Prime Minister (2003) *Sustainable Communities: Building for the Future*, ODPM, London.

Power, A. and Tunstall, R. (1995) *Swimming Against the Tide*, Joseph Rowntree Foundation, York.

Strategic Forum for Construction (2002) *Accelerating Change*, Rethinking Construction, London.

Trotter, E. (1997) *Lifetime Homes*, Joseph Rowntree Foundation, York.

Wilcox, S, (2003) *UK Housing Review 2003/2004*, CIH and CML for the Joseph Rowntree Foundation, Coventry and London.

Willmott, P. (1963) *The Evolution of Community*, Routledge and Kegan Paul, London.

Willmott, P. and Young, M. (1957) *Family and Kinship in East London*, Routledge and Kegan Paul, London.

CHAPTER 5:
Core housing management functions

1. Introduction

The previous two chapters have looked at the financing and development of social housing. This chapter moves on to examine the key tasks involved in managing social housing. It starts by attempting to define what is meant by housing management, and then considers some historical approaches to the function before looking in more detail at those key tasks which housing managers perform; such as letting houses, collecting the rent, dealing with empty properties, carrying out repairs and maintenance to the housing stock, and managing tenancies.

2. Defining housing management

In 2002 local authorities in the UK owned over 3.541 million homes with a further 1.688 million properties owned by housing associations, all of which have to be managed. (Wilcox, 2003). So what are the key tasks which have to be undertaken by housing professionals in managing these properties? The Social Exclusion Unit's Policy Action Team on Housing Management concluded that:

> *There is no single definition of the housing management task. It can vary between landlord and estate. Its nature depends on what local circumstances demand.* (DETR, 1999, p. 18).

However although this view is often repeated there is a surprising level of agreement as to what housing management involves, for example:

> *Most previous studies of housing management have focused mainly on 'traditional landlord functions': that is services provided primarily for tenants and funded from rental income. These functions include rent collection and arrears management, repairs and maintenance, voids and allocations, tenancy and environmental management and tenant participation.* (Scott, 2001, p. 6).

The government's framework for assessing housing management performance under the Best Value regime provides the following definition:

> *The housing management function on the authority's own housing stock where it still retains ownership:*
> * *allocation of tenancies, including lettings to homeless households;*
> * *response repairs;*

- *planned maintenance; cyclical maintenance; capital works;*
- *redevelopment and renewal;*
- *tenancy management, including tenancy sustainability and anti-social behaviour;*
- *estate management;*
- *tenant participation;*
- *leasehold management/Right to Buy;*
- *energy efficiency;*
- *equalities and diversity;*
- *regeneration;*
- *rent setting and collection*
  (Office of the Deputy Prime Minister, 2003, p. 5).

This list of activities closely reflects the activities of social housing staff from the north of England studied in a research project into the changing nature of housing management. The study found that housing officers spent a large proportion of their time on the key housing tasks, and the proportions are shown in Table 5.1.

Table 5.1 Percentage of time spent on key tasks

Task	Mean percentage of time spent by generic housing managers	Mean percentage of time spent by all respondents
Dealing with nuisance/anti-social behaviour	23.2%	20.3%
Lettings	22.2%	14.4%
Rent setting and collection	11.3%	11.0%
Repairs	8.0%	4.7%
Liaison with tenants' groups	6.1%	4.7%
Regeneration of estates	5.8%	4.6%
Developing strategies for under-occupation	4.0%	2.4%
Planned maintenance	2.8%	2.7%
Developing community safety strategies	1.0%	3.0%
All key tasks	**84.4%**	**67.9%**

Source: Grainger, Harding and Kirk, 2003, p. 13

Housing management therefore is essentially about four key tasks:

- letting houses;
- collecting the rent;
- maintaining the properties in good condition;
- managing tenancies and the environment in which tenants live.

The rest of this chapter will look at these key tasks in greater detail.

3. The historical development of housing management

Looking back often gives us pointers to the future and many of the current debates about housing management have their roots in discussions which were taking place in Victorian England. This section starts by examining the work of Octavia Hill, who is sometimes cited as the founder of modern housing management, and considers the principles which she adopted and discusses how applicable they are to contemporary housing managers.

Octavia Hill; the founder of housing management?

Housing management in itself is not intrinsically complex (although it is often demanding); the core tasks of lettings, rents, repairs and tenancy management are performed by all of those who manage housing. How then has housing management developed as a separate profession? In the nineteenth century many landlords who owned a few properties would have carried out the housing management tasks themselves, (as many private landlords do today). Others would have employed agents to carry undertake this work. These would often have been other professionals who undertook these duties as a sideline, such as surveyors, land agents or factors.

In other situations the owner would have employed a middleman who would undertake repairs in exchange for a share in the rent. This system encouraged middlemen to overcrowd properties to maximise their rental income and to minimise expenditure on repairs (Power, 1987).

However, in the late nineteenth century a housing manager emerged who was to exert great influence on the way in which housing management was undertaken in the twentieth century and whose philosophy is still discussed by housing managers today. Octavia Hill was born in 1838 to a middle class family and was persuaded between 1865 and 1866 to take on the management of a small number of dilapidated properties in the Marylebone area of London. Octavia Hill managed this housing herself and she took steps to improve what she saw were the poor housing management practices prevalent at the time. She considered that an essential element of good housing management was the necessity for close personal contact between landlord and tenants.

> *In its early days, her management, operating on a small scale, was often intensely personal; Octavia Hill's principles that people and their homes could not be dealt with separately, and that a sound landlord/tenant relationship must be based on mutual recognition and discharging of responsibilities, were put into practice by her followers* (Smith, 1989).

Only by ensuring that there was close contact on a regular basis could landlords ensure that the investment in their property was safeguarded. Such visits were an opportunity to check on the condition of the property, to ensure that tenants were not abusing the property, to collect the rent and to deal with any necessary repairs. She took a firm line on arrears and would evict those who did not pay their rent and she took a similar line against those who were guilty of persistent anti-social behaviour. The visits were also seen as a means by which tenants, who inevitably were poor and of lower class, could be educated into a better standard of behaviour. She was keen to encourage a sense of community and responsibility amongst her tenants and would also advise tenants on health and diet as a way of improving their standard of living (Power, 1987).

What echoes does this have for contemporary housing management? The emphasis on close contact between landlord and tenant is a key theme underlying local housing management. Those who argue for local offices suggest that one of the failings of centralised housing management has been that landlords have been too distant, both geographically and socially, from the tenants they house. The same idea underlies much of the support in recent years given to tenant participation and the need to work more closely with tenants.

Even so, it is important not to take Octavia Hill's influence too far. Octavia Hill, according to Spicker, was a 'moralistic and authoritarian' landlord and this is something which most modern advocates of tenant participation and local management would want to avoid.

> *...the legacy she left to housing managers has been baneful. She founded a tradition which is inconsistent with the rights of tenants and destructive of their welfare* (Spicker, 1985).

This criticism of Octavia Hill's approach is that she failed to treat tenants with respect. It suggests that her approach was based on a belief that the working classes were inclined to get into debt, to neglect their houses and to indulge in unacceptable behaviour. This tendency could only be overcome by strict housing management, which emphasised the need to pay the rent, to reduce the overcrowding which led to immoral behaviour and to encourage communal areas to be kept clean by tenants.

As Spicker goes on to say;

> *Octavia Hill's principles were misconceived at the time she formed them. Booth's research in the 1880's found that a third of the population did not have enough for the most basic sustenance-food, clothing, fuel and shelter. Landlords were "lax" about rent collection because tenants could not pay. Debt and bad housing were the result of poverty, not indolence.*

Spicker suggests that her management practices were based on a misunderstanding of the circumstances in which tenants found themselves.

It assumed that tenants would not pay; in fact tenants in many cases simply could not afford to pay. Of course one of the effects of Hill's management style was that she would weed out the poorest tenants and only house those who could afford to pay the rents she charged.

And the problem according to Spicker is that the practices which she advocated are still seen today as 'good' housing management; the heavy emphasis on rent payment as a priority, preventing transfers if there are any arrears on the account, the use of Notices of Seeking Possession as a management tool, the emphasis on cleanliness, and the treatment of problem tenants by transferring them to worse estates.

The relevance of Octavia Hill to contemporary housing management

It is fairly easy to suggest that many of Octavia Hill's practices were indeed paternalistic and many would no longer be seen as acceptable today. So why is it that her approach is still revered by many housing professionals? Perhaps it is because that whilst the motivation behind some of her practices may no longer be acceptable the means are increasingly seen as positive housing management. In particular her emphasis on personal contact between landlord and tenant has become adopted as good practice by contemporary housing managers and has been linked to other initiatives such as decentralisation and tenant participation. However, supporters today of a personal approach, tenant participation and decentralisation would do so from a position which accorded tenants significant rights as consumers of a service.

She has also clearly influenced the thinking of those who now advocate the social/welfare role of housing management. Many contemporary housing managers would argue that although the key tasks of management remain rents, repairs and lettings they need increasingly to take on welfare roles with tenants; advising them on benefits, working closely with social workers, the police and other agencies to overcome some of the problems faced by tenants living in housing estates. This issue is discussed in more detail in the last chapter.

Some supporters of Octavia Hill also bemoan the passing of the traditional 'housing visitor' whose main role was to carry out regular inspections of tenants' properties and gardens and who would take strong action against tenants whose homes were not up to standard. They also regret the passing, in some places at least, of the housing application forms which asked housing visitors to grade the state of prospective tenants' homes as 'clean', 'satisfactory' or 'dirty'. This approach is very much in the Octavia Hill tradition but one which is increasingly viewed as unacceptable by today's housing managers.

Developments in contemporary housing management; gold service and incentive schemes

In recent years, however, there has been an interesting innovation in housing management which is reminiscent of the Octavia Hill approach. In the late 1990s Irwell Valley Housing Association based in Salford began to develop an incentive based approach to housing management. Under the Irwell Valley Gold Service, tenants who complied with their tenancy agreement by paying their rent and not causing a nuisance to neighbours, would receive a range of extra benefits as members of the Irwell Valley Gold Service scheme such as;

- a payment of £52 a year in 'BonusBonds' (vouchers that can be used in a wide range of retail outlets);
- an enhanced and quicker repairs service;
- access to discounted services negotiated by Irwell Valley;
- a members' magazine with special discounts and benefits exclusive to Gold Service members;
- priority in improvement programmes.

This model of management was developed as a way of focusing the organisation on high quality customer service and giving 'good' customers a better service. It was also designed to encourage tenants to meet the conditions of membership. The scheme has been a great success with over 70 per cent of the Association's tenants now members, with significant reductions in arrears and empty properties as a result. The scheme, with its emphasis on firm housing management and reward tenants was controversial, but is increasingly being adopted by other councils and housing associations with the explicit endorsement of the government.

4. Letting properties

One of the key tasks of housing management is the letting of homes. Every year local authorities and housing associations have to let many thousands of homes. Some of these are newly built or refurbished homes which are being let for the first time (new lets) but the overwhelming majority are lettings of existing homes where the previous tenant has moved or died, creating a vacancy to be let (re-lets). In England there were a total of 450,000 lettings of social housing dwellings in 2001/02 as set out in the table below;

Table 5.2: Lettings 2001/02 by local authorities and housing associations in England

	Total lettings	To existing tenants (transfers)	To new tenants
Local authorities	291,000	94,000	198,000
Housing associations	159,000	41,000	118,000

Source: Wilcox, 2003.

In Scotland in 2002/03 there were 38,191 lettings to new tenants, in Northern Ireland 8,824 lettings to new tenants (2001/02), and in Wales 13,941 lettings to new tenants (2001/02).

In England 31 per cent of the new local authority lettings were made to homeless applicants, with 11 per cent of the new housing association lettings to this client group. In Scotland the comparator local authority figure was 27.7 per cent and in Wales 15.8 per cent (Wilcox 2003).

Who are homes let to?

As discussed in chapter two, demand for social rented housing is usually greater than the available supply of properties. This means that when there is a vacancy to be let the social landlord is often faced with a number of people who wish to be considered for that vacancy. In these circumstances the social landlord needs to decide which of the competing applicants should be offered a tenancy.

Of course, if landlords face a situation where there is little demand they will have the problem of identifying suitable applicants in order to minimise rental loss and to prevent vandalism. In some parts of the country and for particular properties this problem of the 'difficult to let property' is a real one and poses significant challenges for housing managers. However in most cases social landlords are faced with the situation where they have more than one person wanting a particular home and they need to decide the basis on which property should be allocated. This is often a complex issue because of the number of potential applicants who may need to be considered, including:

- people whose homes have been demolished through clearance programmes;
- homeless applicants;
- keyworkers;
- existing tenants who wish to transfer to this type of property;
- applicants who are not already tenants but who are on a central or common register (or 'waiting list') held by the landlord for rented housing;
- refugees and asylum seekers;
- applicants on a national register of people wanting to obtain rented housing in another area through the *National Mobility Scheme* (called HOMES).

Figure 5.1 shows many of the categories of people competing for social housing tenancies.

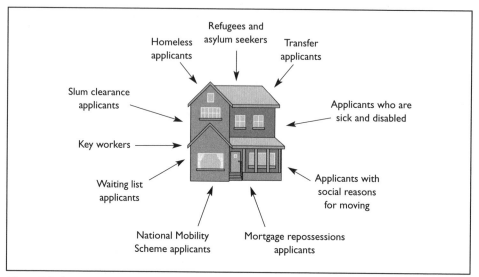

Figure 5.1: Groups competing for housing

All of these people will have pressing needs; so how does the social landlord decide who should be prioritised for one of their homes.

What the law says

All social landlords have to take account of the legislation about their policies and procedures for letting their houses and this is now contained in a number of different pieces of legislation, which do not always apply equally to housing associations and/or local authorities.

Housing Act 1985 (Housing Scotland Act 1987)

All local housing authorities have a duty to consider the housing needs of their area and the need that might exist for additional accommodation.

Housing Act 1996 (as amended by the Homelessness Act 2002)

The 1996 Act set out for the first time clear procedures for local authorities in England and Wales to follow in relation to the allocation of housing. Section 159 of the Act requires local authorities to allocate their housing in accordance with the Act, including nominations to housing associations.

Under the terms of the Homelessness Act 2002, local authorities are no longer required to keep a housing register or waiting list. This provision was intended to pave the way for new and innovative approaches to allocations and lettings, which are considered later in this chapter.

Section 167 of the 1996 Act requires every local authority in England and Wales to establish and publish an allocation scheme which sets out clearly how they will allocate their housing. The allocation scheme must give 'reasonable preference' to the following groups:

- people occupying insanitary or overcrowded housing or otherwise living in unsatisfactory housing conditions;
- people occupying housing accommodation which is temporary or occupied on insecure terms;
- families with dependent children;
- households consisting of or including someone who is expecting a child;
- households consisting of or including someone with a particular need for settled accommodation on medical or welfare grounds;
- households whose social or economic circumstances are such that they have difficulty in securing settled accommodation.

It should be noted that homeless applicants do not come within the groups who should be given reasonable preference although it is likely that their circumstances either prior to becoming homeless or whilst in temporary accommodation will enable them to qualify under one or more of the above headings. These categories are broadly similar to the provisions set out in the 1985 Housing Act which had given reasonable preference to:

- to people living in unsanitary or overcrowded accommodation;
- to people with large families;
- to the statutory homeless;
- to persons living in unsatisfactory conditions.
- (Scotland only) to people living in housing below the tolerable standard.

Under Section 106 of the 2002 Homelessness Act, where a local authority is satisfied that an applicant (or a member of the applicant's household) is guilty of unacceptable behaviour serious enough to make them unsuitable to be a tenant of the housing authority, it can decide to treat the applicant as ineligible for an allocation. The only behaviour which can be regarded as unacceptable for these purposes is behaviour by the applicant or by a member of their household that would – if the applicant had been a secure tenant of the housing authority at the time – have entitled the housing authority to a possession order on the grounds of behaviour such as conduct likely to cause nuisance or annoyance, and use of the property for immoral or illegal purposes. The housing authority will need to satisfy itself that the applicant is unsuitable to be a tenant by reason of the behaviour in question – and in the circumstances at the time the application is considered. Previous unacceptable behaviour may not justify a decision to treat the applicant as ineligible where that behaviour can be shown to have improved or be explainable because of particular circumstances. Housing authorities who decide that applicants are ineligible because of unacceptable behaviour must give them written notification of the decision. The notification must give clear grounds for the decision, which must be based firmly on the relevant facts of the case. Applicants have the right to request a review under the allocation scheme of any decision as to eligibility and a right to be informed of the decision on review and the grounds for that decision.

Earlier legislation, which is still in force, requires authorities to provide accommodation to those displaced by slum clearance programmes and they also use their 'best endeavours' to house farm workers displaced from tied accommodation.

Housing Act 1988

Housing associations (in England and Wales) must supply a copy of their lettings policy for assured tenants to the local authority and the Housing Corporation (or the National Assembly for Wales). The Housing Corporation's Regulatory Code and guidance for housing associations also covers this issue (see Figure 5.2).

Figure 5.2: Housing Corporation Regulatory Code

- Lettings and sales policies are flexible, non discriminatory and responsive to demand, while contributing to the need to be inclusive and the need to ensure sustainable communities.
- Associations are able to demonstrate their co-operation with local authorities in homelessness reviews, in the formulation of homelessness strategies and in the delivery of the authority's homelessness functions.
- When requested to do so by the local authority and to such an extent as is reasonable in the circumstances, associations provide a proportion of their stock to local authority nominations and temporary accommodation to the homeless.
- Criteria are adopted following consultation with local authorities for accepting or rejecting nominees and other applicants for housing.
- Applicants are excluded from consideration for housing only when their unacceptable behaviour is serious enough to make them unsuitable to be a tenant and only in circumstances that are not unlawfully discriminatory.
- Lettings policies;
  - are responsive to local authority housing duties,
  - take account of the need to give reasonable priority to transfer applicants including applicants from other associations,
  - are responsive to national, regional and local mobility and exchange schemes,
  - are demonstrably fair and effectively controlled.

Homelessness provisions (Housing Act 1996 (Part V11) as amended by the Homelessness Act 2002)

The law in England and Wales effectively requires local authorities to secure permanent accommodation for those applicants who were unintentionally homeless and in priority need. In assessing whether an applicant is entitled to permanent housing the applicant has to jump over a number of hurdles:

- Is the applicant homeless or threatened with homelessness?
- Is the applicant in priority need?
- Is the applicant unintentionally homeless?
- Does the applicant have a local connection with the area?

Although the definitions of a *homeless applicant*, *intentionality*, *local connection* and *priority need* were largely unchanged from the 1985 Act, the Homelessness Act 2002 extended the priority need categories so that they now include:

- a pregnant woman or a person with whom she resides or might reasonably be expected to reside;
- a person with whom dependent children reside or might reasonably be expected to reside;
- a person who is vulnerable as a result of old age, mental illness or handicap or physical disability or other special reason, or with whom such a person resides or might reasonably be expected to reside;
- a person who is homeless, or threatened with homelessness, as a result of an emergency such as flood, fire or other disaster;
- homeless 16 and 17 year olds;
- care leavers aged 18, 19 and 20;
- people who are vulnerable because of time spent in care, the armed forces, prison or custody; and
- people who are vulnerable because of violence.

There are some exceptions in the case of 16 and 17 year olds and care leavers who are owed a duty by the social services authority. However, in circumstances where the social services authority and the housing authority are one and the same, the only question is on the nature of the assistance to be provided.

Homelessness provisions in the Housing (Scotland) Act 2001 and Homelessness etc. (Scotland) Act 2003

The 2001 Act required each Scottish local authority to have a homelessness strategy, to conduct an assessment of homelessness in the area and provide free advice and temporary accommodation to homeless people. The 2003 Act went further and strengthened the rights of homeless people and was part of a co-ordinated approach to tackling and preventing homelessness. Under previous Scottish legislation, homeless people had to meet three tests in relation to homeless:

- Is the applicant in priority need?
- Is the applicant unintentionally homelessness?
- Does the applicant have a local connection?

The 2003 Act began to phase out the restrictions in the priority need classification so that by 2012 all people will be encompassed by the definition and the priority need test will be redundant. However, initially priority need has been extended to include those having:

- a chronic illness;
- suffered a miscarriage or had an abortion;
- been discharged from hospital;
- left a prison or the regular armed forces.

In addition, people living or who might reasonably be expected to live with someone in priority need are included as eligible persons, along with 16-17 year olds, 18-20 year olds who run the risk of sexual or financial exploitation through misuse of drugs and alcohol, people at risk of violence or harassment because of race, colour, ethnicity or sexual orientation or a person who runs the risk of domestic violence. As can be seen this is similar to the English and Welsh amendments to the homelessness legislation, but it is clear that the Scottish Parliament is extending the compass of its homelessness legislation and it is anticipated that by 2006 there will be a further extension of the definition of priority need.

Race Relations Act 1976

The selection of tenants and the subsequent allocation of properties to successful applicants is governed by the laws on discrimination. In their Code of Practice for rented housing (published in 1991) the Commission for Racial Equality indicated that a number of research studies clearly demonstrated that ethnic minorities suffered severe discrimination in housing. This has occurred in two main ways. The first in access to housing registers, where people from minority ethnic groups may not have been accepted. The second in the type and quality of accommodation offered to minority ethnic groups. In a number of research studies these groups were shown to have been offered poorer accommodation than white applicants.

The Commission for Racial Equality launched a number of investigations into the selection and allocation policies of local authorities and found discrimination to be a significant problem. For example the Commission for Racial Equality's report into Liverpool City Council found that white people were twice as likely to get a nomination to a housing association home compared to a black applicant; four times more likely to get a new home; four times as likely to get a garden and twice as likely to get a property with central heating. The CRE's detailed Code of Guidance (1991, and so now rather out of date) sets out what housing organisations should do to avoid discrimination in their allocations and selection policies and procedures.

Race Relations Amendment Act 2000

This Act strengthens the 1976 Race Relations Act. The most important change was to place a new, enforceable duty on public authorities to promote racial equality. This requires most public bodies (including local authorities, the Housing Corporation, but *not* housing associations) to make the promotion of racial equality central to their work and to take the lead in promoting equality of opportunity and good race relations and preventing unlawful discrimination. In particular they have to publish detailed Race Equality Schemes which makes it clear how they meet the requirements of the Act. Although the Act applies in Scotland, the Scottish Parliament has the power to set specific duties for Scottish public authorities.

Sex Discrimination Act 1975

This requires that landlords should not discriminate on the grounds of sex in the allocation of their property.

Types of lettings systems

All landlords need to have established a procedural system to decide who should be offered the housing that they have available to let. Under the 1996 Housing Act these procedures must be published and made available to anyone who asks for them. The scheme must give reasonable preference to those applicants set down in the Act.

Date order system

Under this system, landlords will house applicants in strict date order making offers to those who have been registered longest on the list. Even where other systems are used date order can still be important. For example homeless applicants usually have priority for re-housing but it is often the case that local authorities will aim to house first those who have been registered as homeless the longest.

Merit systems

With this system the decision as to who is allocated a particular property is based on the merits of each applicant's case. Usually the organisation will have a lettings policy and applicants are considered against the criteria set out in the policy to determine who is in the greatest need. A common problem with merit systems is that the decision to allocate a property is often based on a very subjective judgement as to which applicant is in the greatest need and therefore the most deserving to get the property. Below is an example of a merit system operated by a housing association.

Figure 5.3: Merit system

In considering nominations from local authorities and in selecting applicants from the association's waiting list the following matters are taken into account:

1. Size, type and location of dwelling available for re-letting and suitability to meet the applicant's housing need.
2. The applicant's housing conditions including:
    *   threatened or actual homelessness;
    *   overcrowding or under occupation;
    *   sharing facilities;
    *   location in relation to work, relatives, friends and services;
    *   state of repair of the present property and ability to influence the state of repair.
3. The applicant's ability to cope with their existing housing conditions including;
    *   income;
    *   health;
    *   stress;
    *   previous housing history;
    *   the needs of dependents.
4. The availability of alternative housing including:
    *   potential access to home ownership;
    *   ability to meet local authority residential requirements.
5. The length of time the applicant has had to tolerate unsatisfactory housing conditions.

Individual applicants are considered against these criteria and the applicant with the 'greatest need' is offered the property. However the key problem is which criteria is given the most weight in the decision making process and in many cases the decision may be difficult to justify given the many subjective judgements that this type of allocation system entails.

Points schemes

These exist where the applicant's circumstances are considered against a scheme where points are awarded for various indicators of housing need. For example 10 points may be awarded to someone living in rented accommodation but 20 points to someone living in tied accommodation. The points are totalled and the applicant with the highest points is usually awarded priority. Such schemes are relatively easy to understand and to query the points score awarded. They are of course subjective in terms of the factors considered and the weighting attached to individual points scores.

Figure 5.4: Example of the points scheme used by a housing association

The housing register
The association operates a single housing register. In all cases applicants, if they are to be accepted onto the housing register, must demonstrate that they are in housing need – the factors which the association considers are:
- Existing housing conditions.
- Ability to cope with these conditions.
- Other prospects for housing. Since our aim is to help those in greatest need, we consider the following as priority examples:
  - Homeless applicants.
  - People in overcrowded, insanitary or insecure conditions.
  - People living in accommodation lacking in standard amenities.
  - People in shared housing who would benefit from moving to a self contained property.
  - People living in under-occupied property.
  - People who would benefit from re-housing for social, emotional or medical reasons.
  - People fleeing violence.
  - People suffering harassment.

Points scheme
The factors which the association will consider and the weighting attached are set out in the points scheme:

1. **Security of tenure**
   The association will not normally award points under this heading for applicants with secure or assured tenancies.
   a. **Homeless applicant** (30 points)
   b. **Applicants without their own home** (20 points)
      People normally falling into this group are detailed below:
      Assured shorthold tenants/licencees.
      Residents of bed and breakfast accommodation.
      Residents of hostels.
      Residents of hospital, prison and other institutions.
      Young people leaving care.
      Applicants living in caravans.   →

Living with family/friends/carers.
Service tenancies and service licences, i.e. tied accommodation.
Sub tenants and persons in rooms with a resident landlord.
  c. **Households living separately**   **(25 points)**
       Applicants who could reasonably be expected to live together as a household including:
       Couples with or without children.
       Families with dependent relative.

2. **Size and type of property**
    In assessing overcrowding the association will take account of an unborn child where a mother
    is more than six months pregnant.
    a. **Overcrowding** (For each bedroom lacking)   **(20 points)**
        We consider a separate bedroom necessary for:
        Each couple living together.
        A parent in a single parent family.
        A single adult over 16 years.
        Each child of 10 years or over who would otherwise have to share with a child of the
        opposite sex.
        (A single bedroom is one bedspace, a double bedroom is two bedspaces.)
    b. **Under occupation**   **(10 points)**
        For each surplus bedroom.
        (One bedroom is allowed above the household's needs)
    c. **People living in flats**   **(10 points)**
        Families with children under 10 years living above ground floor.
        Elderly people living in flats above first floor without a lift.

3. **Condition of property**
    a. **Lack of basic facilities** (for any lack of amenity)   **(40 points)**
        No kitchen facilities.
        No bathroom.
        No inside toilet.
    b. **Property in need of major repair**   **(50 points)**
        Property declared unfit to occupy.

4. **Sharing any facilities**   **(10 points)**
    (except for applicants living with their family)
        Living room.
        Kitchen facilities.
        Bathroom.
        Toilet.

5. **Disability/medical circumstances**   **(30 points)**
    If anyone included in the application is in poor health or has a disability which
    could be assisted by re-housing.

6. **Social needs**   **(25 points)**
    These points may be awarded to take account of other housing related problems or needs
    including:
        To move to be nearer family.
        To move to be nearer work.
        To move to be nearer community support.
        To move to be nearer carers.
        To avoid harassment/nuisance or violence.
        To assist applicants with high rents/housing benefit restrictions.

Group or band systems

A group system operates where applicants are initially placed into different groups (or bands) and the organisation then allocates homes to people from individual groups. It will normally use a quota which indicates the specific proportion of allocations for each group. The groups can be few or numerous but typical schemes will include groups for:

- homeless families;
- medical cases;
- elderly;
- special needs.

Within each group applicants can be ranked by a variety of means: merit, date order or points. If an organisation has adopted a group system it will need to decide which group should receive which proportion of lettings.

Combined systems

Most landlords will operate a variety of allocation schemes. For example, even where a landlord has a points scheme they may still use other systems within it. Some applicants may be given priority over others on the list so that homeless applicants may have priority over people with very high points on the waiting list. In addition it may be difficult to compare people on the transfer list who want a move to more suitable accommodation, with those living in unsuitable private accommodation. It is the case that many local authorities will say that they will let a certain percentage of their properties to applicants off the transfer list, and the choice of the transfer applicant will go to the person with the most points.

Nominations to housing associations

Housing associations are normally expected to offer local authorities **nominations**. This means that the housing association agrees to re-house people referred (nominated) by the local authority. The precise arrangements for nominations differ from local authority to authority. In some cases the local authority will give the association a number of possible applicants to consider and the association will make its choice. In other cases perhaps only one applicant will be put forward for each vacancy. The association must retain the right to refuse a nomination if it feels that the applicant does not meet the association's own lettings criteria. Where local authorities give free land or other financial support to associations they will often require 100 per cent nominations to be given.

Transfers of existing tenants

Any lettings policy also has to consider the needs of existing tenants who may wish to move to a different home. This can be for a variety of reasons:

- Medical: where the current home is unsuitable (e.g. a two storey house occupied by someone with a heart problem who has difficulty climbing stairs).
- Social: where someone may wish to move home to be nearer family, friends, school or work.

- Increased family size: where the property is no longer large enough to meet the household's requirements.
- Other reasons such as a wish to move away from an undesirable area.

In designing its lettings policies and procedures it is essential that the landlord considers the needs of those who wish to transfer. If it does not then these people may end up trapped in housing which is unsuitable for them. Most landlords will therefore devise a transfer policy which sets out the rules by which people may transfer and usually indicates the level of preference which will be given to transfer applicants relative to others on the waiting list. For example if a council has a bungalow available it may consider allocating it first to a elderly tenant living alone in a three bedroom house. This means that the elderly tenant's housing needs are met and the resulting vacancy of the three bedroom house can then be let to someone off the council waiting list, such as a homeless family. (All landlords will have different views as to the preference which they give to transfer applicants but they are required to make clear in their published policies and procedures how they deal with transfer applicants).

Size of waiting and transfer lists

As all housing organisations have a different approach to dealing with allocations issues it is difficult to make an accurate estimate of the numbers of people on housing lists who are seeking accommodation. However the government has estimated that in 2001/2 around 700,000 households – equivalent to around three per cent of all households – contained someone who was on a waiting list for council or housing association accommodation (Mew *et al.*, 2003, p. 20).

Mutual exchanges

A mutual exchange is where one tenant swaps their tenancy with another tenant, usually of the same landlord but not necessarily so. The rules on such transfers are complex but normally such transfers have to be approved, unless the tenant has rent arrears. It is important to recognise that a mutual exchange is technically an *assignment* of the tenancy. In other words there is not a new tenancy created but the outgoing tenant passes on (*assigns*) their existing tenancy to the incoming tenant. This is important because it means that if a secure tenant exchanges with an assured tenant the person who was the secure tenant now takes over an assured tenancy. The assured tenancy has fewer rights than a secure tenancy, for example the Right to Buy does not apply to assured tenants, and an exchange can lead to changes in the rights of the tenants involved. Social housing landlords will wish to encourage such exchanges as they are a means by which tenants can move to more suitable accommodation and they may assist the process by means of computerised exchange lists or simply by means of a display board in the housing office.

Nationally, local authority and housing association tenants can swap tenancies by means of the HOMES National Mobility Scheme which operates across the United Kingdom (see www.homes.org.uk). Under the scheme, participating organisations agree to re-house a certain number of their new lettings to applicants referred through the scheme. This enables a person who wishes to move to a different part of the country, usually for work or employment reasons, to do so. The HOMESWAP scheme is a database of 50,000 tenants wishing to exchange homes throughout the United Kingdom and the website enables applicants to search for possible exchange partners and to view homes on line.

Common housing registers

One issue which has recently been the subject of much debate in housing is whether local authorities and housing associations working in the same area should attempt to develop common housing registers or lettings systems. This is to deal with the all too frequent problem of a person seeking housing having to register on the waiting list of the local authority and all the local housing associations to maximise their chance of re-housing. This can mean in some cases completing up to ten application forms for housing, all of which ask for very similar information. In order to resolve this problem a number of local authorities have taken the initiative of developing common allocations policies. In some cases this amounts to the local authorities and housing associations devising a common application form which is logged centrally and then made available to all housing providers. This saves the applicant having to complete numerous forms. In other cases the landlords have gone further by not only having a common waiting list but by developing a common allocations system in which all social housing landlords agree about the priority to be attached to every applicant so that when a vacancy arises in any of the participant's stock the highest priority applicant for that vacancy is selected no matter who the landlord is. This is much more difficult to achieve as many landlords have different allocations policies and it may be difficult for a number of associations and the local authority to agree on a system.

New approaches to lettings

Increasingly concerns have been voiced about the operation of some of these approaches to allocating social housing. Approaches based on waiting lists have been perceived as being time consuming and bureaucratic, typified by large application forms on which applicants are required to give lots of information before their application is even considered. Traditional approaches can be seen as being designed to meet administrative requirements, as the housing professional retains all of the information to allow them to make an allocation decision, especially since there may be administrative difficulties, particularly in keeping information updated. If information is out of date time can be wasted making offers of accommodation to people who may not still be in need or whose needs may have changed since making their application. Those approaches can also be open to criticism as being closed and secretive, particularly as confidentiality requirements prevent unsuccessful applicants from being given full information about why another applicant was allocated a dwelling that they may have wanted. This can also lead to concerns that any system which cannot be easily seen to be open and fair may be failing to provide equal opportunity to all members of the community.

The government's response to such concerns was flagged in its Housing Green paper, *Quality and Choice – a Decent Home for All*. Within the paper, the government highlighted a desire to re-think traditional approaches to housing provision. Subsequent legislation in the Homelessness Act 2002, amended some existing legal restrictions in relation to the letting of local authority dwellings. These changes included the abolition of the requirement to operate a waiting list or housing register, and paved the way for more innovative approaches to lettings. In addition, the Housing Excellence Framework requires local authorities to have introduced or be considering choice based lettings as an option for the allocation of their dwellings. Market Harborough was the first choice based lettings scheme to cover all the social housing stock in a local authority area (Brown *et al.*, 2002). Essentially, it required housing officers to move from a culture of 'allocation' to one designed to assist homeseekers in their search for a new home.

The government funded 27 pilot schemes in 2002/03 to consider different approaches to allocating social housing in which customer choice could be made central whilst need remained a factor in the allocation of social housing. Many of these pilots were based on variations of the 'Delft' model of choice based lettings, which developed in the Netherlands during the late 1980s and early 1990s. The pilot schemes included a mixture of 'stand alone' schemes in which the properties of one landlord alone were included, and common approaches in which different landlords within the same geographical area signed up to a 'joint scheme'.

Figure 5.5: Home Connections Choice Based Lettings Scheme in Central and North London

Home Connections is a choice based lettings pilot funded by the ODPM in 2002 for £1.5m. It was set up as a partnership of five local authorities (Camden, Barnet, Westminster, Kensington & Chelsea and Islington) and two associations (St Pancras & Humanist HA and Ujima). It developed a choice based system with the following elements:

- all vacant properties were advertised each week on the internet and in newspapers and in public buildings, such as council offices and libraries;
- applicants registered with Home Connections could bid for each property, either in person, by post, over the internet or by an interactive voice recording telephone system;
- when bids were received each week the applicant with the highest number of points (as determined by the council lettings scheme) was offered the property.

The pilot scheme was very successful in terms of:

- increasing choice and customer satisfaction;
- reducing time properties were empty as only people who bid for the property would be offered it (there was a big reduction in refusal of offers);
- developing more customer focused approaches to lettings;
- increasing access of homeless and other disadvantaged groups to housing.

Following the end of the pilot in April 2003 the partners agreed to maintain the scheme and more landlords joined the scheme. In 2004 the LB Camden and LB Barnet agreed to include all of their vacant stock in the choice based scheme and others are likely to follow.

Visit www.homeconnections.org.uk for more information.

Choice models will continue to be a feature of housing policy in England in the 2000s. However, while choice based lettings has caught the imagination of English housing policy makers, in Scotland, a more cautious approach has been adopted with only Edinburgh City Council and Berwickshire Housing Association having set up a choice based allocations systems so far (Housing, Dec 2002/Jan 2003).

5. Rents and arrears management

For all landlords the setting and collection of rents, and the recovery of rent arrears are core housing management functions and this section considers the different approaches which housing organisations adopt.

Setting the rents

As we saw in chapter three, rents are the main source of revenue income for landlords and as such landlords need to establish a mechanism for setting their rents. For social housing organisations a number of factors need to be taken into account in deciding the system they intend to use:

- the system needs to ensure that the landlord is able to recover enough money from its tenants to meet its costs of providing and managing its homes;
- the system needs to be easily understood by tenants and staff;
- the system needs to generate affordable rents;
- the system needs to be seen as fair and equitable;
- the system needs to comply with the law and guidance from regulatory authorities (such as the Housing Corporation).

Law and rent setting

Following changes to government policy first flagged in the Green Paper *Quality and Choice for All* all social landlords in England are now required to restructure their rent setting procedures to achieve convergence in their approaches over the ten-year period to March 2012. This is a major change to the way in which rents are calculated and will be explored later in this section. This change does not apply elsewhere in the United Kingdom, where landlords have more freedom to set rents. It is important therefore to have an understanding of the variety of rent setting processes used by landlords.

Types of rent setting systems

This section outlines the types of rent setting systems which landlords have used in the past (but as noted above these are now being superseded, in England only, by the requirements of rent restructuring).

All landlords raise income from rents to meet their costs of providing the dwelling, managing that dwelling, and carrying out repairs and maintenance. However, if a landlord owns a number of dwellings they need to establish a system for deciding what rents to charge for what properties. For example, if a landlord owns 1,000 homes and needs to create an income of £45,000 each week to cover costs, they need to work out what rent to charge on each property. Of course, the landlord could simply charge all properties the same rent (£45 pw in this example) but this may not be seen as reasonable if someone living in a bedsit in a tower block ends up paying exactly the same rent as someone living in a brand new four bedroom house on a new estate.

Cost rents

Perhaps the simplest approach is for a landlord to charge what it costs to provide the individual dwelling. At its simplest, this will involve the landlord calculating what is pays out for each property in terms of:

- loan repayments;
- management and maintenance costs;
- provisions for voids and bad debts.

They then would charge a sufficient rent to cover all of these costs. Although this appears a straightforward system it does lead to a number of problems, not least that for many landlords it may be difficult to calculate exactly what an individual property has cost. It would also lead to a number of anomalies such as rents being reduced when loans were eventually paid off and properties built at times of lower interest rates having a lower rent than those built when interest rates were higher. Properties which face higher maintenance costs (such as system built) properties would have higher repair costs and so higher rents. It would also mean that similar properties in the same area built few years apart might have very different rents because of interest rate changes and this would very difficult for landlords to explain to their tenants.

In the early days of local authority housing this cost rent system was used by councils to set their rents but they soon found that the disadvantages of the system outweighed its benefits. They began to *pool* all of their costs to seek to recover the costs from all of their tenants in a different way, not linked to the costs involved in providing individual properties. However, cost rents are still quite common in the housing association sector, particularly for developments that have been funded since the 1988 Housing Act with the help of a private mortgage. With these developments the association will know what it has cost to provide the properties and will seek to recover the costs on a scheme by scheme basis.

If rents are not linked to the costs of providing an individual property then it is necessary to devise a system for charging rents on individual properties and four main systems have traditionally been used.

Values based rents

Many landlords have used the value of their stock as the basis of charging rents with properties of greater values paying higher rents. Two main variants on this theme have been adopted:

- Gross values
- Capital values

i. Gross values

Landlords may undertake stock valuations on the basis of the rental income a property might generate if the landlord was responsible for the cost of repairs, insurance and maintenance and was influenced by factors such as the size of a property, its age, location and state of repair. The landlord simply adds up all the gross values of its properties and then works out the proportion of the total rent to be collected which each individual property should pay on the basis of its individual valuation using the formula:

$$\text{Rent paid for an individual property} = \frac{\text{Gross value of property}}{\text{Total gross values of stock}} \times \text{Total rent required}$$

Figure 5.6: Example of rent setting using gross values

A local authority needs to collect £18,000,000 from its 10,000 homes.

The gross value of its homes amounts to £3,500,000 as assessed by the landlord's valuer. An individual property has a gross value of £450 and its rent is calculated using the formula:

$$= \frac{\text{Gross value of property}}{\text{Total gross values of stock}} \times \text{Total rent required}$$

$$= \frac{450}{3,500,000} \times 18,000,000$$

$$= \text{£2,313 pa}$$

$$= \text{£44.48 pw}$$

The key benefit of this system is that all properties are given a gross rateable value which reflects size, amenities, location and state of repair and as such would be easily understood by tenants. However, valuation is an inexact science, and although location and size are important factors in valuations this does tend to lead to tenants who happen to live in more desirable areas paying significantly higher rents. But perhaps the biggest problem with using the gross valuation system is that values quickly became out of date and updating valuations is expensive.

ii. Capital values

A similar system to the gross valuation one is to use capital values. This is where every property is given a capital valuation as if it were to be sold and the rent is related to this. In this system the tenants of a property worth £80,000 would pay twice as much rent as a property with a value of £40,000. This method obviously requires all properties to be valued and given a capital value and this is then used to calculate the rent payable on an individual property using a similar formula:

$$\text{Rent paid for an individual property} = \frac{\text{Value of property}}{\text{Total valuation of stock}} \times \text{Total rent required}$$

A main advantage of the capital value system is that valuations will normally be done by an independent valuer and most people can understand the basis on which the rent is calculated, particularly as values will reflect property attributes such as size, location and state of repair. But obtaining valuations may be costly as landlords will often need to commission a surveyor to carry them out and they need to be updated on a regular basis. A further problem is that again the system leads to larger properties in more desirable areas attracting higher capital values and therefore rents. This may penalise those tenants who live in those areas or property types. Indeed it may make large properties or properties in desirable areas unaffordable to people on low incomes and this will have implications for a landlord's policies on both affordability and equal opportunities.

Points based rents

A number of landlords have set up a points system where properties are given points for individual attributes. Factors which may be relevant include:

- number of bedrooms;
- purpose built or modernised;
- flat, house or bungalow;
- heating systems;
- garden;
- amenities;
- location;
- age of property;
- condition.

Once a list of attributes is produced it is then necessary to assign points to each of these attributes to generate an overall points score for a property. Again the system involves the landlord totalling up all of the points in its stock and using the formula to decide individual rents as follows:

$$\text{Rent paid for an individual property} = \frac{\text{Points score for property}}{\text{Total points of stock}} \times \text{Total rent required}$$

Using a points system enables differences in stock characteristics to be reflected in different points awards, the system does not require experts from outside the organisation to value the stock, and much of the work on identifying stock characteristics can be done in-house. It also enables those characteristics which should lead to lower rents being reflected through the scores (for example properties in less desirable areas could be given a negative points score for the location characteristic). The system is a flexible one and can be adjusted over time, both in terms of amending the property attributes and the points attached to each one. But if too many attributes are used the system can be complicated to operate and the weighting attached to individual characteristics is inevitably a subjective decision. Each property needs to be assessed to decide the points score to be awarded and of course the points score may not reflect the actual costs or value of a property

Formula based rents

A variation on the points system is a formula system. Here an average rent is determined by dividing the rent to be collected by the number of properties. This average rent is then adjusted by percentages depending on the characteristics of a property. For example if the average rent of a landlord owning 10,000 properties and collecting £25,000,000 a year is £48.08 pw then the formula system can be used in the following way to determine the rent of a three bedroom house:

Figure: 5.7: Example of rent setting using a formula

For example the formula for a three bedroom house might mean that the average rent had to be adjusted by these percentages:

3 bedroom house	+2.00%
Downstairs WC	+0.25%
No garden	-0.05%
Full central heating	+0.75%
Refurbished property	-1.00%
No car parking	-0.05%
Unpopular location	-1.00%
Total change required	**+0.90%**

Average rent £48.08 + (0.09% x £48.08) = £48.51 per week

Rent restructuring in England

As was seen in chapter three the government in England has introduced rent restructuring in England for all local housing authorities and housing associations. Rents will be restructured over a ten year period from 2002-2012 so that they converge, so that similar properties in the same area will have very similar rents regardless of ownership or how the home was financed.

Under rent restructuring, rents are set according to a formula which looks at:

- size, condition and location;
- local earnings;
- property size.

The rent level by 2012 will have two elements: 30 per cent of rent will be based on relative property values and 70 per cent of rent will be based on relative local earnings. A bedroom factor is also applied so that smaller units have lower rents. This is expressed as a formula where weekly rent is:

70 per cent of average rent for the housing association sector
    multiplied by relative county earnings
    multiplied by bedroom weighting

plus

30 per cent of the average rent for the sector
    multiplied by relative property value

This will set the target rent for an individual unit which will increase by RPI + 0.5 per cent each year. (Service charges should only increase by RPI). Property values will be based on 'existing use value' (i.e. the sale price on the open market). The base year used will be values at January 1999.

This new regime was introduced for both local authorities and housing associations in 2002/03. For some landlords in the higher value areas of London and the south east this has led to potentially large rent increases. To mitigate this, the government capped rent rises to a maximum of £2 pw on top of the RPI + 0.5 per cent increase. Similarly in other areas target rents were lower than those being charged and reductions were also capped at £2 pw.

Housing association rents

Although English housing associations are now within the rent restructuring framework they do have some rents which are outside this regime. Housing associations have two main types of tenancies; secure tenancies and assured tenancies. Tenants of housing associations whose tenancies commenced before 15 January 1989 will normally have secure tenancies as defined by the Housing Act 1985. These tenancies are almost identical to those enjoyed by local authority tenants, except in relation to rent setting. After 15 January 1989 all new housing tenancies have been assured tenancies under the 1988 Housing Act. Assured tenancies have fewer statutory rights (for example they do not have the Right to Buy). Rent restructuring applies to the majority of tenants because they are assured tenants, but not to the declining minority of secure tenants.

Secure tenancies and rents

Housing association secure tenancies have their rents set not by the housing association but by the rent officer. The rent officer is an independent government officer who is charged with determining, amongst other things, a fair rent for housing association secure tenants. Fair rents are reviewed every two years and in determining fair rents the rent officer has to set a rent which reflects the 'age, character, location and state of repair of the property', with the aim of setting a rent which is fair to both the landlord and the tenant. In coming to a decision on the level of rent to set the rent officer is not allowed to take into account the personal circumstances of tenant or landlord. As rents are not set by the housing association the landlord here has no direct say over the rents which are charged for secure tenants, although landlords have to suggest what they feel the rent should be in their application to the rent officer to set the rent.

Assured tenancies

Since 1989 all new housing association lettings (both re-lets of previously secure tenancies or brand new lettings) have been let under assured tenancies and these properties are no longer subject to fair rents. Housing associations in the past were free to determine their own rents. In some housing association tenancies a formula may be stipulated (for example that rents are increased annually by the increase in the retail prices index for the previous 12 months). If the tenancy agreement does not specify the formula by which rents will be increased then the landlord is able to set a new rent each year (but within the guidance set under the rent restructuring policy in England). This must allow the tenant to have the right to refer the proposed increase to the Rent Assessment Committee for the determination of a market rent. A Rent Assessment Committee composed of property professionals will then independently decide what a *market* rent should be for this type of property. Of course, most housing associations rents are below the average market rent in an area and if housing association tenants refer their rents to the Rent Assessment Committee for a determination they may find that their rent is increased further than that originally proposed by the housing association. In determining their assured rents housing associations have to pay attention to the Regulatory Code published by the Housing Corporation. The Code says that:

> *Housing associations must set rents which move towards target social rents and are on average below those in the private sector for similar properties and which reflect size, property value and local earnings.*

The Code of guidance goes on to advise that:

> *Rents are set in accordance with the rent restructuring formula. All residents have information about their landlord's rent policy and rent levels across the association's stock and in the relevant local authority area. All residents have information about their service charges including costs that their charges cover, how charges are budgeted and increases calculated.*

The guidance prior to rent restructuring advised that associations should ensure that the rents they charged for assured tenancies are affordable for people in low paid employment, and not to discriminate in their rents between people on housing benefit and those who are not in receipt of benefit. The revised guidance no longer refers to this requirement as the rent restructuring formula effectively determines the rent which is to be set.

Collecting the rent

For both local authorities and housing associations, rents are by far the most important source of revenue. (The importance of rents for the financing of social housing organisations is examined in more detail in chapter three). Unless landlords collect the rent due to them then they are not able to fund their repairs service, service their mortgage loans or pay for their housing management staff.

The amount of rent which social housing landlords collect is an important indicator of their financial health, and is monitored closely by government in relation to local authorities. Similarly in the housing association sector, rent collection and the level of arrears is monitored closely by the Housing Corporation (or its equivalents in Scotland, Wales and Northern Ireland). Social housing landlords are required to tell their tenants in their annual report how much rent they have collected each year and there are a range of performance indicators collected nationally for arrears and rent collection.

Boards of housing associations and local authority members will also wish to see regular reports from their officers about how well the organisation is doing in these areas. Auditors of local authorities and housing associations will also comment on the amount of rent which their clients collect, and particularly in the housing association sector, banks and building societies who have lent money to housing associations will want to receive regular reports on rent collection rates. This is because a housing association which is struggling to collect its rents may find itself in difficulty in relation to the payment of mortgages.

Within the housing association sector the Housing Act of 1988 allowed private finance for housing associations' new development. Grant funding to associations (through what was then Housing Association Grant) was reduced significantly and housing associations were encouraged to borrow money from banks and building societies to pay for their new housing development. This has meant that most new housing association developments now carry substantial mortgages which must be repaid each year from rental income. Any shortfall in rental income may make it more difficult for the housing association to meet the loan repayments on their mortgages and because of this housing association committees (and their regulators) now pay much closer attention to levels of rent arrears than was previously the case.

The extent of rent arrears

The level of rent arrears has always been of concern to government and other agencies involved in the regulation of local authorities and housing associations.

Any but the most limited and temporary arrears are damaging to the interests to all concerned; to the tenants involved, who have to manage a mounting of debt; to the landlord authorities which are deprived of resources in their housing revenue account; to the other tenants who thereby suffer higher rents or inferior service; and to ratepayers who in many cases have to bear the cost attached to meeting a larger deficit on the housing revenue accounts. This inefficiency in the use of resources also damages the case for allocation of resources to local authorities for housing (DOE Circular 18/87).

Over the last twenty years there have been a number of influential reports on the extent of rent arrears. These include those in Figure 5.8.

Figure 5.8: Reports on rent arrears

Audit Commission 1984 – Bringing council tenant arrears under control
This report looked at rent arrears in London, the English metropolitan district councils and twenty eight of the largest shire districts where the arrears problem was thought to be the worst. This report highlighted the extent of the problem of rent arrears and made a number of recommendations to local authorities as to how they should combat the increase in rent arrears which the report identified.

Audit Commission 1986 – Managing the crisis in council housing
This report indicated that many local authorities had taken on board the recommendations of the earlier report but that in a minority of councils rent arrears were still increasing.

Audit Commission 1989 – Survey of local authority rent arrears
This report showed an increase in rent arrears in 1988/89 with the main reason for the increase in arrears being the housing benefit changes introduced in 1988. These changes had led to a reduction in housing benefit payable to some households together with changes in the rates at which benefit was withdrawn as incomes rose (the so called tapers).

Department of the Environment – Rent arrears in local authorities and housing associations in England (Gray *et al.*, 1994).
This major piece of research on rent arrears showed that arrears had increased from 1982/83 to 1991/92 from £161 milliion to £458 milliion. Arrears expressed as a percentage of the debit (the annual amount of rent collectable) rose from 4.8 per cent to 8 per cent of the debit.

Accounts Commission 2000 – Managing rent arrears – getting the balance right
This report looked at the performance of councils and associations in Scotland and made a series of good practice recommendations. It set arrears targets of 3 per cent in semi urban and rural areas and 7 per cent for city and urban areas.

→

Audit Commission/Housing Corporation 2003 – Rent collection and arrears management by housing associations in England
This report examined a range of data sources on the issue of rent collection and arrears management, together with in-depth studies of twelve housing associations. This research identified that average rent arrears for housing associations in England rose from 4.7 per cent to 6.8 per cent of the debit between 1996/7 and 1999/2000. In addition the report showed that in 2001/2 current housing association tenants owed £231 million, an increase of 10 per cent on the previous year.

Audit Commission 2003 – Local authority housing rent income
This report looked at the increase in local authority current rent arrears from £335 million in 1997 to £403 million in 2002, with former tenant arrears increasing by 42 per cent from £172 million to £244 million.

Table 5.3: Key rent arrears statistics (local authorities) as at March 2002 (England and Wales)

Current tenants' arrears	£403 million
Average arrears owned by each tenant	£348
% of tenants owing 13+weeks	30%
Arrears as a % of rent roll	2.8%
Former tenants' arrears	£432 million
Former tenants' arrears as a % of rent roll	3.0%
Rent collection rate	97%

Source: Adapted from Audit Commission, 2003b

The Audit Commission report makes it clear that rent collection performance also varies significantly between local authority types ands regions. London councils had the lowest collection rates whilst those in the east of England were the best. Comparative statistics for gross arrears show the following picture over time in Tables 5.4 and 5.5.

Table 5.4: Gross rent arrears statistics (local authorities in England)

1982/83	4.8%	£161 million
1991/92	8.0%	£458 million
2001/02	5.8%	£770 million

Source: Adapted from Audit Commission, 2003b

Table 5.5: Key rent arrears statistics – housing associations, 2003 England

Rent arrears at 31 March 2002	5.61%
Arrears	£233 million
Arrears due to HB delays	1.52%

Source: Housing Corporation, 2003

In Scotland the Accounts Commission (similar to the Audit Commission) sets out details of Scottish councils' performance in arrears (Performance indicators 2002/03; Housing and Social Work).

Table 5.5: Scottish rent arrears quarter 31 March 2003

Current arrears	£28.5 million
% of rent roll	7.4%
Tenants with >£250 arrears	4.8%

Source: Accounts Commission, 2004

Performance ranged from 2.5 per cent arrears in Perth and Kinross to 18.2 per cent in West Dunbartonshire.

Collection methods

A number of methods are used by social landlords to collect the rent owed by tenants. Research published by the Audit Commission in 2003 looked at the different ways in which associations collected their rents and this showed some significant differences between landlords. All of the landlords included within the study used standing orders from those tenants with a regular income. 58 per cent of landlords allowed payment by direct debit. 75 per cent of landlords took cash or cheques at the housing office or through a bank. The same proportion had arrangements whereby tenants could make rent payments at the post office, and an increasing number were adopting swipe card systems through which rent can be paid using the 'Allpay' or 'Pay point' facilities in shops and other locations. Only 16 per cent of landlords would accept payment by credit card.

Table 5.6: Summary of rent payment methods used by local authority and housing association tenants %

	Local authority	Housing associations
Door to door	24	5
Office	44	15
PO Giro/Voucher	24	18
Bank/Giro/Standing Order/Direct Debit	8	27
HB Direct	n/a	24
Other	2	11

Source: Centre for Housing Policy, York ,1993

The Audit Commission also noted a trend away from generic working towards the use of specialist officers to deal with rent arrears, particularly amongst larger associations. At the same time a Housing Corporation survey in 2000 identified that one-third of associations that have adopted a specialist approach report a steady decrease in arrears.

i. Door to door collection

A number of research studies in the past have shown that door to door collection was the most common way in which rent was paid. The rent collector often carried out other roles in addition to receiving rent payments; such as taking repair requests or receiving transfer application forms. Door to door collection is usually associated with lower levels of rent arrears. This is because the collector calls on a regular (usually weekly or fortnightly) basis and it is more difficult for tenants to miss a rent payment. In addition, if a payment was missed it would be picked up very quickly and the arrears recovery staff could begin to take appropriate action to recover the missing payment. In recent years the popularity of door to door collection has declined for a number of reasons. Door to door collection is labour intensive and as more and more landlords have had to review the cost of their service it has often been door to door collection which has been cut. As an increasing number of tenants have been in receipt of full housing benefit the number of tenants paying rent themselves out of their own income has declined which has meant that the amount of rent to be collected by a door to door service has fallen. And of course one of the most significant reasons for the decline in popularity of door to door collection has been the threat of robbery and assaults on door to door collectors.

Door to door collection is most cost effective on estates where there are a large number of tenants from whom to collect the rent. This may well explain the significant difference in door to door collection rates between local authorities and housing associations. Housing association properties on the whole are scattered and there are very few housing association estates with a large number of properties.

ii. Office collection

The Audit Commission research found that most landlords used some form of housing office collection. This may be the main office of the landlord or in some cases will be a decentralised local housing office. In most of these offices the landlord may well have installed secure cash receiving facilities where tenants can pay their rent, usually through a computerised till which issues the tenant with a receipt for the rent paid and automatically updates the tenant's computerised rent account. For landlords there are significant benefits in having office rent collection. It can be more cost effective to have a cashier based in the office than rent collectors out on their patch doing rounds, cash tills can be made more secure and the use of computerised tills means that tenant's accounts can be updated immediately. For the tenant coming in to the office to pay their rent they will usually have the opportunity to raise other tenancy matters with the staff in the office. However, the main problem with office collection in terms of arrears levels is that payment of rent is at the discretion of the tenant. There is no door to door collector knocking on the door requesting that the rent be paid. This means that tenants may find it easier to miss a rent payment and the research evidence suggests that levels of rent arrears are higher with office collection than they are with door to door. If landlords use an office collection system it is essential that the arrears recovery procedure can quickly identify a missed payment so that appropriate action to recover the missing payment can be instigated.

There tends to be a lower level of office collection for housing association tenants as compared to their local authority counterparts. This may be explained by the fact that housing association tenancies may be spread over a large area. Many housing associations will only have one office and this may not be accessible by a majority of the association tenants. In these circumstances housing associations need to offer alternative methods of rent payment to their tenants.

iii. Post office Giro and voucher payment

A significant number of tenants pay their rent through the post office where the post office staff will issue a receipt for the rent paid and send the rent and data collected to the landlord. In other cases tenants may be able to pay their rent through the post office Giro system, where rents are processed by the post office Girobank and payments credited to the landlord's account. The Audit Commission research shows 75 per cent of housing associations taking rent payments through this system. Again the evidence suggests that payments by these methods is associated with higher levels of arrears and this can largely be explained by the fact that there is no external pressure on the tenant to pay the rent and it takes longer for missing payments to be identified. In recent years swipe cards have replaced the Giro paying in slip and other methods such as Allpay or Paypoint cards have been introduced.

For example, Oxford Citizens HA changed from Giro payments to a plastic swipe card with Allpay.net. Using the card tenants can pay their rent at post offices and PayPoint outlets and the payment details are transmitted to the association from Allpay. This electronic transmission has saved staff from having to manually enter payment details into the rent system and it is estimated that they have saved two person days a week as a result (CIH, 2001a).

iv. Bank payment systems

Tenants can also pay their rents through a bank standing order or direct debit, transferring money from their own bank account into a landlord's account. In addition some landlords have issued tenants with bank Giro books where tenants can use these paying-in books to pay their rent into a bank nominated by the landlord. Research has shown this type of system to be more popular within the housing association sector than with local authority tenants. In some landlords on line payments are now being introduced to enable tenants to make payments direct from their own accounts.

v. Rent direct

A majority of social housing tenants are now in receipt of housing benefit to assist them with their rent payments. For local authority tenants the housing benefit is rebated from their rent (in other words it is deducted at source by their landlord). For housing association tenants a rent allowance is paid to the tenant to assist them with meeting their rent payments and these tenants can opt to have their housing benefit payments transferred directly to their housing association landlord. Most housing associations will prefer their tenants who are in receipt of housing benefit to opt for their benefit to be paid directly to their landlord. This means that the landlord can be certain of receiving housing benefit which is due to the tenant. However, unless the tenant is in serious arrears, such arrangements cannot be made compulsory.

The link between collection methods and rent arrears

Over the last 20 years there has been a great deal of research into the causes of rent arrears. Key themes arising from the research include those shown in Figure 5.9.

Figure 5.9: Factors showing a significant association with higher levels of rent arrears

- Young households (below 60 years old).
- Existence of multiple debts.
- Living in an area of above average social/economic deprivation.
- Living in London.
- Dependent children.
- Receipt of housing benefit.
- Experience of problems related to housing benefit.
- Payment at a post office.
- High rents.
- Experiencing a change in household circumstances in relation to more dependent children or a reduction in household earners.
- Unemployment and ill health.

The Survey of English Housing 2001 reviewed the reasons why social tenants had said they got into arrears. These are outlined in Table 5.7.

Table 5.7: Reasons why tenants said they were in arrears

	Problems with housing benefit	Debts	Unemployment	Other job related problems	Domestic related reasons	Illness problems	Increase in rent	Other reasons
Council tenant	38	26	23	14	13	15	3	15
HA tenant	38	20	27	14	7	16	6	16

Note: % do not add up to 100 because some people gave more than one reason
Source: Office of National Statistics, 2002

The Survey showed that social housing tenants have low incomes and the majority of tenants are now in receipt of some form of Social Security benefits. Around 60 per cent of all tenants now receive housing benefit to assist them with their rent obligations. Tenants in serious arrears tend to have larger households and thus lower disposable incomes. If income falls because of illness, unemployment, relationship breakdown or the birth of a baby it is likely to lead to higher levels of rent arrears.

The Audit Commission review of local authority arrears in 2003 said that:

> *Council tenants are now more likely to be on low incomes, dependent on benefits and more vulnerable than previously. Only 31% of council tenants were in paid work (full or part time) in 2000-01, compared with around 50% 20 years ago.*

Refusal to pay

The 2003 study identified a small core of tenants with little intention of paying, particularly younger single tenants unconcerned about losing a tenancy, particularly in areas of low demand where other landlords appear prepared to offer them a new home. The study also identified a small minority of tenants withholding the rent on principle, for example where they feel they have had a poor service from the landlord or perceive the rent as being too high. A minority were also identified as 'playing' the system, prioritising other expenditure and paying enough to prevent eviction action at key points in the landlord's rent arrears recovery process.

Prevention of rent arrears

Social housing organisations need to give as much attention as possible to the prevention of rent arrears in the first place and there are a number of steps which social housing landlords can take to stop tenants getting in to rent arrears.

At the commencement of a tenancy it is essential that tenants are given proper advice and counselling about all aspects of their tenancy. Housing staff should ensure that tenants claim any housing benefit which is due to them as well as giving them advice and assistance with claiming other welfare benefits. A number of research studies have shown that tenants who have rent arrears also have other debts and it is essential that tenants' income is maximised. In a number of housing organisations specialist officers have been employed to assist tenants in maximising their claims for the benefits which are available.

As part of this pre-tenancy counselling it is essential also that housing officers stress to tenants the need to maintain regular rent payments and to advise tenants as to what action the landlord will take if the tenant falls into arrears. This is to generate a *payment culture*. From the organisational perspective it is also important that landlords ensure that sufficient staff are available to deal with their rent arrears. In some cases this may mean establishing a separate 'arrears team', but where arrears' work is decentralised to more generic (all purpose) housing officers it is important that the numbers of properties which they manage is small enough for them to effectively control rent arrears in their patch.

When arrears develop it is essential that these are spotted quickly by housing staff and attention should be given to the information technology which is available to enable arrears action to be started as soon as possible.

Tackling rent arrears

Rent arrears policy and procedure

If staff are to effectively tackle rent arrears it is essential that the organisation has thought about and written down the policy and procedure it wishes to adopt for rent arrears. These procedures should reflect the good practice which a number of organisations have developed over recent years.

i. Early action

It is important when a rent payment is missed that the tenant is contacted by the organisation to remind them of the missing payment. As soon as the payment is missed it is advisable to contact the tenant and certainly within two weeks of a missing payment a letter or a personal visit should have been actioned by the landlord. Clearly an important issue here is for the housing organisation to have an information technology system available which can identify missing payments promptly.

Home Housing Association has undertaken *payment tracking* as part of a corporate review of key business processes, to identify the value of different elements of rent collection and arrears work their staff undertake. They identified some confusion over post office payments and have prioritised the improvement of rent receipts so that tenants have more accurate information on the precise amount of rent due and understand that late payments will result in their accounts showing arrears. Home HA also identified that properly submitted, completed HB forms with all appropriate supporting documentation resulted in an average time for HB to be posted to the rent account of 16 days. For those forms not properly completed the average rose to 83 days. As a result of this knowledge resources were focused more on 'front end' welfare benefit support to help tenants get their claim right first time and to prevent arrears accruing whilst the claim is being processed (Audit Commission, 2003a).

ii. Personal contact

If there has been no response to an arrears reminder letter then it is advisable that personal contact is made by a housing officer to ascertain the reasons for the non payment of rent and to offer the tenant any assistance which may be required to reduce the rent arrears. In some cases this might mean helping complete a housing benefit claim or in other cases negotiating a suitable arrangement to reduce the arrears by instalments. It must be remembered that tenants in rent arrears may also have other debts and that they may not respond to a letter sent to them. In these circumstances a personal visit is likely to lead to greater chances of success.

iii. Legal action

However, if letters and visits fail to achieve a reduction in arrears then the landlord will need to take legal action in the courts to recover the debt. For local authority and housing association tenants the first step is usually to serve a Notice of Intention to Seek Possession. This is a legal document which advises the tenant that if they fail to repay the arrears the landlord may take the matter to court to seek a Possession Order on the property.

iv. Arrangements

When negotiating arrangements to repay arrears by instalments it is essential that these arrangements are satisfactory for both the landlord and the tenant. It might be possible for the landlord to arrange to reduce the arrears through the payment of housing benefit direct to the landlord or by the arrears direct method, through which deductions for arrears are made from income support and paid direct to the landlord.

v. Incentives

A number of social landlords have introduced incentive schemes which reward the tenants for prompt payment and encourage a culture of responsibility. One of the leading schemes is the Irwell Valley Housing Association 'Gold Service'. This rewards tenants who have a clear rent account for six weeks, or those in arrears who have made an agreement to clear and maintained it for twelve weeks. Benefits include 'bonus bonds' worth £1 per week accepted at 20,000 retail outlets, negotiated discounts with a range of businesses and improved housing services such as a more responsive repairs service (ODPM, 2003b).

vi. Other measures

As an alternative to seeking possession of the properties through the courts it may possible for landlords to investigate other measures by which they might recover the debt. This could include making claims in the small claims court or if tenants are working seeking an attachment of earnings order, where the court can order an employer to make deductions from earnings and pay the money direct to the landlord.

vii. Former tenants' arrears

A significant part of the total debt owing to housing associations and local authorities is not owed by current tenants but are arrears of rent owed by former tenants. The CIH suggest that less than 10 per cent of former tenant arrears is recovered (CIH, 2001).

In many cases the landlord will not know the whereabouts of the former tenant and it may be very difficult to recover the arrears in these circumstances. However, when the landlord does know the whereabouts of the former tenant then it needs to seek to recover the debt from them. Clearly as the former tenant is no longer occupying a property owned by the landlord then the sanction of repossession is no longer available. In order to recover former tenants' debts, the landlord has to use all of the remedies available in the civil courts for the repayment of debt. The landlord should consider whether it may be more cost effective to sell the debt to a debt collection agency, write it off or attempt to pursue the debt in-house. In practice, most landlords will seek to recover the debt using their own staff and only if this has failed will it be passed onto an outside agency and then written off.

Figure 5.10: Key good practice points

Prevention of rent arrears
- Pre-tenancy counselling on the total financial obligations of taking up a tenancy.
- Maximising of individual tenant's income through appropriate advice.
- Creation of a payment culture with tenants being made fully aware of the landlord's policies on rent collection and that eviction is the ultimate consequence of non payment.
- Supporting tenants to submit properly completed HB forms promptly, where this is necessary.
- Developing a management organisation with suitable information technology support to enable a rapid response to emerging problems of arrears.
- Providing tenants with up to date information on their rent account, including differentiation between arrears due from the tenant and those due to payment of HB in arrears.

Management of rent arrears cases
- The development of a management information system which gives clear and unambiguous records of the state of a tenant's rent account to enable the landlord to take early action.
- Notification within two weeks of missing payments.
- Negotiation of a workable repayment arrangement with the tenant.
- Avoid taking court action where arrears are due to HB delays (Although such action might be appropriate in cases where partial HB is paid and the tenant's contribution is not being paid).
- Eviction should remain as a final sanction against a persistent minority of non payers.
- Landlords should pursue former tenants for arrears where there is a realistic prospect of recovery. Specialist teams working on former tenant arrears are recommended.
- Consider introducing incentive schemes that reward tenants with clear rent accounts and those who maintain repayment agreements.
- Establishing a specialist arrears team where the arrears situation of the organisation is serious.
- The consideration of alternative recovery methods such as through the small claims court, rent direct or the attachment of earnings.

The 2003 Audit Commission report advised that local authorities should respond to arrears at both the strategic and operational level. These responses included:

Strategic responses
- Creating a clear corporate approach and commitment to tackling arrears.
- Establishing effective management arrangements with clear and challenging targets for staff, coupled with good management information systems.
- Ensuring a tenant focus with flexible payment options.

Operational responses

- Placing an emphasis on prevention.
- Working closely with housing benefit teams.
- Developing effective recovery polices and procedures.
- Maintaining a focus on former tenants who owe arrears and pursuing them more effectively.

Rent arrears are a key issue for all social housing landlords and with the increasing poverty of council and housing association tenants it is likely that the recovery of rent arrears is going to be an increasingly difficult task for housing managers. In this context it is essential that housing managers implement fair and effective recovery procedures.

6. Managing empty properties

Introduction

Letting properties is not simply about identifying applicants and then offering them the properties. It is a much longer and more complex process. All social housing landlords need to ensure that they keep the time that their properties are empty (their void periods) to a minimum. This is because every week a property is left empty there is a lost week's rent with the added danger of crime and vandalism to the empty properties.

Table 5.8: Empty properties in England at 31 March 2002

	Total empties		
	2002	%	2003
Private (including owner occupied and private rented)	605,398	3.5%	603,275
Local authority	76,637	2.9%	62,017
Housing association	37,625	3.0%	43,731
Government & other public sector	10,110	9.4%	9,637
Total	729,770		718,720

Source: Adapted from HIP 2002 and 2003 Raw data. (see www.emptyhomes.com)

Data supplied by the Office for National Statistics for 2003 is shown in Table 5.9.

Table 5.9: Vacant social housing stock England 2003

	LA	HA
Total vacant homes	62,600	44,780
As % of housing stock	2.6%	2.8%
Of which available to let	30,400	21,073
As % of stock	1.2%	1.3%

Source: Adapted from ONS, 2003a

Scottish local authority data as at 31 March 2003 is set out in the Table 5.10.

Table 5.10: Vacant stock in Scotland 2003

Total vacant homes	20,780
As % of vacant homes	4.0%
Of which available to let	8,138
As % of stock	1.6%

Source: Adapted from Housing Trends in Scotland, 2003, Scottish Executive, Edinburgh (www.scotland.gov.uk)

In Wales, the latest data is for March 2001 which is shown in Table 5.11.

Table 5.11: Empty local authority homes in Wales

Total vacant homes	21,658
As % of housing stock	11.5%
Of which available to let	14,101
As % of housing stock	6.5%

Source: Adapted from Local Government Development Unit Wales website (www.lgdu-wales.gov.uk)

One of the key ways of traditionally measuring how well a housing organisation is performing is to look at the number of empty properties. This is usually expressed as the number of voids (empty properties) as a percentage of their stock. So if a social landlord has 10,000 properties and at any one time 200 are empty then it has two per cent of its stock empty (or a void rate of two per cent).

Table 5.12: Void management and re-lets

	West housing association	East housing association
Stock	5,000	10,000
Voids at 31 March	154	100
Voids %	3.08%	1.0%
Re-lets in year	500	200
Turnover %	10.0%	2.0%

This table shows a somewhat confused picture. East housing association seems on the face of it to performing better. It has fewer actual number of empty properties at the end of March and these voids represent a much smaller percentage of its total stock. However although this is true it does not give a full picture as to the performance of each association in minimising voids.

The other piece of data which needs to be considered is the total number of dwellings becoming empty in the year which each association needs to deal with.

West association has to deal with 500 re-lets each year (10 per cent of its stock). The East association has much less work to do; it only has to deal with 200 re-lets each year, representing just two per cent of its stock. In this context the ability of West HA to keep its voids at the year end down to 154 looks much more impressive and suggests that they are able to let each property that becomes vacant quite quickly.

The one piece of information which we now need in order to demonstrate that this is indeed the case is the **average re-let interval** (or the time that each property on average is empty before being re-let) of each property that is let. In terms of performance this is the most important indicator as it shows how quickly empty properties are brought back into use. The relationship between the three variables can be expressed crudely as:

> Voids rate = Average re-let time x turnover rate

For example, assume a landlord has a stock of 120 dwellings and each year 12 become vacant (at an average of one a month). If it takes on average just over 26 weeks to let each one then at the year end it will have let 6 of the homes that become vacant in the year but will have 6 more still to be let. So it will have a voids rate of 5 per cent. Using the equation above we can demonstrate this is the case.

> Voids = 5% of the stock (i.e. 6 out of 120)
> Turnover = 10% of the stock (i.e. 12 out of 120)
> Average re-let time = 26 weeks (0.5 of the year)

Using the formula we can demonstrate that the average re-let interval will be 26 weeks if the voids rate is 5 per cent and the turnover 10 per cent:

> Average re-let interval = Voids rate/turnover
> = 0.05%/0.10%
> = 0.5 year or 26 weeks

This may seem a strange calculation at first but it becomes clearer by working back with our example of West HA. It has a turnover of 10 per cent of the stock and a voids rate of 3.08 per cent. Using the formula we can calculate that it will have an average vacancy interval of 16 weeks.

> Average re-let interval = Voids%/turnover
> = 3.08%/10%
> = 0.308 year
> = 16.06 weeks

For the East housing association there is a voids rate of 1% (0.001). The turnover is 2% (0.002) so the average vacancy interval is 26 weeks.

```
Average re-let interval   = Voids%/turnover
                          = 1%/2%
                          = 26 weeks
```

Clearly East HA is the worst performer in that it is taking significantly longer on average to re-let each empty property. But on the crude statistics we might have thought that it was performing well. Of course it is not always this simple as there may be reasons to do with poor performance to explain the high turnover rate of West HA. Nonetheless it does seem to be able to deal more quickly with more voids than its neighbouring association. We can also look at this in the context of rent loss as a result of voids. In West HA there are 154 voids a year on which it loses 16 weeks rent on each so its rent loss is 2,464 rent weeks. If the average rent is £40pw this amounts to £98,560. If it performed as badly as East HA it would take on average 26 weeks to let each void and so its rent loss would be £160,160 – a significant difference.

The Audit Commission in their influential report on housing management in 1986 argued strongly against focusing on the voids rate as a key performance indicator and they suggested that the turnover rate and the time taken to re-let each property were more significant performance indicators.

In their publication, *The Challenge of Empty Housing*, Smith and Merrett (1988) produced a matrix which enables the vacancy interval to be calculated using the void rate and the turnover. Figure 5.11 shows the void rate associated with each vacancy generation rate (turnover) and average vacancy duration.

Reasons for void properties

There are many reasons why properties are empty at any one point in time. They may be empty whilst a new tenant is being found and in some cases they may be awaiting minor repairs. In fact these two categories account for the overwhelming majority of empty properties. In other cases, properties are empty often for long periods because they are in need of major repair or refurbishment. Indeed, some may be awaiting demolition because they are no longer in a fit state to be lived in or because they are to be included in a major redevelopment scheme.

Of course, it is never the case that having nil voids is a sensible or achievable option. There will always be people moving home, transferring, or properties required to be empty for major repairs, however, what is important is that the period that they are left empty is minimised.

THE VACANCY MATRIX: WHAT IT IS AND HOW TO USE IT.*

Average vacancy duration (in weeks)

Vacancy generation rate per annum (%)	2	4	6	8	10	12	14	16	18	20	22	24	26	28	30	32	34	36	38	40	42	44	46	48	50
1	0.04	0.08	0.12	0.15	0.19	0.23	0.27	0.31	0.35	0.38	0.42	0.46	0.50	0.54	0.58	0.62	0.65	0.69	0.73	0.77	0.81	0.85	0.88	0.92	0.96
2	0.08	0.15	0.23	0.31	0.38	0.46	0.54	0.62	0.69	0.77	0.85	0.92	1.00	1.08	1.15	1.23	1.31	1.38	1.46	1.54	1.62	1.69	1.77	1.85	1.92
3	0.12	0.23	0.35	0.46	0.58	0.69	0.81	0.92	1.04	1.15	1.27	1.38	1.50	1.62	1.73	1.85	1.96	2.08	2.19	2.31	2.42	2.54	2.65	2.77	2.88
4	0.15	0.31	0.46	0.62	0.77	0.92	1.08	1.23	1.38	1.54	1.69	1.85	2.00	2.15	2.31	2.46	2.62	2.77	2.92	3.08	3.23	3.38	3.54	3.69	3.85
5	0.19	0.38	0.58	0.77	0.96	1.15	1.35	1.54	1.73	1.92	2.12	2.31	2.50	2.69	2.88	3.08	3.27	3.46	3.65	3.85	4.04	4.23	4.42	4.62	4.81
6	0.23	0.46	0.69	0.92	1.15	1.38	1.62	1.85	2.08	2.31	2.54	2.77	3.00	3.23	3.46	3.69	3.92	4.15	4.38	4.62	4.85	5.08	5.31	5.54	5.77
7	0.27	0.54	0.81	1.08	1.35	1.62	1.88	2.15	2.42	2.69	2.96	3.23	3.50	3.77	4.04	4.31	4.58	4.85	5.12	5.38	5.65	5.92	6.19	6.46	6.73
8	0.31	0.62	0.92	1.23	1.54	1.85	2.15	2.46	2.77	3.08	3.38	3.69	4.00	4.31	4.62	4.92	5.23	5.54	5.85	6.15	6.46	6.77	7.08	7.38	7.69
9	0.35	0.69	1.04	1.38	1.73	2.08	2.42	2.77	3.12	3.46	3.81	4.15	4.50	4.85	5.19	5.54	5.86	6.23	6.58	6.92	7.27	7.62	7.96	8.31	8.65
10	0.38	0.77	1.15	1.54	1.92	2.31	2.69	3.08	3.46	3.85	4.23	4.62	5.00	5.38	5.77	6.15	6.54	6.92	7.31	7.69	8.08	8.46	8.85	9.23	9.62
11	0.42	0.85	1.27	1.69	2.12	2.54	2.96	3.38	3.81	4.23	4.65	5.08	5.50	5.92	6.35	6.77	7.19	7.62	8.04	8.46	8.88	9.31	9.73	10.15	10.58
12	0.46	0.92	1.38	1.85	2.31	2.77	3.23	3.69	4.15	4.62	5.08	5.54	6.00	6.46	6.92	7.38	7.85	8.31	8.77	9.23	9.69	10.15	10.62	11.08	11.54
13	0.50	1.00	1.50	2.00	2.50	3.00	3.50	4.00	4.50	5.00	5.50	6.00	6.50	7.00	7.50	8.00	8.50	9.00	9.50	10.00	10.50	11.00	11.50	12.00	12.50
14	0.54	1.08	1.62	2.15	2.69	3.23	3.77	4.31	4.85	5.38	5.92	6.46	7.00	7.54	8.08	8.62	9.15	9.69	10.23	10.77	11.31	11.85	12.38	12.92	13.46
15	0.58	1.15	1.73	2.31	2.88	3.46	4.04	4.62	5.19	5.77	6.35	6.92	7.50	8.08	8.65	9.23	9.81	10.38	10.96	11.54	12.12	12.69	13.27	13.85	14.42
16	0.62	1.23	1.85	2.46	3.08	3.69	4.31	4.92	5.54	6.15	6.77	7.38	8.00	8.62	9.23	9.85	10.46	11.00	11.69	12.31	12.92	13.54	14.15	14.77	15.38
17	0.65	1.31	1.96	2.62	3.27	3.92	4.58	5.23	5.85	6.54	7.19	7.85	8.50	9.15	9.81	10.46	11.12	11.77	12.42	13.08	13.73	14.38	15.04	15.69	16.35
18	0.69	1.38	2.08	2.77	3.46	4.15	4.85	5.54	6.23	6.92	7.62	8.31	9.00	9.69	10.38	11.08	11.77	12.46	13.15	13.85	14.54	15.23	15.92	16.62	17.31
19	0.73	1.46	2.19	2.92	3.65	4.38	5.12	5.85	6.58	7.31	8.04	8.77	9.50	10.23	10.96	11.69	12.42	13.15	13.88	14.62	15.35	16.08	16.81	17.54	18.27
20	0.77	1.54	2.31	3.08	3.85	4.62	5.38	6.15	6.92	7.69	8.46	9.23	10.00	10.77	11.54	12.31	13.08	13.85	14.62	15.38	16.15	16.92	17.69	18.46	19.23
21	0.81	1.62	2.42	3.23	4.04	4.85	5.65	6.46	7.27	8.08	8.88	9.69	10.50	11.31	12.12	12.92	13.73	14.54	15.35	16.15	16.96	17.77	18.58	19.38	20.19
22	0.85	1.69	2.54	3.38	4.23	5.08	5.92	6.77	7.62	8.46	9.31	10.15	11.00	11.85	12.69	13.54	14.38	15.23	16.08	16.92	17.77	18.62	19.46	20.31	21.15
23	0.88	1.77	2.65	3.54	4.42	5.31	6.19	7.08	7.96	8.85	9.73	10.62	11.50	12.38	13.27	14.15	15.04	15.92	16.81	17.69	18.58	19.46	20.35	21.23	22.12
24	0.92	1.85	2.77	3.69	4.62	5.54	6.46	7.38	8.31	9.23	10.15	11.08	12.00	12.92	13.85	14.77	15.69	16.62	17.54	18.46	19.38	20.31	21.23	22.15	23.08
25	0.96	1.92	2.88	3.85	4.81	5.77	6.73	7.69	8.65	9.62	10.58	11.54	12.50	13.46	14.42	15.38	16.35	17.31	18.27	19.23	20.19	21.15	22.12	23.08	24.04

Note: * The vacancy quotient is expressed as a percentage, e.g. the figure in the second row, thirteenth column means a one per cent vacancy quotient. Similarly the vacancy generation rate indicates the number of vacancies which appear in a stock of dwellings in any given year divided by that stock and expressed as a percentage. The vacancy generation rate is written per year and the void duration in weeks for ease of comprehension.

What it is

The matrix uses three statistics: vacancy duration, vacancy generation rate and vacancy quotient.

Vacancy duration (D): the columns refer to how long dwellings are empty on average from when they first become vacant to when they cease to be vacant and it is measured is weeks.

Vacancy generation rate (G): the rows refer to the ratio between the number of dwellings becoming void in any given year (e.g. through newbuild and turnover) as a percentage of the total stock at the start at the year.

Vacancy quotient (Q): the ratio of all vacancies to the total stock at the end at the year. This is the mass of figures appearing in the main body of the table.

As a general guide Q is equal to G multiplied by D divided by 52.

How to use it

Two examples.

First, you know Q and G are respectively 5% and 10% You want to know D. Read along the row G equals 10% until you reach 5%, then read up the column to see D equals 26 weeks.

Second, you know G and D are respectively 8% and 8 weeks. So Q equals 1.23%. How will the vacancy quotient increase if transfers policy raises G to 12% but leaves D unchanged in its average value? Read along the 12% row to the 8 weeks column to see that Q will rise to 1.85%. If your total stock is 10,000 units, voids will rise as a result of the policy change from 123 up to 185.

This matrix is published by the School of Advanced Urban Studies, University of Bristol and is the creation of Stephen Merrett and Robert Smith.

Source: Smith and Merrett, 1988

Figure 5.11: Vacancy matrix

Improving the management of voids

Having empty properties can be an expensive business, both in terms of lost rent but also in terms of the costs of additional repairs if empty properties are vandalised. It is important then that all landlords have policies and procedures designed to minimise the time that properties are empty. The Audit Commission recommended that a benchmark for performance outside of London is that voids should be let within three weeks (Audit Commission, 1986a). A higher figure was suggested for London because of the difficulties of achieving the three week target in some of the most deprived parts of the country.

Identifying a void and getting four weeks notice

Most tenancy agreements specify that a tenant should give four weeks notice of their intention to end the tenancy. In most cases it is likely that the housing organisation will get much less notice. Often the first they know is when a house is broken into or when a neighbour reports that a house appears empty.

However, it makes sense to encourage tenants to give four weeks notice so that a new letting can be arranged in the meantime and any essential repairs carried out. Some organisations will make an incentive payment to any tenant who gives four weeks notice to encourage this to happen. Other organisations will also continue to charge four weeks rent as if notice had been given.

Securing voids

One of the main causes of additional expenditure with empty properties is the vandalism which is caused to empty properties. In many areas thousands of pounds worth of damage can be caused to an empty property within hours.

Figure 5.12: Properties with Sitex security screens

It is essential that steps are taken to make secure those empty properties which are vulnerable to vandalism.

Many landlords will secure void properties by using plywood boards to cover the windows and doors but these are relatively easy to remove. An alternative approach is to fix steel screens to windows and steel doors. These are much more difficult to vandalise and have been shown to be successful in a number of locations.

Some housing organisations have found it necessary to put alarm systems into empty properties, whilst others have employed security guards to protect individual properties or to patrol areas where there are voids.

Pre-inspection and arranging for minor repairs
If four weeks notice is given it is possible for a housing officer to visit the property and carry out an inspection. This will:

- identify whether the property can be re-let immediately the existing tenant moves out;
- identify whether a decoration allowance should be paid to an incoming tenant if the state if the decoration is poor (or if the property should be redecorated);
- enable essential repairs to be identified;
- ensure that any costs of repair or redecoration which are to be recharged to the current tenants are agreed.

Identifying potential applicants
If the housing manager has received notice that a tenant is about to leave they can then identify in advance a new tenant for the property. The ideal situation would be for the new tenants to take up occupation on the day that the outgoing tenant leaves. In order for this to happen the organisation needs to identify who the potential tenant is, make an offer of the accommodation to that tenant, and, if the offer is accepted, make arrangements to start a new tenancy.

Whenever a void property becomes available it is necessary to identify an applicant for it. This means that the landlord's waiting list must be accurate and up to date so that time is not wasted making offers of properties to people who may already have been housed, have moved or who do not want the type of property or the areas in which it is located. It will usually involve organisations seeking to confirm on at least an annual basis that the details held on their waiting list are indeed accurate.

Offering the property
To assist in maximising the chances of take-up it is helpful if a housing officer can accompany the prospective tenants around the property which they are being offered. This enables the housing officer to establish a personal relationship with the applicant and to allow the applicant to ask any necessary questions about the property.

Cleaning of properties and repairs

Empty properties will often need at the very least to be cleaned out before prospective tenants are shown round and most voids will need some repairs doing to them. It is usually good practice only to carry out the essential repairs required before the new tenant moves in. This will save time and therefore reduce the void period. However, although this is sensible it can sometimes mean that a prospective tenant may refuse the property because it does not appear to be in a fit state of repair. In these circumstances it may be necessary to do more than those repairs which are strictly necessary.

If only the basic repairs are to be carried out before the tenancy commences then it is essential that all of the outstanding repairs are done to the property very quickly after the new tenant moves in.

Redecoration

Most landlords will not redecorate a property when it becomes empty, although they may make an exception for the elderly. However, in some cases it may be necessary for the landlord to offer an incentive to a tenant to accept a property if the decoration is poor. This may be in the form of a cash incentive, a decoration allowance, (or a rent free period of occupation) or in other cases the landlord may provide decorating materials for the incoming tenant.

Furniture

Many tenants find it difficult to furnish their new home and this has been exacerbated by the difficulty some have to access the Social Fund, where tenants have to borrow money from the Benefits Agency to purchase furniture. In some cases tenants will accept a tenancy, move in and then very quickly give up the tenancy because they cannot afford to furnish their home. There are a number of ways in which landlords have responded to this. Some have supported the establishment of furniture projects which make available a package of second-hand furniture to new tenants, whilst others have introduced furnished tenancies where the rent will include an element for furniture. This has been particularly successful for housing young single people in some areas.

Signing up

The most important stage in a new tenancy is at the start where a new tenant signs their tenancy agreement. This should be done by the member of staff who will be managing the tenancy and is an opportunity for the terms and conditions of the new tenancy to be explained in detail and answer any questions which the new tenant might have. At this stage also housing benefit claim forms can be completed so that the tenant claims whatever benefit is due to them. Arrangements should also be made for the member of staff to visit the new tenant a few weeks after they have moved in to make sure that they are settling into their new home and are not experiencing any difficulties.

Management of voids

Voids management inevitably involves a number of staff, working in different sections of the organisation. Housing management staff will be involved in receiving the terminations of tenancies, whilst technical staff may need to inspect the void and arrange any necessary repairs. At that stage contractors may need to be brought in and their work supervised. Allocations staff will also need to begin the process of identifying a new tenant and showing them round the property.

With so many staff involved in the management of voids there is a danger that things may slip and it is essential that someone has overall responsibility for void management who can chase people when a property is standing empty longer than it should. This will mean that there needs to be accurate and timely information produced about the progress of a void so that people know at what stage each void is at.

Void policies and practices

The 1993 York study of housing management of local authorities and housing associations in England (*Managing Social Housing*) looked at the policies and procedures relating to voids management. The study showed that:

> ...*in general both local authorities and housing associations had adopted good practice guidelines in the management and control of empty dwellings* (Centre for Housing Policy, York, 1993).

Table 5.13: Void policies and practices in England

	LAs (%)	HAs (%)
Pre-allocation during notice period	69	82
Inspections before tenant leaves	41	60
Inspections after tenant leaves	97	93
Charging outgoing tenants for damage	71	56
Cleaning prior to re-letting	39	34
Additional security to voids usually required	12	10
Decoration incentives offered	96	86
Target periods for re-letting voids	75	65

Source: Centre for Housing Policy, York, 1993; adapted from Table 10.1

Although the implementation of good practice guidelines is important in improving voids performance the survey found that there was also a strong link between an organisation's voids performance and the relative level of deprivation in each area. Using a z score (which is a measure of relative social deprivation) the survey found a correlation between those organisations with a low voids rate and a low z score. Organisations with a higher z score (and therefore higher levels of social deprivation) tended to have higher voids rates.

7. Repairing the stock

Introduction

Repairs and maintenance are key issues for housing managers. For almost all housing organisations repairs to their stock represents a very significant element of their revenue expenditure. For tenants the repairs service has been shown in numerous studies to be the most important service that they receive from their landlord and outside of paying the rent it is the service with which tenants have most contact.

As we saw in chapter two, the government introduced a new Decent Homes Standard for social housing landlords in July 2000 which required that:

> *All social housing meets standards of decency by 2010, by reducing the number of households living in social housing that does not meet standards by a third between 2001 and 2004 with most of the improvements taking place in the most deprived local authority areas* (ODPM website, *A Decent Home: the revised guidance*, February 2002).

The estimated cost of undertaking comprehensive repairs to the local authority and housing association sector alone is £8.5 billion. Given this enormous backlog of repairs required to the social housing stock it is essential that housing managers spend their repairs and maintenance budgets wisely and adopt coherent strategies to deal with the significant problem of disrepair within the existing housing stock.

Table 5.14: Housing conditions, repair costs and unfitness England 2001

	Total repairs £m	Total cost to remedy unfitness £m
Owner occupied	59,483	5,247
Private rented	12,552	2,877
Local authority	6,651	638
Housing association	1,968	211

Source: Wilcox, 2003

In England 4.2 per cent of the housing stock is considered to be unfit (with 4.1 per cent of council homes and 3 per cent of housing association homes in this category). In Wales the comparable figure is 9 per cent. In Scotland 1 per cent of the stock is below the tolerable standard.

As can be seen the total costs in England of bringing the social housing stock up to a decent standard to remedy repair and unfitness is considerable. Undertaking this work is a significant challenge for social housing managers.

Organising an effective repairs and maintenance service involves housing management staff working closely with their technical colleagues and external contractors to ensure that the repairs service is of the highest quality. This section considers some of the key elements of providing a high quality maintenance service in social housing organisations.

Types of maintenance work

Repairs and maintenance work involves ensuring that the housing stock is kept in good condition. Over recent years the rate of new house building has been falling which means that the current housing stock needs to last much longer than was originally intended. To ensure that properties remain habitable it is necessary to keep them in good state of repair and also to improve them over time to ensure that they continue to provide a good standard of accommodation.

Jobbing or responsive repairs

Most repairs will be of the *jobbing* or responsive nature. These will be the small, everyday repairs that most households face and include examples such as:

- leaking taps;
- faulty electric sockets;
- damaged roof tiles;
- doors and windows which need easing;
- faulty heating systems.

Cyclical repairs

These are works which can be predicted on a fairly regular basis. A good example is the external painting of woodwork and any necessary pre-painting repairs to external joinery. Most housing organisations will have a policy of repainting the outside of their homes every four or five years and where this is done the woodwork is normally inspected and any necessary pre-painting repairs to joinery carried out. Another example would be the servicing of gas appliances, which under the Gas Safety Regulations landlords need to do every 12 months.

Planned maintenance

There is other maintenance work which, although not on a cyclical basis, needs to be carried out on a planned basis and landlords will normally schedule this work well in advance. Examples include re-roofing of properties, replacement of heating systems and replacement of windows. This type of work is usually organised in larger contracts and happens less frequently than cyclical repairs.

Major repairs/improvements

On occasions landlords will want to undertake major repairs or modernisation programmes to their properties. For example replacing electric circuits, providing new kitchens, new bathrooms and heating systems. Often these works are done when a property is not occupied and they are treated as a building contract with architects and surveyors appointed to undertake the work. These types of works are often funded by borrowing or grant and are capital rather than revenue projects. However, local authorities face restrictions in the amount of money which they can borrow to finance capital works and in some cases these works might be funded from rental income.

Some landlords carry out some significant works around the tenant. This means that the tenant does not have to be moved out (*decanted*) but this will only be possible if the works are such that the tenant can safely remain in occupation. Often kitchens and bathroom and windows, for example, can be replaced with the tenant in situ although other types of major repairs or improvements may be harder to organise in this way. With the introduction of new Health and Safety laws (the CDM regulations in 1995) such an approach to major repairs may be more difficult to organise in the future.

Why are these definitions important?

Jobbing repairs tend to be an expensive way of undertaking essential maintenance. Indeed the Audit Commission (1986b) in their influential report, *Improving Council House Maintenance* suggested that a one-off job can cost up to 50 per cent more than the same job done as part of a planned programme. This is because the works are not planned in advance, they can not be predicted and often they need to be done quickly. This usually means higher costs because the jobs are small, the contractor has to include travelling times to from jobs and the landlord cannot benefit from economies by having a contractor deal with the same problems on a number of properties.

Landlords normally deal with cyclical and planned programmes in a different way to their jobbing repairs. Because they know in advance that the work needs to be done they will normally draw up a detailed specification of the works required, go out to competitive tender to a number of contractors and achieve a cheaper price by virtue of both competition and the fact that works are usually grouped together. For example, a social landlord might arrange for all of the houses on an estate to be painted as part of the same contract. This will allow a contractor to have a team of painters on one estate for a number weeks and will almost certainly mean that a more competitive price can be agreed.

The landlord will also be able to closely supervise the work with a clerk of works or a surveyor and this is likely to mean that a better job will be done. (With responsive repairs it is unlikely that many jobs will be able to be supervised by the landlord whilst the works are underway). The roles of a surveyor and clerk of works are looked at in more detail in chapter four on developing social housing.

The law and repairs

Landlords have certain statutory obligations relating to the repairs and maintenance of their homes. These are mainly set out in the Housing Act 1985 and the Landlord and Tenant Act 1985. In addition to the statutory obligations most landlords will also have obligations for repairs and maintenance which are set down in their tenancy agreements and are contractually binding on the landlord.

i. Landlord and Tenant Act 1985 (England and Wales)
Housing (Scotland) Act 1987 (Scotland)

Under section 11 of the Landlord and Tenant Act 1985 (section 113 of the Housing (Scotland) Act 1987) all landlords are required to:

- keep in repair the structure and exterior of the dwelling (including drains, gutters, and external pipes);
- keep in repair and proper working order installations for the supply of water, gas, electricity and sanitation (including basins, sinks, baths and sanitary conveniences, but not other fixtures, fittings and appliances for making use of the supply of water, gas or electricity);
- keep in repair and proper working order the installations for space heating and heating water;
- in Scotland, provide and maintain the house in all respects reasonably fit for habitation.

For tenancies let after 15 January 1989 there is also a repairing obligation in relation to the common parts of buildings and installations such as communal heating systems.

This means that all landlords have clear repairing obligations for the structural and external elements such as doors, windows and roofs. In addition they have obligations in terms of electrical installations, water supply and sanitary equipment. However, whilst many repairs are encompassed within these statutory obligations other repairs are not. If an internal door is damaged and in need of repair this would not come within the statutory requirements. Similarly if a kitchen unit needs replacing this is not one of the statutory obligations of the landlord.

Social housing landlords often carry out far more repair work than is statutorily required and in the tenancy agreement they will usually indicate the repairs for which the tenant is responsible. Landlords will typically require tenants to be responsible for items such as:

- chimney/flue sweeping;
- door furniture;
- drain/waste blockages;
- electric fuses;

- glass(door/windows);
- internal decoration;
- plugs/chains.

ii. Defective Premises Act 1972

This Act places a duty of care on landlords (in England and Wales) in respect of any building works that they carry out. Under the Act landlords and those engaged in building works (such as contractors and consultants) have a statutory duty of care to carry out works in a professional manner, to use proper materials and to ensure that the property is left in a state fit for human habitation.

iii. Occupiers' Liability Act 1957
Occupiers' Liability (Scotland) Act 1960

This Act (in England and Wales) places a duty of care on the occupier of a dwelling in relation to all visitors to a dwelling. Although this is applicable to an occupier it can apply to a landlord insofar as they occupy part of the stock, for example in relation to lifts, communal entrances and other common parts of an estate.

A similar provision exists in Scotland under the **Occupiers' Liability (Scotland) Act 1960**, although in Scotland a landlord is given a specific duty of care to *any person* on their premises.

iv. Housing Act 1985 s 96: the Right to Repair
Housing Scotland (Scotland) Act 1987 s 96

Following criticisms, particularly of local authorities' performance in dealing with repairs, the government introduced a Right to Repair for council tenants under section 96 the 1985 Housing Act. The original scheme, which was very complex and involved the tenant being able to call in a contractor to undertake repair works where the landlord had failed to respond, was replaced with a revised scheme under the **1993 Leasehold Reform, Housing and Urban Development Act**.

Under the procedure for local authority tenants (introduced in 1995) a landlord can be instructed to issue a further repair order if the original request is not completed within a prescribed timescale. If the repair is still not completed the tenant can claim compensation of £10 plus an additional £2 for each day the repair is outstanding up to a maximum of £50.

For housing association tenants the Housing Corporation has introduced a similar scheme, although in the housing association scheme each individual association itself can determine which repairs come within the scheme and the timescales for completion. The compensation levels (£10 plus £2 a day thereafter up to a maximum of £50) are the same as the local authority scheme. In Scotland, there is a scheme which offers a £10 compensation payment if an emergency or urgent repair is not carried out within a specified period of time.

In Scotland the scheme is broadly the same as applies for English and Welsh local authorities. For Scottish housing associations there is a voluntary right to compensation for failure of the repairs scheme with a flat rate payment of £10 for each repair not carried out within a specified timescale and which jeopardises the health, safety or security of the tenant.

v. Environmental Protection Act 1990

This provides legal remedies for statutory nuisance where the premises are 'in such a state as to be prejudicial to health or a nuisance' defined as premises which are 'injurious or likely to cause injury to health'.

vi. Housing (Scotland) Act 2001

This Act now incorporates some common law duties into statute including a duty to inspect a house prior to the commencement of a tenancy to check that it is habitable, wind and watertight.

vii. Gas Safety (Installations and Use) Regulations 1998

These regulations require landlords to carry out an annual safety check of gas appliances and to ensure records of such inspections are kept and made available to tenants.

Issues in repairs and maintenance for housing managers

a. Organising the repairs function

In the past, the repair of homes was often seen as a technical issue and housing management staff may have had little to do with repairs other than pass repair requests from the tenant to a contractor. However, in recent years it has been recognised that housing managers, if they are to deliver an effective housing service, must have greater control over repairs. This involves housing management staff setting timescales for work, passing orders to contractors, monitoring performance and paying the bills.

Because many repairs are undertaken either by contractors or another department then it is necessary for the housing department to act as a client; issuing repairs orders, monitoring the performance of contractors and checking the quality of work undertaken on its behalf by contractors. Local authority housing departments increasingly have taken over this client role.

The repair reporting aspect of the repairs service is most likely to be partly or fully decentralised to local offices. This is not surprising since if there is a local office tenants are most likely to make repairs requests at that location. However, in the majority of local authorities and housing associations tasks such as pre and post inspections of repairs and the management of external repairs contracts are most likely to be fully centralised (based in a central office), reflecting the fact that these are normally handled by specialist technical staff rather than the more generic (all purpose) housing staff at local offices. (The distinction between specialist and generic staff is covered fully in the chapter six).

b. Reporting of repairs and issuing repairs receipts

Most repairs are reported by tenants over the telephone or in person. Clearly if there is a local office it is often housing management staff who receive repairs requests and it is essential that housing staff taking these repairs requests have some understanding of the technical issues involved. A number of training courses can be provided for non-technical staff. Some organisations have produced booklets for tenants about repairs which advise tenants of the technical terms that they should use to ensure that a repair is properly reported in the first place. In other cases tenants have access to a repairs manual in the office and can indicate exactly what their problem is.

Good practice also suggests that tenants should be issued with a repairs receipt which will confirm the repair requested, the date of the repair request, any appointment time and the target time for completion.

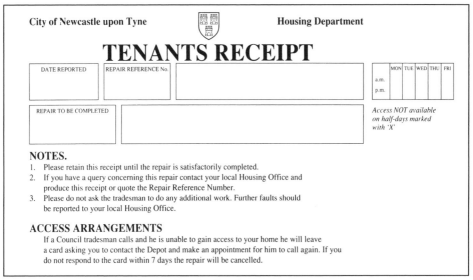

Figure 5.13: Newcastle City Council Repairs Receipt

c. Pre-inspections of repairs

For responsive repairs most landlords will receive a repair request from a tenant in person, in writing or over the telephone. If a job is straightforward, such as a leaking tap, it may be passed by the housing officer directly to the contractor. In other cases it may not be clear what the problem is and in those circumstances a technical officer may be sent to inspect the property and identify the problem.

Clearly if works are inspected before an order is placed it is more likely that clear instructions and specifications can be given to the contractor and greater control exercised over what is to be done. For example, if a tenant reports a leaking tap and the work is not pre-inspected an unscrupulous contractor may be able to go and replace the whole of the tap rather than the leaking washer.

d. Response times

Another key performance area which concerns both tenants and housing managers is the speed of response in dealing with repairs. All landlords should indicate target times for the completion of a repair from the time it was first reported and every organisation needs to establish systems to ensure that it can effectively monitor performance in meeting those response times. Many landlords have established response times such as:

Category of repair	Target
Dealing with emergencies	24 hours
Urgent repairs	5 days
Responsive repairs	28 days

Jobs which are completed outside the target time should be identified and outstanding jobs similarly recorded. Contractors who fail to perform can be penalised and eventually stopped from receiving any further work if they fail to improve their performance.

The government expects both local authorities and housing associations to report annually to tenants on their performance in meeting repairs and the Housing Corporation publishes league tables of performance in this key area.

e. Appointments for repairs

In recent years there has been an increasing trend to offer tenants appointment times for repairs to be done. In some organisations this is little more than agreeing that they will call on a particular morning or afternoon rather than a specific time. Many landlords argue that the volume of work they have makes it impossible to deal with appointments, although a number of organisations have now successfully introduced appointments systems.

f. Local repairs teams

Having a local repairs team is one of the ways in which a better repairs service can be delivered. A local team will know the estate and its problems and because they always work on the estate there is a stronger incentive to ensure that they do a good job the first time around. If they do not do so they will face criticism from tenants and will also be called back to the original job to put it right. Having a locally-based team means that they can respond more quickly to deal with problems and some costs such as travelling time can be reduced.

An alternative model is a zoned maintenance system which does not rely on an estate based team but is a system where a repairs team calls on an estate on a regular cycle and all non-urgent responsive repairs are packaged together for the team to deal with when they are next on the estate. This may well be appropriate where there are areas which do not have enough properties generating repair work to support an estate based team.

g. Post inspections

When works are not regularly inspected before an order is placed it is even more essential that landlords monitor the work that has been completed to ensure that a reasonable job has been done, that the work was carried out in a professional manner and that a reasonable price has been paid for the work. Many landlords will have a system of post-inspections where completed jobs will be inspected before an invoice is paid. This will rarely be all jobs because of the cost of inspections but often a sample of 10-15 per cent of jobs will be looked at. Many organisations will also have a policy that works with invoices over a certain level will always be post-inspected.

h. Satisfaction surveys

It is increasingly common for social landlords to assess tenants' views about the repairs service by way of a satisfaction survey. These will usually be by a pre-paid questionnaire which asks tenants a number of questions about their repair; the results of which are then collated and analysed. This might be supplemented by satisfaction surveys carried out by technical staff when carrying out post-inspections of repairs. An example of a repairs satisfaction card is given in Figure 5.14.

TEES VALLEY HOUSING ASSOCIATION

Job Number:

Your views on our Repairs Service

When the repair you have requested has been completed please would you complete the questionnaire and return it to us. You do not need a stamp

Please tick one box for each question

	Excellent	Good	Satisfactory	Poor
1. How do you rate the staff at Tees Valley who dealt with your repair request?				
2. How do you rate the time taken to complete the repair?				
3. How do you rate the quality of the completed repair work?				
4. How do you rate the courtesy of the contractor who did your repair?				

If you have any other comments please write them in the box below

Figure 5.14: Tees Valley HA repairs satisfaction card

j. Reducing levels of responsive maintenance and increasing planned maintenance programmes

The Audit Commission recommends that no more than 10 per cent of all responsive repairs should be emergency repairs and that a target spend ratio should be set of 70:30 for planned to responsive maintenance. Given that it is more expensive to undertake responsive repairs many landlords have attempted to reduce the amount of responsive or jobbing repairs they do. This has been done by:

- Attempting to increase the amount of planned work to reduce costs and to minimise the number of responsive repairs. For example, a regular programme of roof maintenance may reduce the number of tiles that need to be replaced as one-off jobs.
- Grouping non-urgent repairs until a number of jobs have been collected to enable some economies to be gained. A contractor may be able to deal with a number of jobs in the same estate in the same day thus reducing the travelling times.
- Negotiating schedules of rates. These fix in advance the price for a particular job as long as an agreed volume of work is provided.

k. Stock condition surveys

One of the key approaches to reducing the amount of jobbing repairs has been to increase the size of planned maintenance programmes. The first step in developing a planned programme is to identify clearly what needs to be done and what the priorities are.

Many housing organisations have now undertaken stock condition surveys in an attempt to quantify more precisely the amount and type of maintenance work that needs to be done. These surveys will usually be on a sample basis taking a small proportion of the stock and carrying out a detailed survey of its condition. This is then used to build up a profile of the condition of the stock now, the remedial works needed immediately and a list of future maintenance works required. The data collected from the sample can then be aggregated to produce a profile for all of the organisation's stock.

Organisations may use their own staff to carry out a stock condition survey or may use external surveyors to undertake the work. In most cases the surveys indicate a significant backlog of repairs that will need to be tackled to bring the stock up to a reasonable condition and from the survey organisations can draw up a list of priorities for planned maintenance. The survey can also be used to plan future programmes of work over anything up to a 25 year cycle.

The development of this approach also requires the involvement of finance staff who need to be advised of the likely costs of the future planned and major maintenance programmes so that they can develop strategies to ensure that these can be funded. In local authorities this exercise will inform the housing strategy bids and their rent setting strategies, as much of this work requires funding from a mixture of capital borrowing and revenue income. Similarly in housing associations, stock condition surveys and the resulting planned maintenance programmes are used to inform bids for major repairs grants, and to build up of major repairs provisions and sinking funds to fund future programmes.

It is also essential that a stock condition survey is not seen as a one-off exercise. All organisations should undertake a rolling programme of surveys to ensure that programmes remain up to date and priorities can be adjusted in the light of developments in the condition of the stock.

l. Partnering

As was seen in chapter four, partnering is now increasingly common in the procurement of both development and maintenance services. Partnering was a key recommendation arising from the *Rethinking Construction* report of 1998 by Sir John Egan.

Increasingly landlords are partnering with contractors to develop improved maintenance and repairs services. Key features of partnering contracts involve:

- long term contracts;
- open book accounting;
- sharing of expertise;
- identification of cost savings in the supply chain;
- development of a quality culture;
- adoption of Best Value targets;
- sharing of IT and management information systems;
- a change in the culture from client/contractor to one of partnership and trust;
- developing good problem solving strategies;
- effective monitoring and measurement processes.

One example of partnering in a housing association is shown in Figure 5.15.

Figure 5.15: Good Practice in Partnering

St Pancras & Humanist Housing Association won the National Housing Award in housing management for its innovative approach to partnering. Benefits of the partnering approach with two key maintenance contactors were identified as:

- a reduction in timescales to complete the jobs;
- reduced void turn around times;
- improvements in payment processing ensuring more accurate accounting and improvements to the contractors' cash flow;
- a joint tenant compensation fund;
- simplification of procedures;
- joint training sessions;
- introduction of agreed appointments with tenants.

Source: CIH, 2001b

Good practice in repairs and maintenance

The Audit Commission and Accounts Commission reports give many examples of good practice in repairs and maintenance and these are available on their websites. Figure 5.16 sets out examples of good practice identified at Canterbury City Council.

Figure 5.16: Canterbury City Council

Good practice includes ensuring:

- responsive repairs let under a contract to Serco in April 1999;
- contract let on a fixed price basis to avoid need for single job invoicing;
- surpluses directed to other innovative repairs programmes;
- tenant involvement in developing the contract; particularly around quality standards;
- a focus on completing the repair to an agreed quality level, first time;
- satisfaction rates at 98.3 per cent.

Source: CIH, 2001b

8. Managing tenancies

Introduction

In the previous sections of this chapter we have looked at the traditional tasks of housing managers; collecting the rent, dealing with voids, letting properties and carrying out repairs and maintenance. However, in recent years more and more time is being spent by housing managers on other tasks such as:

- dealing with neighbour disputes;
- dealing with the results of crime and vandalism on estates;
- ensuring that common parts of estates are properly managed and maintained;
- liaison with other agencies providing services to estates; such as, police, health service, schools and community centres.

Dealing with neighbour disputes

In recent years many of the most difficult problems which housing managers have faced have involved the increasing incidence of nuisance and harassment on social housing estates. This can take many forms from noisy and inconsiderate neighbours, to drug dealing from and around properties, to gangs of young people roaming the streets and terrorising whole communities to serious public disorder. As the problem has grown and the expectations of tenants of the housing officer's ability to resolve the problem has increased, housing managers have had to learn new techniques to deal with anti-social behaviour and neighbour disputes.

Of course, in many cases the problems complained of are criminal matters for the police but housing managers increasingly are called upon by tenants to take action themselves to deal more effectively with the problems. In the past the typical reaction of a housing manager to a neighbour dispute might have been to interview the alleged perpetrator and if the case was proven, to issue a warning letter. In some cases a Notice to Quit or Notice of Seeking Possession might have been served but very few cases ever reached the county courts for possession.

However, more recently housing managers are developing a wider range of techniques to deal with this problem. For the typical neighbour dispute staff are often given training in interviewing and mediation skills. Indeed in some areas, such as Bolton MBC, independent mediation services have been employed in order to attempt to resolve disputes between neighbours. (The Independent Housing Ombudsman (IHO) regularly makes use of mediation in an effort to resolve disputes between associations and tenants). The Chartered Institute of Housing with the Joseph Rowntree Foundation has published a series of Action Frameworks aimed at governing bodies, managers, officers and tenants entitled, *Tackling anti-social behaviour* (Nixon and Hunter, 2001).

Social landlords are also making use of a wider range of legal powers to deal more effectively with the problems. As an alternative to seeking possession orders in the county court a number of landlords have pioneered the use of county court *injunctions*, requiring anti-social tenants to stop acting in a way which is contrary to the provisions of their tenancy agreement. In some cases these injunctions have been extended to visitors to the tenant's household and in a small number of cases have been obtained against individuals who are not tenants of the landlord but who are causing problems on the landlord's estate. The use of injunctions requiring tenants to comply with the terms of their tenancy agreements have now been used successfully in a number of areas to deal with persistent offenders and in other cases social housing landlords have obtained possession orders in the courts to evict people from their homes. Under the 1996 Housing Act the courts are empowered to attach the power of arrest to injunctions if there is a threat of violence to victims. This enables the police to arrest someone immediately of there has been a breach of the injunction order.

In order to improve the chances of successful court action some landlords have taken the step of employing dedicated officers to investigate serious complaints of nuisance and harassment and to prepare the necessary statements and affidavits of Court. For example, Middlesbrough Borough Council's Housing Department employs a specialist team of Housing Enforcement Officers whose remit includes ensuring that proper statements and investigation of cases are taken prior to court action. The council has successfully obtained a number of injunction orders against tenants. Of course, one of the benefits of an injunction is that if the tenants breach the terms of the injunction they can be committed to prison. This is often a very powerful deterrent to people who are causing a problem on estates.

In some areas social housing landlords have also employed professional witnesses. These are paid staff whose job is to witness anti-social behaviour and to provide signed statements to that effect. This initiative has been developed to overcome the reluctance of witnesses to give evidence in court proceedings because of their fears (often justified) of retaliation or intimidation.

Increasingly in particularly problematical geographical areas social landlords are developing initiatives with the police to reduce the problems of anti-social behaviour. The types of initiatives which have been developed include the establishment of police stations or offices on estates, often based in the local housing office. This gives the police a direct presence on estates and also allows much closer liaison between the police and housing officers. In other areas protocols have been agreed between the police and housing organisations about the sharing of information and the assistance which police and housing officers will give each other. Newydd Housing Association has set up a formal agreement with social services, environmental health and the police on the management of neighbour complaints.

With the development of Closed Circuit Television (CCTV) surveillance systems these are increasingly being placed on housing estates to increase the levels of security. Similar surveillance systems utilising alarms or miniature cameras have also been developed to put into empty properties to enable the police to deal more effectively with those causing vandalism to empty properties.

At an operational level the police crime prevention officers work very closely with housing managers on identifying ways in which the security of existing homes can be improved through the installation of alarms, door locks and security lighting, so called target hardening initiatives – and through advice on crime prevention features to be incorporated into new housing developments. Indeed many new housing developments which incorporate particular crime prevention features are awarded the police 'Secure by Design' certificate. Other social housing landlords have employed private security firms to patrol estates and intervene directly with anti-social perpetrators.

1998 Crime and Disorder Act: Anti-Social Behaviour Orders (ASBOs) and Acceptable Behaviour Contracts (ABCs)

The 1998 Crime and Disorder Act introduced significant new powers for landlords to tackle anti-social behaviour. These included:

* *Anti-Social Behaviour Orders*
  These can be obtained from the magistrates' court to restrict people from entering certain homes or estates in an effort to curb anti-social behaviour of people who may or may not be tenants (and for which the eviction or injunction route may not be applicable). These orders have been somewhat easier to obtain in the magistrates' courts and have been accompanied by the development of Acceptable Behaviour Contracts where landlords agree acceptable forms of behaviour with tenants as away of enforcing good behaviour; obviously the breach of an ABC can be used in evidence in court. Following amendments to the legislation housing associations can now apply for these orders in their own right after consultation with the police and the local authority.
* *Child curfews*
  The Act introduced powers to allow curfews to be introduced where problems with children and young people roaming the streets is perceived as a significant problem.

Introductory tenancies

The use of introductory tenancies, where tenants are not given security of tenure for a period of twelve months has been widely adopted since local authorities were given the option to introduce an introductory scheme in the 1996 Housing Act. Local authority landlords adopting such a scheme must apply it to all new tenants, not only those whom they consider to be a 'risk'. Although these types of tenancies have been criticised by some landlords because they only deal with new tenants and only last for twelve months a number of landlords undoubtedly make use of them as an additional weapon in their armoury to deal with anti-social behaviour.

Many housing associations have policies of granting assured shorthold tenancies to new tenants to fulfil similar requirements of giving new tenants a 'probationary period' after which eviction will be relatively easy if the tenant fails to behave appropriately.

In Scotland, the 2001 Housing (Scotland) Act introduced probationary tenancies for tenants with a history of anti-social behaviour (known as short Scottish secure tenancies). In addition, a standard tenancy can be converted to a short tenancy if an Anti-Social Behaviour Order is served on a tenant or a member of the household. In addition the Right to Buy is suspended where a Notice of Possession is served.

Tackling racial harassment

Racial harassment is an acute form of anti-social behaviour as well as being a criminal offence. The Race Relations Amendment Act 2000 places local authorities and other public bodies under a statutory duty to promote equality of opportunity and good race relations between different racial groups.

As a result many landlords have reviewed and strengthened their policies and procedures for dealing with racial harassment.

Advice from the government in *Tackling Racial Harassment* suggests the following as Good Practice tips:

- refer victims to effective and sensitive counselling services;
- where threats of violence are made by identifiable perpetrators use ex parte (without notice) injunctions to protect victims and witnesses;
- provide safe, good quality temporary housing for victims if required;
- arrange access to telephones for victims and interpreters if necessary;
- develop means of assessing victims' satisfaction with the process. (Source: DTLR, 2001).

9. Performance monitoring

Introduction

In recent years there has been a growing interest in performance monitoring within most public sector organisations. There are a number of factors which are behind this increased concern for monitoring performance.

Financial constraints

The increasing financial constraints on local authorities and housing associations have led all housing organisations to review how they deliver their housing services in the face of declining resources. The concern to maximise value for money has inevitably led most organisations to establish systems for setting performance targets for key areas of work, such as rent arrears, voids and repairs and monitoring the performance of the organisation against these targets.

Influence of external bodies

The influence of external bodies has to be considered, such as the Audit Commission and the Housing Corporation, Communities Scotland, and the National Assembly for Wales – all of whom have been powerful advocates of performance monitoring and who have been able to influence the internal working of housing organisations. This has led to the development under the Labour government since 1997 of a significant 'inspection' culture, with local authority housing being subjected to Best Value inspections, Comprehensive Performance Assessments by the Housing Inspectorate and with housing associations coming into the Inspection regime in 2002.

Legislation

Legislation has set specific requirements on local authorities and housing associations to monitor and report on their performance.

1989 Local Government and Housing Act
Under this Act local housing authorities in England and Wales have a duty to provide their tenants with an annual report on their housing management performance. The government sets out the contents of such reports which are compiled at the end of the financial year in March each year and issued to tenants by the 30 September each year.

These annual reports to tenants include performance information on most of the key housing management activities such as rent arrears, voids, re-let intervals and repairs response times. Local housing authorities are increasingly encouraged to provide more detailed performance information to tenants in excess of that which is required by the legislation.

In Scotland, the requirement to produce an annual report on housing management performance was introduced under the Leasehold Reform, Housing and Urban Development Act of 1993.

Housing associations

Interestingly there is no statutory requirement on housing associations to publish performance information to their tenants. However, the Housing Corporation's Regulatory Code does require housing associations to annually publish information on their performance on a range of housing management activities to their tenants on issues such as rent arrears, repairs performance and voids.

The impact of performance monitoring on housing organisations

Performance monitoring, the setting of performance targets and reporting on performance, and dealing with inspections are now common features of almost all housing organisations in Great Britain. All local housing authorities and most housing associations now publish annual reports to their tenants which include detailed performance monitoring information on their services.

The performance monitoring culture now permeates housing organisations at all levels. Housing committees and boards of housing associations regularly receive performance information at their committee meetings. Senior staff of housing organisations will review their key performance data on a regular basis and in most area housing offices staff will collect information on arrears performance, voids and repairs and compare how well they are doing to their colleagues in other offices.

In almost all of the housing management tasks discussed earlier in this chapter most housing organisations have established performance monitoring systems to check how well the organisation is performing in each of these areas. For example, most housing organisations will collect information on arrears performance, the numbers of tenants in arrears and the amount of rent collected as a percentage of the rent debits. With empty properties, almost all housing organisations will collect performance data on the numbers of empty properties, the time they are empty and the rent lost as a result. Many of these approaches have been encouraged by a series of government policy initiatives, most recently the introduction and development of Best Value, which is considered in the next chapter.

Tenant satisfaction

Ultimately, the test of how well any housing organisation is performing is the views of customers. The Housing Inspectorate's approach to inspection is to view the service quality from the customer perspective and in addition both the Audit

Commission and Housing Corporation expect housing landlords to gather data on tenant satisfaction using the same methodology. This data is usually gathered from large scale satisfaction surveys carried out every three years. Table 5.15 presents an indication of the overall satisfaction levels of tenants in local authorities in England in 2002.

Table 5.15: Tenant satisfaction (tenants saying they are satisfied or better with the overall service provided) England March 2002

	All	BME tenants
Local authorities	75%	70%
London boroughs	67%	62%

Source: Audit Commission website, BV PI indicators, 2002

The discrepancy between black and minority tenants is of concern and is replicated in the housing association datasets. Research is underway to attempt to identify reasons for the differential satisfaction rates by ethnicity.

References and further reading

Accounts Commission (2000) *Managing rent arrears – getting the balance right*, Scottish Executive, Edinburgh.

Accounts Commission (2004) *Housing and Social Work Performance Indicators 2002/03*, Scottish Executive, Edinburgh.

Audit Commission (1984) *Bringing council tenants arrears under control*, HMSO, London.

Audit Commission (1986a) *Managing the crisis in council housing*, HMSO, London.

Audit Commission (1986b) *Improving council house maintenance*, HMSO, London.

Audit Commission (1989) *Survey of local authority rent arrears*, HMSO, London.

Audit Commission/Housing Corporation (2003a), *Rent collection and arrears management by housing associations in England: Housing association rent income*, Audit Commission, London.

Audit Commission (2003b), *Local authority rent income*, Audit Commission, London.

Brown, T., Dearling, A., Hunt, R., Richardson, J. and Yates, N. (2002) *Allocate or Let?* Chartered Institute of Housing and Joseph Rowntree Foundation, Coventry and York.

Centre for Housing Policy, University of York (1993) *Managing Social Housing*, HMSO, London (referred to as the York Report).

Chartered Institute of Housing (2001a) *Good Practice Briefing Managing Rent Arrears*, CIH, Coventry.

Chartered Institute of Housing (2001b) *Good Practice Briefing Repairs and Maintenance*, CIH, Coventry.

Department of the Environment (1994) *Rent Arrears in Local Authorities and Housing Associations in England*, HMSO, London.

Department of the Environment, Transport and the Regions (1999) *Report of Policy Action Team 5 on Housing Management*, DETR, London.

Department of the Environment, Transport and the Regions/Department of Social Security (2000) *Quality and Choice: A decent home for all*, DETR, London.

Department of Transport, Local Government and the Regions (2001) *Tackling Racial Harassment: Code of Practice for Social Landlords*, HMSO, London.

Egan, J. (1998) *Rethinking Construction*, Department of the Environment, Transport and the Regions, London.

Grainger, P., Harding, J. and Kirk, R., (2003) *Changing Organisations: Changing Roles?: The Work of the Housing Manager*, Housing & Community Research Group Discussion Paper No.2, Northumbria University.

Housing Corporation (2000) *Rent Arrears Standard: A guide to managing rent arrears for RSLs*, Housing Corporation, London.

Housing Corporation (2003) *Housing Associations in 2002 Performance indicators*, Housing Corporation, London.

Mew, H. *et al.* (2003) *Housing in England 2001/02: A report of the 2001/02 Survey of English Housing carried out by the National Centre for Social Research on behalf of the Office of the Deputy Prime Minister*, ODPM, London.

Nixon, J. and Hunter, C. (2001) *Tacking Anti-social Behaviour*, CIH for the JRF, Coventry and York.

Office for National Statistics (2003) *Social Trends 33*, HMSO, London.

Office for National Statistics (2003a) *Housing Statistics 2003*, HMSO, London.

Office of the Deputy Prime Minister (2003a) *Best Value in Housing and Homelessness Framework*, ODPM, London.

Office of the Deputy Prime Minister (2003b) *Incentives and Beyond: the Transferability of the Irwell Valley Gold Service to other Social landlords*, ODPM, London.

Power, A. (1987) *Property Before People – The Management of Twentieth Century Council Housing*, Alan and Unwin, London.

Scott, S. (2001) *Good Practice in Housing Management: A Review of the Literature*, Scottish Executive, Central Research Unit, Edinburgh.

Scottish Executive (2003) *Housing Trends in Scotland 2003*, Scottish Executive, Edinburgh.

Spicker, P. (1983) *The Allocation of Council Housing*, Shelter, London.

Smith, M. (1989) *Guide to Housing*, Housing Centre Trust 3rd edition, London.

Smith, R. and Merrett, S. (1988) *The Challenge of Empty Housing*, SAUS, Bristol.

Spicker, P. (1985) 'Legacy of Octavia Hill' in *Housing*, June 1985.

Wilcox, S, (2003) *UK Housing Review 2003/2004*, CIH and CML for the Joseph Rowntree Foundation, Coventry, London and York.

CHAPTER 6:
Organising the housing service

1. Introduction

This chapter looks at how social housing landlords organise the delivery of their housing service. In the social housing world there are significant differences between landlords ranging from the large metropolitan district council managing over 30,000 properties with 2,000 plus staff to the very small housing association owning 10 properties with no paid staff. However, whilst there are significant differences between landlords, all social housing landlords have to undertake a number of common tasks.

In the local authority sector most councils in the past were organised on strict departmental lines and in some cases the work involved in managing a housing service was distributed amongst several different departments. In recent years there has been a tendency to bring more of the work involved in the management of social housing within a single department, in order to provide a *'comprehensive housing service'*. This move to a comprehensive housing service has also been associated with decentralisation of services delivering housing services from local estate based housing offices.

In the housing association sector the management structures have been somewhat different, largely because of the smaller size of most associations compared to their local authority counterparts.

This chapter will explore the historical development of the housing service and the move towards a comprehensive housing service. It will also consider the reasons why social housing landlords have increasingly looked to decentralise the delivery of their housing services. Alongside this decentralisation of services there has also been a move towards less staff specialisation, with the development of *generic*, or multi-skilled, housing officers.

The chapter will also look at more recent influences on the way in which housing services are delivered. In particular the impact of Compulsory Competitive Tendering, Best Value, tenant participation, care in the community and Supporting People will all be explored.

2. Organising the delivery of housing services

Introduction

Chapter one described in detail the development of local authorities as landlords since the first world war. As local authorities became landlords of significant numbers of homes very few of them had a co-ordinated approach to the management of their housing services. This was because the housing management function was relatively new and involved a number of local government disciplines and perhaps it was not surprising that the task of providing and managing social housing fell to a number of different departments.

In the inter-war years it was still relatively rare to find a local authority housing department which carried out most of the key housing management functions itself. However, as the numbers of properties owned by local authorities increased then the need for a more co-ordinated approach to housing management led to more and more functions being brought together into a separate housing department. Practice varied from local authority to local authority and even in the 1950s and 1960s it was still common to find a number of different departments undertaking housing responsibilities.

This fragmentation of service delivery was a cause for concern for the housing profession and in 1969 the influential Cullingworth Report, *Council housing; purposes, procedures and priorities,* advocated the establishment of a separate housing department responsible for all housing functions of the local authority. This was echoed in 1972 by the Institute of Housing in their report, *The comprehensive housing service; organisation and functions*, which influenced the way in which housing services were organised in the new local authorities which were established in the 1974 review of local government.

However, even in the 1980s a significant number of local authorities still had not set up a housing department with responsibility for the key housing management functions. The Audit Commission in 1986 commented that among local authorities:

> *...some have all of the housing functions under the direct control of a chief housing officer; others operate with the financial aspect outside the housing department under the treasurer; yet others have no separate housing organisation at all, typically with the treasurer in control of the management of all council housing* (Audit Commission, 1986).

In their report the Audit Commission had indicated that 12 small housing authorities had no separate housing department, whilst 108 authorities had the treasurer responsible for rent collection, rent accounting, arrears recovery and housing benefit.

The Audit Commission strongly advocated the creation of a single housing department and since the 1986 report local authorities have increasingly recognised the benefits to be obtained from having one department co-ordinating all housing activities. In 1993 the Centre for Housing Policy at the University of York found however that a truly comprehensive housing department was the exception rather than the norm. The research showed that only 29 per cent of local authorities had a separate housing department which carried out *all* housing management functions.

On average 30 per cent of housing management work was carried out by departments other than housing.

Perhaps not surprisingly, the local authorities which were most likely to have a housing department carrying out most functions were those with the most properties. Indeed 85 per cent of local authorities with 30,000 properties carried out more than 70 per cent of housing management functions in the housing department alone compared to only 40 per cent of authorities with less than 5,000 units.

The Audit Commission in their 1986 report suggested that the department most likely to be involved in housing management activities outside of the housing department was the borough treasurer. Although the 1993 research reported that over 20 different types of local authority departments were involved with housing management, it was clear that the treasurer's department was most likely to be undertaking some aspect of housing management work, whether rent collection, rent arrears recovery, or managing housing benefit.

In most local authorities the key housing management functions of lettings, void control, rent collection and arrears recovery are now carried out within a housing department – although this is still not universally the case.

The government's Social Exclusion Unit Policy Action Team on Housing Management in their report in 1999 recommended further developments in the organisation of housing management. The report recommended comprehensive 'on-the-spot' neighbourhood housing management to provide comprehensive locally based services which linked into other initiatives aimed at renewing and sustaining local communities (Policy Action Team 5, 1999).

This approach has continued to inform policy on housing management. *The National Strategy for Neighbourhood Renewal: A Framework for Consultation*, for example, suggested that:

> *Deprived neighbourhoods also need services that are tailored to their particular needs. Key ideas include On-the-spot delivery, where there is a case for more service provision within deprived neighbourhoods. Ideas include more On-the-spot housing management, and better use of local buildings* (Social Exclusion Unit, 2000).

As a result, the government has funded a number of innovative neighbourhood management schemes to act as demonstration projects for the effectiveness of such initiatives.

The organisation of housing association services

Most housing associations are very small compared to local authorities; a medium sized housing association will own between 1,000 and 5,000 homes, which of course would be considered small by local authority standards. There are significantly more housing associations than local authorities and within the housing association sector there is greater diversity in terms of the number of homes that associations manage ranging from almshouses with perhaps a couple of homes to large national housing associations with over 40,000 homes under their management. Many housing associations, unlike local authorities, are not based in one geographical location and may well operate in a number of local authority areas or even nationally, such as the Anchor Trust.

In contrast to local authorities, some housing associations will specialise in meeting the housing needs of a particular client group rather than aiming to meet general needs, which is the remit for a local authority. For example, Habinteg is a national housing association which concentrates on meeting the needs of people with disabilities. In recent years a number of Black and Minority Ethnic (BME) associations (such as Asra and Ujima) have been established to meet the housing needs of BME communities and act as examples of good practice in doing so.

Given these significant organisational differences between housing associations and local authorities it is not surprising that housing associations often deliver their housing service in a different way to local authorities. Perhaps the most significant difference is that housing associations are more likely to directly control *all* of their housing management services. Local authorities have a wide range of responsibilities to their local population and a number of different departments exist to meet these needs, including some which will carry out housing management responsibilities. A housing association however is established solely to provide housing.

This was confirmed by the 1993 York research which showed that housing functions were unlikely to be outside the direct administrative control of housing associations, with over 90 per cent of associations directly controlling rent collection and arrears recovery, void control, repairs and lettings. Some associations will of course have to contract out some of their work to outside agencies, whilst remaining in control of the work as the client. This may be because they do not have the staff or expertise within the association to carry out these functions. For example, the York research showed that 47 per cent of associations employed an outside agency to administer at least one of their key functions, with services such as training, computer services and the management of supported housing the most likely to have been contracted out to another body. The management of supported housing is likely to have been contracted out by those associations which did not have the expertise in-house to manage such properties. The contracting out of training services may reflect the fact that many associations do not have the resources to employ their own training officers and need to use outside agencies. The contracting out of IT services may reflect the costs involved in maintaining a computer system, probably making it more appropriate for associations to purchase services from an outside agency.

The 1993 research suggested that this difference between local authority and housing associations reflects the different context in which they work:

> *...housing departments exist within a relatively large bureaucracy with a great many functions, in which tasks outside the immediate expertise of the department may well be handled by specialists in another department, housing associations are 'housing only' organisations and may therefore be obliged to seek outside help with areas outside their main functions* (York, 1993).

3. Decentralisation of housing services

Introduction

One of the most important trends in housing management over recent years has been the decentralisation of housing services by both local authorities and housing associations. This trend towards the decentralisation of services has been encouraged by the housing profession, the Audit Commission, and the Priority Estates Project amongst others, and this section will explore in more detail what is meant by decentralisation, the extent of decentralisation within local authorities and housing associations and the associated trend towards more generic working by housing staff who now undertake a wider range of housing responsibilities.

The move to local housing management

In the 1980s there was an increasing recognition both within and outside the profession, that housing management, particularly within local authorities, was in a crisis. Problems of rent arrears, difficult to let estates were all in the news. The Audit Commission's influential report in 1986 said:

> *'Crisis' is a heavily overworked word. Yet it is difficult to find a more appropriate way to describe the state of much of the stock of... council owned dwellings in England and Wales... A combination of short sighted national housing policies since the 1960s and shortcomings in local administration has produced a major management challenge in many urban areas* (Audit Commission, 1986).

The crisis which the Audit Commission identified included problems such as:

- defective dwellings;
- deteriorating stock;
- shortages of housing for rent;
- increases in homelessness;
- low rents;
- weak management control.

In response to these problems a number of housing organisations had already taken steps to improve the way in which they managed their housing particularly by moving towards the decentralisation of housing management. Although many housing professionals had long advocated the benefits of a more personal approach, not least of these being the Victorian housing reformer, Octavia Hill, it was the case that the move towards more integrated housing departments tended to be accompanied by an increase in the number of staff based in town hall offices, rather than on estates.

Prior to the 1980s there had been a number of efforts to re-establish local housing management. As far back as 1948 Leeds City Council decided to decentralise its housing management service to a number of estate management offices (Donnison and Maclennan, 1991).

However, it is widely acknowledged that the more recent trend towards the decentralisation of housing management began in the 1980s with decisions of some inner city local authorities, such as the London Borough of Islington and Walsall Metropolitan Council in the West Midlands, to set up local housing offices. These initiatives were quickly emulated by a large number of other housing organisations and in particular the Priority Estates Project (PEP), originally a government backed project established to look at best practice in managing difficult to let estates, very strongly advocated the establishment of local offices for the worst estates. Anne Power from the PEP wrote:

Housing management is about relations between tenants and landlords. If tenants cannot reach their landlord quickly and easily and vice versa, the relationship will quickly deteriorate (Power, 1991).

This emphasis on tenant involvement underpinned all of the PEP's work.

Defining decentralised housing management

Whilst many housing organisations have now decentralised their housing services there is no agreed definition of what it is. The following can all be features of a decentralised housing service:

A local management base

All decentralised housing management involves the delivery of some services through a local, estate based, office, rather than through a central housing department based in the town hall or head office. In some cases almost all of the core functions, such as rent collection, arrears recovery, lettings, void management and housing benefit administration are carried out from the local office. In other cases a much more limited service is offered, perhaps with the local office dealing with arrears and tenancy matters, but with rent collection, housing benefit and lettings being carried out centrally.

Local decision making

Another common feature of decentralised housing management is the delegation of some decisions on housing management issues to locally-based housing managers. For example, where lettings are devolved to a local housing office, the local manager will be able to decide who is allocated housing on the estate. This local control over decisions is also closely linked to control over resources. In some decentralised services local housing managers have control over some budgets, such as repairs budgets, to enable them to provide a more responsive service.

Local political control and decision making

In a smaller number of housing organisations, political or committee control over the housing service is decentralised. For example, there may be an area housing committee, which oversees work of the local housing office. This committee will often be given delegated powers by the main housing committee in respect of key housing management activities in their area.

This may also be linked to the greater involvement of tenants in the management of their estates at local level, which may take the form of residents' associations which are consulted by the local housing manager or the direct representation of local residents on area housing committees.

In some cases, decentralisation of housing services will amount to a local housing office being opened on an estate, with responsibility for a very limited range of housing services. In other cases, a local office will be established, carrying out the full range of housing management services, with control over a sizeable budget and with an area committee which exercises political control over the housing service in the area.

The extent of decentralisation of services

Those who advocate the adoption of decentralised housing management believe that it leads to improvements to housing management services and performance. Staff who are working from a local office are expected to be more responsive to problems on their estates and in turn the service can be made far more accessible to tenants.

In their 1993 research, the Centre for Housing Policy at the University of York found that a large number of local authorities had decentralised some of their housing services to local offices. Indeed 59 per cent of local authorities had local offices with larger local authorities more likely to have decentralised their services. 91 per cent of local authorities with a stock of between 10,000 and 20,000 and all of those with a stock of over 20,000 had established local offices. In smaller authorities with 5,000 or less properties only 26 per cent had decentralised some of their housing services. This difference is likely to reflect the fact that in smaller local authorities the problems of managing their stock may be less acute and also they may find it more difficult to provide the resources to deliver a local housing service.

Decentralisation and housing associations

As was noted earlier most housing associations are relatively small; only 11 housing associations in England have over 20,000 dwellings and just 44 have more than 10,000 (Housing Corporation, 2004). It would not be surprising therefore if the pattern of decentralisation of services was significantly different for associations as compared to local authorities. Unlike local authorities which have all of their stock in one district, many of the larger housing associations will operate over a number of local authority areas and a key question for housing managers in these associations is how best to deliver the service. If an association has a substantial stock holding in a particular area or town it may be possible for the association to open a local office to provide key services to tenants in the area. However, where stock is scattered it will not be cost effective to establish a separate housing office.

For example, a small housing association with only 500 properties in a particular town is likely to only have one housing office. But a larger national association like North British Housing Association (part of the Places for People Group) will provide its services through a network of regional offices throughout the country. Although these large national associations may have a number of regional offices they are still unlikely to provide local, estate based offices, in the same way as local authorities. This is largely because most housing associations do not have large estates in one area.

The York study found that 46 per cent of associations only had a central office. Like the local authorities it was the larger housing associations which were more likely to have decentralised services to local offices, with 88 per cent of housing associations with more than 3,000 homes having established a local office.

How successful has decentralised housing management been?

Many housing organisations have decentralised their housing management service in order to improve their performance. The leading advocate of decentralised housing management has been the Priority Estates Project. This was originally set up as a consultancy by the then Department of the Environment in 1979 to advise on how to improve the management of difficult to let estates. The Priority Estates Project believed that the concept of local housing management was derived from the work of Octavia Hill in the nineteenth century, with a housing manager responsible for all aspects of the housing management service in a particular area. The Priority Estates Project advised a number of local authorities in the 1980s and 1990s on decentralised housing management and they indicated that there were 10 key elements to successful local housing management:

- A local office.
- Local repairs.
- Local lettings procedure.
- Local rent arrears control.
- Estate budget.
- Resident caretakers for flatted estates.
- Tenant participation.
- Co-ordination and liaison with other services.
- Monitoring performance.
- Training.

In 1987 the PEP reported on the performance of nine estates where they had been working. This report showed that in most of the nine projects there had been a significant improvement in performance in key areas such as:

- Fewer empty dwellings.
- Improved repairs.
- Cleaner environment.
- More tenant involvement.
- Reduced crime and vandalism.
- Lower rent arrears.
- Quality of dwellings.

In five of the projects there had also been a lower turnover of tenants. Often these improvements were accompanied by greater staff satisfaction with their work and greater tenant satisfaction with the service (PEP, 1987).

In 1995, Anne Power of the Priority Estates Project together with Rebecca Tunstall published a further report which looked at 20 difficult to let estates over a period from 1978 to 1995. This research, *Swimming against the tide: progress or polarisation on 20 unpopular estates*, showed that local housing management had played a significant part in improving the conditions on the estates. Even though the process of residualisation (where council estates increasingly housed the very poorest in society) had accelerated the report did confirm the earlier Priority Estates Project study that local management had led to an improvement in the performance of core housing management activities: voids had fallen on the whole, rent arrears had fallen generally, estates were now kept cleaner and local repairs budgets had improved the way in which repairs service operated.

The report concluded that the improvement in the popularity of estates was largely due to the efforts of local housing staff and residents and that the local management together with resident involvement had resulted in improvements in key housing management areas. However, in order to maintain conditions the estates needed a housing staff with the ability to control the management of their estates in permanent local offices.

4. Development of generic housing management

Introduction

An almost inevitable result of decentralising services to local housing offices is that local housing staff take on a wider range of responsibilities. In centralised housing departments there may well be a separate lettings section, repairs section, housing benefits section and rent section, all of which will have separate staff. A small local office with perhaps six or seven staff providing services to 2,000 plus properties will be unable to specialise to the same extent and staff will undertake a wider range of functions.

One feature of local housing management has therefore been the development of housing officers with a range of skills and knowledge about all of the key housing management activities – the generic housing manager. In many respects this is a return to the estate management tradition advocated by Octavia Hill, outlined in chapter five, where a housing officer would be responsible for all of the housing management activities relating to an individual tenancy. But if staff are to undertake a wider range of functions it is essential that the organisation has in place effective staff training and development programmes to them to do so. Clear policies and procedures should be in place for all aspects of work to ensure that services are delivered in an effective and equitable manner. Given that staff in close contact with tenants may also be under significant pressure to deliver services, effective information technology systems and good support from managers are also crucial.

The Department of Environment in their efficiency report on housing management training said that:

> ...the pressures on staff were graphically evident from visits to estate offices... these impressions are given statistical support in the Glasgow study (on the efficiency and effectiveness of housing management in England) where in an interesting and important finding, it emerged that 44% of staff in metropolitan authorities believed they were expected to carry out too wide a range of functions (p. 37).

This finding was echoed by the York *Managing Social Housing* report in 1993, where about half of the staff interviewed found themselves overstretched mentally and physically by their work. If these problems are to be avoided and organisations are to maximise the benefits to be obtained from generic working it is essential that staff are properly trained and supported.

5. Recent trends in the provision of housing management services

Introduction

We now consider some important recent changes in the way in which housing services are delivered, from Compulsory Competitive Tendering in the early 1990s to the establishment of arm's length management organisations in the early 2000s.

Compulsory Competitive Tendering

In July 1991 the government published a White Paper on the Citizens' Charter in which it proposed to extend the Compulsory Competitive Tendering (CCT) regime for local authorities to include housing management. Under CCT, councils were required to place some services out to tender, with the aim of bringing private sector competition into the provision of what were seen as monopoly local authority services.

Under the subsequent CCT Regulations, 95 per cent of certain housing management activities (called defined activities) had to be included in a housing management contract to be let by means of competitive tender, where the local authority's in-house bid had to be considered alongside the bids of competing prospective landlords. During the CCT era the activities that had to be tested in this way against private competition were:

- Rents and service charges.
- Collecting rent and service charges and dealing with arrears.
- Letting of properties.
- Dealing with applications after allocations have been made and exchanges.
- Vacant properties.
- Taking tenancy terminations.
- Inspection of voids and arranging repairs.
- Preventing vandalism of voids.
- Managing tenancies.
- Enforcing tenancy conditions.
- Dealing with illegal occupants.
- Dealing with neighbour disputes.
- Repairs and maintenance.
- Assessing repair requests and ensuring works are carried out.
- Carrying out stock condition survey.
- Assessing the Right to Repair claims for compensation.
- Assessing claims for compensation under the right to improve.
- Caretaking and concierge services.
- Assessing the condition of common areas and arranging necessary works.
- Operating reception and security services.

The first set of contracts were let from April 1996 in England.

The impact of housing management CCT on the organisation of housing services

CCT had a significant effect on the way in which local authorities delivered their housing service. CCT required a separation of roles which influenced organisational structures and service delivery. The two main roles were the 'client' role and the 'contractor' role. These are not unfamiliar to housing organisations and as was seen in chapter three all new development activity involves clients and contractors.

a. Client role

With CCT every local housing authority had to develop a 'client' function. This was responsible for drawing up the housing management contracts, supervising and administering the tendering process, awarding the contract and monitoring the performance of the successful contractor. As a result of CCT, many authorities established a separate client unit in the housing department. The process of preparing specifications required them to think carefully about the housing services that they provided and the way in which they were delivered. For many authorities this encouraged a thorough review of housing management policies and practices with consideration being given to new ways of carrying out the services.

b. Contractor role

Under CCT a contractor was appointed following a competitive tender process to undertake the defined activities as set out in the housing management contract. In most cases the local authority's in-house team won the contract and performed this role, but in some cases it was an external contractor who won the contract. Because of the importance of winning the contract many local authorities restructured their housing services to establish a separate contractor section within the housing department to bid for CCT contracts. This section acted as a service delivery arm of the housing authority and enabled the authority to have a clear client/contractor split within its staffing structures. Contractor sections were established to undertake all of the activities within the housing management contract. Staff who worked in the contractor section needed to acquire a range of new skills in:

- Understanding contract conditions and specifications.
- Writing method statements.
- Performing to a detailed contract with penalty clauses.
- Performing the contract to the agreed price.
- Negotiating variations to the contract.
- Budgeting and cash management.

These were new skills for many housing managers and reflected very much the skills which private sector contractors had acquired over a number of years. Indeed some local housing authorities, such as Sunderland City Council, went as far as referring to their housing managers as Business Unit managers.

The desire within local authorities to win housing management contracts also impacted on service delivery. Many authorities who wished to maintain the benefits of local housing management produced contract specifications in such a way that the service continued to be provided through local decentralised offices.

Others took the view that their current decentralised structures were too expensive and sought to rationalise the service in order to ensure they could deliver a more cost effective service.

The introduction of CCT significantly changed the way in which the housing service is delivered by a housing authority. At the very least it required new roles to be performed and prompted a variety of organisational responses. In the larger authorities where there were a number of CCT contracts there was a possibility of different contractors providing the housing management service in the area and this inevitably complicated the way in which the service is delivered. In reality, the CCT regime, which was phased out in the late 1990s after the election of the Labour government in 1997, did not lead to a big expansion in private sector companies taking over contracts. In a small number of areas they did win contracts (such as Pinnacle Housing Services in a number of London boroughs) and in others local housing associations competed to win contracts (usually when invited to bid by the local authority). However, although few contracts were 'lost' to the private sector, CCT had a major impact. Arguably it paved the way for the development of skills within the sector to enable stock transfers to be handled more effectively by councils and for the successful transition to arm's length management organisations (ALMOs) to take place. It also represented a 'culture' shift towards a more business-oriented approach to the management of social housing services.

And for elected members, CCT also meant major changes in the way they were involved in the delivery of housing services. Under CCT, members were involved in the decisions about the specification of the housing service to be provided and decisions about the way in which the organisation should structure itself to meet the challenges of CCT. They were also involved in the monitoring of the successful contract but elected members became *much less* involved in the day to day delivery of services as this was now left to the contractor.

Best Value

The election of a new Labour government in 1997 meant the end of the CCT regime in local government. However, somewhat surprisingly, it was not abolished immediately as the government was keen to have an alternative in place to ensure that councils examined their service delivery on a rigorous basis. In due course, CCT was replaced by the Best Value regime. This required councils to examine their services with a view to ensuring they were obtaining 'Best Value'. They were required to draw up a programme of reviews which would expose each service to the 'four Cs':

- **Challenge** – the authority must show that it challenges the way in which housing services are provided.
- **Compare** – the performance of housing services must be compared with that of other local government and non-local government providers.

- **Compete** – the authority must show that it has embraced the principles of fair competition in deciding who should deliver housing services.
- **Consult** – the authority must show that it has consulted local service users and residents on their expectations of the service.

The review process had also to show that the authority was continuously improving the way in which it delivered its housing services.

The new regime meant that authorities no longer had to place their housing service out to competitive tender but instead could subject the service to a series of Best Value reviews. Some councils undertook such a review of the whole service but in most cases reviews have been conducted on parts of the service (such as repairs, or lettings or sheltered housing services). In order to test the rigour of the Best Value reviews the government extended the remit of the Audit Commission and established a new Housing Inspectorate (which commenced inspections in April 2001). This Inspectorate's initial role was to test the rigour with which councils had carried out Best Value reviews and then to comment on how good the service was and whether it was likely to improve.

The work of the Housing Inspectorate in England and Wales

In July 1998 the Secretary of State for Transport, Local Government and the Regions confirmed the creation of a Housing Inspectorate, in a paper on the outcome of the Comprehensive Spending Review of Housing and Regeneration. The Housing Inspectorate is now part of the Audit Commission. From April 2003 the Housing Inspectorate assumed responsibility for inspecting registered social landlords in England. The role of the Inspectorate is to look at how local authorities:

- provide direct services to their communities as a landlord;
- fulfil their roles in the private sector within the local housing market;
- respond to those who are homeless or are threatened by homelessness; and
- enable good quality housing and housing services to be provided by others, to support the housing needs of their community.

The Audit Commission's website says that:

The Housing Inspectorate will:
- *search for and support excellence while challenging poor performance;*
- *focus on outcomes, not just processes;*
- *be on the record and in the public domain;*
- *work across local government and housing to encourage a learning environment; and*
- *be open, approachable and in touch with service providers.*

The Housing Inspectorate aims to recognise good performance and promote excellence, as well as to chastise bad performers. Above all, the Inspectorate's role is to help local housing authorities to provide high-quality services, within their available resources, in response to the aspirations of their communities (www.auditcommission.gov.uk, 2003).

The Commission inspects the whole range of housing services. To ensure that inspections are grounded in reality and customers' experiences, inspectors look at the housing service being provided as well as checking that the review complies with the 'four Cs' of Best Value. Where reviews have specified standards for housing services, inspections assess the extent to which those standards are being achieved from the customer's viewpoint.

The judgements made by housing inspectors

At the end of each housing inspection, the inspectors make two judgements:

1. How good are the inspected services? Rated from three stars (excellent) to no stars (poor).
2. What are the prospects for improvement? Rated on a scale that runs from 'excellent' to 'promising' to 'uncertain' to 'poor'.

The inspector's report will set out the evidence that led to these judgements, and will make recommendations to help the authority achieve improvements.

Set out in Figure 6.1 is the graphical description of the Audit Commission's report into Dudley MBC Strategic Housing Services published in 2004 by the Housing Inspectorate.

Figure 6.1: Housing Inspectorate verdict on Dudley MBC Strategic Housing Service

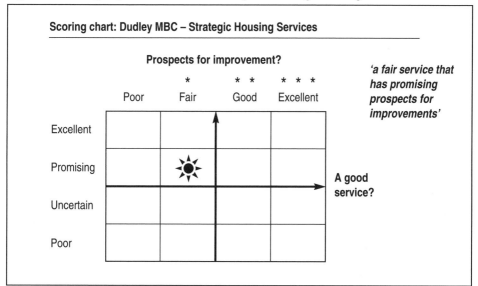

Source: Audit Commission Inspection report, 2004a

As can be seen from this table Dudley received a one star rating which says that the service is fair but that it has promising prospects for improvement.

The housing inspection programme for local authorities

The Housing Inspectorate inspects the housing services provided by all 354 housing authorities in England (even those which have transferred their stock and do not manage housing themselves) and all 22 Welsh local authorities. Inspections of local authority housing services take place under a number of different circumstances:

- Following Best Value Reviews (BVRs). These reviews are required to cover all housing functions. Authorities can choose to review all their housing functions in a single year or to spread the reviews over a number of years.
- All inspected services which score zero stars, i.e. are judged to be providing poor services, are re-inspected within 18 months.
- Arm's length management organisations (ALMOs) established by local authorities for their housing are inspected as a requirement for the release of central government funding.
- Housing services can be inspected where no BVR has taken place and where there is a need to meet national inspection requirements for Comprehensive Performance Assessment.
- Supporting People programmes are inspected by specialist teams within the Housing Inspectorate.
- The Secretary of State or the authority's external auditors can also direct the Housing Inspectorate to carry out an inspection.

The programme of inspections is based on the review timetables submitted by local authorities in their Best Value performance plans and current national inspection priorities. Over time, the lead housing inspectors will build close relationships with the housing departments within their respective regions so that inspections can be planned for a suitable time.

Inspection of housing associations

Whilst the Housing Corporation has long regulated the work of housing associations it was only in 2001 that it formally set up an inspection programme similar to that operated by the Housing Inspectorate for local authorities. The Housing Corporation inspection regime was designed to answer two key questions;

- How good is the service?
- How good is the association at continuous improvement?

The improvement question is slightly different to that for local authorities.

The inspection process was piloted in 2001/02 and commenced properly in April 2002. However, the existence of two similar inspection regimes run by different organisations operating a slightly different methodology was seen by many as wasteful and in September 2002 the Deputy Prime Minister decided to combine inspection activities for all social housing landlords into one organisation. As a consequence, in April 2003 the responsibility for the inspection of housing associations transferred from the Housing Corporation to the Audit Commission's Housing Inspectorate. The Housing Corporation Inspection regime produces slightly different inspection findings in relation to the absence of a star rating and a different question in relation to improvement. This can be seen clearly in Figure 6.2.

Figure 6.2: Housing Inspectorate summary verdict on Anglia Housing Group

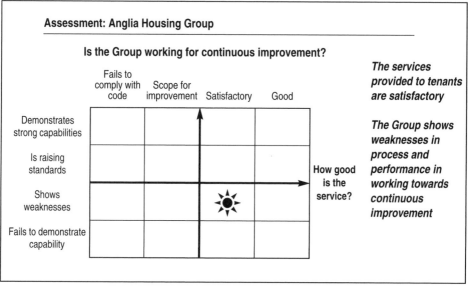

Source: Audit Commission report, 2004b

The Housing Inspectorate in early 2004 indicated it wished to develop a star rating for housing associations and agree the same assessment for improvement. It is likely that a unified assessment regime will be introduced in late 2004.

Inspection in Scotland

In Scotland, *Communities Scotland* has the obligation under the Housing (Scotland) 2001 Act to implement a single regulatory framework for all social landlords and homelessness functions in Scotland. Its first report into East Lothian Council's housing and homelessness services was published in January 2004. In each inspection three key questions are asked;

- How good are the services inspected?
- How well are the council and its services being managed?
- Are the services and the council likely to improve?

Inspection reports assess each area with four grades (A being excellent through to D, being poor). Figure 6.3 sets out the assessment for East Lothian Council;

Figure 6.3: East Lothian Assessment

These are the inspection grades achieved by East Lothian Council		
Housing Managment	C	The Council delivers a fair housing management service with some strengths, but with significant areas where improvement is needed.
		We consider that prospects for improvement in the housing management service are uncertain.
Property Management	C	The Council delivers a fair property management service with some strengths, but with significant areas where improvement is needed.
		The prospects for improvement in the property management service are promising.
Homeless	D	The Council delivers a poor homelessness service with major areas where improvement is needed.
		We consider that prospects for improvement in the homlessness function are uncertain.

Source: Communities Scotland; Accounts Commission Inspection report, January 2004

Arm's length management organisations

The government first introduced the concept of arm's length management organisations (ALMOs) in its Housing Green Paper *Quality and Choice: A Decent Home for All* (2000) and this was re-affirmed in the *Sustainable Communities Plan* in 2003.

ALMOs are companies set up by a local authority to manage, maintain and improve its housing stock. A key point to remember is that the local authority remains as the landlord (and continues to own the housing stock) and tenants remain secure tenants of the authority. An ALMO does not trade for profit and is managed by a board of directors comprising council representatives (usually councillors), elected tenants and independents, usually on a third/third/third basis.

As an incentive to establish ALMOs the government decided that local authorities pursuing this option could secure additional capital funding if the new arm's length body had received a 'good' rating (two or three stars) from the Audit Commission's Housing Inspectorate. To access this additional funding an authority must:

- have established an arm's length management organisation to manage its housing stock and associated investment;
- have demonstrated a high level of performance as measured against the Best Value national housing indicators and a 'good' rating (two or three stars) following a Housing Inspection;

- have demonstrated sound financial planning, management and long-term financial viability through a high quality business plan; and
- have provided a clear plan showing how it proposes to move to a structure of rents and a lettings scheme that is in line with the reforms agreed following the Housing Green Paper.

In July 2000 the government announced the resources it would make available to such authorities. To secure improvements to around 90,000 homes, £160 million was available in 2002/03 and a further £300 million in 2003/04. In *Sustainable communities: building for the future* the Deputy Prime Minister announced an additional £1.4 billion for ALMO expenditure to April 2006. With this funding, local authorities and their ALMOs are expected to achieve the Decent Homes Standard for their housing stock by 2010.

6. Involving tenants in the management of the housing service

Introduction

The extent to which tenants are involved in the management of housing services varies from landlord to landlord and from a situation where tenant involvement is at the legal minimum through to housing co-operatives where tenants fully control and manage all aspects of their housing stock.

Statutory requirements

The legislation relating to the involvement of tenants in housing management is fairly weak as under the Housing Act 1985 local authorities and housing associations are only required to *consult* their secure tenants on a limited range of housing management matters.

Section 105 of the 1985 Housing Act requires landlords of secure tenants in England and Wales to consult them on changes to certain housing management practices or policies (with the significant exception of changes to rents and service charges). Consultation is not defined in the legislation but should involve the landlord seeking the views of tenants affected by the change and the landlord considering the views of tenants before making any final decision on a matter subject to consultation. In addition, landlords of secure tenants have to publish details of their consultation arrangements and make these available to tenants on request.

For housing association assured tenants there is no statutory requirement for consultation. However, the Housing Corporation's Regulatory Code states that:

> *Housing associations must seek and be responsive to residents' views and priorities: reflecting these interests in their business strategy; giving residents*

and other stakeholders opportunities to comment on their performance, enabling residents to play their part in decision-making, providing opportunities for residents to explore, and play their part, in how services are managed and provided. The association is effectively accountable to all its stakeholders. Current information about the association's activities is widely available to residents and other interested parties. Residents, housing applicants and others have ready access to an effective complaints and compensation policy, administered effectively. Independent Housing Ombudsman recommendations are implemented. Residents have the opportunity both to influence the association's activities and to become involved. The association considers a range of methods and opportunities to consult and obtain feedback from residents. It seeks to make an agreement, developed in partnership with residents, setting out how they will be involved, consulted and informed and how this will be resourced, measured, monitored and reviewed. Where they so wish, residents are supported, enabling them to obtain the knowledge and skills to play an effective part in investment in, and management of, their homes and neighbourhoods. They are encouraged and supported to explore such options (Housing Corporation Regulatory Code, 2001).

The ladder of involvement

Although the legislation only requires housing organisations to consult tenants, tenants may be involved in the management of the housing at a variety of different levels. Indeed this involvement can work at a number of different levels ranging from:

- Information giving.
- Tenant consultation.
- Tenant participation.
- Tenant control.

a. Information giving

Working with tenants at this level involves providing tenants with more information about the housing service, the standards they can expect and the levels of services to be provided. This information might be given in the form of newsletters, leaflets and other publications or it might be in the form of resident meetings or one-to-one communication.

b. Tenant consultation

This involves housing officers actively seeking the views of tenants on housing issues. Tenants might be consulted, for example, about a change to allocations policy or rent setting policy. Consultation involves a commitment to ask tenants what they think but involves no commitment to fully take account of their views. But it does enable tenants, usually through surveys, meetings or face-to-face communication to influence the housing service which is provided.

c. Tenant participation

With tenant participation tenants are actively involved in the decision making process. They may not have the ability to decide every issue but they will have a real voice in decision making. For example, a form of participation might include tenant representatives sitting on an area housing committee with a vote and a true voice in the proceedings, or it might be seen in an estate committee, where residents have control over a small improvements budget. Where tenant participation occurs tenants have a real influence over the decision making process.

d. Tenant control

This involves tenants controlling most or all aspects of their housing service. There are a number of models of tenant control which can be seen in Britain today. In estate management boards residents control most aspects of the housing service on their estate and usually employ staff directly. In housing co-operatives tenants are shareholding members of their co-operative housing association and are fully responsible for the housing service which the co-operative, as landlord, provides. In some cases co-operative members may undertake the housing management work themselves or they may employ staff directly or indirectly, through a secondary housing co-operative to provide the housing service.

Tenant involvement is now a feature of most housing organisations although the extent of that involvement does vary. However, involving tenants in the management of the housing services is a relatively recent phenomenon and as late as 1977, the Green Paper on Housing Policy proposed a new Tenants' Charter which would encourage tenant participation in housing. The ideas as set out in the 1977 Green Paper were eventually incorporated into the 1980 Housing Act in the Tenants' Charter, but the extent of tenant involvement was limited to a requirement for consultation rather than participation or control.

Under the 1988 Housing Act (1988 Housing (Scotland) Act) council tenants were given the right under the Tenants' Choice legislation to transfer their homes to a new landlord. At the time this legislation was passed there was an expectation from government that large numbers of dissatisfied council tenants would vote to transfer to a new landlord. However, in practice very few such transfers took place, but one of the interesting effects of the 1988 Act was to force many local authorities to consider more seriously ways of improving their communication with tenants and involving them more actively in the management of their homes.

Estate management boards and housing co-operatives

Whilst many tenants are happy simply to receive information from the landlord and to be consulted by the landlord on changes to housing management policy and practice there have been a number of models established through which tenants can exercise much greater control over their housing.

Where estate management boards have been established tenants control the housing management and maintenance of their estate by involvement in an estate management board which is a legally constituted organisation which undertakes the management of an estate from a local authority under the terms of a management agreement. Through the estate management board model residents control the management of their estate through the board with much of the day to day management being undertaken by paid staff.

Housing co-operatives

One of the more advanced forms of tenant participation and control is through the establishment of housing co-operatives. A housing co-operative is where a group of tenants come together to form a legal entity which manages and in some cases owns the houses in which the tenants live. There are a number of different forms of housing co-operative including:

Par value co-operatives

This is a co-operative in which the shareholding members who are normally tenants or prospective tenants only hold a one pound financial stake in the co-operative. The homes which they live are owned collectively by the co-operative of which they are shareholding members. As the co-operative is the landlord, all housing management functions are undertaken by the co-operative and in many cases housing management tasks are delegated to individual co-operative members, such as collecting the rents and arranging repairs. However, as this poses an additional burden on tenant members many housing co-operatives have decided to employ paid staff themselves to carry out the day to day housing management work under the direction of co-operative members or have employed another housing association or secondary housing co-operative to provide such services under the terms of a management agreement.

Tenant management co-operatives

A tenant management co-operative is normally constituted in much the same way as a par value co-operative with the difference that the co-operative only manages and does not own the homes of the tenants. For example, the Langridge Crescent tenant management co-operative in Middlesbrough was established when the local authority agreed to transfer the management of a small estate to the tenant management co-operative. Under the terms of the management agreement with the local authority, the co-operative undertakes certain housing management and maintenance functions on behalf of the local authority and receives a fee from the authority for undertaking this work.

Although most tenant management co-operatives have been established on local authority estates there are a number of examples where housing associations have transferred the management of some of their estates to tenant management co-operatives under the terms of a management agreement.

The impact of tenant involvement on the delivery of housing services

There are many ways in which tenants have been involved in changing the ways in which organisations deliver their housing services and the organisational forms they establish to provide housing services. Some of this influence will come through the consultation process where tenants' views will affect the work of the organisation.

However, the more significant impact comes where tenants have a direct say in service delivery either through their participation in tenant forums, area committees or through co-operatives. In these situations tenants can have a very real influence in the service which is delivered and the distribution of available resources amongst competing priorities.

The York study found that tenant participation was still 'relatively undeveloped' by many social landlords, with the lowest levels of tenant participation occurring in the smaller non-urban organisations.

More recently, the government's Neighbourhood Renewal agenda has advocated neighbourhood management, local wardens, community investment and development. This is particularly vital to create some level of what Mumford and Power (2002) refer to as an 'urban renaissance' in the north of England.

7. Care and Support – from Care in the Community to Supporting People

Introduction

During 2003, the government implemented its '*Supporting People*' policy which changed the way in which care and support services are funded. The policy built on and developed existing policies on care in the community and has had implications for the management of housing services.

Care in the Community

In the 1980s there were a number of reports published about how best to meet the care needs of vulnerable persons, the most important of which was the Griffiths' Report, *Community Care: Agenda for action*. This report showed how services for vulnerable people were fragmented with no single agency assuming full responsibility for the care needs of individuals and that there was often conflict and confusion between the various agencies involved in care services such as the health service, the local authority social services department and housing department and private or voluntary sector agencies. However, at the same time there was also a concern about the costs of residential care and nursing care, the bulk of which was being funded through the social security system and much of which was provided by private sector care homes. This generated worries that large numbers of dependent and vulnerable people were entering residential care and nursing care at high cost to the state when a more appropriate and cost effective solution might have been to provide domiciliary care services in their own home. As a part of the service delivery, Griffiths wanted each vulnerable person to have a single 'keyworker' to whom they could refer (Meteyard, 1994).

The government largely supported the conclusions of the Griffiths' Report and in the White Paper of 1989 *Caring for People: Community Care in the next Decade and Beyond* the government set a number of key objectives in relation to care in the community. These included that:

- Dependent people should be able to live as normal a life as possible in the community with the right amount of care and support to achieve independence.
- Dependent people should be able to stay in their own homes for as long as possible.
- Dependent people should have a greater say about the services they needed with more choice available to them.

The government also accepted that the local social services authority should be given the lead responsibility to provide community care services and these principles were included in the National Health Service and Community Care Act of 1990 which came into effect in 1993. Under this legislation social service authorities became the lead agency responsible for meeting social care needs in their areas and in addition had responsibilities to produce and publish community care plans after consultation with health authorities, housing authorities, community care service users and other interested parties.

The key feature of the 1990 Act was that social services were responsible for assessing the care needs of individuals and designing packages of care which met the user's assessed needs taking account of the need to ensure value for money.

The concept of care in the community has been supported by all parties for 30 years, although with little clarity as to what this actually meant. In general terms, the concept reflects a move away from the provision of care from large institutional settings where people who were mentally ill, or who had learning disabilities, or physical disabilities or who were old were taken to receive care. This model of care took people with high dependency needs away from their own communities to isolated and segregated settings (Platt, 1995).

A key thrust of the government's care in the community reforms was therefore a switch in emphasis away from institutional care to the provision of more domiciliary, day care and respite care to enable individuals to live in their homes in the community. One of the more dramatic results of this policy change was the closure of a large number of long stay beds in hospitals which were previously occupied with people with mental health problems or learning disabilities in particular, and the transfer of these individuals into the community often to much smaller registered care homes or nursing homes.

Housing and community care

As more and more individuals no longer received care services in large institutions then suitable alternative accommodation had to be provided for these individuals, frequently by local authorities or housing associations or the private/voluntary sector. Indeed in recent years a significant development has been the growth in small registered care homes providing housing and care services for 6-12 individuals who might previously have lived in a long stay hospital.

In addition, with the emphasis on enabling individuals to remain in their own homes, it has been increasingly necessary to ensure that accommodation is made more suitable to the needs of individuals who might find it difficult to cope with existing accommodation. For example, as the elderly become more infirm it may become necessary to provide a range of aids and adaptations to enable them to remain living at home, such as the provision of ramps, handrails and walk-in showers.

The impact of community care: changing the way housing services are organised

Under the community care legislation the lead organisations for community care are the social services authorities. However, in any community care package the provision of suitable accommodation is a key component and as such housing authorities and housing associations both have important roles to play in the successful implementation of the community care programme.

A number of the larger local authorities have established separate community care sections within the housing department which have a responsibility for liaising with their social services colleagues on both the community care plan and the provision of accommodation to meet the needs as set out in the community care planning process. Within housing associations there has also been a significant expansion in the provision of accommodation for people with special needs, and associations have been required to establish much closer links with social services colleagues than was the case prior to the implementation of the 1990 Act.

At the operational level, housing officers in both local authorities and housing associations have been required to develop a greater understanding of the workings of the community care legislation. They may be required to liaise with social workers who are seeking to find more appropriate accommodation for their clients as they are moved from long stay hospitals, or housing officers can be required to investigate funding for possible adaptations to enable individuals to remain within their own homes. Indeed in some areas housing staff are now involved in the care assessment process undertaken by social workers.

'Supporting People'

Supporting People radically overhauled the way housing related support is strategically planned and funded. Local authorities receive a single, cash limited grant for funding support services in their area. The *Supporting People* grant replaced several funding mechanisms including:

- Housing benefit paid to claimants for tenancy related support services (HB is still payable for housing costs).
- Income support paid by the Department of Work and Pensions on support services provided to leaseholders.
- Probation Accommodation Grants – Home Office funding for local probation offices, to pay for accommodation and support.
- Supported Housing Management Grant (SHMG) paid to housing associations for support services.
- Housing Revenue Account local authority funding for council tenants, which can be used to provide housing related support.

Supporting People funding is only available for 'housing related support', it cannot be used to fund housing management or personal or health care for which other sources of funding are available. During the transition to *Supporting People* before April 2003 many landlords identified a need to change the way in which they operate and budget for services. Some social landlords found that they were required to separately account for housing management and support costs so that appropriate amounts could be charged to tenants (and in turn claimed as housing benefit or Supporting People grant by those eligible). Together with the rent restructuring proposals detailed in chapter five, *Supporting People* required those landlords who had 'pooled' the rent – spreading the whole cost of the service across some or all of their budgets – to now account (and charge) separately for all rent and support costs.

One of the unforeseen impacts of the introduction of Supporting People was a big increase in the amount of money being charged to Supporting People funds by landlord providers. This occurred because of a switch of funding from health and social services authorities who saw an opportunity to charge support costs to Supporting People and to reduce their own grant and support expenditure. The resultant huge increase in Supporting People costs led to the Treasury instigating a review of Supporting People in January 2004.

References and further reading

Accounts Commission (2004) *Inspection of East Lothian Council*, Communities Scotland/Scottish Executive, Edinburgh.

Audit Commission (2004a) *Inspection Report Dudley MBC*, HMSO, London.

Audit Commission (2004b) *Inspection Report Anglia Housing Group*, HMSO, London.

Central Housing Advisory Committee (1969) *Council Housing: Purposes, procedures and priorities*, HMSO, London.

Centre for Housing Policy, University of York (1993) *Managing Social Housing*, HMSO.

Centre for Housing Research, University of Glasgow (1989) *The Nature and Effectiveness of Housing Management in England*, University of Glasgow, Glasgow.

Department of the Environment (1990) *Efficiency Report and Action Plan: Training, education and performance in housing management*, HMSO, London.

Donnison, D. and Maclennan, D. (1991) *The Housing Service of the Future*, Longman/CIH, Harlow and Coventry.

Griffiths, R. (1988) *Community Care: Agenda for action*, HMSO, London.

Housing Corporation (2001) *Regulatory Code and Guidance*, Housing Corporation, London.

Housing Corporation (2004) *Housing Associations in England: Key facts 2003*, Housing Corporation, London.

Institute of Housing (1972) *The Comprehensive Housing Service: Organisation and functions*, IoH, London.

Meteyard, B. (1994) *Community Care Keyworker Manual*, 2nd edition, Longman, Harlow.

Mumford, K. and Power, A. (2002) *Boom or Abandonment: Resolving housing conflicts in cities*, CIH, Coventry.

Office of the Deputy Prime Minister, (2003) *Sustainable Communities: Building for the future*, ODPM, London.

Platt, D. (1995) 'Housing and Community Care' in Smith, M., *Housing Today and Tomorrow*, 2nd supplement to the *Guide for Housing*.

Policy Action Team 5 (1999) *National Strategy for Neighbourhood: Report of the Policy Action Team on Housing Management*, DETR, London.

Power, A. (1991) *Housing Management: A guide to quality and creativity*, Longman, Harlow.

Power, A. and Tunstall, R. (1995) *Swimming against the Tide: Progress or polarisation on 20 unpopular estates*, Joseph Rowntree Foundation, York.

Priority Estates Report (1987) *PEP Guide to Local Housing Management, Volume 2*, DoE, London.

Social Exclusion Unit (2000) *The National Strategy for Neighbourhood Renewal: A Framework for Consultation*, SEU, London.

Websites

www.housingcorp.gov.uk
www.auditcommission.gov.uk

Chapter 7:
Meeting the challenges

1. Introduction

The previous chapters have explored the evolution and role of social housing in the United Kingdom and analysed the work which housing professionals do in relation to finance, development and housing management. Although these areas have been reviewed in separate chapters we have tried to highlight throughout this book that the task of managing social housing requires the integration of a wide rage of skills and knowledge. For example, the successful development of a new housing scheme requires housing managers to have a thorough grasp of development, finance and management issues in order to address all of the complex issues which have to be resolved.

As explained in the earlier chapters, social housing has been affected by significant changes over the last 20 years, with the result that the role of different providers has been changing substantially. This in turn has had an impact on the work of housing professionals. This final chapter looks ahead at the likely key challenges facing housing professionals in the first decade of the 21st century and the impact these will have on their work. Our choice of issues is necessarily selective but few commentators would disagree about their significance for social housing. However, policy developments in housing do change, sometimes significantly, over time, and readers should keep abreast of policy developments in the specialist housing press.

2. What are the key challenges in the 21st century for social housing?

Earlier in the book we documented some of the big changes that took place in social housing during the 1980s and 1990s. In many ways, the challenges now faced by the sector are the product of these earlier changes and – to a great extent – the problems which they caused or left unresolved. In the last two decades of the 20th century, public investment in housing fell in real terms by nearly three-quarters in England (it also fell, but less so, in Scotland, Wales and Northern Ireland) (see Smith *et al.*, 2000; Sim, 2004; and Paris, 2001). For many years, housing policy was dominated by an emphasis on home ownership, which grew from 56 per cent to almost 70 per cent of households in the UK over the twenty years, largely as a result of the Right to Buy and similar initiatives.

Local authority housing was subject to tremendous pressures; it bore the brunt of spending cuts, it lost stock through Right to Buy, and it found its ability to build homes reduced virtually to zero. At the same time as the quality of the stock declined – so that in England the backlog of disrepair reached £18 billion – rents were also rising as subsidy fell. More and more tenants were dependent on housing benefit, and the combination of high rents and reduced supply meant that, in contrast to the 1970s, houses were increasingly let to the poor, elderly, single parents and/or the unemployed. This change is often called the 'residualisation' of council housing.

Conditions were somewhat better for housing associations, which enjoyed an increasing share of an admittedly declining budget for social housing, but boosted from 1988 onwards by the ability to raise private finance. The sector expanded not only through new building but also through a massive shift of ownership of social housing from councils to housing associations, through large scale voluntary transfer. Nevertheless, because their rents too were forced upwards by government (to enable grant funding to be reduced), and because of the shortages of council housing and rising levels of homelessness, they too were increasingly accepting poorer and more vulnerable tenants, whose rents are paid through housing benefit.

The challenges facing social housing in the 21st century are – in short – how to deal with this legacy of under-investment, residualisation and political antipathy, and rebuild the social housing sector so that it is no longer a 'last resort' for people with little choice, but an attractive option for people who at various stages in their lives want or need to rent rather than to buy a home. If the challenge is not met, the future would appear to be one in which social housing is increasingly a minor tenure catering only for society's most poor and vulnerable – as is the case in the United States. The alternative requires increased investment but also much more – a new perspective for the future of the sector, a response to its changing role in the wider social environment, and even a new image for what it offers and for the professionals that work in it.

This short chapter cannot do full justice to all of these issues, but it does provide a taste of the debate taking place and the stance being taken by the government and by those concerned for social housing's future

The changing political response

The direction of housing policy is clearly a political issue but, surprisingly, the Labour government which came to power in 1997 did not initially have a significant housing agenda, although it did seek to stem the decline in investment by allowing the 'reinvestment' of the unspent proceeds from earlier council house sales. This was one of the few exceptions to the government's initially very tight fiscal policy.

In 1999, the Chartered Institute of Housing's submission (to the IPPR's forum on the future of social housing) argued that the aims of housing policy should be:

- A housing stock reflecting modern standards of space, design, accessibility and construction.
- Sufficient houses to meet demand and allow for mobility.
- Houses at affordable costs in relation to incomes.
- Sufficient choice between buying and renting.

The report argued that, in order to achieve these aims, we need a 'sustainable housing system', which ensures that we:

- Have sufficient homes, so that all housing requirements can be met.
- Sustain and develop a high quality housing stock, which is built efficiently and well managed.
- Achieve economy and flexibility in the use of resources for housing, to support economic prosperity.
- Combat poverty and disadvantage.
- Promote a healthy, secure and sustainable environment.
- Have choice and accountability, with systems which empower the customers.
- Sustain communities, with well-planned neighbourhoods and adequate facilities, which avoid the segregation of rich and poor.

In relation to social housing, the CIH argued for a 'more European approach' (pp. 11-12) which implies:

...a more independent non-profit sector, which operates in a more commercial way and has a wider client base, with less clear-cut divisions between tenures...but the challenge is to do this and not lose sight of social objectives (p. 12).

There have been two major government papers which set out the government's thinking on housing policy:

- April 2000 Green Paper: *Quality and Choice – A Decent Home for All,* (DETR, London, 2000).
- February 2003: *Sustainable Communities: Building for the Future,* (ODPM, 2003).

The Green Paper
This, in particular, represented the first government attempt to set out a comprehensive policy for housing, covering all tenures, since the mid 1970s. As its title suggests, the thrust of the new policy was 'improved quality' both in the housing stock and in housing services, and greater choice both between landlords and between renting and home ownership.

Along with changes specific to housing, the government launched its attack on 'social exclusion', with a dedicated Whitehall team and a range of 'policy action teams' drawn from the public sector, voluntary agencies and the wider public, looking at issues such as neighbourhood management, anti-social behaviour, unpopular housing and many more. In parallel, an inquiry by Lord Rogers focused on the future of the inner city, and these two threads of policy were later brought together in the National Strategy for Neighbourhood Renewal which now has a dedicated unit within the ODPM. Later, in response to racial conflict in northern cities like Bradford and Oldham, the government began to attach a high priority to what it has called 'community cohesion'. The report by Ted Cantle into the causes of the disturbances led to a special unit being established in the Home Office and to a number of practitioner groups being set up, of which housing is one. A CIH publication (Anderson and Sim, 2000) *Social Exclusion and Housing*, examined in detail the relevance of inclusion and inclusive policies and practice in housing. They concluded that:

> *...there are clearly a number of ways housing can contribute to social inclusion...however, housing policies and practices cannot yet be described as inclusive* (Anderson and Sim, 2000).

In its second term, the Labour government made the reform of public services a high priority. The Treasury's Spending Reviews led to more money going into public services like education and the health service (and to a lesser extent housing), but with 'strings', as made clear by Tony Blair in a Fabian Society pamphlet in 2002:

> *Our public services, despite the heroic efforts of dedicated public servants and some outstanding successes, are not all of the quality a nation like Britain needs* (Blair, 2002).

Although in his Fabian pamphlet, *The courage of our convictions: why the reform of the public services is the route to social justice,* Blair reviewed the Labour government's approach to public services, he fails to mention housing once. And although Labour scrapped the previous government's Compulsory Competitive Tendering of public services, including local authority housing management, it put in place a range of measures to drive up performance, through the Best Value regime. In housing, the pressure to achieve a good assessment by the Audit Commission's inspectorate (in England and Wales), and the rewards that a good result can secure, are the incentives that have replaced the pressure of private competition (which never in fact materialised on any scale).

In summary, there are a number of clear themes running through Labour's approaches to housing and related social policy:

- A multi-tenure approach, promoting choice and recognising the widespread desire for home ownership.

- Acceptance of the need to improve stock condition across the social housing sector, and doing this through a combination of greater public investment and also continued reliance on private investment through stock transfer.
- Recognition of the twin problems of low demand in many parts of the north and midlands, and high demand and shortages of housing in the south.
- A commitment to tackle the social exclusion of the poorest sections of the community and achieve more sustainable communities.
- Driving up standards of performance in social housing through Best Value and Comprehensive Performance Assessment, and the development of the inspection regime in housing.

As we have seen, better housing and better housing services are also important in Labour's wider agenda of improved services like education and health, in tackling anti-social behaviour, in renewing deprived neighbourhoods and in creating greater community cohesion.

The Sustainable Communities Plan

The Deputy Prime Minister introduced the *Sustainable Communities: Building for the Future* Plan early in 2003. It had a number of elements designed to ensure the creation of sustainable communities in the 21st century. In many ways it summarises current housing policy, embracing many of the elements in the earlier Green Paper.

A key objective of government housing policy is providing homes where people want to live. This simple statement hides what is a hugely complex issue. In large parts of the south east of England there is a gross shortage of housing in all tenures leading to house price inflation, high market rents and a shortage of affordable rented homes, leading to long waiting lists and thousands in temporary accommodation. In spite of this problem, house building in both the private and social housing sectors, as we have seen, has been in decline for decades. Local authority house building effectively stopped in the 1970s and the level of investment by housing associations has not kept pace with the level of need.

Table 7.1: Housing starts in the UK

	1970	1980	2002
Local authorities/new towns	153,198	44,433	243
Housing associations	8,594	14,911	18,226
Private sector	169,154	102,175	177,139
Total	**330,946**	**161,519**	**195,608**

Source: Wilcox, 2003

In the private sector too, house building has failed to keep pace with the demand for home ownership. As the Communities Plan states:

Successive governments have failed to tackle the issues and the gap between the need for new housing and what is being provided is widening (ODPM, 2003).

In London and the south east the key housing problem is a lack of affordable housing for rent or sale. The box below sets out some stark housing statistics from the Communities Plan, 2003.

In England 155,000 new households are projected to form each year, while the net housing stock is currently growing at 120,000 annually.

For every social housing home added to the stock in the last few years at least two have been sold under the Right to Buy.

Over 300,000 privately rented homes have been vacant for over 6 months, with nearly a quarter in London and the south east

Source: ODPM, 2003, p. 30

The government's strategy to increase supply in London and the south east has a number of elements:

i. Enabling private developers to build more homes of the right type in the right place

A key action here is to improve the planning framework to make it easier and quicker for new development to proceed. The government is committed to improving the planning framework and the Audit Commission will be required to assess how well local authorities are geared up to deal with the planning responsibilities to achieve a significant expansion in house building. The government has decided that the additional new housing should be located in four growth areas:

- *Thames Gateway*, which covers the north and south banks of the Thames into north Kent as far as the Isle of Sheppey and south Essex as far as Southend.
- *Milton Keynes/South Midlands*, to the north of London.
- *Ashford*, in Kent, to the south east of London.
- *London-Stansted-Cambridge corridor*, which extends broadly to the north east of London up the M11. In February 2004 Peterborough was added to this growth area.

The government is also likely to issue planning guidance to reduce the number of larger private homes built and to encourage the development of higher density and smaller dwellings

Delivery of the extra 200,000 new homes planned in these four areas by 2016 is a massive task. In order to achieve this target, the government will be:

- allocating additional resources to these Growth areas for site assembly, improving brownfield sites, additional housing and provision for local infrastructure;
- setting up new delivery vehicles to ensure that growth happens (such as Urban Regeneration Companies, and new Local Development Bodies with planning powers);
- agreeing new planning guidance for these areas;
- making sure that transport is integrated more effectively into the new developments.

ii. Funding the provision of more affordable housing for the homeless and keyworkers
The funding made available to the Housing Corporation will increase over the next few years with £3,286 million being allocated during 2003-04/2005-06 to boost the supply of new housing in the south east of England over this three year period. English Partnerships (which is responsible for the government's landholdings in England) will be given additional funding to assemble sites for housing development, to work alongside the Housing Corporation.

For keyworkers, the government is committed to increasing its support for the Starter Home Initiative, which enables keyworkers to buy a home on the open market with the help of an interest free loan. As an indication of the support for keyworker housing the government is likely to allocate £1,000 million over the three years from 2003-04 compared to the £100 million allocated in 2002-03.

The government remains committed to promoting home ownership through the encouragement given to the private sector to produce more homes, through continued support for home ownership programmes by housing associations (such as Homebuy, shared ownership) and a continuation of the Right to Buy for council tenants.

iii. Making better use of the existing housing stock
One of the paradoxes is that in a time of massive housing shortage there are large numbers of empty homes available in the public and private sector. Often there are good reasons for the properties being empty, such as the need for major repairs or modernisation, but in other cases it is difficult to see why the homes are not put back into the market. The government in its Communities Plan has indicated that it wants to bring more of these long term properties back into use through proposals such as:

- allowing local authorities to lease (compulsorily) long term empty homes;
- charging the owners of empty homes up to 90 per cent of the council tax;
- encouraging social housing tenants to relocate from high demand areas to lower demand areas;

- supporting choice based lettings schemes;
- funding and supporting care and repair partnerships which can ensure that older properties can be adapted for the use of older tenants.

iv. Other reforms to improve delivery

The changes announced in the Communities Plan (in particular the expansion in the provision of housing across all tenures) is also accompanied by some radical changes to the way in which housing is delivered. Changes to improve the planning system and the speed in which it operates have already been mentioned. Greater co-ordination between key stakeholders will be a feature of the new arrangements. Other reforms include the creation of Regional Assemblies with housing responsibilities and Regional Housing Boards, discussed in chapter three. These are intended to ensure that housing strategies, and the allocation of finance, best reflect the needs of the particular region. Their activities will be watched with some interest.

Dealing with low demand and abandonment

In some parts of the north of England and in the midlands the housing problem is the reverse of that in the south east, with an excess supply of housing, low average house prices, a glut of rented homes leading to empty estates and vandalism. This low demand is not a new problem and the first signs were noted in the north east in the early 1990s but it has accelerated ever since. The reasons for low demand are complex but are linked crucially to economic conditions and the availability of jobs. Over the last 50 years, the large manufacturing base, often concentrated in the urban areas of the north and midlands of England, central Scotland, south Wales and parts of Northern Ireland, has all but collapsed. With this, there has been a reduction in jobs, increased unemployment and a migration of people, often from conurbations to the more attractive suburbs and rural areas, where the economy is more buoyant. The outcome has been an excess of housing supply in some areas.

The Communities Plan sets out the government's strategy to deal with the dilemma of how to bring back life to those areas where there is low demand for housing. In some cases there is wholesale abandonment of homes and a need to re-build sustainable communities where people want to live.

The government's approach to these serious problems has been to create nine Market Renewal Pathfinder Areas. These areas cover almost 50 per cent of the homes which have been affected by low demand and abandonment and where 20 per cent of all of the English non decent homes stock is situated. *Pathfinders* are partnerships between the local authorities, housing associations, the Housing Corporation, English Partnerships, Regional Development Agencies and other key stakeholders in the relevant area and have been tasked with producing strategic plans for the revitalisation of the total housing market in these areas on a permanent basis. Plans for each Pathfinder area will of course differ but they are likely to include actions such as:

- demolition;
- refurbishment;
- building new homes of a kind that people want;
- the development of sustainable communities;
- wider use of compulsory purchase orders of land and property;
- use of 'gap funding' to subsidise developments where the costs of development exceed estimates of sale values;
- community safety;
- encouraging economic development through Regional Development Agencies and Business Links.

The government is making additional resources available to these Pathfinders to make a lasting impact on their areas, with £525 million being allocated for the period 2002/03-2005/06. In addition the government expects other funding to go into low demand areas through programmes such as the Neighbourhood Renewal Fund and the New Deal for Communities. In the north of England, the government will be reviewing planning policies to seek to reduce the amount of urban fringe greenfield development and to seek to increase development of urban brownfield sites.

This approach taken to tackling low demand and neighbourhood regeneration is not entirely new. Previous initiatives have included Housing Action Areas and General Improvement Areas (to improve private sector housing), Estate Action and Estates Renewal Challenge Fund (to tackle poor quality council housing), City Challenge, and Single Regeneration Budgets. However, what is new about the 2003 Communities Plan is the priority and emphasis attached to tackling the problem of low demand and abandonment. This emphasis is to be welcomed but we will need to wait to see whether it is successful on the ground.

In addition, there is a growing realisation that low demand is not exclusively an urban problem, though policies have so far concentrated on urban areas. Many former mining villages in the north of England, for example, exhibit problems of low demand similar to their larger, urban cousins, but because they are situated in rural areas they are, as yet, largely overlooked by policy initiatives.

The Barker Review: Review of Housing Supply: Interim and final Report and Analysis (2003 and 2004)

Following on from the publication of the Communities Plan, the Chancellor of the Exchequer commissioned the Barker Review in April 2003 with a requirement to:

- conduct a review of issues underlying the lack of supply and responsiveness of housing in the UK;
- in particular to consider:
  - the role of competition, capacity, technology and finance of the house building industry; and
  - the interaction of these factors with the planning system and the government's sustainable development objectives;

- consult with key stakeholders to establish views and inform analysis; and
- if appropriate identify options for government action, including the use of fiscal instruments
  (Barker 2003)

Kate Barker published her interim findings in late 2003. Her introduction stated that:

Housing has a huge impact on individual's quality of life. Being adequately housed, and living in a pleasant environment is fundamental to well being. The housing market also has a major effect on the economy. An inadequate housing supply, or a poorly functioning housing market, constrains economic growth. Demand for housing in the UK continues to grow. Population growth, changing patterns of household formation and rising incomes are all fuelling demand for homes, yet in 2001 the construction of new homes fell to its lowest level since the second world war. Over the ten years to 2002, output of new homes was 12.5 per cent lower than for the previous ten years.

The interim report made it clear that more homes should be produced but that they needed to be of the right type and in the right location. In relation to population growth and household formation estimates, Barker advised that the current shortfall in England was 39,000 homes each year, 8,000 of which were for sale at market prices together with 31,000 affordable homes. In addition she indicated that there was a current backlog of 450,000 homes to build.

These estimates are startling and much greater than the government is planning to produce through its Communities Plan. As Barker said in the interim report:

The Government has already acknowledged that more houses are needed. Sustainable Communities: Building for the Future sets out the Government's ambition to deliver an additional 200,000 homes by 2016 over and above those currently planned for through Regional Planning Guidance. However if the Government wishes to deliver a better functioning housing market, more houses may be required.

In March 2004 Barker published her final report. She confirmed that in 2001, around 175,000 houses were built in the UK. This was the lowest number since the second world war. In the last 30 years, UK house prices have gone up at double the average rate of increase in the EU. In real terms, prices have increased by 2.4 per cent a year, compared to the EU average of 1.1 per cent.

One way to reduce the pressure on house prices is to increase the number of houses available. 70,000 new private sector houses would be needed to reduce the price trend in real house prices to 1.8 per cent. To get that inflation down to 1.1 per cent, house builders would need to build an additional 120,000 private sector homes per annum. Just to meet the needs of social housing, 17,000 more homes must be made available each year. To make real differences to the present backlog of people in most need, along with the other recommendations, would require up to 23,000 additional social homes a year. All of this would mean additional investment of between £1.2 billion and £1.6 billion.

The main recommendations in the final report were:

- Government and the bodies responsible for planning need to take more notice of changes in house prices and levels of affordability when setting targets for housing and allocating land.
- A regional planning executive should be set up to bring together regional planning and housing boards.
- The allocation of land needs to be more in line with the needs of the local area. If demand for housing is unexpectedly high, reserves of land should be released for development.
- A Community Infrastructure Fund of £100 million-£200 million should be set up to cover infrastructure blockages and facilitate development.
- Land for housing can be worth as much as 300 times its value as agricultural land. Landowners and developers generally see big windfalls when planning permission is granted, and these increases in value should be shared with the community. This would mean considerable reforms to simplify the current system.
- The house building industry needs to improve. It should deliver better service and improve on investment in skills and innovation.
  (Barker, 2004)

A range of possible issues arising from the Barker Review was highlighted in *Inside Housing* (26 March 2004). Peter Williams, deputy director of the Council of Mortgage Lenders (CML), suggested, firstly, that associations with the greatest capacity to borrow (i.e. those with least assets assigned to debt) may not be in the places where new homes are most needed. Secondly, in relation to affordability, he pointed out that increased supply will not necessarily resolve excessive house price inflation. House prices and housing supply are not directly connected, as many factors other than supply also influence house prices. Others have expressed concern that house construction also demands a range of additional resources to provide essential infrastructure, particularly transport, and it is not clear who will be willing or able to fund this. There are also concerns that residents will wish to be involved in decisions to increase supply in their areas, and that nimbyism ('not in my backyard') may be a factor. Barker herself recognises this, and suggests a need for good design to help overcome local fears. Finally, according to Jim Coulter, chief executive of the National Housing Federation, the critical issue will be whether the government responds [to the Report] with additional resources, as... 'That's, in essence, the test of whether this is reality or rhetoric'.

3. The key challenges

In due course the government will need to respond to the Barker Review proposals. What is clear however is that the next 20 years will see an increased emphasis on new house building for the first time in a generation. At the bottom end of the scale will be the 200,000 new homes envisaged by the Communities Plan but the clear implication of the Barker review is that this will not be enough. In addition, the Barker Review places more emphasis on the need for more affordable housing to be produced (either for rent or shared ownership).

It is likely therefore that housing managers over the next 20 years will be working in an environment in which much more affordable housing will be produced. The challenge will be to ensure not only that enough new housing is provided, but that it is built cost effectively to high standards, that it is well managed and maintained and that the mistakes of the past are avoided.

It is clear that this challenge cannot be met by one body alone; tackling the shortage of housing requires a *partnership* between central government, local government, funders, associations, developers and housing managers. Delivering homes and services of high *quality* will require housing managers to work closely with technical staff, residents and other agencies. And building homes is not going to be enough; the challenge of building *sustainable communities* where people want to live also needs to be addressed. The rest of this chapter looks at these three main challenges, drawing together a number of key issues which have been explored in earlier chapters:

- The quality challenge.
- The sustainability challenge.
- The partnership challenge.

4. The quality challenge

In a time of significant expansion in the provision of new homes (as suggested by the Communities Plan and the Barker Review) the temptation is to build quickly and cheaply. The legacy of a similar expansion of housing supply in the 1950s and 1960s remains in terms of unpopular high rise blocks, large anonymous estates on the outskirts of towns devoid of facilities and community spirit, and problems of disrepair caused by the use of unsuitable and low quality building materials. Much of the housing policy of the 1980s onwards has been about tackling the legacy left by this earlier period of expansion of social housing. It is essential in the next few years that policy makers and housing managers remember the mistakes of the past and do not repeat them.

The omens however do not look particularly good. There is a clear government pressure for an increase in affordable housing provision but to do so as cost effectively as possible. Pressure is being placed on housing association developers to reduce their development costs, grants are being offered to developers to produce affordable homes, emphasis is being placed on Modern Methods of Construction (a modern day version of prefabrication and systems built housing) and high density housing is back in fashion.

What are the responses to this challenge?

The responses to this challenge cover a number of interrelated areas; the remainder of this section will concentrate on three key areas;

- ensuring that the existing housing stock is brought up to a decent standard such as that required in the English Decent Homes Standard;
- ensuring that landlords have the resources to tackle the improvement agenda through large scale voluntary transfers, PFI or the ALMO route;
- ensuring that landlords provide high quality housing and services.

Providing Decent Homes

Although the government is keen to see more house building there is now a clear political imperative to improve the existing housing stock; stock whose maintenance has often been neglected by landlords in the past as a result often of a lack of resources. This policy challenge is clear in the Decent Homes Standard which requires all social housing homes to meet the Standard by 2010.

The results of the 2001 English House Condition Survey, published in 2003 by the ODPM, show that an alarming 33.1 per cent of all dwellings are 'non decent'. This is a total of nearly 7 million homes, nearly 1.6 million of which are in the social housing sector, where 37.7 per cent were counted as 'non decent' in the 2001 survey. The requirement for LA stock to meet the Decent Homes Standard was accompanied by the introduction of Major Repairs Allowances, paid into the new Housing Revenue Accounts (see chapter three). However, it also led to a realisation that local authorities needed to examine a range of other options to achieve the standard, which are examined in the next section. Within the housing association sector, the challenge of meeting the Decent Homes Standard is less acute given the fact that the stock is more modern than that of councils, LSVT associations had built improvement plans into the transfer strategy, and there is greater freedom to borrow to finance the necessary improvements.

Ensuring sufficient resources

Decent Homes is a new standard and a challenging target given the huge problems of disrepair in the English housing stock. Early evidence from local authorities is that many will fail to meet this standard without a significant increase in investment. The government's response to this dilemma is stark:

*Local authorities will be able to choose the right approach for additional
investment in housing stock which they own from the three existing options;
stock transfer, the Private Finance Initiative (PFI) and, for high performing
authorities, Arm's Length Management Organisations (ALMOs). Authorities
that do not use these options cannot expect increased investment in their stock
above that from the Housing Investment Programme. Authorities can use
different options from this list for different parts of their stock, as part of an
overarching strategy* (ODPM, 2003).

English councils have been told by the government that they must complete a
Stock Options Appraisal by the summer of 2005 (as part of their business plan),
which explores the preferred vehicles from the three options for delivering Decent
Homes:

- LSVT – voluntary transfer to a housing association.
- ALMO and obtaining increased resources from government.
- Private Finance Initiatives.

The government is therefore clearly saying to English local authorities that if
stock transfer is not chosen as a route, then the only ways in which to get the
additional investment which is required is either through ALMOs or PFI.

In the housing association sector the challenge of Decent Homes is requiring
associations to examine their business plans carefully (particularly as, for many,
rent restructuring has reduced their ability to raise rents to pay for improvement
programmes). Some associations are withdrawing from development and therefore
hindering the growth objective of government in an effort to provide resources for
Decent Homes. For example, Peabody Trust decided to significantly scale down
its development aspirations in 2004 in order to ensure its resources could be
directed to meeting its Decent Homes target.

i. Large scale voluntary transfer (LSVT)
As was seen in chapter three the 1988 Housing Act enabled the voluntary transfer
of stock by local authorities themselves. Since 1988, there have been a large
number of large-scale, landlord-initiated transfers, known as *large scale voluntary
transfer* (LSVT). The first council to transfer was Chiltern District Council in
Buckinghamshire which transferred its 4,650 homes to a new housing association
it had set up following a successful ballot of tenants.

*This started a quiet revolution in social housing which spread over the next
two years to other places in the South East, then expanded across England.
Confined initially to the leafy suburbs, in 1996 stock transfer arrived in inner
city estates (Walsall and Manchester) and now looks likely to result in the
disposal of the whole council housing stock in cities such as Coventry,
Birmingham and Sunderland* (Perry, 2000).

(In fact the transfers in Coventry and Sunderland were able to achieve the support of tenants but the transfer in Birmingham was surprisingly rejected in 2002.)

The main driving force behind stock transfer since 1988 has been the conflicting need to finance the necessary backlog of improvements and repair in the council housing stock and the government's need to restrain public borrowing. The 2000 Housing Green Paper identified the repairs backlog in England of around £18 billion and it is clear that this level of investment cannot be met by the public sector. A key issue in relation to housing finance, is the restrictive role of limits on public sector borrowing, and the government's definitions of public spending (see chapter three) where local authority capital expenditure on housing counts as government borrowing and, as a result, has been subject to severe restrictions by successive governments. In contrast, while the grants made to housing associations in the form of Social Housing Grant count as part of public expenditure, any private finance which they borrow does not. If council stock is transferred to a housing association, as part of a large scale voluntary transfer for example, then the borrowed funds used to finance this lie beyond central government control.

For some councils an undoubted additional attraction has been the prospect of a significant capital receipt to invest in the area (often in new house building) although some proceeds now need to be returned to government in the form of a transfer levy of 20 per cent of the capital receipt. Transfer to an LSVT also offers some protection from a continuing loss of stock through the Right to Buy; new tenants do not have a Right to Buy although existing tenants are given a preserved Right to Buy.

The purchase price for the stock from the local authority together with costs of the improvement programme has to be raised from the private sector by borrowing from banks and building societies. This partly explains why LSVTs to date have been largely in English shire districts, areas with relatively few stock condition or management problems which makes it much easier to obtain finance for the transfer. By March 2003 LSVTs had involved a total of £5.5 billion paid in transfer prices and private finance of more than double that (to fund both the transfer price to the selling local authority and the necessary modernisation and improvement programme).

The local authority must use the proceeds of LSVT to repay housing debt, with any remaining sums available for other purposes. LSVT does not free councils of their statutory obligations to those in housing need, such as the homeless, but these obligations may be met by nomination rights to the new association, or the local authority may maintain its own accommodation for this purpose. Many have made large sums available to the new association via grants to fund essential repairs and rehabilitation.

Table 7.2 shows the numbers of LSVT transfers in England since 1988.

Table 7.2: LSVT transfers England 1998-2003

Year	Number of councils	Dwellings transferred	Total transfer price £m	Loan finance at transfer £m
1998-89	2	11,176	98.4	130.7
1999-90	2	14,405	102.2	123.5
1990-91	11	45,512	414.4	708.4
1991-92	2	10,791	92.1	176.5
1992-93	4	26,325	238.0	319.0
1993-94	9	30,103	270.5	455.3
1994-95	10	40,510	406.3	745.4
1995-96	11	44,595	477.8	963.1
1996-97	5	22,248	192.6	419.5
1997-98	6	24,405	259.6	498.2
1998-99	11	56,072	484.1	938.0
1999-00	14	80,405	658.9	1,191.0
2000-01	17	132,360	795.2	1,859.0
2001-02	7	35,390	377.7	647.5
2002-03	18	162,769	635.5	2,006.3
TOTAL	**129**	**737,106**	**5,503.3**	**11,181.4**

Source: Adapted from Wilcox, 2003

In Scotland and Wales the number of homes transferred has been much lower, as shown in the Table 7.3.

Table 7.3: Stock transfers in Scotland and Wales 1988-2002

	Scotland	Wales
1988-89	649	11
1989-90	251	0
1990-91	416	0
1991-92	2,791	206
1992-93	4,481	2
1993-94	1,876	444
1994-95	2,955	42
1995-96	3,940	90
1996-97	2,337	95
1997-98	448	102
1998-99	241	36
1999-00	13	40
2000-01	79	45
2001-02	1,558	14
	22,035	**1,127**

Source: Housing Statistics 2002, Extracted from Table 6.7

In Scotland by 2003 there had been four LSVTs (the much earlier Berwickshire transfer and the post-devolution transfers in Dumfries and Galloway, the Scottish Borders and, of course, Glasgow). However, smaller scale transfers have taken place, often to community based housing associations (unique to Scotland, these are managed by a locally based committee). Communities Scotland (formerly Scottish Homes) has provided substantial funding for such transfers, and itself transferred some 18,000 homes from its own (ex-Scottish Special Housing Association) stock (Sim, 2004). So far in Wales there have only been small-scale transfers but one LSVT is in prospect in Bridgend (Smith *et al.*, 2000).

Although obtaining resources for stock improvement has been the key driver it should be remembered that LSVT has not been advocated by government simply for financial reasons:

> *Local authorities should separate their landlord function from their strategic housing responsibilities. Best Value reports show that landlords' concerns often dominate local authorities thinking on housing when they should be considering strategies for whole local housing markets* (ODPM, 2003).

The Labour government was concerned that the retention of a landlord role prevented some local authorities from taking a strategic overview of all housing tenure in their area, which builds on the previous Conservative government's views in the 1980s that local authorities should be *enablers* rather than *providers*.

Transfer however has not been the saviour for all local authorities. As seen above in a number of cases tenants have not supported the transfer (most notably in Birmingham where a massive transfer proposal was rejected). In other areas there are financial obstacles in that the value of the housing stock (discounted to take account of the repair backlog) may be less than the outstanding HRA debt; leaving councils with no housing stock but a continuing debt to service if a transfer were to proceed. In such cases the government has on occasions been prepared to clear the residual debt to enable transfers to take place – for example, in the case of Glasgow.

Stock transfer is a tried and tested route, and as a result of the Communities Plan it is likely that transfer will continue. However, each transfer still requires the support of tenants and this cannot be taken for granted. Local opposition and the need to win ballots may continue to prevent some local authorities going down the transfer route. Even so, the government is clearly saying to English local authorities that if stock transfer is not chosen as a route then the only ways in which to get the additional investment which is required are either through ALMOs or PFI.

ii. Arm's length management organisations (ALMOs)

Examined also in chapter three, an ALMO is a separate, council-owned company which manages the houses, but where ownership of the stock remains with the local authority. A typical ALMO will have a board made up of councillors, tenants and other independent members. In return for setting up an arm's length body the government then gives additional capital allocations to councils for their ALMOs, so long as they obtain a two star rating (until July 2002, the requirement was for three stars) in their Housing Inspections. It is likely that, in the next few years, there will be a steady increase in the number of ALMOs across England. As indicated in chapter three, the Audit Commission has praised the significant improvements in service delivery which the first round of ALMOs were able to achieve.

Already, by 2003, there were 33 ALMOs in England, which covered 530,000 council homes and which had bid for £3.2 billion of extra government resources. So in just a few years ALMOs have almost achieved the same significance as stock transfers. However, in January 2004 the ALMO vehicle was challenged when the London Borough of Camden's proposed ALMO (a three star housing authority which had decided that stock transfer was neither politically acceptable nor likely to obtain the support of tenants in a ballot) was rejected by tenants in a secret ballot.

iii. Private Finance Initiative

PFI or the Private Finance Initiative is a well developed funding vehicle in the public sector generally, which was examined briefly in chapter three. PFI has been slower to take off in housing, but the model usually involves a PFI consortium (usually of a developer and a housing association) agreeing to modernise and maintain council housing stock for a period of up to 30 years, in return for a fee from the local authority paid annually. This fee is linked to how well the stock is managed under the performance contract. This model is attractive to government because the large sums of capital investment paid up front do not count against Public Sector Net Borrowing, even though the public sector is actually meeting the costs in the annual payments made to the contractor over many years. Effectively, it substitutes a revenue cost for a capital one, so is not borrowing.

The government has indicated that it:

> ...will make it easier for local authorities to refurbish homes through the PFI, for instance through resolving outstanding technical and legal issues, standardising documentation and providing more support. We will develop proposals to enable local authorities to build new social housing under PFI as part of a refurbishment scheme (ODPM, 2003).

This is a clear indication that the government has recognised some of the weaknesses in making the PFI scheme work and will be seeking ways to make PFI a more attractive option to those local authorities who do not wish to proceed down the stock transfer or ALMO routes.

The need for investment in Scotland, Northern Ireland and Wales

In Scotland the position is similar to England. The estimated cost of bringing the Scottish housing stock up to a modern standard is £5.5 billion and the last Scottish House Condition Survey found that 11 per cent of owner occupied housing was below the tolerable standard (similar to the fitness standard in England).

Unpopular housing is also a problem, with all local authorities and 57 per cent of housing associations advising that they are managing some low demand areas. Yet high demand is also an issue; 400,000 homeless cases during the 1990s; about 40,000 a year and combined waiting lists of 200,000 (Housing, June 2002).

Stock transfer is the primary route which the Scottish Executive has set out for local authorities, and it has made available a New Housing Partnership Programme of £323 million. The transfer programme is designed to increase investment in the housing stock, tackle poor quality housing, cover overhanging debts and encourage community ownership. The Executive is not making available other options such as ALMOs or PFI. Early successes were the massive Glasgow City Council transfer (the largest so far in the UK) and smaller transfers in Berwickshire, the Scottish Borders and Dumfries and Galloway. Transfer, particularly in Glasgow, will lead to a massive injection of new cash to tackle the backlog of disrepair.

The Housing (Scotland) Act 2001 demonstrated the higher profile being given to housing policy by the new devolved Scottish Parliament. The Housing Improvement Task Force was set up in December 2000 with a remit to review policy issues relating to the quality and investment in private sector housing. Its first report in March 2002 identified over 100 issues in improving quality in private houses and a second review is now underway to identify solutions to the problems, including:

- changes to the Scottish 'tolerable standard';
- a new index of housing quality;
- new legislation;
- additional resources.

In Northern Ireland, housing policy has been developed by the Northern Ireland Assembly when the Assembly has been operating and by the Northern Ireland office in periods when the Assembly has been suspended. The bulk of social housing is owned by the Northern Ireland Housing Executive, and is in better condition than social housing on the mainland and the NIHE generally has a good reputation as a housing provider. Current thinking is to devise a means by which private finance can be levered into the NIHE without breaking up the landlord into a larger number of smaller landlords.

In Wales, the Assembly has a Quality standard which is similar to the English Decent Homes Standard. The Deputy Housing Minister for Wales advised in February 2003 that the repairs backlog was around £2 billion, much higher than the previously quoted figure of £750 million in 1999, which would encourage many more Welsh local authorities to proceed with stock transfers. The Welsh Assembly has required all 22 local authorities to develop costed business plans to show how they will meet the new quality standard. Unfortunately the Assembly has not prioritised housing investment and until recently Welsh councils have continued to see declining resources.

Council housing in the next 10 years

The problems of stock improvement will not go away and, in England, the government is still clearly committed to stock transfer and ALMOs as the main options for councils, with PFI as a secondary possibility. In Scotland and Wales, transfer appears to be the favoured solution. It is likely therefore that the transfer programme will continue, but with modifications to ensure that the model is attractive to urban authorities (which tend to have much higher levels of outstanding debt). Of course, the need to win tenant support could still be a major obstacle to the success of this strategy. What is certain is that the role of local authorities as landlords will be much reduced in the next ten years as a result of the effects of the Right to Buy and stock transfers. John Perry (2000) suggests that by 2010 there could be as few as 0.5-1.5 million homes in council ownership compared to the 5 million council homes in England in 1979. Where councils still own houses, it is increasingly likely that they will not be managed directly by the authority, but by arm's length management organisations or through new management bodies set up through PFI arrangements. The end of councils' landlord role, a goal of successive Conservative governments, may well come closest to being achieved by a Labour one.

High quality management

Alongside the need to ensure that homes are brought up to a decent standard and that new homes meet the high standards which tenants have a right to expect is the need to ensure that services provided by landlords are of the highest standard.

Design of both new and existing housing plays a hugely important role in building sustainable communities but even more important is the quality of housing management. As we saw in the earlier chapters the core tasks of housing management can be described as collecting rents, letting homes, repairing them and managing tenancies. It is this last task that is becoming particularly pressing.

As well as the 'traditional' housing management tasks, modern day housing managers have to tackle anti-social behaviour, deal with drug dealing, possibly confront organised crime, and be able to address the issues of social exclusion in the areas where they work. One could argue that these have always been the tasks of housing managers but in recent years they have grown enormously in importance and profile. As public services have reduced so have resources which used to be deployed in the support of housing managers from social workers, the police and other agencies. Often it is the housing manager who is on the front line left to manage the social issues on some of our difficult estates.

In responding to the management challenge housing managers are developing innovative approaches to management. Spurred on by the government's Social Exclusion Unit, neighbourhood management is becoming a more common feature of estate management, where a manager takes responsibility for a wider range of services on an estate provided by a range of different providers. Neighbourhood wardens are undertaking security and community safety duties once undertaken by the police. Housing managers are involved in a wide range of regeneration projects ranging from Single Regeneration Budget schemes, Neighbourhood Renewal Projects, local Crime and Disorder Reduction Partnerships...the list is endless.

In high density estates, many of which will be new produced under the Communities Plan, housing managers will need to develop plans to manage these estates effectively. In low demand areas, housing managers will need to be closely involved and in some cases leading Market Renewal Pathfinders and other regeneration projects to ensure that the community which remains can live in a home and not a prison.

And linked to this is the whole issue of 'choice'. The government's housing policy has been keen to introduce choice into social housing and over recent years landlords have been moving away from the traditional waiting list system of lettings to one where potential tenants can exercise some choice in their housing aspirations. The pilot projects introduced in 2001 have already demonstrated that choice can work in both low demand areas as well as high demand areas such as London. It is likely that choice based lettings system will be the model for allocations systems in the future.

Inspection and quality

As can be seen by the introduction of the Housing Inspectorate and its remit to review the provision of services by local authorities, housing associations and ALMOs, the Government is clear that landlords need to demonstrate quality in their services provided. The star rating introduced for local authority and ALMO services is likely to be extended to housing association inspection in 2004 to enable a better comparability of service standards in the social housing sector.

It is also likely that in the future landlords who obtain high inspection ratings will be rewarded; possibly by not being subject to as frequent inspections, allowing additional borrowing (so called prudential borrowing as set out in chapter three) or access to additional Social Housing Grant for housing association development.

The two key features of the inspection regime are about the quality of services from a tenant's perspective and how good the landlord is at continuous improvement. These are issues which need to concern all staff working for a housing organisation. Housing management staff are often at the forefront of customer services, but finance staff also have a critical role to play in ensuring that adequate resources are available for service delivery and that customer services are provided effectively (such as rent collection and rent postings).

Technical and development staff also play a big part in ensuring that repairs and improvements are carried out to a high standard and that new estates are designed and built to meet the needs of residents.

4. The sustainability challenge

Basil Jellicoe, the founder of St Pancras Housing, in 1924 said 'Housing is not enough'. This was born out of a recognition that building new homes did not create a community and that communities require facilities such as shops, schools, medical centres, and communal spaces (*Housing is Not Enough*, SPH Housing, 1999). More than this, the people in those communities need to feel that they 'belong' there and it is vital that residents, collectively, have a commitment to the area, if high turnover and, ultimately, abandonment are to be avoided in future. However, as you learned in chapter four, the properties themselves nevertheless remain important, and it is this aspect which is examined next.

Sustainable properties

We know that successful 'homes' must have layouts which 'work' for the families who live there, they need to be warm, secure, safely built and not require excessive amounts of maintenance. They need decent kitchens, bathrooms and WCs, appropriate to the size and nature of the inhabitants. Concepts such as 'Lifetime Homes' (or, in Scotland, 'barrier-free' homes) have been developed to try to ensure that properties are suitable for the changing needs of households, as they age or become infirm. All of these factors must be considered in new and refurbished house design, and it is a key reason for the development of design 'yardsticks' such as the scheme design standards developed by the Housing Corporation. We have, hopefully, learned a great deal from past mistakes about what households seek from their homes and must continue to strive to apply the best design practices in future.

Additionally, of course, as a society, we seek to ensure that our production and consumption decisions do not make excessive use of the earth's natural resources. The design of properties must therefore attempt to minimise energy use, the depletion of non-renewable resources and the emission of harmful chemicals and gases. It should try to ensure that sustainable, renewable resources are used, so that future generations do not find that our homes have added to the many environmental problems that they will face. We also need to try to be more efficient in our use of resources, and this is a key reason why the Egan report (see chapter four) encouraged much greater use of factory-produced components in house building. The recent partnership agreements, introduced by the Housing Corporation, will require increasing compliance with this objective from housing associations.

Of course, getting the homes 'right' is only one aspect of the physical challenge of sustainability; there is also the key issue of the homes in their setting, the design of the estate, and the significance of the locality.

Sustainable estates

There are many unpopular estates at present where the properties themselves are perfectly adequate, yet few want to live there. This is partly for social and economic reasons, which are examined later in this section, but in some cases it is the estate design which has failed. Just as the properties need to 'work' for their inhabitants, so too does the design of the estate. Do residents feel safe to walk along the streets, can cars be left safely, is vandalism or drug use deterred because perpetrators can be observed? Are there safe places where children can play, without causing annoyance to other residents? Future estate design is likely to be particularly challenging, given that government guidance is urging much higher densities (to make best use of available land), so residents could feel rather too close to their neighbours without sensitive planning of layouts.

As you saw in chapter four, the concept of 'defensible space' has become more important over recent years, to ensure that residents can monitor activity on their estate to deter many forms of anti-social behaviour. Too many estates in the past had areas for which no-one felt responsible, and which were allowed to deteriorate to the point that they became unpleasant parts to be in or pass through. There were 'hidden' areas, where individuals and groups could engage in anti-social acts without fear of being seen or challenged. Most rehabilitation projects over recent years have concentrated on (amongst other things) eradicating such no-go areas.

Of additional importance, however, are the facilities available on the estate. Are there child care facilities and schools, shops, community facilities, a doctors' surgery? Is public transport conveniently and regularly available? The need for community infrastructure, such as these types of facilities, must be 'built into' any estate design at the outset, and a key challenge for those developing the much needed affordable, new homes in the south east of England, for example, will be to ensure that they work with other organisations, individuals and groups to deliver this essential infrastructure.

However, a key challenge of the new house building boom predicted in the next 10 years must be to heed the words of Basil Jellicoe and to ensure that the design of new housing is such that communities and not simply estates are developed. If the community is not sustainable, then the estate and its properties are unlikely to be sustained effectively. We turn next to this essential element, beginning with a review of the problems created by social exclusion, generally a key element in fragile and unstable communities.

Social exclusion

The term social exclusion is widely used to describe the multi-faceted disadvantage suffered by some communities. This will include significant economic disadvantage, with unemployment, poverty, welfare-benefits dependency, low skills and low educational attainment as key features. The residents are often demotivated, with low aspirations and expectations (Page, 2000). In many areas, this economic disadvantage is closely related to economic restructuring, as the old traditional industries (such as mining, ship-building, and manufacturing) have closed down, to be (inadequately) replaced by new, lower paid, service sector jobs. The most able members of the community move away in search of better jobs and incomes, resulting in a greater concentration of poor households and, potentially, declining demand for properties in that area. This is compounded by the fact that poverty hampers the involvement of residents in wider activities, so they may become disconnected from mainstream culture. Research by Page in 2000 suggested that, as a result:

> *Estate life was important because it occupied such a large part of their lives and provided most of their social contacts* (p. 2).

Unfortunately, socially excluded communities tend to suffer significant social problems on their estates, ranging from truancy, poor parenting, teenage pregnancies, and anti-social behaviour (particularly by disaffected, young people), to crime, drug abuse and drug dealing. As Wilson (1996) argues:

> *High rates of joblessness trigger other neighbourhood problems that undermine social organisation, ranging from crime, gang violence and drug trafficking, to family break ups and problems in the organisation of family life* (quoted in Martin and Watkinson, 2003, p. 1).

The government is well aware of the problems created by social exclusion and tackling this is high on the political agenda. Of course, social housing organisations have a key role in tackling issues such as crime and anti-social behaviour, and the government has developed a number of initiatives – such as Anti-Social Behaviour Orders (ASBOs), and private sector licensing schemes – to assist them in this. Local partnerships, involving statutory, voluntary, private and community agencies, also form an important element in tackling these multi-dimensional problems and improving services in disadvantaged communities. These can help to provide more help for families, better health care, environmental improvements, safer streets, less anti-social behaviour and vandalism (Gregory, 1998; Nixon and Hunter, 2001). The value of partnerships is taken up again in the next section.

Another key policy has focused on creating more mixed tenure estates, to introduce new residents who are better connected with mainstream culture, are more likely to be employed, and have higher incomes (better to sustain local services). We examine these tenure policies next.

Mixing tenures

Right to Buy was the first significant policy intended to create mixed tenure on social housing estates, and, in numerical terms, it has been spectacularly successful. However, research by Martin and Watkinson (2003) showed that it has not been particularly successful in slowing or reversing the decline of unpopular estates because:

- purchasers are often older residents, lacking the income to maintain their properties adequately;
- significant numbers of properties transferred to the private rented sector which may be poorly managed and create further problems.

In a number of localities, the private rented sector contributes significantly to community instability, with properties in poor condition, very high rates of turnover and problems of anti-social behaviour, often due to inadequate vetting. In the worst cases, properties are simply abandoned and left to decay, causing further stigmatisation of the area, falling house prices and further abandonment by owners unable to sell. In some cases, tenants evicted by social landlords simply relocate, often in the same street, in the private sector. Hence, partnerships with private landlords have become an increasingly important strategy for dealing with unstable communities.

A rather more effective policy has been to sell vacant properties, which attract new, middle income residents, often with children at school. It may, of course, be necessary for the social landlord to be able to buy the properties back when they are subsequently re-sold, to ensure that they are not taken over by private landlords who have no regard for the other residents.

Martin and Watkinson (2003) cite the example of the Joseph Rowntree Housing Trust at New Earswick, which has a policy of allowing 50 per cent of re-lets to be sold (either full sale or shared ownership), achieving a 22 per cent tenure switch by the end of 2002. Perceptions of the village have improved, property prices have risen, and there is high demand from new families wishing to move in. In their wider survey of social landlords which have active programmes to mix tenure in this way, Martin and Watkinson report that all claimed improved sustainability, with:

- higher prices;
- lower turnover;
- higher resident satisfaction;
- increased demand;
- reduced stigmatisation;
- improved household mix.

However, although there seem to be significant benefits in terms of greater stability and satisfaction, there remain concerns about the extent to which these approaches improve the 'social connectedness' of the pre-existing residents. This may require a greater focus on community development, which we turn to next.

Community involvement and development

Community development refers to actions which help to strengthen the social resources and processes in a community, developing relationships, networks and activities outside the household, to make the area a better place (in the judgement of the residents) in which to live and work (Gregory, 1998). Community involvement aims more narrowly to ensure that communities are involved in making decisions which affect them, so that the actions taken have a better chance of addressing the concerns of the residents.

The earliest approaches beginning in the late 1980s focused mainly on community involvement in regeneration, when it was recognised that estate and property refurbishment were not necessarily, in themselves, sufficient to promote more sustainable communities. However, research by McArthur *et al.* in 1996 found that the effectiveness of community involvement in regeneration was somewhat varied. They found that the most effective community involvement occurred when there was:

- A history of community activism.
- A high level of community activity with a range of different organisations.
- A sophisticated degree of organisation of activists with extensive networking.
- The prior existence of one organisation perceived as the estate's mouthpiece.
- Minimal factionalism.
- A readiness to change.

In other words, where the sense of community and its social resources and processes were already well-developed. This suggests that, in unstable and fragile, socially-excluded communities, there may be a need for considerable community development before any meaningful involvement can occur.

The Community Development Foundation's experiences suggest that while there has often been a focus on developing community *leadership*, there has been an inadequate concern for developing *membership* (Thomas, 1995). Thomas argues that the two key elements of membership are a sense of belonging and a sense of identity. These depend on the extent to which people recognise each other as neighbours, having contact, sharing information and participating in community activities. This suggests a need for community facilities, such as pubs, churches, shops, cafes, etc.; active organisations which bring people together; daily routines that promote contact (such as walking children to school); social and recreational networks, including those based on mutual aid. Professional enablers, such as youth and community workers, can greatly enhance local efforts to achieve these. In addition, initiatives such as choice-based lettings policies, through which prospective tenants have significantly more control over where – and in what – they choose to live, will hopefully, over time, contribute to the development of more sustainable communities. Residents are more likely to feel satisfied with their home and neighbourhood when they have had some control over those location decisions.

5. The partnership challenge

As you have seen throughout this book, the government has encouraged the use of partnerships in all aspects of social housing. This is in the belief that no single organisation or individual can possibly achieve as much, or perform as well, as a number of organisations and individuals working together, bringing their different perspectives and experiences to the problem – whatever it may be. It also stems from a desire to use public subsidy more efficiently and effectively, by encouraging private partners to become involved to provide funding, financial expertise and also to share some of the risks. Hence, the theme of partnerships has pervaded all of the previous chapters, dealing with finance, development, and management issues. Partnerships are certainly essential to meet the previous two challenges examined in this chapter, quality and sustainability. This section will show how partnerships in all of these key aspects are expected to result in improved social housing stock, improved management and strengthened communities.

What partnerships?

To secure more housing
There has been a growing belief that partnerships can help to secure more housing, and more quickly, than would be possible for an individual organisation working alone. It began with a requirement by central government that local authorities work more closely with housing associations in their area. They were also asked to produce housing strategies for their areas, which addressed the needs, not only of social housing, but also those of the private rented and owner occupied sectors. The funding bodies encouraged the development of partnerships, not only for the provision of housing, but also for its finance. Housing associations now borrow finance from a wide range of financial institutions, and have had to work hard to build up these relationships. Crucially, all local authorities can help to assemble land banks, and can subsidise housing associations through the provision of low cost land. They can expedite planning consents and building regulations approval, as well as supporting the use of section 106 agreements to ensure that new social housing remains available for local households in need. Hence, they have a key role to play, in partnership with others, in securing affordable housing in their areas.

To reduce the costs of development and improve quality

The publication of the Egan Report heralded new 'partnering' arrangements for development, refurbishment and repairs and maintenance, so that the client organisation works in genuine partnership with all parties to the process, involving all parts of the supply chain. Local authorities are now expected to demonstrate that they have explored the creation of partnering arrangements for their repairs service, to assist them to create a climate of continuous improvement. Partnering for new development and refurbishment has been promoted particularly strongly in England by the Housing Corporation, which has also initiated partnership agreements with selected housing associations, in order to promote continuous improvement in efficiency terms, in the development of new social housing. These partners will secure the bulk of future SHG funding and it is anticipated that they will be able to produce more homes as a result, more quickly, and to high standards. Social Housing Grant is also to be made available to selected private developers, thus widening the range of partnerships. The Housing Corporation has also formed partnerships with private firms to produce a range of approved housing layouts for use by associations, both to speed up the design process and scheme approval by the Corporation.

Egan also suggested that greater use of off-site manufactured components would improve the efficiency of house building, which has required new partnerships with manufacturers. The Housing Corporation has also taken the lead in promoting this, by earmarking a minimum proportion of SHG for non-traditional construction techniques.

To improve the quality of existing homes

Key concerns for the government include not just ensuring that we have sufficient homes for present and future households, but also that they are of the right quality. But it is important to recognise here that many policies to promote quality involve the creation of new partnerships, for example, in securing the extensive repairs needed in many council homes to achieve the Decent Homes Standard. Of course, central to achieving effective and successful refurbishment is tenant participation in the decisions that are made, including the detail of the design and more sensitive issues such as demolition.

Many local authorities have had to create new partnerships with their transfer organisations and ALMOs, and they, in turn, have developed new partnerships with developers and the communities they serve, in order to secure better quality homes. Local authorities also have had to become involved with financial institutions when they seek to set up transfer organisations. A number of Scottish inner-city housing associations, in particular, have faced difficulties in trying to secure the refurbishment of multi-tenure blocks of tenement properties, which have been resolved only by working in close partnership with the residents and funders.

To develop and empower communities

As indicated in the previous section, over the last couple of decades, there has been a growing awareness that it is not sufficient simply to provide decent housing, important as this is. Communities need infrastructure and facilities if they are to thrive. However, they also need to contain individuals who have a commitment to, and feel involved in, that community. It is primarily through members of the community working together with housing managers, the police, youth workers and health workers etc., to achieve common goals, that improvements can best be made to the overall quality of life. As indicated previously, there has been a recent focus on community development and involvement, with training for residents in a variety of skills, and the promotion of resident involvement in community activities such as setting up crèches, youth activities, training facilities, etc. Community empowerment – enabling the community to feel that it can and should push ahead with projects, seek funding, take more control over its own future – can be highly effective, as well as providing a very positive, confidence-enhancing experience for the individuals concerned. Nowhere has this been more evident than in Scotland, where the encouragement of community based housing associations has enabled thousands of tenants, working together with Scottish Homes, then Communities Scotland, to take full control over their housing (Sim, 2004).

Recent research into urban regeneration through partnership (Carley *et al.*, 2000) has suggested that partnerships must involve health trusts, the Employment Service, the Benefits Agency, and the police, but also, crucially, private businesses. Most importantly, they must address community capacity building from the outset, and measure success in terms of the development of community skills, as well as residents' satisfaction. In this way, once the physical regeneration is complete, the residents will have significantly improved opportunities to ensure that the community can sustain itself.

To address anti-social behaviour

As indicated in the last section, problems of anti-social behaviour can have a rapid, negative impact of communities, and problems of low demand and abandonment in some localities have forced many housing organisations to take steps to address these kinds of damaging activities. These problems are generally particularly acute in the most disadvantaged, socially excluded areas. However, they can be tackled most effectively in partnership with many others, including the local community (to identify problems and provide evidence), the police, community workers, and often schools and other institutions. Where the problems arise in other tenures, there is a need to try to engage with other landlords and with owners, and many local authorities have set up landlord organisations to promote regular interaction with private landlords in their area. A number, too, have initiated the development of private sector licensing schemes, which should not only improve the quality of homes but also promote the greater involvement of private landlords with the local authority.

To achieve more balanced communities

There has been a new commitment in recent years to achieving more balanced communities, ones in which there is a range of income groups and household types, rather than ghettos of poverty or enclaves of wealth. As indicated in the last section, this has involved the promotion of mixed tenure estates, initially mainly through Right to Buy, but more recently through sales of vacant properties. For new build estates, partnerships with private developers, to introduce a range of housing options in a locality for different needs, are becoming much more significant. These new estates will include not only social rented housing but also shared ownership, low cost home ownership and full cost home ownership. This has required effective partnerships between private developers, housing associations, funding bodies, financial institutions and councils.

These estates must be attractive and desirable to buyers, or the developer will be unable to sell, but increasingly, too, tenants have choice, so these estates must attract them also. This ability to choose has arisen in some areas partly through the introduction of choice based lettings, as well as the existence of excess supply and surplus properties in some localities. In such areas, there are no longer lengthy waiting lists from which to select new tenants for allocation to particular properties, so potential tenants can be much more selective about the properties they accept. By allowing tenants to play a key role in allocation decisions, it is hoped that there will be a better chance that they will value their home, take pride in it and its surroundings, and feel that they have a greater stake in the community they have chosen to live in.

6. A new future for social housing?

Given the scale of the problems and challenges we have described in this chapter, it is not surprising that there have been recent efforts to set out a vision for a new future for social housing, a route by which the problems of under-investment, residualisation and unpopularity can be overcome. To some extent the government has faced the issues in policies such as the Communities Plan and the wider National Strategy for Neighbourhood Renewal. But the profession itself has also tried to take a longer term view and set out a vision for what social housing might become. One important example was the inquiry carried out in 2000 by the Institute for Public Policy Research, a 'think tank' close to government policy making. Its report, *Housing United*, called for social housing to become a 'sector of choice rather than stay a sector of last resort'. It should be a 'mainstream choice, not an ever-more residualised symbol of failure'.

Its key message was to break down the barriers between tenures, so that people can move more freely from one to the other, so there is a less rigid distinction between owning and renting, and also that social housing becomes – over a period of time – less physically distinct from private housing. It is not a vision that can be achieved overnight but one which – the report argues – is the right goal for social housing over the next twenty or thirty years. Housing professionals should be willing to commit to such a vision, and work towards it over that period. The alternative, according to IPPR, is an increasingly marginalised form of social housing which will be less and less attractive – only a 'last resort'.

The report argued that independent landlords of the sort being created through transfer and ALMOs were the logical future for social housing, and that local authorities should no longer be direct managers of housing stock. Instead, there should be various different types of 'community housing organisation' which would run social housing as community based, non profit businesses, freed from many of the constraints which currently hamper local authorities. Ideally there would be a single form of tenure either for social renting or for rented housing generally, and there would be choice between providers in a local authority area so that people could 'vote with their feet' for a better landlord or better quality house.

The National Housing Federation (the representative body in England for housing associations) also became increasingly concerned about the lack of public awareness of the significant role which housing associations played, in providing quality housing in pleasant neighbourhoods. They argued that there was:

- *Growing public prejudice against social housing and our customers*
- *Declining satisfaction and higher aspirations among our customers*
- *A persistent perception in government and partner organisations that we are competitive and complaining*
  (NHF/inbiz, 2003, p. 3)

As a result, from 2001/3, the NHF undertook a radical re-think of 'what we stand for, what we do, how we do it and how we present ourselves' (NHF/inbiz, 2003, p. 3). This resulted in the creation of a new, national alliance of associations in England, re-branded as iN Business for Neighbourhoods, with the logo iN.

iN made three key commitments, setting out what English HAs intended to do to make the new brand 'a reality, not just a promise' (p. 3). Unsurprisingly, these broadly echo the main thrust of current housing policy objectives for social housing, and are identified in Figure 7.1 overleaf.

In *Who we are, what we do* (2003b), iN emphasises that they are in business for their neighbourhoods, to create places where people want to live, provide a range of services as well as homes, while working in partnership with others. In other words, they are committed to addressing the three key challenges identified in the previous sections, of quality, sustainability and partnerships. These are challenges that no social housing provider can afford to ignore.

Figure 7.1: iN Business for Neighbourhoods: Action for Change commitments

1. **To neighbourhoods**
   - We will put neighbourhoods at the heart of everything we do.
   - We will promote neighbourhoods where there is a place for everyone, with positive support for diversity of people and places.
   - We will work in partnership with local people, councils and other agencies and will champion local needs .
   (p. 3)

2. **To customers**
   - Customers are the driving force behind our business.
   - We will listen to them, respond to their views.
   - We will offer them respect, choice and support.
   - We will do everything we can to prevent neighbourhood problems.
   (p. 8)

3. **To excellence**
   - We will pursue excellence and improvement.
   - We will make the changes needed, so our organisations can rise to the challenge of being iN.
   - We will work with regulators and inspectors to build a culture of challenge and change.
   (p. 12)

Source: iN Business for Neighbourhoods, 2003, Action For Change, NHF

7. Conclusion

Few commentators and observers would disagree that there are and remain huge challenges in social housing. This book has shown the work which housing professionals in the United Kingdom are doing to meet these challenges. The provision of decent and affordable housing requires an understanding of finance, development, housing management, policy and strategy and this book has attempted to give a flavour of what is involved in providing high quality social housing.

For the first time in a generation, today's housing professionals are faced with the prospect of a major expansion in the provision of new homes, including affordable housing. The challenge is to be able to achieve all of this whilst ensuring that the quality of these new estates, as well as of existing developments, will contribute to the creation of sustainable communities. We cannot afford to fail.

What is clear is that the challenge needs to be met by housing professionals who understand the context in which they are operating and have a firm grasp of the wide range of issues which makes for the development of sustainable communities.

Almost inevitably, housing policy will change over the coming months and years and housing professionals need to ensure that they remain up to date with the latest developments. The only real certainty about housing in the UK is that it will change; the challenge is to make sure it changes for the better.

References and further reading

Anderson, I. and Sim, D. (2000) *Social Exclusion and Housing*, CIH, Coventry.

Barker, K. (2003) *Delivering Stability: Securing our Future Housing Needs*, HM Treasury, HMSO, London.

Barker, K. (2004) *Review of Housing Supply*, HMSO, London.

Blair, T. (2002) *The courage of our convictions; why the reform of the public services is the route to social justice*, Fabian Society, London.

Cantle, E. (2001) *Community Cohesion Review Team*, Home Office, HMSO, London.

Carley, M., Chapman, M., Hastings, A., Kirk, K. and Young, R. (2000) *Urban Regeneration Through Partnership*, Policy Press, Bristol.

Chartered Institute of Housing (1999) *Social Housing in the 21st Century – the key issues*, CIH, Coventry.

Department of the Environment, Transport and the Regions (2000) *Quality and Choice – A Decent Home for All*, DETR, London.

Gregory, S. (1998) *Transforming local services*, York Publishing Services, York.

Holmes, M. (1999) *Housing is Not Enough: The story of the St. Pancras Housing Association*, SPH, London.

Housing Magazine, October 2002, CIH, Coventry.

Housing Statistics 2002, HMSO, London.

iN Business For Neighbourhoods (2003a) *Action for Change*, inbiz.org website, National Housing Federation, London.

iN Business For Neighbourhoods (2003b) *Who we are, what we do*, inbiz.org website, National Housing Federation, London.

Inside Housing (2004) 'Meeting the Barker Objectives', 24 March.

Institute for Public Policy Research (2000) *Housing United – report of the IPPR Forum on the Future of Social Housing*, IPPR, London.

Martin, G. and Watkinson, J. (2003) *Rebalancing communities by mixing tenures on social housing estates*, JRF Findings, York.

McArthur, A., McGregor, A. and Hastings, A. (1996) *Less than equal? Community organisations and estate regeneration partnerships*, Policy Press, Bristol.

Mumford, K. and Power, A. (2003) *Boom or Abandonment: Resolving housing conflicts in cities*, CIH, Coventry.

Nixon, J. and Hunter, C. (2001) *Tackling Anti-social Behaviour*, CIH, Coventry.

Office of the Deputy Prime Minister, (2003) *Sustainable Communities: Building for the Future*, ODPM, London.

Office for National Statistics (2003) *Social Trends 33*, HMSO, London.

Page, D. (2000) *The reality of social exclusion on housing estates*, JRF Findings, York.

Paris, C. (ed.) (2002) *Housing in Northern Ireland*, CIH, Coventry.

Perry, J. (2000) 'The End of Council Housing' in Wilcox, S, (2000) *UK Housing Review 2000/01*, CIH/CML/JRF, Coventry, London and York.

Sim, D. (ed.) (2004) *Housing and Public Policy in Post-Devolution Scotland*, CIH, Coventry.

Smith, R., Stirling, T. and Williams, P. (2001) *Housing in Wales*, CIH, Coventry.

Thomas, D. (1995) *A review of community development*, CDF Publications, London.

Wilcox S (ed), (2003) *UK Housing Review 2003/04*, CIH/CML/JRF, Coventry, London and York.

Index

Notes:
1. Acts of Parliament are only included in the index in cases where there is more than one reference in the text.
2. The index covers the main text but not the Glossary or references.

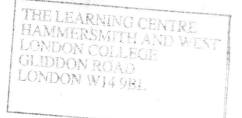

THE LEARNING CENTRE
HAMMERSMITH AND WEST
LONDON COLLEGE
GLIDDON ROAD
LONDON W14 9BL